Women's Transborder Cinema

WOMEN'S MEDIA HISTORY NOW!

Series Editors
Kay Armatage, Jane M. Gaines, Christine Gledhill, and Sangita Gopal

This series is global in scope and investigates the significance of women's contributions to film, television, broadcast, audiovisual, print, digital, and social media history. Taking advantage of archival discoveries and new materials, the books in the series explore women's media histories through a variety of lenses.

For a list of books in the series, please see our website at www.press.uillinois.edu.

Women's Transborder Cinema

Authorship, Stardom,
and Filmic Labor
in South Asia

ESHA NIYOGI DE

UNIVERSITY OF
ILLINOIS PRESS
Urbana, Chicago, and Springfield

Earlier versions of chapters 1, 3, and 5 have appeared in *Dissident Friendships: Feminism, Imperialism, and Transnational Solidarity*, edited by Elora Halim Chowdhury and Liz Philipose (Urbana: University of Illinois Press, 2016); *Feminist Media Studies* (August 2020): 1–18; and *Third Text* No. 170 (May 2021): 373–388.

Library of Congress Cataloging-in-Publication Data
Names: De, Esha Niyogi, author.
Title: Women's transborder cinema : authorship, stardom, and filmic labor in South Asia / Esha Niyogi De.
Description: Urbana : University of Illinois Press, [2024] | Series: Women's media history now! | Includes bibliographical references and index.
Identifiers: LCCN 2024017897 (print) | LCCN 2024017898 (ebook) | ISBN 9780252046209 (cloth) | ISBN 9780252088285 (paperback) | ISBN 9780252047473 (ebook)
Subjects: LCSH: Women in the motion picture industry—South Asia. | Women motion picture producers and directors—South Asia. | Motion picture actors and actresses—South Asia. | Motion pictures and transnationalism—South Asia.
Classification: LCC PN1995.9.W6 D396 2024 (print) | LCC PN1995.9.W6 (ebook) | DDC 791.43082/0954—dc23/eng/20240614
LC record available at https://lccn.loc.gov/2024017897
LC ebook record available at https://lccn.loc.gov/2024017898

To Suranjan
for his quiet energy and his incredible kindness

Contents

Acknowledgments

The debts I have accumulated in researching and writing this book are innumerable and are owed to people and institutions located in several different countries.

For a book that wants to put female practitioners into the practice of film production, I must express first and foremost my deepest gratitude to all the women filmmakers who have spoken to me as well as to the researchers, observers, and fans in their orbits. In Pakistan, the conversations I had with Samina Peerzada, Meenu Gaur, and Farjad Nabi provided me the first insights into the generations of star and non-star filmmakers active in South Asia. Khwaja Najam-ul-Hasan, leading producer at the Pakistan Television Corporation, and Sarwat Ali, renowned music critic, told vibrant stories about Noorjehan, Sangeeta, and the film and gramophone cultures of Lahore. My extensive study of the late Urdu star-director Shamim Ara and her company Shamim Ara Productions would have been impossible had I not had the privilege of meeting with Shamim Ara's brother Irshad Ahmed Khan and son Salman Carim in London and with her crew members Syed Hafeez Ahmed in Washington, DC, and Raja Riaz Khan in Lahore. I am utterly thankful to Salman Carim and Irshad Ahmed Khan for welcoming me to their home and sharing rare memories of Shamim Ara, to Syed Hafeez for sending me photographs and memorabilia from the private archive of Shamim Ara Productions, and to Raja Riaz for taking me on a memorable tour of the Evernew Studios of Lahore. My debt to Salima Hashmi is immeasurable for chasing down acquaintances in Lahore's film and media world in order to make contacts on my behalf and, together with her daughter Mira Hashmi, for telling me stories about female cinemagoing and fandom in 1980s Pakistan.

In India, filmmakers Aparna Sen and Gauri Shinde carved time out of their busy schedules to give me extended interviews, with Aparna graciously agreeing to meet multiple times over the years and allowing me glimpses into her evolving practice. I am very grateful to film journalist Monojit Lahiri for putting me in touch with both. I sincerely thank the veteran Bengali stars Nirmal Kumar and Madhabi Mukherjee for sharing colorful tidbits about an earlier era of the Kolkata film industry, their daughter Mimi Bhattacharya for setting up the interviews, and actress-director Sudeshna Roy for painting a dynamic picture of the new Bengali cinema for me one afternoon at a café in Kolkata. In Bangladesh, I am greatly indebted to the women filmmakers Rubaiyat Hossain, Nargis Akhter, and Shameem Akhtar, who taught me to think in different ways about gender activism in film and infrastructure building. I am grateful as well to filmmaker Tanvir Mokammel for telling stories about the film clubs movement of Bangladesh. A special word of thanks is due to Md. [Mohammed] Fokrul Alam at the Bangladesh Film Archive for his unbounded enthusiasm for Bangla film industry research and an encyclopedic knowledge of relevant facts and details. Not only did he share rare memorabilia and stories and set up contacts for me, but he also brought me to a film shoot at the Film Development Corporation of Dhaka that was rounded out with a ten-course lunch! I am thankful as well to Faridur Reza Sagar, CEO of the leading Bangladeshi conglomerate Impress Telefilm, for kindly meeting with me and generously gifting me with an invaluable archival album of their productions.

Research for this book was carried out at the National Library of Pakistan, Islamabad; the National Film Archive of India, Pune; the Jadavpur University Archive of Bengali Cinema, Kolkata; the National Library of India, Kolkata; the Bangladesh Film Archive, Dhaka; the Dhaka University Library; and the UCLA Library. I am very grateful for the enthusiastic help I received for my cross-border project from the research and reference staff at all of these venues. Particularly worthy of mention is Akbar, the clerical staff member at the National Library in Islamabad who stayed after the library had closed down for the Eid holiday and helped me finish my research as my visa to Pakistan was about to expire (to do so, he delayed his miles-long bicycle journey home).

The Regional Fulbright Research Scholars Program both funded the research for this book at the initial stage and helped me to cross national borders in South Asia. I extend thanks for all their help and guidance to Catherine Johnston Matto in Washington, DC; Zulfikar Ali Bhutto in Islamabad; Shevanti Narayan in Kolkata; and Shaheen Khan in Dhaka. Zulfikar is owed a special word of gratitude for going beyond the call of duty to help me sift through Urdu film magazines at the National Library in Islamabad. The American Institute of Pakistan Studies strengthened my research ties by funding a workshop that enabled me to return to Pakistan and visit Lahore.

My deepest gratitude to all colleagues and friends who have stood by this project, offering crucial help and advice at various stages. Shu-mei Shih

(UCLA), Ketu Katrak (UC Irvine), and Asif Agha (University of Pennsylvania) most helpfully supported my idea for this book early on. More recently, Iftikhar Dadi (Cornell University) very generously shared with me the digital archive of *Eastern Film* and some other primary sources from Pakistan discussed in this book. Kamran Asdar Ali (University of Texas at Austin) steadily encouraged my evolving work on Pakistan and gave valuable guidance. Jane Gaines (Columbia University) looked with much interest at an early version of the table of contents, taking time to talk it through with me and offer heartening feedback. Elora Halim Chowdhury's keenness for my study of gender, Bangladesh, and cross-border South Asia has been truly meaningful. To Gwendolyn Sarah Kirk (Indiana University), my debt is boundless both for her insights on my work and her help with translating some of the Urdu passages and transliterating the Urdu.

Beyond those named above, others who have energetically supported my research and whose scholarship inspires my own include Madhuja Mukherjee, Abhijit Roy, and Moinak Biswas at Jadavpur University; Ali Khan and Zebunnisa Hamid at Lahore University of Management Sciences; Nasreen Rehman at Beaconhouse University; Shaiful Alam Bhuiyan and Fakrul Alam at Dhaka University; Fahmida Akhter at Jahangirnagar University; Marta Elena Savigliano at UC Riverside; Barnita Bagchi at University of Amsterdam; and Shahnaz Rouse at Sarah Lawrence College. At UCLA, I thank Kathleen McHugh for motivating me to think about women's cinema, Vinay Lal for help with identifying student assistants versed in Urdu, and Purnima Mankekar and Akhil Gupta for encouraging my cross-border project on women. Anna Morcom, a new colleague and friend, has been warmly enthusiastic about this book, and for that I am grateful. I owe a special debt to Karen Leonard (UC Irvine) for reading some chapter drafts, giving valuable feedback on the ethnographic aspects, and all in all, for keeping faith in my research.

Huge thanks go to four student research assistants for playing dynamic roles in the development of this book. In Bangladesh, Elizabeth D'Costa assisted with the initial research and interviewing, and, more recently, Samiha Tahsin chased down rare sources despite the COVID-19 lockdown. At UCLA, Malik Hussain Bakshi and Lubna Saira have been expert and excited translators of Urdu passages discussed in these pages.

The tremendous support and guidance I have received from the University of Illinois Press has made this a much better book. My heartfelt thanks to Mariah Mendes Schaefer for reading and commenting on significant portions of the manuscript and for thinking so astutely with me about improvements. I am truly appreciative of Danny Nasset for an abiding interest in the project and for acute guidance at the early stages. I thank the editors of the series Women's Media History Now!—Kay Armatage, Jane Gaines, Christine Gledhill, Sangita Gopal—for their support. The deeply insightful and detailed comments given by the three anonymous reviewers who assessed the proposal and the manuscript, as well as the clarifications that followed, have improved this book in remarkable ways. My sincere gratitude to Jill R. Hughes for copyediting the manuscript with meticulous diligence, to Tad Ringo for expertly shepherding the project, and to Susan Stone for preparing the index.

My spouse, Suranjan, has contributed to every step of this book—keeping faith in my project before I knew my way, making sure I had time for the research and writing, actively participating through his insightful readings of films and help with Bangla translations, and simply being there in little and big ways.

A Note on Translation and Transliteration

This book uses a simplified transliteration of Bangla and Urdu terms for wide readability. The following rules have been used:

- Transliteration of Bangla words follows the Library of Congress romanization guidelines.
- Transliteration of Urdu words follows guidelines developed by Frances W. Pritchett, most commonly used in the United States.
- Titles in the bibliography omit all transliteration.
- Bangla and Urdu terms widely used in English are spelled according to their common usage (*jatra, bhadralok, Muktijuddho, izzat, ashraf,* etc.)
- Proper names of people are listed in English based on common usage. Following a convention shared by all three linguistic cultures studied in this book (Bangla, Urdu, Hindi), I have sought to retain clarity and consistency by using the first name rather than the surname in subsequent references. Some exceptions have been made based on common English usage, such as *Ray* to refer to Satyajit Ray.
- Film titles are based on common usage and guided by IMDb listings. Periodical and newspaper titles are also based on common usage.
- Quotations of non-English words from English language sources reproduce the source and retain variant spellings.

All translations and transliterations of Bangla words are mine. Translations from Urdu were done by Malik Hussain Bakshi, Lubna Saira, and Gwendolyn Sarah Kirk. Transliteration of Urdu words was done by Gwendolyn Sarah Kirk.

"I Must Be Famous to Be Heard"

Star-Authors, Female Fictions, and Transborder Modes of Women's Cinema

In the last weeks of 2013, I was just beginning my journey across South Asia to explore histories of women's filmmaking and industrial structures of opportunity. My comparative interest lay in linguistic cultures of the northern region that share both artistic and geopolitical histories impacting cinema. I was hoping to expand the historical lens by reaching into neglected archives of women's creative labor in film industries while I held onto the core scholarly idea of what women's cinema is. I think of this cinema both as being *authored* by women—taking a substantial creative role as director, producer/scriptwriter, cinematographer, costume and set designer—and as being about women and gender politics (Butler 2002, 8). In select cases, the works I was to find fulfilled the third criterion often associated with women's cinema: that of fiction films made primarily for women, even though, like all South Asian mainstream cinema, they are always made for general audiences as well.

Early in my journey, I had the privilege of having two extended conversations with Samina Peerzada, renowned Pakistani director, producer, and female star of Urdu and Punjabi motion pictures and television serials. Before getting to Pakistan, I had read on the internet about a bold motion picture on marital rape titled *Inteha*, directed and produced by Samina Peerzada and made in a Lahore film studio in 1999. I greatly anticipated my conversation with the filmmaker, hoping to learn about the production of women's cinema in Pakistan from a historical perspective preceding those more readily available.[1] The more visible records of women's cinema in Pakistan are those of a new generation of women directors active in the 2000s. Indeed, most scholars position South Asian women authors as directors of oeuvres that are seen as being in line with elite national or transnational traditions of feminist, art-house, or mainstream cinema.[2] The oral account I received from Samina

Peerzada, pieced together with motion pictures related to her name (in some capacity), impelled me to reconsider at least two paradigms common to the aforementioned studies and, till then, influential on my own approach. I could not but ask if these frameworks occlude a whole range of female authorial labors that might lie beyond internationally recognizable forms. As noted by Edward Said, provocative moments of departure are key to historical readings because they "*enable* what follows from them" (1979, 16; italics in original). The paradigms whose limitations I began to question are those of the film director as an auteur whose individual labor is historically analyzable solely in relation to an oeuvre,[3] and of women's cinema as an invariably subversive tradition undermining structures of gender domination. To detail the interpretive departure that followed from conversations with Samina Peerzada, I must begin with my manifold assemblage of sources as well as the formative role of oral histories therein.

Piecing Together an Archive of Female Authorship: Sources and Method

My effort to assemble sources from across the northern region of South Asia, while it found a plenitude, arose from issues of archival gap and closure. Scholars have noted that official archives are either incomplete or absent in the countries under consideration. Both India and Bangladesh do have national film archives. However, their collections, as discussed by historians Debashree Mukherjee (2015) and Lotte Hoek (2014), are at once partial and enclosed by nationalist goals of preservation and exclusion. No national film archive exists in Pakistan (Siddique 2019; Dadi 2022), although an archive of paper preserved by the National Library of Pakistan partially compensates for the absence at an official level. Beyond this, any search for diverse collections on women's cinema at the national film archives reveals that the ubiquitous emphasis on national heritage is especially delimiting to this purpose. At the National Film Archive of India, I found ready records mostly of women-directed motion pictures that had won national awards or gained recognition at national or international levels. Moreover, the archive as a whole is determined by linguistic nationalism insofar as it preserves materials largely on cinemas made in Hindi, the national language of India, or in Marathi, the language of the region in which the archive itself is located (along with a scattering of materials on nationally visible auteurs, studios, and stars from other linguistic regions of the country). The Bangladesh Film Archive similarly preserves women-directed films that have won government grants and awards. While this archive's publications do record an array of production roles taken by women in Bangla cinema, typically these are positioned as constituting support work for the national male heritage of auteur-directors and film entrepreneurs.[4]

My attempt has been to do "the fugitive work of gender" around these archival closures (Burton 2010, vii). What has been most helpful for building my archive is well characterized in Salma Siddique's words (said in reference to Pakistan) as a "democratic nebula" of independent archivists flourishing across the countries (2019, 197). The independent archivists range widely. They include scholarly collectors and curators of image and paper;[5] private collectors or researchers, including film crew and film fans; as well as storytellers about experiences of filmmaking, production venues, and film viewing. Among the stories discussed in this book are oral histories narrated to me by the film-makers Samina Peerzada, Aparna Sen, Gauri Shinde, Shameem Akhtar, Nargis Akhter, Rubaiyat Hossain; by film personnel, film archivists and journalists, and family members of women filmmakers; and by "embodied" spectators (Siddique 2019, 198). The latter comprised individuals who were motivated by memories of fandom and sometimes turned into impromptu researchers on my behalf. Noteworthy was the fan in Islamabad who not only told me a story about popular Pakistani women's cinema in the 1980s but also brought me a set of degraded-quality DVDs. Fortuitously, I had gained access to the "pirate archive" circulating in Pakistan and across South Asian countries (Cooper 2015; Tanvir 2013). These DVDs were to launch my exploration of a "pirate mode" of transnational cinema, which this book studies using an eclectic array of visual, print, digital, and oral sources found from official, unofficial, and ephemeral archives.

Of these, the oral accounts have been formative for my method in more senses than one. Characteristically shifting and contradictory, these oral stories were far from free of the archival spirit of claiming "competence" in heritage narratives (Derrida and Prenowitz 1995, 10). Nonetheless, they alerted me to gaps in the extant information by offering tidbits on female practice and filmic context that refused to cohere with the sight lines of history. Beyond that, my interactions with storytellers taught me a way of historicizing stories and images from other worlds of creative practice through forging, as it were, bodily relations with voices, fictional images, and contexts. Alessandro Portelli argues that how narrators "plot" or arrange the fragments of recollection to tell the story or intensify its import—how they stage meanings through the rhythm or "velocity" of speech, for example—has much to suggest about how the speaking subjects relate to historical context (2006, 35–36). The perfor-mance of subjectivities and beliefs should be analytically considered "as much the business of history" as documented "facts" (36). As I understand, Portelli calls on historical analysts to relate not only to informational details but even more to performative and disjunctive textures, the tonal plots of detail. I find here what I like to call an "intersubjective" way of reading that is helpful for approaching both oral matter as well as visual or print matter. For one thing, it offers an ethnographic approach to historical analysis that easily encompasses sources beyond the oral. An "ethnographic stance" in research, notes Sherry B. Ortner, helps to contextualize both "fieldwork and archival research" because, at minimum, it is a way of "understanding "another life world using the self— or as much of it as possible—as the instrument of knowing" (1995, 173).[6] This method of reading can alert us to how details and voices push back or pull another way such that not all our encounters with other historical worlds come to be "unpacked with hermeneutic finesse" (Stoler with Strassler 2006, 284). We must research around the remnants of detail to see where else they might lead us. From this ethnographic perspective, I read filmic texts and orbital visual and print material as archives bearing traces of women's "inhabitation" in the cultural fabrics of production, technology, and society (Dadi 2022, 19). Visual sources are pieced together with available oral and printed matter in the attempt to "plot" the textures of women's claims to creative authority in specific contexts of film production and circulation. Defying hermeneutic finesse, the plots shed light on "the categorical blind spots and conceptual taboos" in received understandings of women's authorial work, including in my own understanding (Gaines 2018, 197). To clarify further, I now turn to my conversations with Samina Peerzada.

Let me start with an odd detail to which I could not at first relate. Throughout the conversation, Samina Peerzada was passionate yet cryptic in insisting on her generic fame, repeating with verve that she had to be "famous" as a female star of industrial Pakistani cinema in order "to be heard."[7] This insistence pushed back my conceptual taboo against linking industrially manufactured female star genres to the oeuvres directed by women who are also stars, a taboo that abides by the notion that an author is the individual who creates an original and unified text. Instead, her steadfast belief in the usefulness of fame, a conviction calling for analysis as a historical fact, forced upon me my first baffled reckoning with the complexities of what I call *female-star-authorship* (De 2020). Not to get ahead of her plot, though, allow me to go to where it commenced.

Samina Peerzada began the account of her film career on the dramatic note that she had wanted to take up directing films in order to depict a family drama in which her lived knowledge of domestic violence could be publicly seen and "heard." Drawing on her experiences of encountering domestic abuse in her neighborhood in Lahore, she had imagined the motion picture *Inteha* (The Limit, 1999). In her words, this was to be an "alternative-in-the-mainstream" narrative that portrayed marital rape and domestic violence by taking on conventional emotions from the Urdu screen and "turning them around." While she used the format of the "Pakistani *masala* [spices] film"—a mixed-mode genre interspersing family melodrama with song and dance, action, and physical thrills—she sought to reverse classic family drama tropes such as the abused but "forgiving" wife and the morally invincible patriarch. Samina related an eloquent story about the struggles of making *Inteha* and getting it released. A number of her male colleagues and crew initially maintained that rape within marriage was not a believable theme for a film. Nor did they agree with her plans for the camera angles and framing of male figures. Thereafter, she ran into a protracted battle with the Pakistan Censor Board. *Inteha* was decertified twice on the charge of including a "vulgar" exposure of intimate relations. As reported by a blog describing the case of *Inteha*, the exposure of intimacy was deemed to be inimical to the family "morals of an Islamic society" (Inam 2009). In the course of public outcry, a theater exhibiting the motion picture was burned down in Karachi. Samina Peerzada went on to recount how, nonetheless, she had forged ahead with her "controversial" vision, pursuing a larger commitment to "feministic" (*sic*) activism in the arts and in society. She further elaborated that her investment in activist art had germinated from early roles in the Marxist feminist theater movement spearheaded in Pakistan by London-trained Sheema Kermani (late 1970s and early 1980s) (Kermani 2015, 8–11); led to an internationally acclaimed performance as Nora in an Urdu version of Henrik Ibsen's *Doll's House* (1992); and to this day motivates her participation in theater and cinema networks bridging the troubled national borders of South Asia.[8] She indicated as well that the project of *Inteha* had received official sanction from the right quarters by stating that it had begun from a seed grant from the First Women Bank of Pakistan.

In this vein, I heard of an elite woman author-director's journey into an oppositional, intentionally nonconformist practice of "women's cinema." In the light of Claire Johnston's pioneering theorization of women's "countercinema" in entertainment film industries ([1973] 2021, 354–355), I could see Samina Peerzada's practice as involving the creator's strategies for "the subversion of [sexist] ideology" both in the fabric of Pakistani masala films and in the extradiegetic male-privileged structures of industry and economy producing films as material objects. Also suggestive was the role taken by women's transnational initiatives and artistic networks in shifting the infrastructures and enabling feminist cinema in an apparently conservative studio system. While working largely in Pakistan and with local resources, Samina Peerzada appeared to extend to a specific national location the practice of a "transnational generational cohort" of women filmmakers. As argued by Kathleen McHugh (2009b, 120–121), this postwar cohort of border-crossing filmmakers—awkwardly located in national space-time—is historically impacted by feminisms both in their "authorial discourse" and in "opportunity structures" (training, funding, and so forth).

Thus far, the plot of Samina Peerzada's authorial discourse sat well at the crossroads of transnationally influenced Pakistani women's movements in the arts and in society, and pro-women national and global discourses on "gender equity" and Islamic social uplift (Weiss 2012, 65–66). The latter had yielded such infrastructures for women's initiatives as the First Women Bank, which had been established in 1989 by Benazir Bhutto, Pakistan's female head of state and an ally of the urban women's movement in the country (Zia 2009, 29–46). The feminist theater initiatives of which Samina spoke, spawned as they were from transnational mobility and training, had burgeoned in the 1980s against the brutal Islamist military dictatorship of US-backed Zia-ul-Haq (under cold war maneuvers around the anti-Soviet war in Afghanistan). By the 1990s, when *Inteha* was made, elite Pakistani women's debates were surging against the domestic violence and honor killings that were widespread in the "long shadow" of the Zia period (Toor 2011, 162–164). Samina's authorial narrative illuminated the staging of female anger in *Inteha* in a particular way. I could read into the diegesis historical traces of contemporary Pakistani feminist debates as well as transnational influence of oppositional feminist aesthetics (see the film analysis in chapter 3).

My difficulty lay, however, in holding on to the reading as I tried to plot in the disjunctive yet insistent details of Samina's generic fame. The analytical categories of opposition, subversion, or nonconformist awkwardness common to feminist thought came up against "unthinkabilities" (Gaines 2018, 197–198). Samina Peerzada's story of feminist activism to an extent had been a "positioned utterance" (Clifford 1986, 12), responding to my excitement about the feminist motion picture *Inteha* I had read about on the internet. Before I knew it, unexpected demands were being made on my attention as her plot drifted to fragmentary accounts of how she was "always saying things controversial" and being "heard." With equal if not more velocity, Samina Peerzada added two paradoxical details. Describing how much the "public" had actually "loved" *Inteha* for its familiar emotions and "stereotypes"—such that it made no less than a Platinum Jubilee at one theater—she went on to evoke her belief in stereotypes in quite another way. She told of the "confidence" she commands in her voice through acting and "emoting" in stereotypical family melodramas. She said that she had moved from performing in activist theater to playing stock roles in studio-made Urdu cinema on the conviction that in order to be heard, she had to be famous. This new trail of details pulled me with libidinal force to attend to another diegetic strand, which negotiates in complicated ways the feminist mise-en-scène of female anger in *Inteha*. This is the audiovisual drama around the mild-mannered humility of a battered wife and mother played by Samina Peerzada herself. Moreover, I was implicitly led to trace these diegetic politics to their historical context by another storyline of how her "gentle" demeanor helps Samina Peerzada make controversial statements and win over audiences.

Correcting my presumptuous word choice in describing the "battles" she had fought for the release of *Inteha*, Samina Peerzada instead described the laborious "gentleness" with which she had worked with the Appellate Censor

Board: for weeks, she would travel repeatedly from Lahore to Islamabad and sit with quiet patience outside the chief's room until the day came when she was told her case was being heard. In the same vein, she depicted how she had, in her words, commanded "respect" and "full attention" from male representatives of the right-wing Jamaat-e-Islami party during a televised debate about "vulgarity in the media," thus clearing a pathway for dance shows and various other programs on television. Although she did not specify the date of this debate, she could very well have been referring to the Pakistani Jamaat campaign in 2004 against the "indecent exposure" of female bodies in advertisements and other visual media (Zia 2009, 37). As I elaborate later (chapters 3 and 5), this orthodox position on so-called obscene exposure rests on an Islamic notion of the male gaze that breeds anxiety about the pious male subject. Samima Peerzada went on to emphasize that she is commonly identified (on talk show platforms, for example) as "Allah's *nāyāb*" (literal meaning "precious")—to go by the translation she volunteered, "God's second in command." We could certainly contextualize Samina's authoritative religious voice in relation to what Charles Hirschkind delineates as the communal practice of *da'wa* widespread to modern Muslim publics, a summons to the "pursuance of greater piety" through which a tradition of Islamic scholarly argumentation is put to "novel uses within contemporary situation[s] shaped by . . . media forms" (2006, 31, 37). As shown by Saba Mahmood (2005), Sadaf Ahmad (2009), and Annelies Moors (2006), among others, elite women are becoming visible as deliberators of modern Islamic moralities in contexts where women grow mobile in urban spaces. It is in a mediated sphere of social transformations that we must situate Samina Peerzada's evocative tale of her "gently" articulate stance on sexually controversial matters (marital violence, dancing female bodies). Her gentle and patient stance—a conformist practice of the Islamic female virtue of modest humility—dramatizes a process common to the Muslim world of working in "culturally appropriate" and selective ways through Western liberal ideals (such as women's rights, freedom of expression, women's ownership of their bodies) (Weiss 2012, 52).

Central to the purpose of this book, however, is the way Samina Peerzada's plot details drifted to link her public performance of moral authority to its *form of mediation*—that is, to the fame she had accrued as a female star persona in mainstream Pakistani cinema. This linkage revealed, in effect, that the genres of femaleness she personified as a famous star of social fictions had turned her into an intimately relatable "stranger" appealing to wide audiences. Hilary Hallet explains that the term "persona" is used in film scholarship to delineate the "star as a text whose complications create ambiguities that can appeal to diverse fans" (2013, 29–30). The fame that film personas like Samina incarnate is a "multilayered performance." It unfolds in diegetic space as well as in the extradiegetic "celebrity rituals" through which the personas cultivate

Fig. 1: Samina Peerzada in a pious mother pose (Source: *Durr-e-Shahwar*, HUM TV, 2012)

intimacy with the ambiguous longings of their fans. A star who seeks to author different fictions for the times could perform persona as a way to dwell in social ambiguities and questions. Samina was performing ambiguous desire at least at two appealing levels—at the level of diegetic imagery and at that of infrastructure building on celebrity platforms (talk shows, film and media periodicals, autobiographical narratives). For one thing, Samina Peerzada's generic persona supported and chaperoned, in a sense, contestations over gender and genre in the images and narratives she directed, scripted, or designed. For another, by stimulating public desire, her appealing persona helped to build "virtual infrastructures" for emergent values and contestations: it worked the "pathways of circulation directly into the eyes and sensoriums" of viewers and fans (Jonathan Beller, qtd. in Larkin 2013, 339). As demonstrated by Samina Peerzada's account, these virtual pathways of desire and controversy opened the gates to physical and financial support structures, such as theatrical venues for exhibition and certification by the censor board.

All in all, I was being pulled by the performative details of Samina Peerzada's story to the profoundly provocative suggestion that female star genres not only had *exchange value* that was prefabricated and circulated for profit as commodified units of sameness, albeit internally ambiguous and tensile. But their famous genres—being tangible repositories of widely appealing ways to be womanly and to work gender relations—also had *use value* for female stars becoming authors of cinema. By anchoring her creative voice in her famous stardom, Samina Peerzada was illuminating a form of fame not derivative from preestablished canons but rather aesthetically cultivated and collaborative: "something the audience could feel it actively participated in" (deCordova 2001, 51).[9] The complex plot of Samina Peerzada's career story depicts the practice of female-star-authorship. It is a *multilayered performative mode of claiming creative authority* that is widespread across the familial workplaces of social cinema in South Asia. This female creative mode constitutes collective reuse of famous conventions and underlying values. Female stars who become filmmakers inhabit their famous personas and work through social desires and ambiguities collaboratively. As intimate celebrities, they invite sensuous collaboration both from target audiences and, in some cases, from film personnel as well. These collaborative ways build opportunity for working social norms and vivifying ambiguous desires (as we see in Samina Peerzada's collaborative negotiations on behalf of women and dance in the media). A continuous, multifaceted labor of meaning production can be traced across contexts of production and media platforms of publicity.

A striking example of the transmedial continuity of star-authorial labors is the reuse of the female star pose. By plotting the multiple lives of the pose beyond the bourgeois patriarchal or nationalist diegeses for which these were first developed, we see female star-authors becoming dynamic bricoleurs of the commodity life of conventions through claiming control of labor.[10] Reuses of the pose not only invest the female body with fresh historical significance, generating new fictions for the contemporary, but they also place, as it were, women's signatures on the generic creative labor of posing as stars for pre-fabricated narratives. Samina Peerzada's pose of pious humility, clipped from widely appealing Urdu social films and television serials (fig. 1), can be trans-medially plotted through her appearances on female-focused talk shows to the screen of *Inteha*.[11] In the narrative of sexual violence staged by *Inteha*, the same pose of feminine humility comes to be newly recognizable "as one of its own concerns,"[12] the flashpoint for a dysfunctional patriarchy needing reform by men (see chapter 3). We see a similar politics at work in the authorship of Kolkata-based Indian director and scriptwriter Aparna Sen. She inhabits her sexy star persona from the popular Bangla screen to interact with urban West Bengali audiences on multiple media platforms (celebrity editorship of women's magazines, talk shows, public appearances). She interrogates morali-ties of taste and consumption and thus claims infrastructural space for the socially subversive films she makes (chapters 1 and 6). A plotting like this of Aparna Sen's creative labors as those of a star-author complicates the typical approach taken in the substantial body of scholarly work on her oeuvre. Plac-ing her motion pictures in the author-director tradition of Indian art-house or feminist cinema, most scholars fail to historicize how her directorial labor is nuanced by the star-celebrity work she does in popular West Bengali media.[13]

A good part of this book will stay with the histories of female-star-autho-rial labors, being that this substantial archive has been largely overlooked or neglected in South Asian studies of film and culture.[14] An emphasis on female-star-authorship allows me to expand the historical lens on women's cinema beyond the borders of both nation-state and social class. I am able to include cases not only from India, whose studies dominate the field, but also from the robust histories of female star-filmmakers in Pakistan and Bangladesh (chapters 2, 3, and 5). Beyond this, Pakistani studio culture has long been led by the entertainer classes who place female artist-entrepreneurs at the helm. By contrast, both parallel and mainstream Indian cultures marginalized the entertainer classes from the 1930s onward, with cinema coming to be dominated by the respectable classes and bourgeois nationalist men (chapters 1 and 4). As such, my parallel reading of a Lahore studio culture led by female entertainer authors offers a striking contrast to India-focused historical studies (chapter 3). Yet, I have already noted that my historical lens stays comparative. The star-author generation, typically engaged in multiple production and publicity roles, is studied in relation to authorship by a new generation of non-star filmmakers flourishing along large-scale infrastructures of film production and brand publicity.

The point of my lengthy discussion of the Samina Peerzada case in this introductory chapter is to develop an ethnographic method for situating the *modality* of female authorship and filmic labor in postcolonial contexts of South Asia, *as practiced by stars or non-stars*. The emphasis on authorial modality aims in a number of ways to complicate the patriarchal notion of the filmic author as a unified identity whose meaning production can be analyzed through "purely text-and-form-based criticism." I am compelled by Lingzhen Wang's (2011, 10–22) reading of authorship in terms of Michel Foucault's position that the author is a "historical and institutional function" (rather than that authorial intention is dead). It follows that the author and her text should be analyzed as "interconnected" in historical terms.

First, my method of plotting the textures and tonalities of meaning production helps me to think of female authors as "negotiating historical subjects" (Wang 2011, 22). In non-Western contexts, these authors engage with multiple force fields of colonialism, national and statist borders, and concomitant cinematic formations. In this vein, I think of female filmic practice as a "historically conditioned . . . continuity . . . [of] performative interactions between the author outside the text and the textual significations" (25). As aptly demonstrated in the case discussion above, I have learned to follow women's labors intertextually: as unfolding both on the gendered screen, in the images they direct and script, and off the screen, in negotiations with the gender mores informing production and publicity practices. Here, gender is understood as the constitutive element of a range of creative and business relationships based on perceived sexual divisions of labor and authority.

Second, this method permits me to see filmic images as dynamic commodities carrying "cryptic histories" of being made and used in time (Marks 2000, 89). These traces are analyzable as pointing in two directions. On the one hand, they suggest how the genre develops, as put by Sangita Gopal, "as a node in a network of associated elements that constitute a field of activity" (2012, 20). This field assembles financial, technological, and sociopolitical practices to constitute the cinematic modern in a particular context. On the other, they suggest how the genre is being reused, how women authors fashion the aesthetic fabric of conventions as they work through the force fields of filmmaking. By plotting the diverse commodity lives of expressive and narrative details—the reuse of a star pose, a familiar trope, a mise-en-scène, for example—we could come upon mimetic pictures of the material scenes in which women as historical subjects work, how they negotiate labor and authority within dominant structures of opportunity.

Third, an intersubjective method of plotting the performative detail teaches me to read sources as much for the primary as for the disjunctive threads, details that push back my reading or that pull me with libidinal force to make unexpected connections[15]—to wit, my insight into how the female star becomes author, narrated above. Finally, and needless to say, I find my intersubjective way in to understanding women's creative labors being greatly enhanced by bringing oral archives of details and intensities into the analytical mix.

My multipronged method of approaching female authorial histories ethnographically informs the case studies in this book as well as my choices of which cases of authorship and textuality to take up from a vast body of work spread across four different film cultures sharing languages and histories (Lahore, Mumbai, Kolkata, and Dhaka). My comparative focus on submerged women's archives also requires that, within the limited scope of this book, I contain the study of filmmakers who are transnationally visible and widely discussed. To develop an account adequate to the archive at hand, then, I have braided two discrete fields of film scholarship. I draw inspiration from both production studies that use ethnography to bring hidden labor to light and from historiographic readings of aesthetic and infrastructural formations, which sometimes elide the labors of practitioners.[16] My attempt is to put female creative practitioners into the practice—specifically, into altering modes of film production and infrastructure formation across the northern region of South Asia.

So I ask, How might female authorial practices shift with the infrastructural conditions, especially with the spatial scale at which capital for filmmaking and film circulation is organized? The following chapters demonstrate that while women's opportunities do seem to expand through the generations and with the transnational scale of support, so do constraints on creative authority and innovation. Constraints could heighten as large-scale markets, visual and viral media, and state politics intersect to reinforce the hierarchies born of nation building and internecine boundary wars in this postcolonial region. My point here is that fictions and production conditions alike become force fields of the postcolonial, with colonization understood as an "extended and ruptural world-historical event" wherein national, statist, and local "subject-matter" entwine with new imperial formations (Stuart Hall, qtd. in Rajadhyaksha 2000, 30). Across modern South Asia, fields of fiction making have been unevenly produced and gendered by anticolonial national, statist, or imperial frameworks. Specific to the northern region are cultural and socioeconomic conditions that are formed of two "partitions"—of India and Pakistan in 1947 and of Pakistan and Bangladesh in 1971—that inflect to local and transnational structures of capital and empire. By juxtaposing two generations of women filmmakers active across Pakistan, Bangladesh, and India, case studies in this book attempt to show that women's creative and entrepreneurial labors are paradoxically authorized and delimited by the shifts. These conditions shape infrastructure, altering the scale at which filmic capital is gathered and authority commanded by women's filmic labor. Such paradoxes of opportunity and inequity—complexly gendered and irreducible to any progress narrative—are suggested by the title *Women's Transborder Cinema*. In the remaining sections of this introductory chapter, I use this central notion to map out the film history to be explored in the rest of the book.

Women's Transborder Cinema and Scales of Female Labor: A South Asian Spectrum

An analysis of women's transborder practice must begin with the opportunity structures that enable women's creative authority in the production contexts of South Asia. I maintain that these opportunities are organic to the production of the "social film," a genre that is ubiquitous to the sound film histories of this postcolonial region. Across film industries, for example, women who assumed positions as star-directors and star-producers rose to fame by acting in social films. The practices of the female star-author cohort constitute a potent instantiation of the argument made by Jane Gaines (2012, 17, 27) that the "genius" of women's innovations in mainstream cinemas should be sought in "genres" that comprise a "vast cultural storage" of choices. These aesthetic choices are made as much by the filmmaker and production crew as they are prompted by the gendered subjects who consume and desire the generic attractions. In the South Asian region, the social film centering on the family and gender relations has been the protean anticolonial genre storing the emotions and tensions of transforming modernities.[17] Historically, the term "Social" was used across film industries of the region to describe motion pictures combining codes of melodrama with social realism to depict narratives focusing on, in its classic form, women and domesticity set in contemporary times. Yet, from the 1930s onward, this genre has been evolving across diverse contexts of theatrical motion pictures. More recently, it has been catching the influence of transnational forms such as urban action and exploitation, travel and flânerie, comedy, horror, and war cinema. Codes of social melodrama have been mutating as well, cross-breeding with conventions of art-house realism.[18] The chapters of this book follow the Social, or social film, through its different lives in the theatrical film cultures of the northern subcontinent. My focus is on the complex creative roles taken by women on all sides of the camera—as star actor, filmmaker, publicist, and audience.

The organic connection of the social film genre to the politics of female authorship in the region begins to grow clear in the light of Neepa Majumdar's important argument that the very rise of a female star system in the colonial subcontinent came with the social film. According to Majumdar (2009, 27–28), the social film inaugurated a "new filmic space for the enunciation of a fiction and of characters . . . incarnated solely by [their] stars." The fact that social films proliferated at the end of the silent era is suggestive. A sound film medium replete with opportunities for character performance was apt for women to build public fame through enacting fictions of the "unknown" (28)—in other words, fictions of social transformation and conflicts over modernity. I draw from Majumdar's argument two implications that are key to my study. First, the fictional space of social films was spawning female public personas who configured appealing ways to contest social changes and ruptures. In these countries, such fictions of change have constituted the staging grounds for the force fields of neo/colonial modernity, nation formation, and state development under global flows. As authoritative figurations, materializing both on the fictional screen and on celebrity platforms, female stars as authors were poised to reorient social fictions and the underlying appeals. Second, female-centric traditions of social film came to constitute a cultural crucible for famous fictions of femaleness and gender—a crucible that would invite the "genius" of female-focused creativity from consecutive generations of women filmmakers, star and non-star. This book examines women's modes of social fiction making under different formations of film business and opportunity, attempting to illuminate the possibilities and limits of female authorship through a comparative focus.

Studies by Ravi Vasudevan (1989; 2000), Iftikhar Dadi (2016b; 2022), Kamran Asdar Ali (2020), Zakir Hossain Raju (2015), and Alamgir Kabir (1979) reveal that in their female-centered engagement with contemporary issues, social films are loosely distinguishable from other genres of the early decades. The latter include the Hindu mythologicals and historical films of India, the Urdu *dāstān* mode or pictorial film of Pakistan, and the classic folk fantasy of East Pakistan/Bangladesh. Across the gamut of social films, gender relates to the "fissures and fault lines" (Ali 2020, 44) that riddled the social fabric of modernizing anticolonial cultures in the years immediately preceding or following nation-state formation in the three countries. These conflicts revolve around "secularized reform," Westernization and cultural authenticity, and "perverse" forms of familial desire riddling national unity (Dadi 2016b; Raju 2015; Vasudevan 2000; Ali 2020). In my view, the pivotal roles of female and family issues described by these studies of the social film are clarified by Mrinalini Sinha's analysis of a politicized domestic. Sinha argues that struggles against imperialism in colonial India resulted in a "politicization of the domestic" (2014, 16), a cultural politics emanating from British colonial policies that were striving to privatize the family as a domain of so-called native traditions requiring reform.[19] Aesthetic productions of womanhood and the family came to constitute the stage for reinventing anti-imperial traditions and debating cultural modernities. Since the British colonial era, these gendered sites of transformation have been revivified in different South Asian contexts of struggle with neocolonial modernities. While they engendered diverse production structures and mediatized audiences for the social film, these generic sites of social debate at the same time were generating the heterogeneity of female authorship studied in this book.

Voices and images of women were central, for instance, to what Elora Shehabuddin calls the "Bengalicisation of the Muslim middle-class" at the turn of the twentieth century (2014, 54). This endeavor to develop a Bengali-Muslim identity was to lead to the anti-imperial Bangla Language Movement in East Pakistan that brought along a robust theater and social cinema culture involving educated middle-class women (Kabir 1979, 20). Through the 1950s and 1960s, we find, on the aesthetic side, Bangla social films politicizing the homes and women of a riverine Bengal delta to position the identity of middle-class Bengali Muslims (Raju 2015, 138). On the production side, we encounter a large cohort of female actress-producers and costume/makeup designers, including star-producer and scriptwriter Kohinoor Akhter Shuchanda, who collaborated in the family film business with her liberation activist husband, Zahir Raihan. In the post–Liberation War era, Shuchanda established her own production house, managing and promoting the business at the same time that she wrote and enacted scripts. She led her two sisters, Gulshan Ara Akhter Champa and Farida Akhtar Babita into a "sororal mode" fiction film that unsettled available patriarchal forms, magnifying the inequities that these suppressed (chapter 2). Down this path, she also steered Babita into small-scale, border-breaching collaborations with the Pakistani star-author Shamim Ara after the partition of Pakistan and Bangladesh (chapter 5).

Considering the parallel register of Bangla cinema in West Bengal, India, Moinak Biswas argues that realist melodramas drew on nationalist literary traditions to configure social tensions and political upheavals on the emotional grid of family relations (2000, 126–127). Studies by Biswas and Sharmistha Gooptu chart the shifts of the West Bengali social film from a "guarded domestic world" of couple romance and maternal reform (1950s), through new forms of female waywardness arising from sociopolitical malaise (1970s and 1980s), to a world of commodity realism enhanced by digital and television techniques (late 1980s till present) (Biswas 2000; Gooptu 2010). The consecutive eras of the Bangla social film constitute the grounds from which actresses such as

Kanan Devi, Manju Dey, Aparna Sen, and Sudeshna Roy step into production, cinematography, scriptwriting, and direction. The multiple authorial roles taken on by these and other women combine into a slim genealogy of women's social cinema that conflicts with male-dominant fictional modes in West Bengal, even as this female-centric practice mutates with the production scale (chapters 1 and 6).

Taking up the Urdu social film, Iftikhar Dadi explains that the bourgeois social film moved by way of a brief period of alignment with an elite Pakistani national imaginary "self-assured [in its] take on gender" (mid-1960s), to a second incoherent phase of action/social film internalizing cultural pressures (1970s/1980s), and a third life in bourgeois Urdu television serials (1980s till present) (2016b, 88–90; 2022, 1–28). The second life of the Urdu social film burgeoned through a parallel new media economy of video piracy that mediatized audiences in homes, fostering the spread of a women's consumer culture fueled by cold war aids. This era of small-scale cinema from the Lahore studios began foregrounding star-filmmakers from entertainer communities, women who were reusing hereditary arts to perform filmic female bodies for a time of brutal Islamist censorship (backed by cold war militarization). Notable for their artistic address to contemporary female publics are heroine social and action films helmed by the prolific star-directors and producers Sangeeta (aka Parveen Rizvi) and Shamim Ara (chapters 3 and 5). Finally, with Samina Peerzada's Urdu melodramas, we arrive upon the third life of the social film, birthed from a coupling of the theatrical motion picture with bourgeois television serials (chapter 3).

The scholarship cited above does not in any way relate genealogies of the social film with the rise of stars as filmmakers. My point is that once we do, we find that the relations are inextricable. The historical interrelation suggests to me a postcolonial modality of community fictions wherein women become the linchpins of a politics of shifting borders. These politics unfold both in diegetic spaces and beyond, within familial production circuits (further discussed below). Jacques Derrida argues that political borders are of two types. In his words, "The first type of border passes among contents (things, objects, referents: territories, countries, states, nations, cultures, languages, etc.)." The other type of borderly limit passes "between a *concept* (singularly that of duty) and an other, according to the bar of an oppositional logic" (Derrida 1993, 17–18; italics in original). Female stars of social fiction films materialize in public as tangible concepts of social and sexual duty, rendered in stereotypical forms of propriety, respectability, foreignness, or deviance. As generic personas, they reinforce borders and divisions specific to their contexts. Yet, the social fiction film, being a protean genre adaptive to contexts, is a storehouse of historical tensions that riddle territorial meaning. As performers of tensile historical forces, famous female stars command the emotional authority to unmoor the divisive concepts of duty stored in their commodified personas. As suggested in the previous section, female stars hold the potential to become small-scale bricoleurs of conceptual value.

The parts and chapters of this book are organized around the core concepts of womanliness and the family found in the social films that are emergent from postcolonial conditions: maternity, domesticity, the couple form, working womanhood, and gender duty in families that have been dismembered or displaced. My case studies follow these concepts into the contents of women-made social films: objects and things such as shot composition, mise-en-scène, storytelling, filmic body performance, and location choice. My point is to illuminate how in women-made films conceptual uses of these artistic objects grow "inadequate relative to what [they] ought to be" (Derrida and Prenowitz 1995, 24).[20]

This mixing of conceptual politics with female authorship has a larger historical implication. It suggests that the politicization of the domestic inculcated in the patriarchal formations of this postcolonial region a dependency on women's aesthetic labor. This dependency calls women into multiple positions of creative authority that, at the same time, rest on sexual divisions of labor and voice. It seems to me that this female pathway to filmmaking is peculiarly durable and wide-ranging in South Asia. It cuts across borders of nation, religion, language, social class, and caste, enabling women to access production positions. It is a cultural infrastructure both preceding and exceeding the opportunities born either of parallel directors' cinema and film society initiatives or of state initiatives spawned by women's movements. We gain this insight from a comparative look at the careers of Sai Paranjpye and Aparna Sen in India—both being directors of feminism- and art house–inspired theatrical films, and the latter a famous female star as well (chapters 1 and 4).

What I am getting at is that we should understand the *contents* of female filmic labor (the handling and the performance of filmic things) as constituting paradoxical forms of opportunity for women's intervention in established concepts of social duty. This contention takes me to the familial mode of film business through which prominent actresses typically command authority over the production of femaleness and gender. Historians observe that filmmaking was born in South Asia as a domestic enterprise, soon to transform into joint family–mode studios, and that to this day it continues to thrive through kin-like ties and close-knit networks.[21] Kinship-based business practice is long-standing in South Asia, being a British colonial–era legacy that extends far beyond film industries (Birla 2009). However, my research reveals that the small familial mode of film business rests on a specific allocation of sexual labor and authority enabling women to do productive work, albeit within limits. This allocation, in my view, rises from what is best described in terms of Madhava Prasad's Marxian study of the early Indian industry as a "heterogeneous" or disaggregated process of creating the filmic commodity "in which the whole is assembled from parts produced separately by specialists" (1998a, 32). The process itself stems from an incompletely capitalized "patchwork of consumerist and pre-capitalist ideologies" prevailing across the smaller production practices of South Asia. Through a meticulous study of the Lahore studios, Gwendolyn Sarah Kirk (2016) demonstrates that to this day they function through tight-knit familial ties that are both real and "fictive." Examining production practices in Kolkata and Dhaka, I show that the familial mode likewise reappears in various forms from the 1950s through the 2000s (chapters 1 and 2). I submit that under the patchwork capitalism of familial production networks, women, in some capacities, take on the authority of specialists to whom at once the crew and target audiences *defer*.

If we return momentarily to Samina Peerzada's extra-cinematic commentaries, we find a ready picture of this disaggregated assemblage of specializations. Let us take an interview given for the magazine *SHE* to Moneeza Hashmi to promote the release of the family-produced motion picture *Nazdeekiyan* (Closeness) in 1986. Describing in detail the creative labor she has put into the production, Samina claims, "This was my own film and I loved working on it. . . . I was incharge [*sic*] of costumes, props, etc." (1986, 53). Another comment suggests that Samina Peerzada's actor-director husband may well have deferred to her creative authority over sexually specialized skills. We learn that Usman Peerzada has been guided by his wife to perform "emotional scenes" in less than tense ways, presumably in *Nazdeekiyan* and elsewhere (1986, 52). These authorial claims pull me to a way of reading images of costuming and couple romance that survive from the teen movie *Nazdeekiyan*, clueing me in to a deft womanly negotiation of the Islamic censorial codes of the time (see chapter 3). If we return to the interview, we see that Samina Peerzada's claim of owning her creative labor blends comfortably with belonging in a powerful patriarchal film-and-theater family lineage that paved her own pathway to both sides of the camera. In her own words: "Peeru [Usman Peerzada] had his famous father. I had Peeru as an image" (1986, 51). We hear the ambivalent authoritative voice of a female specialist who publicly positions her labor as an essential source of capital for the family business precisely by deploying gender hierarchy. On the one hand, she publicizes a disaggregated mode of building gender capital for the product reliant on her capacities not only as a performer but also as an informal filmmaker. On the other, her story suggests that what accrues capital on the print media platform of a female celebrity interview are multiple contents of sexually specialized labor. These include designing and staging costumes and deportment, constructing the mise-en-scène of couple emotions appropriate for the audience and market and completing other unnamed and laborious "etc." tasks. All in all, the public authorization of women's specialized, productive work rides on the assumption that these intimate female subjects will take on additional women's work in the reproductive domain.

We find here a sexually complicated and labor-intensive pathway to commanding labor power. This allows women who participate in patriarchal film businesses to reuse available concepts in the collective production of new commodity value. The case studies that follow illuminate how such pathways—built of patriarchal cultural dependency—enable women to step into the gaps or breaches of male-dominant businesses and statist machineries. Building on the insights of economic geographers like Linda McDowell (2001), I would characterize the disaggregated mode of production enabling female authority as *quintessentially small-scale*.[22] Women's work of taking initiatives and making decisions is managed at the levels of the body and the familial—levels considered to be the most "local or closest-in" of spatial scales (229). That being said, this scalar argument becomes more complex in the case of female film workers who are also stars and public celebrities. The "body work" done around stardom obviously dwells within large-scale consumerism. I maintain that, nonetheless, the production initiatives and decision work continue to be small-scale as long as the "locus" of forging and managing "cross-scalar relations and connections" continues to be that of star-authors' bodily labors (McDowell 233). My discussion of Samina Peerzada's star-authorship has sought to illustrate this intensive localization, a closing in of scalar relations around multiple forms of body work. These include her labors as a director and designer of gendered forms, as a star-actress, and as a celebrity reusing the star pose to gather capital (media platforms, revenue channels) for women in the media. As we will see in chapter 5, cross-scalar work by star-filmmakers has also had a compelling transnational reach, building bridges across troubled geopolitical borders in South Asia. A small-scale transnational practice of coproductions was actively managed by the Pakistani and Bangladeshi star-filmmakers Shamim Ara and Babita through a range of cross-scalar aesthetic work: sharing food to forge business relations across state boundaries, as stars of national value building capital for the contentious concept of women's companies crossing borders, and directing and performing (in Babita's case) filmic dramas of border-breaching kinship.

The familial access structure for women in South Asian film businesses somewhat resembles the "family system of production" found in early twentieth-century United States. Jane Gaines and Radha Vatsal have shown that within the family production system, "boundaries between family and business were often blurred" in ways allowing women's participation in diverse roles of filmmaking; the family system and couple mode of production could also turn the motion picture set into "a newly gender-mixed workplace" (2011, 8–9). Moreover, Karen Mahar studies how a gender-divided culture of reform and uplift permitted women filmmakers from respectable family backgrounds, such as Alice Guy-Blaché and Lois Weber, access to the film industry in the first decades of the twentieth century (2006, 79–81, 88–92). Note, however, that unlike the early American familial mode of female access, the South Asian mode is neither a passing nor a monolithic historical phase. This difference suggests to me that the two histories of familial access are basically incommensurable. Since family fictions are central to the politics of belonging and otherness in postcolonial cultures, women have a durable, if paradoxical, position of privilege as cultural bricoleurs. They are able to engage with prevalent concepts of family, community, and the body by way of carrying out the gender labors that are essential to familial production modes—at least, as long as the filmic space is incompletely capitalized and small-scale such that decision work stays disaggregated. For within the disaggregated mode of commodity production, bodies and hands of female specialists remain the locus of negotiating gender concepts and amassing gender capital at a small scale.

Then how might the modality of female filmic authorship mutate with the geographic scale of media capital?[23] This book explores that question by examining the filmic space of the 2000s, in which a new generation of women directors, mainly non-stars, has grown apace. My point is to examine how generic fictions of femaleness and difference are being processed in the new filmic space supported by large-scale capital. As a point of contrast, I turn briefly to a context in which an organized women's movement generated nation-scale dependency on the woman's "voice," momentarily accruing support for women from both state-governed media and industrial sectors. Considering 1980s India, I note that mainstream women directors like Sai Paranjpye, functioning as relatively independent professionals, partially controlled multi-scalar connections and produced gender fictions that were subversive to large-scale agendas. The bigger point I take from this comparison, though, is that women's independent relations with large-scale structures of filmic capital and desire seem less sustainable than their positions as negotiating subjects who work through existing hierarchies and familial networks. Feminist fictional modes evolve accordingly. This brings me to the filmic space of the 2000s and to what differs.

Today geographies of the film business expand at an exponential rate to support women and marginal groups as well as myriad small film firms. Yet this transnationally expansive and flexible new space, being conditioned by advanced neoliberal capitalism, reveals two contradictory trends. On the one hand, familial networks continuing to provide women points of entry grow increasingly liberal and egalitarian in their outlook on women's film work. Typical to the spaces of this new author cinema across South Asia are equalizing couple- or partner-mode film firms steered by female and male heads from the privileged classes. This liberal familial mode of partner entrepreneurship spans the careers of Gauri Shinde in Mumbai/Bollywood;

Sudeshna Roy in Kolkata; Nargis Akhter and Rubaiyat Hossain in Dhaka; and Mehreen Jabbar, Meenu Gaur, and Sabiha Sumar in Pakistan; among many others. Moreover, the familial networks of access are enhanced by liberal infrastructures for large-scale distribution and exhibition that enable many women. In recent years, women-made fiction films have been crisscrossing the spaces of high-end multiplex and single-screen theaters in urban South Asia and of international film festivals across the world. A good number of the latter have grown inclusive through "advocacy" involving programming and outreach (White 2015, 18).

The complex contradiction of the new filmic space, on the other hand, lies in the fact that it inexorably interrelates the geographic scales of production and circulation to a regulatory, aggregate mode of decision work. According to economic geographers (McDowell 2001, 230–238), a workplace or organization being a "social relation" slips into increasingly complex "multi-scalar connections" with "regulatory systems" in globalizing spaces. As such, more small-scale or local conceptual innovations come to thrive through national corporate and transnational structures of opportunity and to be contained by dominant interests. Typical to neoliberal late capitalism is a flexible logic of brand formation that produces conceptual inclusions and occlusions. Opportunities for filmmaking and innovative critique come to be determined by the way tastes are trending and at which venues. My case studies of new filmic spaces in South Asia suggest that branded fictions are produced by present-day corporate cultures of conglomeration that inflect to the workings of the state. Moreover, the same brand logic of trendy concepts seems to link the production culture to a determinate range of distribution and exhibition venues. These include high-end film theaters and DVD circuits in South Asia, media platforms accessible to diasporic audiences in the global North, and international festivals and award systems.

I got a vivid sense of this inclusive yet aggregate mode of brand production from an exclusive interview given to me by Faridur Reza Sagar (2014), CEO of the leading Bangladeshi television/film conglomerate, Impress Telefilms. We met at the company's headquarters in Tejgaon, Dhaka. Much of the interview was devoted to a discussion of gender inclusivity. I learned of the many works by women directors qua authors being produced by Impress Telefilms (see chapter 2 for details). I was also introduced to woman filmmaker Gita Hasan. She told me that she was preparing to direct a film about Kazi Nazrul Islam, the revolutionary poetic voice of the anti-British struggle in colonial Bengal and now the posthumous national poet of Bangladesh. My discussion with Faridur Sagar proceeded to the topic of the film trade. He explained that the business model of Impress Telefilms parallels the media conglomerates in India. Multiple "brand partner" consumer economies are being deployed to produce "*unnato* [developed/advanced]" Bangla motion pictures aimed for the Oscars and international film festivals. In his preface to the *Impress Telefilm's Movie Album*, which he generously handed to me at the end of the interview, Faridur Sagar makes the same points in greater clarity and detail. It states that "quality feature-film productions" from Bangladesh are reaching audiences in all "six continents" (2011, 3). As also pointed out by Sagar, the economies of new cinema in neighboring India work according to the same logic of conglomerate brand formation. Studying the new Bollywood industry, Sangita Gopal astutely observes that what once were family firms of film business now have their own brand identities (2012, 70). This brings us, then, to the flexible aggregation principle of brands.

Examining the culture industry of brands, Scott Lash and Celia Lury (2007, 4–6) maintain that brand values do not circulate in the same way that commodity values do. The brand sells the value of an identity by way of a range of commodified products that flexibly "instantiate" the same concept by marking the distinctiveness of that conceptual value from all other ranges (of commodity-as-value). In other words, the brand being a "sign-value" operates at a higher and more regulatory scale of abstraction than a commodity that could be both exchanged and reused (i.e., revalued) hand to hand. By contrast to the tangible circulation of commodities, the circulation of brands is coordinated through sets of interactions between users who come to be "oriented . . . towards one another . . . in relation to an object" (18). It seems to me that the conglomeration of "brand partner" consumer economies found in the new filmic space aims precisely at coordinating expectations and orienting values of users/audiences across target geographic spaces—spaces that are accessible to elite respectable classes of audience. As such, the scale at which brand value circulates constitutively differs from that at which commodified star-author value circulates. This is not to claim that star–commodity value does not exchange in abstract and binary form. To the contrary, stars as commodities circulate within large-scale affective economies of goods and services,[24] often lending glamorous heft to a line of merchandise by embodying it. What I have been arguing is that female stars as authors could also enliven personas that are replete with public concepts and tensions so as to reuse them collaboratively with fan publics and invest the concepts with contingent new value. What the difference implies overall is that the range of gender concepts being included and aesthetically valued in the branded fiction films in South Asia are relatively determinate by comparison to the heterogeneity of some small-scale star-author productions that are historic to the South Asian region. With that said, let me restate the question I raised earlier: How might the modality of female filmic authorship be altering under the contradictory momentum of the new filmic space?

The case studies to follow situate women directors within the contradiction, shining light on how creative authority varies with the scale of structures supporting production. On one side of the spectrum, we find a Bollywood director and entrepreneur such as Gauri Shinde cofounding a couple-mode firm and leveraging brand-partner economies on a global scale to expand the reigning concept of the heroine body in transnational Bollywood cinema. Chapter 4 approaches Gauri's work as an archive of process, examining how female difference (in age, clothing, habit, language) is made commensurable to the prevalent liberal brand of valuable Indian womanhood. Yet an intertextual reading of the diegetic with oral and print materials in its orbit reveals traces of ambivalent choice and memory—the disjunctive remains of a successfully branded production. On another end of the new filmic spectrum, we find independent director and scriptwriter Rubaiyat Hossain in Bangladesh deploying (privileged) family and social networks of finance and publicity to radically unsettle nationalist fictions of female heroism in 1971's Bangladesh Liberation War of Independence. The case of Rubaiyat's debut fiction film, made for theatrical release, shows how new liberal filmic capital could be made to work against regulatory national frameworks, even if only for a moment. Yet what threads together my case studies of female authors in the new filmic space is a curiously inexorable teleological tendency. Authors and oeuvres develop only through moving into transnational fields of filmmaking activity that tend to be informed by a few trending concepts. The trending brands, while they inflect to specific political and industrial histories, converge on a few *timely* values of the liberal ethnocentric dispensation. Brand value is identified in female/gender freedom from regressive heteropatriarchies (across South Asia); in the companionate soft hero or the vulnerable man (across the historically patriarchal spaces of Indian cinema); in the middle-class female savior-activist (in Bangladeshi developmental cinema); and in the retrograde or terrorizing patriarch who is profiled disproportionately as Muslim (a brand hovering over transnational South Asian festival films in a time of escalating Islamophobia).

Generally speaking, my cross-generational approach to female authorship cautions me against a progress narrative based on visible numbers (of women filmmakers, funding opportunities, venues of exhibition). Instead, I settle for thinking about the differing conditions of opportunity and constraint that have enabled women to claim conceptual authority in their interactions with prevalent social film genres. The overarching argument of this book, then, is that the generative labors of the female authors working the infrastructures of theatrical cinema in this region are best understood as comprising a *transborder legacy* of women's cinema. Building on Derrida's observations (1993, 10, 16), I take the analytic of transborder to mean an "interminable experience" of traversal replete with paradoxes. Crossing borders and becoming "hospitable" to the social and sexual other also comes with being duty-bound to boundaries, both in aesthetic and everyday senses. Women's gender-bound destinations can range from complicity with heteropatriarchal nationalist concepts of belonging to conformity to state- or market-driven forms of censorship regulated by transnational brand values. Thus, bordered destinations evolve with the historical contents (filmic objects, things, and referents). My case-based approach focuses on specific connections and ruptures between women's experiences.

Archives in Female Focus: The Plan of the Book

As should be evident by now, my lens on women's cinema archives is deeply indebted to feminist theorization on film history and labor geography. To develop a framework adequate to the complexities of women's authorial claims, however, I have had to rethink the paradigm of subversive "counternarrative" that is widespread to feminist film scholarship (as discussed earlier in this chapter). I eschew the framework that cinema qua women's in postcolonial contexts comprises only declared political projects that resist "patriarchy and (neo) colonialism" (Shohat 2006, 39).[25] Building on Derridean deconstruction, I use instead a female-focused transborder analytic. This female-focused analytic looks for women's decision work around theatrical films that bear women's names in some productive capacity and that are concerned with prevailing postcolonial fictions of womanliness and gender relations. My transborder female focus builds on a rare variety of visual, print, and oral materials: filmic texts, posters, televised talk shows and promotional "hype" events, blogs, published life narratives and interviews, film periodicals, women's magazines, gossip columns, and oral histories. Through the transborder lens, the objects and things to do with women's creative labors are seen as diverse in reference. They evoke both socially subversive counternarratives and socially conservative or seemingly compliant negotiations with prevailing concepts. Yet in one unsettling way or another, female authorial labor continues to interact with and disrupt gender hierarchy in the fields of production and of diegeses.

The three main parts of this book are organized around concepts that are generic to fictional cinema across postcolonial South Asia. These shared concepts serve as lenses for examining how selected women directors and film entrepreneurs negotiate generic logics and lay claims to creative authority in different contexts of anticolonial nationalism and transnational capital. The point of part 1 is to illuminate how social film genres could become crucibles for such claims of authority by women. It demonstrates that the genre of motherliness is an opportune concept for both star and non-star filmmakers of the Bengal region to traverse. Taking on maternal stereotypes and entering related social debates in front of and behind the camera have permitted women on both sides of the national border to access infrastructures of film production. The two chapters combine to locate this generative concept in a shared anticolonial field of Bengali national aesthetics that twines the influence of regional traditions with evolving modern constructions of respectability. Together the chapters also account for historical difference. They show that the spatial binarism in the Indian Hindu nationalist concept—of the respectable woman as a domesticated goddess-mother—mutates into a relatively ambiguous maternal genre in the Muslim-majority contexts of nationalist activism (1960s) and state development (1980s) in Bangladesh. This genre of the proactive "public mother" is found in the diegetic field as well as in the many extradiegetic production roles that women from the respectable classes have taken in the Bangladeshi film industry. Nonetheless, what runs through the cases drawn from both Bengals is women's tendency to stage the motherly in ambivalent relation to spaces occupied by respectable male heroism, whether these spaces are domestic or public and state-governed. Following reuses of the maternal concept in women-made social fiction films, the chapters consider what changes occur as the fields and scales of business opportunity evolve.

Chapter 1, "Decoupled Maternities: Female Stars in Production Modes, Kolkata," mainly elaborates how female stars manage authorship and negotiate large-scale change at the levels of the familial and of star body appeal. My first case in point is the work of Kanan Devi, the star-producer and director who pioneered the female production mode in Kolkata by successfully running a small-scale company and participating in its directorial team after the demise of the male-dominant joint family studio system in the 1940s. Exploring the maternal melodrama *Mej Didi* (Middle Sister; 1951) in relation to Kanan's autobiography, I investigate the text for clues to Kanan's hand in the cinematography and set design, skills she had taught herself on the job. Turning to the elite star-author Aparna Sen, I consider the feminist maternal social films *Parama* (1984) and *Paromitar Ek Din* (House of Memories; 2000), both of which she directed and scripted. I demonstrate that although Aparna is widely held as a politicized author spawned by state-level women's cinema initiatives, her authorship of gender critique has been sustained at a small scale by a vernacular star persona and fan cultivation on multiple media platforms (women's magazines, television). My argument for juxtaposing these two Bengali star-author personas is that although their practices of the motherly range from the conservative to the subversive, their works share a curious tendency. They want to reclaim the maternal home and domestic femaleness through decoupling the heroine from the bourgeois hero. While much of this first chapter uses these case studies to illuminate a previously unnoticed genealogy of women's cinema evolving in West Bengal from the 1950s through the 1990s, it ends with a look at how maternal fiction shifts under the new Bollywood-oriented brand scale of Kolkata cinema. I briefly consider *Mayer Biye* (Mother's Marriage), released in 2015 by actress-director Sudeshna Roy from her partner-mode film firm.

Chapter 2, "Public Maternities: Women's Companies and a Sororal Production Mode, Dhaka" takes a deeper dive into film entrepreneurship through the lens of women's companies, which reappear through decades of cinema in Bangladesh. I show that uses of the mother genre alter with the level at which the infrastructures women rely on for their film businesses are controlled by financiers and the state. My first case in point is the social action film *Tin Konna* (Three Sisters; 1985), produced and costarred in a small-scale sororal mode with sisters Babita and Champa by scriptwriter and company owner Kohinoor Akhter Shuchanda. I note that this ensemble heroine fiction puts the motherly to irreducibly ambiguous use and thus magnifies the hierarchies in contemporary cinema and society (under a military-bureaucratic regime). I find in the sororal aesthetic mimetic traces of a disaggregated entrepreneurial field allowing star value to diverse femaleness. The chapter follows women's companies to the large-scale filmic space of Bangladeshi "world cinema" populated by author-directors in the 2000s. I examine an NGO-sponsored company whose productions carry traces of resisting televisual censorship and invading brands of patriarchal heroism prevalent in state-supported new Bangla media. However, complexities give way to teleology as the company becomes more entrenched in the force fields of large-scale national and global capital. A maternal activist-savior brand comes to replace the reformer hero. The case at hand is an AIDS movie series directed and produced from her all-women media company by Nargis Akhter: *Meghla Akash* (The Cloudy Sky, 2001) and *Megher Koley Rod* (Sunshine in the Clouds, 2008).

Part 2 of this book looks more closely at the way aesthetic conventions differ with the spatial scales of women's film capital and related force fields of nation-state activity. Taking a contrapuntal approach to national language cinemas, this part studies the small-scale star-author work on Urdu cinema done by women in globalizing Lahore in parallel with the large-scale brand-making work done by female Hindi film directors in gentrified Bollywood. The cases are analyzed in relation to social film conventions of the public female body, the body being the site of acute contestation in globalizing postcolonial societies that demand middle-class women be publicly mobile (i.e., working), aggressive, and immersed in self-loving consumption. Part 2 contextualizes the aesthetic politics of female publicness, on the one hand, in a studio film culture shaped by cold war flows and heightening censorship in Islamizing Pakistan (late 1970s and 1980s) and, on the other, in a large-scale multiplex film culture shaped by nationalist and Hindu brands (2010s). The latter arise from an Indian state-supported film industry. Combined, the chapters in this part plot a counterintuitive insight about the staging of female bodies and corporeal arts. They suggest that whereas social contestations are irreducible in the first context, they are more contained and conceptually overarched in the second, despite the fact that multiplex aesthetics offer a plethora of social details.

Chapter 3, "Performing Bodies: Entertainer Authors and Small-Scale Urdu Cinema in Lahore Studios," shines light on an efflorescence of Urdu women's cinema led by female star-directors and producers from hereditary entertainer backgrounds. I explore how this national-language cinema, close to state censorship and middle-class mores, addresses the complexities of an expanding middle-class women's workforce and media culture (with video and television networks bringing entertainment to homes). My position is that the arts of performing female bodies and fictions found in this legacy are traceable not only to middle-class audience address but also to women's hereditary practices of entrepreneurial and creative work. The chapter discusses how familial businesses dependent on women adapted for the times a legacy of (implicitly) agonistic survival arts practiced by hereditary entertainers and artisanal poster painters of the region (agonistic vis-à-vis respectable establishments). In this light, I situate the "working woman" melodramas *Society Girl* (1976) and *Mutthi Bhar Chawal* (A Handful of Rice; 1978) directed and starred in by Sangeeta (aka Parveen Rizvi) in relation to the small-scale production house run by her screenwriter mother Mehtab Bano. Then, I turn to the action-heroine social film *Miss Hong Kong* (1979/1980), directed and produced by the illustrious star Shamim Ara, reading the production in relation to the author's publicity work in reinventing her "respectable" Urdu social film persona for the times. The chapter situates the female homosocial heroine films created by the above two entertainer authors in comparison to Samina Peerzada's female-lead heterosocial melodramas *Nazdeekiyan* and *Inteha*. The latter represent a minority respectable-class presence in the Lahore studios. Combined, these women's productions enhance a politicized impetus in the Pakistani Urdu social film tradition, that of exposing national fault lines.

Chapter 4, "Timing Bodies: Hindi Cinema and a Female Brand Author at Bollywood Scale," explores female authorship of Hindi fiction films that take up Indian nationalist concerns over middle-class women's public success as income earners and consumers within contexts of urban and global change. I study the case of Gauri Shinde in Bollywood, the female author-director and writer of a successful female-lead fiction film titled *English Vinglish* (2012), in relation to another successful mainstream female author of the 1980s, Sai Paranjpye, director and scriptwriter of the gender-centric social comedy *Chasme Buddoor* (1981). My argument is that even though both women forge multi-scalar relations with infrastructures whose locus of decision making lies beyond their own, the modality of female filmic authorship constitutively changes between these generations. Born of a context of feminist debates around the female body and gender inequities, Sai's production inhabits contemporary infrastructures of realist "middle-cinema" while unsettling their patriarchal assumptions. The work dramatizes the unequal landscape of gender, class, and consumerism in urban neighborhoods of the period and renders it irreducible. By contrast, I find Gauri Shinde leveraging multiple scales of opportunity and partner economies (of costuming, location choice, and hero branding) to develop a niche-realistic brand of Indian womanhood out of an untimely story of a mother. I situate her mode of brand authorship in line with a cohort of female directors and entrepreneurs who negotiate the liberalizing patriarchal networks of 2000s Bollywood in order to place their "signatures" on trending brand identities. The chapter situates these shifting cases of Hindi/Bollywood female authorship within an intermittent genealogy of women's production roles in the Mumbai (previously Bombay) film industry. I consider if this might relate to the development of patriarchal nationalism as the Hindi grew to be the national film industry of India. Thinking about women's production history in the Hindi filmic field in a comparative regional light, I also point out that women have had relatively more opportunities to *sustain* complex authorial roles in Urdu (Lahore) and West Bengali (Kolkata) production fields. These were fields of filmmaking activity that lost resources to pre-Bollywood Hindi cinema due to the India-Pakistan partition such that patriarchal infrastructures shifted or gave way.

Part 3 thickens the texture of women's film history in South Asia by turning to regional transnationalism taken in two senses: as transnational film work *in* the region and, to a more limited extent, as transnational cinema *about* the region. The chapters follow the family-centered social film into transnational women's productions that relate female-prone kinship to regional historical trauma (the two partitions of the northern subcontinent; internecine boundary wars; militarized state formation under global/local warfare). All the female practices studied in this part are transnational in one or more senses of the term. The production processes network beyond borders rather than being limited to one national culture or normative order; they target audiences across divides of nation and difference; and they dramatize migratory or displaced identities and cross-border relations.[26] Like the previous parts of the book, part 3 situates the transnational practices in relation to different geographic scales of infrastructure. What this part adds is a comparative regional perspective on the way new media geographies enable or constrain women's creative and entrepreneurial authority. It juxtaposes a small-scale transnational cinema spawned in 1980s Pakistan and Bangladesh by the new media environment of video piracy with women's productions that traverse large-scale visual and digital networks in the brand space of the 2000s. Studies in this concluding part further complicate my reading of brand capital in earlier chapters. I demonstrate that feminist authors working with the heft of star capital or independent resources could make neoliberal capital inflect against regulatory frameworks, at least to an extent. They could create transnational counternarratives of displaced, precarious, or found kinship that refuse to compromise with nationalist sexual concepts. Nonetheless, authorship relying on large-scale connectivity in the new filmic space of the 2000s trends invariably toward timely concepts of femaleness and family, implicitly assuming branded limits. By contrast, small-scale authorial collaborations bred by transnational video piracy generate forms of family and sociality that are irreducible to borderly limits.

Chapter 5, "Families Out of Bounds: The Pirate Mode and Women's Coproductions across Pakistan and Bangladesh," shines light on a previously ignored repertoire of border-crossing cinema coproduced in the 1980s by Pakistani and Bangladeshi female star-filmmakers who were inhabiting pirate geographies in that the filmmakers were working through the infrastructures of reproduction and consumption generated by video piracy. The chapter examines two "superhit" Urdu action-heroine films: *Miss Colombo* (1984), directed by Pakistani star Shamim Ara and coproduced with a female star from Sri Lanka; and *Lady Smuggler* (1987), directed by Shamim Ara, coproduced by the Bangladeshi star Babita. The original Urdu version of *Lady Smuggler* was released by Shamim Ara Productions in Pakistan in 1987, and a print of the same fiction film dubbed in Bangla was released by Babita Movies in Bangladesh in 1990. While these action spectacles pirate attractions from the video market, they displace borrowed forms of patriarchal and neoliberal-female heroism. Instead, these innovative ensemble heroine films pit female homosocial kinship against violent masculinities and statist injustice. I read the heterogeneous spectacles and (fugitive) records of these action-heroine social films as comprising the ephemeral archive of a sexually paradoxical mode of film business. This mode involved women's body work in the fields of both production and publicity. Star-authors Shamim Ara and Babita alike deployed their famous personas on domestic media platforms in Pakistan and Bangladesh, respectively, to reinforce norms of national cinema and licit entertainment while generating infrastructures of desire for a piratical heroine cinema made by women. Collaboratively made and transnationally exhibited, the productions bear the traces of a migratory "pirate mode" creativity, a form of textuality worked on by many gendered hands. They embody a practice that thrived through crossing regional borders of nation-state, language, religion, and taste.

Chapter 6, "Families Torn and Found: Feminist Modes and Transnational Bangla Media," situates feminist social films in relation to media geographies proliferating in the Bengal region of the 2000s. My main cases in point are star-author Aparna Sen's corporate production of horror/partition comedy *Goynar Baksho* (The Jewelry Box; 2013), and non-star author Rubaiyat Hossain's independent family-mode production, for theatrical release, of the Liberation War film *Meherjaan* (2011). The first uses a multigenerational female drama as the lens on the mass displacement and linguistic gentrification in West Bengal following the partition of India and Pakistan; the second dramatizes a broken family and unrequited cross-border romance as subversive ways in to national memories of wartime genocide and rape. Both of these cases of transnational cinema in the region reveal that prevailing genres of regional heritage and war memory are gendered anew in the feminist fictions. These counternarratives are enabled, in the first production, through female star capital claiming partial control of corporate resources, and in the second, more radical production, by independent familial networking for funds, publicity, and exhibition. However, the conundrum in sustaining such legitimate feminist infusions of genre lies in the fact that critical choices become bounded by brand criteria of national timeliness or legitimacy. A ban subsequently imposed on Rubaiyat Hossain's *Meherjaan* shows that brand markets are shaped by a viral media undergirded by statist and global politics. Hossain's pathway takes us, finally, to the racial complexity of making transnational cinema *about* a postcolonial region. The chapter finishes by briefly considering that the flexible infrastructure of international film festivals, while it increasingly includes the global South, can come with its own brand concepts about "other" regions. Inclusion might be premised on imperial logics of Orientalism, Islamophobia (heightened by the War on Terror), and developmental aid.

In excavating women's cinemas from across the industries of a quickly transforming postcolonial region, this book builds on the argument I have recently made for moving beyond the "spatial containers" of area studies through deepening scholarship on regional cinematic relations.[27] This means that we reconsider approaches to the cinema contained by nation-state boundaries and think, instead, about processes of formation and fissure that zigzag across the region and blend with new imperial developments. Extending my earlier argument, this multi-sited book strives for what Gayatri Spivak calls a "textured" way to "region-think" on the interrelated modes by which women have made authorial claims on public meaning production in South Asia (2008, 226, 212). The chapters chart a genealogy of women's cinema beginning with the 1940s and through the 2010s. My attempt is to thicken the textures of female authorship and filmic labor as these evolve with major historical shifts. These shifts and formations range widely. As nations arise in the wake of the partitions of 1947 and 1971, male-dominant film businesses recede through the loss of resources in Lahore, Kolkata, and Dhaka, or, conversely, they consolidate in pre-Bollywood Mumbai. As inequities and brutalities escalate under state development in the 1970s through 1980s, mainstream cinema inflects to sociopolitical disturbance while catching the influence of social movements led by women, workers, and youth. As nation-states are globalized or militarized, legitimate and parallel media networks take shape. In the following pages, my attempt is to pry out a few ways in which under these conditions postcolonial cinema might become women's cinema, a creative legacy in which lives and hopes are traceable to female hands and bodies.

PART I

Maternal Modes and Infrastructural Access

Decoupled Maternities

Female Stars in
Production Modes, Kolkata

Part 1 takes up this book's primary argument about female filmic opportunities in South Asia. The chapters attempt to demonstrate that spaces of social films, spawned by the conceptual politics of domesticity and identity, invite women's participation on both sides of the camera. Female-centric family dramas being the emotional grid for staging anticolonial debates with modernity enable women's access to both creative work and entrepreneurial work. Focusing on the eastern region of South Asia, this part of the book shines light on previously ignored or overlooked histories of how women's creative practices of directorship, scriptwriting, and shot and set design entwine with infrastructure building (which includes setting up film companies of their own but is not limited to this form of entrepreneurship). The two chapters illuminate this genealogy by plotting the path of "motherliness" through different historical moments of social fiction making in West Bengal, India, and Bangladesh. The point is to consider how a nationalist concept like maternity, bred of cultural traditions of the Bengal region, generates "respectable" opportunities for women filmmakers. While much of part 1 dwells on the small-scale labors of female star-author entrepreneurs, managed at the localized levels of familial and celebrity relations, it proceeds to the related question being asked by this book. Both chapters consider how female authorship might mutate as the spatial scales of filmic capital expand or alter in the outreach. Roles taken by nation-states and by neoliberal brand markets are germane to the discussion. Focusing on the West Bengali industry located in Kolkata (previously Calcutta), the present chapter begins with the case of a woman widely recognized as the auteur of a politicized avant-garde repertoire spawned by state-level initiatives. The history of how her authorship of gender critique has been sustained by a celebrity persona and fan cultivation is often overlooked by scholars. The introduction brought up the case of Aparna Sen to discuss the limitations of using the auteur paradigm for a film worker who is also a major star. Here, I round out that discussion by situating her practice in a longer genealogy of female star-authors of Bangla cinema in West Bengal, India.

Renowned as an Indian woman director and scriptwriter, Aparna Sen turned to filmmaking in the early 1980s. Directing motion pictures in both English and Bengali, she rode the crest of a feminist women's cinema that arose in the latter years of a male-dominant New Wave cinema in India (Sawhney 2015). Her cohort comprised women directors such as Aruna Raje, Vijaya Mehta, Sai Paranjpye, Prema Karanth, and Kalpana Lajmi. Not unlike the rise of feminist cinema, together with supportive audiences elsewhere in the world (Cook 1998, 244), the context for the Indian women's wave was a burgeoning movement that raised public debates on a range of issues, including women's "legal rights . . . education, employment, health, sexuality, [and] domestic violence" (Sawhney 2015, 153–154). Yet Aparna Sen differed from the cohort in her point of access to filmmaking. She had already earned star fame by acting in Bengali social films. Hindi film director and editor Aruna Raje makes this point in a retrospective account. She implicitly positions Aparna Sen—one "who had been acting" before she directed her first film—as somewhat of an outlier to an emergent "film fraternity." This fraternity is described by Aruna as entering the industry through film school training or prior roles in film and media production in the late 1970s through the 1980s (Raje, qtd. in Gargi 2013, 47–48). Aparna's own perspective on access adds further insight.

In an interview published in 1984 in the periodical *Filmfare* to mark the release of her first Bengali-language motion picture, *Parama* (made in a Hindi version as well), Aparna notes that film direction and acting offered parallel "channels" of opportunity for her "creative efforts" and that it had been relatively easy for her to crisscross between the respective positions (A. Sen 1984, 80–81). In the same interview, Aparna Sen avers that she garners "respect" (albeit "indulgent") for her directorship from male colleagues in the industry while also maintaining that she would continue to perform the "commercial film" roles in which she had developed "competence" (81). The implication seems to be that cultivating multiple competencies in film work is useful for her. In recent personal conversations with me, Aparna has responded to my question about access in a similar vein. When I asked if getting to the production position of director and scriptwriter had been difficult for her "as a woman," she asserted that it had never been a problem and voluntarily added "*āmi to celebrity chilām*" (I was a celebrity; phone interview, 2013). In light of her adaptive relations to available infrastructures for creative output, it is significant that Aparna's productions of female-centric fiction films have far outlived the period of the women's wave described above. That fleeting wave had been enabled by progressive male patronage—or in the colorful words of Aruna Raje, by the inclination of male directors "to take on girls as assistant directors because it was more fashionable and the 'in' thing to do" (Raje, qtd. in Gargi 2013, 48). By contrast, Aparna Sen's authorship of gender-critical fiction films appears to have been sustained by her competent interactions with generic Bengali femaleness on both sides of the camera.

This chapter demonstrates that although Aparna Sen's entry into directing certainly was enabled by the state-sponsored women's wave of the late 1970s and '80s, her authorial position intersects with a longer genealogy. If we turn a female-focused lens on the preceding decades of Bangla cinema, the decades following the partition of Bengal and Indian independence in 1947, we find a slim but telling strand of small-scale female-star-authorship setting the context for Aparna Sen's creative authority in the Bangla production culture. Her signatory tropic interventions in established concepts of respectable maternity and Hindu couple formation—in *Parama* and thereafter—are more holistically illuminated as well if seen in the light of the previously neglected activities of her cultural forerunners. The pages that follow in this chapter plot reuses of the pivotal gender concepts of Bengali nationalist modernity—motherhood, the couple form, and respectable domesticity—through selected moments of women's production history in West Bengal.

The bulk of this chapter situates Aparna Sen's feminist Bengali productions in the 1980s and 1990s in relation to female star-entrepreneur Kanan Devi's activities of genre remaking in the 1950s. Kanan's authorial activities encompassed shot and costume design, film company entrepreneurship, and tutelage of Kanan's own company's directorial collective. My attempt here and elsewhere in this book is to examine how female authorship—understood as performative interactions with given genres of femaleness and gender relations—loops through production contexts into the diegetic contents of works whose making is steered by women. How male-centric objects (tropes or mise-en-scènes) generic to the field of Bengali social cinema are *restaged* in works made by Kanan Devi and her successors suggest shifts in the material referents. In other words, artistic changes carry traces of how female star-filmmakers negotiate authority on a small scale, unsettling gender relations in the historically male-dominant production and publicity circuits of Kolkata cinema. Staying with my comparative focus on the scales at which women negotiate creative control, the chapter ends with a briefer look at maternal cinema in 2000s Kolkata. My lens is the trendy repertoire of director/producer/actress Sudeshna Roy. The present-day environment of Kolkata cinema is not unlike others across India and South Asia in including an unprecedented number of women in production roles. What I note, however, is a curiously recursive shift in the portrayal of *maleness* in 2000s woman-made maternal fiction film, a generic shift that seems to be branded on a large scale at both the local and pan-Indian levels. To get to these specifics, I must begin by situating women's cinema in relation to the genealogy of gender in the Bangla filmic spaces of Kolkata, mainstream and parallel.

Women's Cinema, the Couple Form, and Maternity: A West Bengali Genealogy

Attempting to historicize the rise of female star-filmmakers in post-partition West Bengal, I find conditions that in significant aspects were not dissimilar to those enabling women to become filmmakers and small-scale film entrepreneurs elsewhere in the northern region of South Asia, albeit the women were functioning in clearly asynchronous contexts. Not unlike their counterparts in Bangladesh and Pakistan, the star-filmmakers of post-partition West Bengal were allowed access and creative control through gendered shifts in infrastructure. As I demonstrate throughout this book, the infrastructures of cinema should be understood as made up at once of economic resources, material tools and technologies, and affective commodities. The latter comprise genres and conventions that pave the virtual pathways of desire and consumption. In our context at hand, gendered hierarchies were being transformed or questioned both within the infrastructures of economic and material resources and in the affective realm. Urban Bengali publics who were consuming cinema desired change. What we must consider is if *women's traversals* of these gendered conflicts over the Bengali contemporary might stand out in the focus and the modality. Questions of a female address and the appeal to women audiences are also germane.

In the wake of the partition of India and Pakistan and subsequent political and social upheavals, this eastern Indian state was beleaguered by refugee influx and uneven urbanization. From the late 1940s through the 1970s, the Bangla film culture suffered not only from the loss of the East Bengali market to partition but also from shifts and fragmentation in resource structures. These shifts enabled female stars and actresses to enter production roles. Aparna Sen's immediate predecessors in production roles were the performer and director of film and music Arundhuti Devi (1924–1990) and the performer/director and producer Manju Dey (1926–1989). Forerunning them all, the pioneer of the female production mode in Kolkata was the singing star Kanan Devi (1916–1992). Kanan set up a small-scale production house in 1949 and ran it successfully for sixteen years while participating in the directorial team. Infrastructures enabling women filmmakers in these decades arose from the ways that both the concepts and the financial contents (property and social privilege) of the patriarchal and caste-based Hindu joint family were coming undone in West Bengal.

On one side, the collapse in the 1940s of a joint family–mode studio system, which had sought a tight hierarchy of cinematic labor, opened the floodgates to many producers, independently valued and contracted stars (sometimes also involved in production), and an unregulated capital flow exacerbated by a parallel war economy (Gooptu 2010, 120–125). Published by India's Ministry of Information and Broadcasting in 1951, the *Report of the Film Enquiry Committee*, with S. K. Patil as the committee chair, documents this transformation, albeit through an unfavorable characterization. It describes a "haphazard growth of the industry under the full blast of *laissez faire* . . . [driven by the] cupidity of gamblers and financiers [and an] . . . overmuch reliance on individual rather than collective initiative." The same report riddles its negative assessment by associating the individual entrepreneurship that replaced bureaucratic studios with a new, postwar "state of prosperity" (171–172). Precisely these so-called haphazard changes in favor of personal initiative were what shifted the caste-based patriarchal division of labor and resource typical of studio-era bureaucracy in Calcutta. In its place came more malleable familial production modes allowing women to stake interdependent partner-like arrangements with both paternal and companionate men. These arrangements accorded a new authoritative status to the sexually divided labors that were always assumed from women professionals, and stratified as well by class and caste, within studio-era industrial practices. The types of women's labor previously extracted without due transactional value in the joint family–studio milieu included both creative work, such as costume design, and domestic-type caregiving work, such as cooking for male colleagues.[1] We learn, for example, from life stories narrated by herself (1973) as well as by her biographer Mekhala Sengupta (2015) that in the studio era, Kanan Devi had regularly sketched out designs for her costumes and sets without receiving due credit. Kanan's evolving career demonstrates that women's creative and corporeal work alike started to accrue independent value and matriarchal capital for film entrepreneurship in the post–joint family studio era. I will get to more details below, but for now let me turn to the generative impact of historical shifts on filmic social fictions of the contemporary. Collective experiences of uprooting from ancestral communities and hierarchies through the India-Pakistan partition and subsequent urbanization engendered new cinematic concepts that decentered patriarchal Bangla aesthetics.

Important historiographies of Bangla social film point to two focal concepts of gender relations on whose emotional grid the collective experiences of ruptured lifeworlds were staged. On the one hand, we find a couple form riddling the patriarchal family structure. Both Moinak Biswas (2000) and Sharmistha Gooptu (2010) aptly demonstrate that what came to dominate the Bengali cinematic modern in the 1950s through the 1970s, across "the categories of 'mainstream' and 'parallel' cinema" (Gooptu 2010, 257), were explorations of heterosexual couple forms and male-female relations. These relations allowed for simultaneous individuation of both the male and the female protagonist (Biswas 2000, 132). Tanika Sarkar's archival reading reminds us that contestations over conjugality and couple romance were hardly new to the paradoxes of Bengali Hindu modernity (1995, 101–106). These politics of the domestic date back to the anticolonial nationalisms of nineteenth-century Bengal. The concept of consensual love—embroiled in "discomforts about mutuality and equality"—had been central to debates that raged among elite male nationalists about how to reform the upper-caste Hindu patriarchal joint family and marital domesticity (106). What arose in the cinema in the turbulent postpartition decades, however, were concepts of respectable middle-class women (*bhadramahila*, or gentlewomen) working outside the patriarchal home or becoming mobile beyond the normative borders of caste and class (Bagchi 1990, 43). In addition, male-female relations were being dramatized anew in the forms of premarital romance (Biswas 1990, 309) and of conjugal and familial relations and conflicts. Recurrent in such fictions of conjugality, on the other hand, was the inclination to situate female roles in relation to what Gooptu describes as "crises of masculinity" or insecurities of urban male youth (2010, 162, 257–263). Along similar lines, Ashis Nandy locates an early version of the dependent Bengali "man in crisis" in pre-partition, studio-era pastoral cinema—specifically, in the archetype of a perpetual lover/son searching for the lost "maternal utopia" (2001, 55).

My female-focused lens complicates the aforementioned genealogical readings of gender in Bangla cinema in at least two ways. To begin with, my approach fills a gap in the scholarship simply by foregrounding the history of women's Bangla cinema. Beyond that, my case studies illuminate how the heroine films made by women from the 1950s through the 1990s curiously come together in posing a veiled rebuttal to prevalent male-oriented concepts of couple formation and maternal domesticity. In other words, women-made fiction films inhabit the field of social genre making in which male colleagues are active and reprioritize values. Veiled or direct reprioritizations of gender worth by women serve to clarify the contrast of even the more unorthodox gender portrayals by the ilk of Satyajit Ray and Tapan Sinha in the art-house and parallel streams or of Ajoy Kar in the mainstream. Across the board, male directors share a tendency to construct agential or companionate women as maternal nurturers of needy masculinities and dependent families. Male protagonists tend to be allegorically feminized (Biswas 2000, 132), although patriarchies at the same time are destabilized or outright critiqued, especially in the art-house stream (in productions by Ritwik Ghatak, Satyajit Ray, or Mrinal Sen, for example). It is arguable that in the recurrent inclination to portray the normative female lead as something of a maternal nurturer, we find in a new guise the nineteenth-century Hindu nationalist trope of the respectable woman as a pure "goddess and mother" figure (P. Chatterjee 1993, 130). This reflexive tendency to magnify the travails of modern Bengali masculinity through the lens of nurturant womanhood was further buttressed by the respectable (*bhadralok*) male stars towering over the eras in question: hero and director Pramathesh Barua in the pre-partition era (Kanan Devi's coworker), and the heroes Uttam Kumar and Soumitra Chatterjee in the post-partition decades. I maintain that while rebuttal to the persistent male orientation in Bengali fictions of maternal domesticity grows explicit in the feminist melodramas directed by Aparna Sen, this rebuttal must be situated in a longer legacy of women's cinema. In this legacy, we find previously unnoticed *transborder* activity. Prevalent genres of Bengali femaleness are repeatedly reworked both in filmic texts and in the infrastructures of film production and circulation. Reuses of generic forms by actresses commanding public appeal open other pathways of audience desire in the transforming urban contexts of West Bengal.

An even passing glance at the works directed by Arundhuti Devi and Manju Dey uncovers heroine narratives decentering male-focused couple forms and motherhood. For example, Arundhuti Devi's directorial debut, *Chuti* (Vacation; 1967), pits an unrealizable ideal of couple romance against dysfunctional conjugality and failed motherhood. The fictional arc of *Chuti* is ambivalently tangled with that of *Jatugriha* (1964), a social film about a divorced couple, casting Arundhuti as the female lead and the iconic hero Uttam Kumar as the focal point. The latter was directed by Arundhuti's spouse, Tapan Sinha. Having set up her own production house, Anindiya Chitra, in 1969 (Rajadhyaksha and Willemen 1999, 83), Arundhuti went on to direct *Padi Pishir Barmi Baksa* (The Burmese Box of Aunt Padi; 1972). The children's literary film, based on a novel of the same name by the woman writer Leela Majumdar, heroizes the pranks of a feisty widowed aunt who outwits both vicious and incapable men. Released the same year as *Chuti* from her independent star-name company, Manju Dey Productions, was Manju Dey's debut feature as director and heroine of *Abhisapta Chambal* (The Cursed Chambal; 1967). This bandit drama depicts the woman as an action heroine and dancing girl embroiled, once again, in experiences of failed romance and unfulfilled maternity. Significant is the cover of a song booklet promoting *Abhisapta Chambal* with the caption "Manju Dey's daring and over-bold picture," and an accompanying image of the director/heroine herself in an "angry woman" facial pose (fig. 2). Neepa Majumdar has argued that in classic Indian cinema, star personification is rooted in pre-cinematic conventions of figuring public fame or notoriety (2009, 21). The persona relies on an "iconic framing" wherein the "external display of legible and recurrent signs" means the revelation of "depersonalized norms" in the form of personal details (143–144). It is telling in this light that the face of Manju Dey's angry revolt is uniquely at odds with the iconic expressions of female stars of era. The facial poses of such famous stars as Suchitra Sen and Supriya Devi towering over the 1960s variously personalize patriarchal norms of maternal pleasance or feminine distress. In view of the oddity in Manju Dey's pose, it is not irrelevant to mention that Manju Dey's star-director persona was depicted for me by her close colleague and fan, the

মঞ্জুদে'র দুঃসাহসিক ছবি—

আভিশপ্ত চম্বল

Fig. 2: Cover of song
booklet for *Abhisapta
Chambal* (1967; dir.
Manju Dey)

octogenarian actor Nirmal Kumar, as that of a dashing woman (roaming the
roads in a flashy car) who had wanted to make films that broke the norm
(personal interview, 2014). Perhaps in the errant details found in the filmic
texts and orbital objects produced by Manju Dey and Arundhuti Devi, we
encounter traces of dissident authorial work on both sides of the camera. The
creative and entrepreneurial labors of star-directors Manju Dey and Arundhuti
Devi await further research.

The following sections explore how the imagery created by both Aparna
Sen and Kanan Devi reveal a tropic tendency of the same vein. The shared
inclination is to control figurations of the maternal and feminine in ways
that pry womanliness away from male-centric couple narratives. Clearly, the
practices of the two women in question diverge, as do the conditions of
their production work. Kanan Devi's artistry as a star-filmmaker, negotiating
the post–studio era transformations noted above, constitutes an ambivalent

attempt to infiltrate genres of respectable womanliness by overcoming her own stigmatized background. By contrast, the feminist counternarratives made by the elite star-author Aparna Sen constitute a "political interpretation of the social text and of the social subject" (de Lauretis 1987, 113). The hermeneutic is fueled by a different set of infrastructural shifts, noted earlier and further discussed below. Thus, in situating Aparna Sen's practice in comparison to Kanan Devi's, we must distinguish between what Gayatri Spivak describes as "traces of the heterogeneous [revealing] difference between radical and conservative resistance to the dominant" (1999, 314). Nevertheless, the differing practices of these two female star-filmmakers of West Bengal do converge in contributing to a particular modality of women-centric cinema. In this modality, the characteristic male orientation of West Bengali liberal traditions gives way. Considering selected maternal dramas directed or codirected and performed by Aparna Sen and Kanan Devi, respectively, I find that the works portray *decoupled* maternal bodies to be *self-sustaining sites* of sociomoral commitment and libidinal desire. However, in following the women-made genre of Bengali motherliness through the phases of its commodity life, I also find that it grows less than self-sustainable as it travels into the large-scale infrastructures of the present day.

Motherly Form, Romantic Vocality: Kanan Devi and the Small-Scale Film Company (1950s)

Kanan Devi may well be seen to have engendered the conflicts of the contemporary in the early decades of the Bangla social film—once she passed the voice test for the transition from silent to sound performance and went on to become the leading female singing star of the 1930s through the 1950s. Sharmistha Gooptu describes Kanan as the "quintessential product" of talkie-era fictions through which the leading studios were constructing their principal actresses as personifications of "demure femininity . . . [and] glorified domesticity connoting respectability" (2017, 145). Gooptu argues for a mutual and circular relationship between the shifts in Kanan's star-to-filmmaker identity and that of the identity of the film industry she signified in the public eye. She maintains that by the end of her career, Kanan had been transformed from a perceived "public woman of easy virtue" and uncertain parentage performing for an ill-reputed industry to a towering star of the good cinema mirroring a respectable industry and targeting middle-class audiences (2017, 152–153). Moving along a similar arc, Kanan Devi's life story, *Sabāre āmi Nami* (My Obeisance to All, 1973; henceforth, Life Story) offers an overt self-rescue narrative. Serially cowritten later in her career with woman journalist Sandhya Sen, Kanan's Life Story narrates her rise from an early life of servitude spent in part in a red-light neighborhood to the reputable stature of maternal star, film company owner, and industry leader with international outreach. We read that in the 1950s and 1960s, she visited Hollywood and British studios and also made her presence felt at international film festivals.

Yet, what if we dwell on the extra tidbits that remain in the folds of the Life Story, adding anecdotal color but not necessarily cohering with the narrative arc? The extra details call on me, with some libidinal force, to pay attention to the actress-filmmaker's interactions with conventions of feminine behavior prevailing both in the film genres and the production practices of her time. Bits and pieces of the Life Story appear to pull together with certain film scenes, soundtracks, and star poses as if to index "fossilized" traces of Kanan Devi's authorial strides and struggles.[2] The struggle seems to have been for claiming artistic control over the female form and voice (her own) by working the conventions and mastering their tools while she negotiated the underlying borders of gender and social privilege. My focus is on the maternal social film *Mej Didi*, seen in relation to extradiegetic images and accounts. Codirected by Kanan Devi and produced in 1950 from her recently established film company, Sreemati Pictures (literally, Mrs./Miss Pictures), *Mej Didi* seems to reproduce techniques for featuring gender relations and domestic worlds that were conventional to the mainstream Bengali screen at the time yet, inexplicably, remains at odds with couple imagery.

The plot of the literary film *Mej Didi* closely follows a short Bangla novel of the same name written in 1938 by the well-known male writer Saratchandra Chattopadyay. In her Life Story, Kanan Devi asserts that she had wanted to build a production house that followed the lead of the good stories and fine artistry of New Theatres productions—the studio in whose employ she had achieved high stardom in the 1930s (Devi 1973, 109). In turning a Saratchandra fiction into film, Sreemati Pictures indeed followed the tradition of the eminently respectable New Theatres and its towering hero/director Pramathesh Barua (himself an aristocrat by birth). At first glance, *Mej Didi* recreates the quintessential Saratchandra-Barua trope of a fragile and anguished pastoral hero uprooted from the maternal care of his utopian village home and hurled into the "soulless . . . rationality" of petty bourgeois urban culture (Nandy 2001, 50–53). It is the tale of a teenage boy named Keshta who is brought from his village to the provincial-urban abode of his stepsister Kadambini after he loses his impoverished yet ever-protective mother to tuberculosis. While the stepsister and family are brutally exploitative of Keshta, having taken custody of Keshta only out of fear of social censure for failing in their family duty, Kadambini's sister-in-law Hemangini tries to protect the orphaned teenager with intense maternal longing. Called "Mej Didi," or second sister, by Keshta, Hemangini is the devout mother of two children of her own. Nonetheless, she comes into conflict with her otherwise loyal husband about protecting Keshta from oppression. Once obstructed in her maternal drive, she begins to waste away from symptoms not unlike those experienced by Keshta's late birth mother. Although husband Bipin at first refuses to confront his older brother and wife for fear of dissension within the joint family, he is eventually persuaded by male elders in the community to stand against family hierarchy in favor of his wife's ethical motherly decision to adopt Keshta.

The plot seems to reproduce what Ashis Nandy characterizes as the Saratchandra-Barua worldview of fragile masculinity and vanishing rural-maternal utopias. This worldview appealed to (male) audiences who faced "the problem of refashioning their selves in response to the changing demands of Indian modernization" in the colonial era (Nandy 2001, 53). Both *Mej Didi* and similar melodramas subsequently released by Sreemati Pictures in the 1950s must be seen as restaging the said worldview in a new era of cinema in the Indian nation-state. The worldview was being made functional not only to a woman-led company but also to a cinematic address that was adequate for audiences facing the consequences of displacement (from village roots) in the first decade after the partition of India and Pakistan. Mother figuration in this work strives, from both sides of the camera, to produce a modern "citizen-self that is (paradoxically) regionally anchored" in the city while it seeks "a fantasy equipoise" between urban/rural identities and locations (Biswas 2003, 94–95). In the simultaneous making and performance of the equipoised maternal citizen—a process that invites reading for an urban middle-class female address as much as a male—the libidinal utopia of homemaking seems to mutate in favor of the enlightened mother rather than of heroes and conjugal patriarchs. At least, up to a point.

Take an early scene in which Hemangini tells a bedtime story that turns into a song as she puts her young daughter and son to sleep. The scene is intermit-tently match-cut with shots of Keshta, fragile with exhaustion, toiling in the haystack to chop hay for his stepsister's cows. Low-angle medium to close-up shots show Hemangini's children curled comfortably in bed as they look up, with utterly reliant adoration, to their mother's face. Her face is contoured in soft focus with key and rim lights lending an ethereal sensuality to the pleasant expression. The soundtrack picks up the soft cadence of Hemangini/Kanan's voice narrating the tale of how a prince lying abandoned in a rubbish heap is awakened from exhausted stupor by the magical sense of a feminine presence by his side reminding him of his long-deceased mother. We hear of how he wakes to a gentle touch upon his forehead with the startled cry of "Mother" on his lips. At this moment, the shot of dreamy-faced storyteller Kanan is audio match-cut with that of Keshta in the distant haystack, remembering his village mother in a flash and also crying out "Mother." Incarnating motherly protection in her *spiritual* tone and tune, singing star Kanan/Hemangini goes on to present the song by the magical mother that in her story had put the prince to restful sleep. By association, Hemangini's own motherly spirit grows magically expansive. The deft techniques of soft focus, meditative song presentation, and match-cuts serve to envelop both the birth children in her lap and Keshta at a distance. As the soundtrack picks up the song lyric of "sleep, my prince" (*ghumāo rājkumār*), we realize that Hemangini/Kanan's voice has become audible to Keshta in the haystack, lulling his thin and tired body to a comfortable sleep in parallel to the children's in the bed.

This iconic framing of everyday mother work in the depersonalized terms of maternal spirituality—equipoised between rural (Keshta's mother's) and educated urban (Hemangini's) ideals of child care—serves to place the fragile and dependent on the receptive periphery while altogether blocking male control. Kanan's motherly pose and voice become the center of sensual contemplation, constituted as it is through the receptive eyes both of her dependent children as well as of the fragile hero, Keshta. In addition, the supramundane space of mother care comes to be guarded from the mundane proprieties and couple-mode pressures of the patriarchal domestic clock. The narrative pretext for the bedtime space is a demand made by her children on Hemangini to which she readily concedes: that of being with them and telling the story rather than going and serving the father his dinner when he returns from work. This way of authenticating maternal space-time paradoxically, by *guarding it* from intervention by male characters within the text *and* implicitly by male stars in extradiegetic space, is even clearer in another scenic configuration. The scene to which I now turn evokes the trope of the mother as a goddess figure familiar to patriarchal Hindu nationalism, noted above, while positioning the patriarch as something of an intruder in the scene of mother worship.

Key and fill lighting combine to brightly illuminate Kanan's face in close-up as she pours out a devotional song, supplicating to the deity of the hearth, Ghanaśyam, so that she gains the capacity to see the way of (maternal) truth and virtue. The camera pulls back to expose Hemangini seated in the worship room with her two children on either side, praying and singing along. We encounter the frontal tableau framing that is common to 1950s Hindi cinema (Vasudevan 2000, 136–138). In the Indian context, the tableau is the grouping of characters into a stable "work of iconic condensation" available for a depersonalized reading in terms of already familiar extratextual images and narratives. Ravi Vasudevan explains that this specifically Indian mode of iconic framing arising from Hindu religious art enables scenic constructions of the devotional practice of *darsana*, a reciprocal gaze exchanged between the devotee and a "living" deity that fulfills the former's supplication (137–140). The iconography of darsana is dynamically deployed on Indian screens (138). We certainly find in this scene a condensed construction of the darsana effect. In the tableau, the mother with children supplicates to the household deity for the true domestic way of maternity, and she is reciprocated with the divine touch. The melodrama of divinely graced maternity not only is dynamically accented by top-lit close-ups; it is also deployed intratextually to polarize the stepsister's mundane and calculative mother work, shot elsewhere in unaccented natural light. Yet the more dynamic and immediate narrative import of the maternal worship scene is that it is sutured to a point-of-view (POV) shot tutoring us to think about centrality and periphery. The POV is that of husband Bipin, who stands outside the threshold of the worship room, later explaining that he had hesitated to intrude lest he spoil the perfection of the scene. His wife looked so utterly "beautiful" with her two children on either side. The scenic sequence serves to highlight the libidinal value of an implicitly decoupled maternal icon. The iconic commodity is guarded from conjugal relations, with men positioned as intrusive or, at most, as contemplators of the sensually self-sustaining female form.

While the commodity value of the divinely touched feminine form recurs in yet another song interlude, the latter is curiously contradictory in the way it illuminates the *performer* in extradiegetic space, beyond the domestic role being played. It seems to me that in this contradictory configuration of libidinal desire for the female form and voice, we see a trace of Kanan Devi's long-standing struggle to gain authorial control over her artistry by overcoming her stigmatized background. It is telling that the scene sequence in question is a flashback that momentarily transmutes the "character role" of mother being played by an older Kanan to the role of a romantic singer-heroine, evocative of the unstable eroticism surrounding Kanan's star fame in the 1930s.

In the studio era, she had often been cast in what journalist Kuldip Singh calls, in his obituary of Kanan Devi, "risqué roles" making up a "glamour queen" persona (1992). While such de-domesticated roles staged the contradictory desires for modernization and anticolonial nationalism among the target male and female audiences, they also served to gesture at Kanan's background as that of a public woman identified with easy virtue. Her roles include a single Christian woman masquerading as married in *Manmoyee Girls School* (1935; dir. Jyotish Bannerjee), a socialite and estranged wife in *Mukti* (1937; dir. Pramathesh Barua), and, most germane to our discussion, a glamorous public performer in *Street Singer* (1938; dir. Phani Majumdar). Calling attention to how signifiers of respectability and class were merged into "sound aesthetics" in the 1930s, Madhuja Mukherjee points to a popular style called *caiti* that Kanan sings in *Street Singer*. Her sonic identification with the caiti, "a faster and vulgar version of the [classical] *thumri*," is melodramatically pitted against the thumri being voiced by the hero and singing star K. L. Saigal, known for his restrained classical style (M. Mukherjee 2007, 15). Clearly, a vulgar popular voice was jostling against the normative singing persona Kanan had sought to cultivate. As narrated with teleological zest in the Life Story, Kanan had strived to develop the style of both a classical vocalist and a "spiritual" exponent, versed in the proper rendition of the highly respectable Tagore song repertoire, for one (Devi 1973, 41–43). As should be evident from the previous pages, *Mej Didi* combines sound with visual aesthetics to reinforce the restrained spirituality of the motherly heroine and her voice. At the same time, the last song interlude navigates the moral contradiction inherent in Kanan Devi's singing-star persona and repositions the latter's commodity value by staging a respectable patriarchal resolution.

The episode begins at a heated moment of conjugal conflict. Hemangini, sickened from grief over Keshta's persistent oppression in the hands of her in-laws, pleads with her husband to arrange for her to adopt Keshta, only to receive a shrewd retort. Bipin refuses to always pander to her mother-goddess-like protective inclinations (in his words, "to behave like the goddess *Jagatdhātri*"). Not only does he refuse to rock the family boat, but he is also unwilling to take on the additional financial burden of an adopted ward (notwithstanding his obvious wealth). Left alone with her frustration, Hemangini recalls the early romantic days of their married life, when Bipin would deny none of her wishes. We see the shot fade into the vibrantly smiling figure of a younger-looking Kanan with ornamented face and flowing hair. Soft and shallow focus shots reveal dreamy-eyed Hemangini/Kanan by herself on the open terrace, singing to the rhythm of the swaying trees a song about the exquisite natural looks of a princess riding a boat of gusty clouds to her prince. When Bipin does arrive on the scene, his words only reinforce the supramundane nature of Hemangini's innate motherly femininity. He begins by saying that the care work for the needy she had longed for in her dreamworld (*swapnalok*)—a world implicitly outside the calculative reasoning of bourgeois domesticity—he has transacted in the earthly world (*martyalok*). He has restored a property to its needy male owner, paying out of pocket and taking a loss to do so. It is significant that although husband Bipin does appear on the scene to complete the romance of the heterosexual couple form familiar to the Bengali screen, both his belated entrance and the dialogue about earthly decisions (in mundane time) are temporally guarded from the ethereally erotic dreamworld of his motherly wife. Yet, precisely this *autoerotic* scene of womanly desires seems to mutate into questions about the identity of the woman and performer.

What Bipin's dialogue also contains is a threatening interpretation of Kanan's decoupled performance—one that dislocates the sensualized performer from couple-mode respectability. Bipin ends by saying that the money he paid to fulfill her wish is the monetary reward Hemangini/Kanan would have received had she sung her song publicly, as a professional performing before a prince or a landowner and being paid for her skills. The reference is to the tradition of public women associated with easy virtue performing professionally for the feudal gentry, as compared to the respectable high-caste/-class women keeping to domestic privacy (the influence of Victorian notions of female respectability and domestic privacy being unmistakable in this anti-colonial nationalist construction of womanhood in India). In this case, the framing by her husband's dialogue of Kanan's song as that like a professional entertainer's seems to serve two radically conflicting purposes. On the one hand, it highlights Kanan Devi's extradiegetic identity as a professional singing star who towers in her own right, thereby clarifying the star-vehicle purpose of this motion picture. On the other hand, it paradoxically identifies Kanan with the disreputable performing classes so as to uplift her identity through the necessary agency of the respectable husband and private conjugality.

Concepts such as these of uplifting conjugality and respectable male-supported maternity loop off-screen into accounts of Kanan Devi's production work, which also seem to concede to the sexual borders of authority and labor in the cine-workplace. Ironically, this conceptual infrastructure allowed her citizenship and creative opportunities in the *bhadra* (genteel) patriarchal context. Traces of how Kanan negotiated the opportunity structure in a way that shifted patriarchal control have to be teased out from stories lodged within her narratives of concession and collaboration.

The credits for *Mej Didi* list Kanan Devi's name only as the female lead, while direction is attributed to the collective "Sabyasachi" and production to the film company Sreemati Pictures. What we learn from Mekhala Sengupta's biography of the late Kanan Devi, which draws, among other sources, from firsthand accounts of such colleagues of Kanan as Tarun Majumdar,[3] is that in the early days of the Sabyasachi Collective, "direction was provided by the entire team" (Sengupta 2015, 140). Far from being unique to Sreemati Pictures, the model of collaborative directorship was common to the Kolkata production space both in the post-studio era and in selected studio-era arrangements. Making this point to me, the octogenarian actor Nirmal Kumar reminisced that what he termed the "unit" process of film directorship could well involve hands-on collaboration between film personnel on the set, including camera operators, sound technicians, and actors (personal interview, 2014). The collective practice of unit directorship seems to have been a variation on the "heterogeneous" film production mode Madhava Prasad detects in the early Hindi film environment (1998a, 32). A group of specialists were contributing a disaggregated range of skills and insights to the making of the whole. In a collective unit like Sabyasachi, located in a company managed by a woman and veteran film professional, the borders of specialization and authority were complexly sexual.

Kanan's Life Story, while it reiterates the arrangement of collaborative directorship, accords a primary authorial role to her husband. We are told that by the time *Mej Didi* was being made, Kanan's husband, Haridas Bhattacharya, not only had joined the Sabyasachi Collective but also had taken on the principal tasks of scriptwriting (credited in the extant print) and casting direction for the part of Keshta (Devi 1973, 126). Indeed, Kanan's Life Story offers a wondrous accolade to the natural creative acumen shown by her husband, resonant with the awestruck tone with which elsewhere it invokes the "high society," and implicitly high-caste, status of husband Haridas (117). Clearly, high-society bhadralok conjugal life was serving to elevate Kanan's own social status such that her reliance on respectable coupledom with Haridas came to be central to the Life Story's narrative of self-rescue. Keep in mind that the Life Story was plotted in conjunction with a woman journalist from the respectable class. Still, what distinguishes our account at hand from that of private conjugality found elsewhere in the Life Story is the portrayal of Kanan's evolving partner-like professional relations with a husband just entering the film business by the side of a veteran such as Kanan herself. Depicting how a "hidden force" had been "awakened" (*supta śakti . . . jagrata*) within Haridas under influence from his environment (126), the narrative about scriptwriting positions Haridas as a gifted novice and Kanan herself as the influential specialist. We learn that she was engaged with him in "numerous discussions" (*anek ālochanā*) on script preparation, albeit she had eventually conceded to his approach of close fidelity to the high literary original penned by Saratchandra. The narrative implies that even though Kanan had conceded some ground, she remained actively involved with script preparation for *Mej Didi*. Perhaps here we find a "condensed cryptic histor[y]" of a cowritten script—a collaborative authorship indexed by the ambivalent centrality of the female figure in the song-and-scene arrangements discussed earlier (Marks 2000, 88).

There is little doubt that the pose of dedicated motherliness developed in *Mej Didi* thereafter became generic to Kanan Devi and, in combination to narratives of needy young men, a prototype for Sreemati Pictures productions. For example, the cover of a song booklet promoting another maternal melodrama titled *Asha*, released a few years later (1956), showcases Kanan's pose as the motherly protector hovering over a young male dependent (fig. 3). The poster names Kanan as the producer and husband Haridas as the solo director. Instated in the role of the primary director and creative decision maker, the elite patriarch certainly makes the respectability of their production house tangible to the eyes of middle-class audiences. No doubt, the foregrounding of the respectable male director and husband helped to strengthen an infrastructure of acceptance for the company, associated as it was with the name of a female star of questionable background. Yet, in doing the fugitive research of gender around the dominant foreground, I am drawn to the many extraneous stories about Kanan's specialized contributions. It seems that a partner mode and collaborative creative practice was essential to the production process at Sreemati Pictures.

Kanan's account of her collaboration with other participants in the Sabyasachi Collective is less concessional and humble than it is matriarchal. The Life

শ্রীমতী পিকচার্সের গীতি-মুখর নিবেদন

আশা

প্রযোজনা ও প্রধান ভূমিকায়
কানন দেবী

স্মৃতি - মা সা রি লি জ এ

Fig. 3: Cover of song booklet for *Asha* (1956; dir. Haridas Bhattacharya)

Story characterizes Sreemati Pictures as a home-like environment managed at the smallest spatial levels of familial and body work by a mother figure. Younger male personnel such as Ajoy Kar, Tarun Majumdar, and the latter's colleagues in the Yatrik Collective are described as receiving their *hātekhari* in the filmic craft, thereafter to become towering directors of Bengali cinema (Devi 1973, 125). The trope of hātekhari literalizes the touch of a maternal tutor, as it means "putting the chalk in the hand" of a child or a novitiate in order to ceremonially initiate the young one into learning. The trope stages the film company as a kinship network ordered by age and expertise. The family image is linked elsewhere in the Life Story to descriptions of horizontal "teamwork" among colleagues who also became *āpanjan*, or close kin (124). The image is significantly embellished with accounts of the physical care given to the personnel by the maternal owner (cooking a special diet for an ailing actor, for example) (29). What the Life Story sketches, generally speaking, is a gendered ecology of work relations within which, in the words of Debashree Mukherjee, the "*sensuousness* of labor [seems to have been] imbricated in the logics of structure" (2020a, 14; italics in original). Explicit is the point that corporeal maternal labor produced the "immaterial" value of "a binding element" (Hardt 1999, 95) for the team of specialists led by Kanan Devi. Yet, if I see the tutelary energies condensed in the familial metaphor of hātekhari—the training received by emergent specialists from the experienced—in relation to other accounts of Kanan's own specialized experiences in camerawork and costume design, I cannot but note a fragmented history of sexually specialized labors. Kanan Devi's leadership in her film company at large and specifically in the directorial collective seems to have involved labors equipoised between corporeal mother work and expert creative work. She collaborated in crafting gender aesthetics in productions such as *Mej Didi*.

Told serially in the Life Story published in 1973 is a previously neglected tale of Kanan Devi's self-taught acumen in photography and camerawork, with the second half of the narrative effectively correcting the import of the first. The first part of the narrative, located in relation to productions such as *Mukti* and the studio-era hierarchy of salaried labor in New Theatres, expresses her dissatisfaction with director and hero Pramathesh Barua's authoritarian ways. We are told that he was inclined to always turn the camera toward his own body and facial expression (Devi 1973, 48–49). The second part is narrated in the context of the post-studio period of flexible contracts when Barua had forged more of a partner-like relationship with Kanan in motion pictures like *Shesh Uttar* (1942). In the latter narrative about camerawork, Kanan expresses eagerness to learn technique from the eminent "cameraman Barua" (91). While the emphasis in both narrative parts is on the technique of filming the couple form, specifically on visually conjugating Kanan with Barua, the bridge between the two is a story of how Kanan Devi had taught herself photography and even bagged a prize at a competition (90). Correcting her earlier allegation against Barua's authoritarian camerawork, the second story suggests that her newfound expertise in photography had alerted her to what is best characterized as the autoerotic camerawork of director Barua—that is, his way of highlighting the signature poses, the "novel [facial] expressions" (*abhinaba expression*), distinguishing hero Barua (91).

The monumental status given to the studio era and its modular artist Pramathesh Barua, both in this two-part narrative of camerawork and elsewhere in Kanan's Life Story, certainly falls in line with the histories of Bengali cinema that frequently appeared in leading film periodicals like *Chitrabani* in the early 1950s (see, for example, *Chitrabani*, January/February issues, 1951). However, the libidinal telos of Kanan's stories of photographic expertise is not any monument or model but rather the personal skills of a star-director. Her focus is on the skills Barua had mastered of simultaneously performing and filming star poses, especially one's own. Kanan avers that all actors should learn photography and command control of camera angles on the set so that their forms and faces make the "meanings of their roles stronger" for audiences (Devi 1973, 91). It is arguable that we see in *Mej Didi* how innovatively Kanan *reuses* the art of autoerotic shot design to displace the patriarchal cinematography she identifies in the Barua style. Both the romantic female form and the maternal voice, key stylistic features of femaleness on the Bengali screen, are at least partially guarded from the male-centric frame. Note that even as a salaried employee at studios, Kanan sought to claim artistic control over her figurations. Not only did she make "pencil sketches of her possible apparel . . . [often becoming] her own costume designer," but she also worked with art directors to rearrange sets (Sengupta 2015, 98).

That being said, the credits on the extant print of *Mej Didi* name Ajoy Kar as the director of photography. The techniques of camera, lighting, and spatial construction are officially attributed to Kar and other members of the Sabyasachi cohort rather than to the performer Kanan Devi. Moreover, some of the same black-and-white techniques we find in *Mej Didi*—soft focus, "affective lighting, vignette close-ups" and stylized studio-built sets (Biswas 1990, 309; Biswas 2000, 140)—were to dominate the signature productions of Ajoy Kar himself as well as those of leading male directors like Tarun Majumdar, who had worked for Sreemati Pictures. Cases in point are *Harano Sur* (1957), directed by Ajoy Kar, and *Chaowa Pawa* (1959), directed by Tarun Majumdar and his Yatrik Collective. The latter reproduces the *Mej Didi* prototype of the terrace as a guarded romantic space within a joint family home. However, what we find in these intertextual linkages of *Mej Didi* with the mainstream Bengali motion pictures of the 1950s is a striking discrepancy. Techniques of evoking the "guarded, domestic world of melodrama" in subsequent works are used to guard the aesthetic space of couple formation from "patriarchies old and new" (Biswas 2000, 127, 137). Guarding as a way to decouple the female form from male-centric configuration is never the objective. No doubt, the literary source of the film *Mej Didi* does not simply provide the narrative pretext for female-centric constructions but actually demands them. However, an intertextual pairing of shot design with the many extradiegetic stories Kanan told of her self-acquired skills in film work provokes another reading. I maintain that the discrepancy in couple mise-en-scènes found in *Mej Didi* is a fossil bearing witness to the hātekhari that male directors had received from Kanan and later reworked into male-centric cinematography.

The agency in Kanan Devi's specialized labors for her small-scale company, Sreemati Pictures, constitutes a far from random case in the South Asian subcontinent. Subsequent chapters of this book demonstrate that the authorial mode delineated above intersects with a larger history of gender work in women-led, small-scale film companies across India, Pakistan, and Bangladesh.

Although the rise of women's film companies is asynchronous and contextually specific, a comparative region-think illustrates that the small-scale women-led practices converge on a transborder enigma. Across the South Asian contexts I examine, a women-led, familial, and sexually apportioned modality of production tends to yield cinema replete with *female-focused arts and concerns*. Staying with the Kolkata film culture of the 1980s and 1990s, this chapter now turns to how the familial mode and female authorship work in relation to a different structural formation: that of large-scale changes helping the woman to become a director and scriptwriter. We see how an elite star-filmmaker like Aparna Sen was directly enabled by the Indian women's movement and state-sponsored directors' cinema initiatives. However, a deep dig into the contradictory sources making up the archive of Aparna's creativity reveals that she radicalized the course of change by managing cross-scalar relations from the locus of her star persona. Becoming a celebrated household name in urban West Bengal, she interacted as an "intimate stranger" with the mediatized publics of a transforming context, intervening in the prevalent sociosexual norms (Hallet 2013).

Decoupling Motherhood: Aparna Sen and Scales of Cinematic Change (1980s/1990s)

Whereas we catch only glimpses of Kanan Devi's command of the cinematic medium in between her depictions of male authority, we clearly learn about Aparna Sen's authorship. The difference demonstrates that large-scale change in the logics of structure make women's creative labor publicly visible and rational. Yet we see that the rationality of male familial support endures as well, dovetailing with state-level change to bolster the respectability of women workers in the historically disreputable public space of cinema (associated with women of easy virtue). Where Aparna Sen's practice as a star-author stands out is that it inhabits the available infrastructures yet grows heterogeneous to the gendered logics of taste and virtue in avant-garde cinema as much as mainstream cinema.

An article written by Aparna Sen in 1999 to mark the exhibition of *Paromitar Ek Din* at the Indian Panorama Festival documents how state support provides authority to the woman director and scriptwriter. The article offers a picture of total authorial agency. Aparna details how once she has prepared the script, she gives hands-on guidance to each of the "departmental heads"—providing her cinematographer with "paintings and photographs to communicate lighting effects," working with the editor on consecutive cuts, and describing to the music director the quality of effect she seeks by "referring to something non-musical" (1999, 45–46). Clearly, the Panorama Festival provided a discursive rationale for the woman director's creative control. As the national component of the annual International Film Festival of India, the Panorama had been born of a state policy to give Indian cinema the respectable status of an auteurist "art form."

Undertaken in 1980 by the "Working Group on National Film Policy" under the auspices of the Ministry of Information and Broadcasting, the film policy initiative intersected with both the "new cinema" wave and the legacy of film societies. With author-directors like Shyam Benegal and Mrinal Sen on board, the policy report asserted that cinema "as a means of creative expression" was coming to be seen in India as "primarily a director's medium" (*Report of the Working Group* 1980, 9). In an interview appended to the *Report of the Working Group*, the internationally acclaimed filmmaker Satyajit Ray, founder of the Calcutta Film Society, added his voice by distinguishing the director's medium of "meaningful cinema" from what he called the "popular medium" of mass entertainment (112). This national drive to promote meaningful director's cinema coincided with the Indian women's movement and debates on sexual issues and women's rights. The Directorate of Film Festivals during this period characterized "India's new cinema" as being dually preoccupied with a "changing society and the status of women" (*Film India* 1981, 12–17). Although the preoccupation with women's "status" hardly correlated to the number of women finding production opportunities (the directorate's list of "good" film directors names mostly men), a state-sponsored movement for a new cinema of "social change" did permit limited openings for women from the educated classes. Government-run film festivals supported women's programs and promoted filmmakers dealing with "previously 'marginal' issues" (*Filmotsav* 1986, 6). However, reports on state-supported "good" films noted as well that the infrastructure was very limited because "established distributors [did] not buy them" *(Film India* 1981, 21).

Eschewing the narrow label of a "woman filmmaker" appealing only to select festival audiences, Aparna Sen herself favors cinema "that will run" (*jetā chalbe*) (personal interview, 2014). She came to filmmaking through her connections with the urban auteur cinema in West Bengal. As discussed by both Sharmistha Gooptu (2010, 263–268) and Abhijit Roy (2000), the regional Bengali cinema market, being economically burdened by the late 1970s, had splintered into two broad strands (the burdens were of taxes as well as competition from big-budget Hindi cinema and television). The more dominant strand addressed urban working-class and village audiences through action and "folk" films, sometimes coproduced with the folk-genre makers of Bangladesh (discussed in chapter 2). A slimmer strand of respectable "middle cinema" made for urban theatrical release forked out of film societies and intersected with a globalizing "local-popular mediascape" of magazines and television programs addressing urban "citygen" consumers (A. Roy 2000). Aparna Sen inhabited the latter space and its contradictions. Her creativity flourished (and still does) on both sides of the camera, in the public roles of a star persona, a director and scriptwriter, and, eventually, a celebrity women's magazine editor. While her path to production did commence with liberal paternalist guidance, undergirded by Indian state discourse, it soon moved past prevalent guidelines of taste and consumption.

As she put it in the 1984 interview for *Filmfare* with which I started this chapter, Aparna's turn to directing offbeat cinema did not "come as much of a surprise," either to the target Bengali public or to male colleagues, because they knew of her father and film family background (A. Sen 1984, 79). Being the daughter of film critic and filmmaker Chidananda Dasgupta, who had cofounded the Calcutta Film Society in collaboration with Satyajit Ray and brought international avant-garde cinema to the family home (Bakshi and Dasgupta 2017, 189), she seemed well poised to become a parallel cinema author in her own right. More detailed accounts of her access and creative authority over the medium, given to me and published in interviews, reveal that the way she got to that position was by moving against sexual divisions of labor with the right male support behind her. Aparna Sen says she had initially begun writing a script of her own to obviate the "dissatisfaction" she felt with how her creative suggestions about her own roles—inspired by the "interest in the craft" she developed on the set—were being ignored by the directors in whose films she starred (A. Sen 2004). In a personal conversation with me (2009), Aparna waxed intense on how she had gone from director to director seeking a maker for her script and receiving the same condescending feedback saying that it was unfilmable. Upon handing the script to her avuncular "mentor," Satyajit Ray, she finally heard that it would make a "wonderful film" that needed a producer only because the director should be none other than Aparna Sen herself. Ray's endorsement not merely of the script but of Aparna's potential to be director came with timely guidance in identifying the right offbeat producer.

The script that turned into Aparna Sen's critically acclaimed English-language debut feature, *36 Chowringhee Lane* (1981), fell in line with what Satyajit Ray had approvingly characterized as the "permissiveness" accompanying "unconventionalism" in Western cinema. Ray had pitted the uninhibited tastes upheld by Western avant-garde films against what he called the "puritanical-hypocritical" conventions of Indian cinema (1976, 90–92). In the same unconventional vein, Aparna's debut feature depicts how racial "subalternity . . . [dwells under the] heteropatriarchal structures" of bourgeois Bengali sexual mores (Bakshi and Dasgupta 2017, 191). The work dramatizes the racially marginalized existence and vulnerable sexuality of an aging mixed-race Shakespeare teacher residing in Kolkata. The isolated woman's unfulfilled desires are exploited by a young Bengali couple, especially the self-assured young man, who pretend friendship in order to use the privacy of the teacher's apartment to have premarital sex in her absence. The support Aparna received for her permissive social critique from both Ray and such industry insiders as the producer of *36 Chowringhee Lane*, Sashi Kapoor, reveals how progressive male establishments were working in line with the liberal state to enable middle-class women's counternarratives at the moment. Seen another way, the government's large-scale decision to promote cinematic uplift, even though it failed in financial networking, spawned an infrastructure of "good cinema" culture that drew resources. The complexity arose around Aparna Sen's Bengali-language practice. In fact, the transborder path of Sen's subversive Bangla productions reveals how nationalist contents very well could constrain the convention-bending perspectives of the male avant-garde establishment, especially where the concept of Bengali motherhood was at stake. Founts of support for the radical decisions animating the feminist melodramas scripted and directed by Aparna in this period must be sought in her own small-scale labors as an influential public persona.

In one of her interviews with me (2014), Aparna Sen staged a provocative "plot" of resistance (Portelli 2006), which effectively clarified why she objects to gender labels for herself (as a "woman" filmmaker) and for her creations (as films about "women"). She began by maintaining that whereas far too often characters were depicted by directors around her through the lens of "gender," she wanted to portray them as "individuals." She went on to point to a tendency she had found in many motion pictures directed by Satyajit Ray: he depicted women as normative "conscience" figures. I heard that Ray himself had affirmed to her in an interview that he saw women to be "morally superior perhaps because they were physically weak." Aparna averred that, notwithstanding her "huge respect" for Ray and his landmark "feminist" works, she felt that women as much as men could grow "corrupt." The point of her scattered stories and ruminations seemed to be that individuating gender portrayal meant granting women as much as men the "corrupt" agency to transgress the normative borders of society and sexuality.

Soon, Aparna was narrating her experience in the role of an adulterous wife in Satyajit Ray's short fiction film *Pikoo* (1980). She said quite plainly that at one point she had disagreed with his direction. In principle, Aparna Sen's star persona sat well with the role. As the foremost urban Bengali woman icon of the turbulent 1960s and 1970s, a time rife with transformations (Gooptu 2010, 169–170), Aparna's social film roles had kept pace with the sexual ambivalence prevailing in respectable Bengali attitudes toward the contemporary. Across the gamut of mainstream and avant-garde Bangla cinema, she materialized as the rebellious woman or sexually liberated urbanite whose independence was pursued by allegations of transgression or the "specter of prostitution" (177). In this vein, Satyajit Ray's permissive melodrama *Pikoo*, made for French television, casts Aparna Sen as a Bengali joint-family housewife caught between her dysfunctional conjugal relationship, her obligations to an ailing father-in-law and the young son Pikoo, and her extramarital relations with a domineering lover. Aparna's point of contention with Ray was about the extent to which she should enact the conflict of a mother betraying Pikoo as against performing the (individuated) identity of a woman leading a life fraught with unhappy demands. Ray had clearly favored the depiction of innate motherliness. As noted earlier, Aparna Sen is inclined to attribute the growth of the "director" in herself out of dissatisfaction with the directors she has worked with. Her disagreement with Ray over the gendering of motherliness in the seemingly permissive *Pikoo* may well be a case in point. Building on their extended interviews with Aparna Sen, Bakshi and Dasgupta stake the claim that the "strong moral judgment" Satyajit Ray's *Pikoo* had sought to invite from audiences drew a "bold feminist rejoinder" from Aparna Sen, a rejoinder that took the shape of *Parama* (Bakshi and Dasgupta 2017, 200). Written and directed by Aparna Sen, this fiction film is also about an adulterous Bengali housewife. Although Bakshi and Dasgupta add that the claim itself is unsubstantiated by Sen, the similarities between the two productions did not go unnoticed in film reviews of *Parama*, as discussed later.

Aparna Sen herself frequently characterizes *Parama* as an explicitly "feminist film." An oft-quoted early scene in *Parama* situates the docile housewife of an upper-middle-class joint Bengali family within a web of relational names— "mother," "aunt," "sister-in-law," "wife"—which hides her own name. This fact of her forgotten name is made explicit by the critical remarks of an expatriate professional photographer and his American woman assistant, who are on an assignment to take photographs for *Life* magazine of the traditional Hindu festival of mother-goddess worship (Durga Puja) being held at Parama's marital family home. The plot evolves into an extramarital affair between the repressed housewife Parama (Rakhee Gulzar) and the expatriate photographer Rahul (Mukul Sharma) after the latter embarks on a fresh Orientalist project of photographing "tradition" for *Life* magazine, that of photographing the "traditional Bengali beauty" of housewife Parama. Rahul's project is soundly supported by Parama's liberal elite husband (Dipankar De), up until the moment the illicit affair is exposed by a copy of *Life* showcasing a photograph taken by Rahul of Parama's partially denuded bust. Thereafter, Parama is ostracized in her marital family home and called a "whore" by the husband, who conveniently ignores the sexual double standard of his own extramarital flings. Driven by abject isolation, she attempts suicide upon learning that Rahul, too, is unreachable (he has left India on another photographic expedition and failed to communicate).

Parama's recovery, at the expensive hospital where her wealthy husband and family have admitted her, is a journey out of abject dependence on relationships to individuated choices. Refusing the psychotherapy recommended by the paternalistic neurosurgeon (Anil Chatterjee) as the way to overcoming her "sense of guilt" and retrieving her proper "place as housewife, wife, and mother," she radically unsettles his assumption of her innate feminine virtue. She declares that she suffers from no such sense of guilt (about her putative "corruption," to use the filmmaker's own words, quoted above). At the same time, Parama is shown to let go of the page of *Life* magazine that tells her where Rahul is now, metaphorically disengaging herself from yet another heterosexual couple form. What Parama settles for is the relatively unrespectable job of a low-paid saleswoman, the only position her divorced professional friend (Aparna Sen) is able to arrange for a woman with her limited qualifications. In this vein, Aparna's script reminds us that Parama's one-time dependent relations with her elite husband and marital family were coded not only by gender but also by her lower-middle-class background and concomitant constraints of opportunity. Yet, the complexity of the narrative flow from relational dependencies and couple formations to individual agency lies in an ending that reopens the story of family from a *maternal* perspective. The final shots depict how Parama reclaims her motherly commitment through the growth of a new bond with her college-going daughter, with the latter shown as finally comprehending her mother's world of longings. Relevant to this ending on the hope of a mother decoupled from patriarchies is an insightful point made by Brinda Bose. She notes that although this piece of "gendered cinema" falls in line with the Bengali avant-garde genre of films about women, it diverges from the tendency shown by male directors such as Satyajit Ray or Mrinal Sen to portray a "sense of sadness, edging on doom, for the woman's future, either arising out of her own transgressions or merely her destiny (as woman)" (1997, 322). *Parama* replaces such feminine signifiers of hopelessness or victimhood recurrent in Bengali social films with a dynamic artistry best described in words drawn from Pam Cook and Thomas Elsaesser. It is a maternal melodrama of "female transgression" (Cook 1991, 251) replete with spectacular excesses of color and sound that give rein to "female desire" as the way to acting "subversively . . . [in relation to] the given historical and social context" (Elsaesser 1985, 169).

Key to my argument in this chapter is a series of scenic constructions that visibly personalize female desire by detaching the woman from a depersonalized iconic order of mother as goddess. The first is a rack focus close-up of Parama's face encircled by a gorgeous red-bordered sari shot in juxtaposition to the resplendently clothed maternal deity, Durga (fig. 4). The tight shot shows Parama's face turned away from the deity, momentarily distracted from her fertility ritual of anointing the mother godhead with the vermilion mark of *sindur* (worn by Hindu Bengali women as a sign of marriage and procreative sexuality). Whereas this instance of Parama's distraction is contained within the orbit of domestic duty (her daughter having asked a question about a

Fig. 4: Parama and the maternal deity Durga (Source: *Parama*)

family chore), the shot and frame of the close-up propels a telos of distractions and desire. Soon to appear is an almost identical close-up shown once again through photographer Rahul's meta-cinematic lens. It depicts Parama turning from her task at hand to look back with alert intensity at Rahul in response to his comment that he will call her by her own name rather than any relational one. The personalizing drama of the close-up takes a subversive turn when Rahul is invited by the family to display a slide show of his photography. When Rahul projects the close-up he had taken at the Durga Puja of Parama's face framed in sexy red, the erotic excess of the "overly composed and decorative" use of color provokes voyeuristic banter (Galt 2013, 94). While a brother-in-law jokes that he feels like running off with Parama, her husband rejoins that he must learn to take photographs (of his own wife) himself. Soon, this staging of clandestine longings is intensified by another long take at close up—one that effectively subverts the erotic adequation of housewife, mother, and self-reneging goddess embodied by Parama's Durga Puja photograph. Parama inadvertently steps in front of her projected image and once again turns a distracted face. Only, this time she responds with confusion to her mother-in-law's approving comment about her feet prettily decked in *āltā* (a red paint worn by married women, another beautifier of the fertile female body). Parama's distraction at the controlling concept underlying her mother-in-law's approval—the concept that the āltā confirms her marital status—arises from the fact that it was Rahul who had helped her to apply the āltā during a photo shoot, igniting what clearly had been their first experience of mutual attraction. This third in the series of identical close-ups upsets the generic reference to domestic conformity and instead drives the diegesis of transgression.

It may seem, though, that agents of patriarchal control merely shift rather than disappear from the diegesis. For a modern couple, romance appears to replace the traditional arrangements of a joint family and patriarchal marriage with the globally mobile photographer blazing the trail of freedom. What complicates any such male-centric reading, however, is the sheer subordination of the photographer's role to that of the woman's as an agent not only of desire but also of choice and change. For one thing, Parama leads the illicit affair, with her pleasures being pointedly physicalized in scenes of lovemaking through a female-focused camera that lingers on her hands and body in favor of his. For another, the final frames in dual focus, with Parama sitting face-to-face with her daughter caressing her hair, stage a self-sustaining world of maternal family that is independent of male encroachments. All in all, it seems to me that the path trodden by female desire in *Parama* is culturally circuitous. It works through male-centric and heteronormative liberal traditions, only to end on individuating Bengali womanliness and habitual maternal relations. Bengali maternity and quotidian domestic care work take center stage in Aparna Sen's subsequent Bengali production, *Paromitar Ek Din*. Here, it is entwined with the tale of a non-normative couple of caregivers inhabiting the interstices of a patriarchal household. One infrastructure bridging the two productions, in my view, is a changing mediascape of gendered opinions and desires steered in part by the creative labor of Aparna Sen. While *Parama* is known to have divided Bengali public opinion, less obvious is how the more radical positions taken in support of the work might have been intertextual with the sensorium of Sen's star persona and the implicit gender trouble. To explain, let me begin with the conflicted viewing positions catalyzed by *Parama*.

As recorded in its day by reviewers, *Parama* was released with tremendous *haichai* (uproar) across Kolkata and adjacent urban spaces (P. Bandopadhyay 1985, 27). According to the filmmaker, it did become a box-office success in commercial theaters rather than at offbeat venues (personal interview, 2014; Sen, qtd. in Bakshi and Dasgupta 2017). The haichai came from a range of "historically distinct viewing positions" (Williams 1994, 4). These positions were contesting the way the sexual role of the respectable Bengali woman was portrayed vis-à-vis motherhood and domesticity. A valuable archive of these distinctly conflicted viewing positions is offered by a 1985 issue of the film society magazine called *Chitravas*. The issue assembles several reviews written by male art-house cineastes alongside a survey of women cinemagoers' opinions. It is striking that all three men writing full-length reviews converge on the view that *Parama* is "unnatural" (*asvābik*) in the characterization of a "traditional" Bengali housewife's unconflicted abandonment of her maternal attachments (P. Bandopadhyay 1985, 27; D. Chakrabarty 1985, 35). That a heteronormative nationalism drives the collective masculine view is explicated as well. One reviewer avers that Aparna Sen must be foreign to what "freedom" could mean for Indian women, since her previous production dealt with an English-speaking protagonist (P. Bandopadhyay 1985, 28; the reference is to *36 Chowringhee Lane*). In a distinctly homophobic tone, another reviewer maintains that since Aparna Sen is basically "suspicious" about "men and women's natural relations" (*naranārir svābik samparkya)*, she is incapable as well of conceptualizing normal forms of "social freedom" (S. Bandopadhyay 1985, 31). Telling in this light is the fact that two of the three male cineastes writing reviews for this art-house magazine pit the balanced realism in Satyajit Ray's portrayal of adulterous motherhood in *Pikoo* in opposition to the aberrant drama of sexuality in *Parama*. The position is that the logical depiction of a mother's "extramarital sexual companionship" is Ray's way of relating the transgression to her young son's "perspective" (P. Bandopadhyay 1985, 27).

By contrast, women cinemagoers' opinions surveyed by *Chitravas* not only are radically split but also could be seen as interwoven with the gender trouble that is immanent to Aparna's cinematic sensorium. If a few women side with heteropatriarchal nationalism, with one going to the extent of alleging that Aparna's portrayal is a "perversion" of Bengali domestic womanhood (Sanyal 1985, 40), a good number support the issues of independence and freedom raised by *Parama* in sociosexual terms. One such favorable commentator celebrates what she finds to be Aparna Sen's fresh vision of companionate intimacy, with Rahul's body becoming a musical instrument in the hands of the player Parama throughout, as against Parama's body being "property" (*bishaya*) in the hands of her possessive husband (Sutapa Bhattacharya 1985, 38). Another focuses on the pathfinding familial "consciousness" (*sachetanā*) cultivated by the work. Rebutting nationalist objections in the very name of the Bengali family, the latter commentator maintains that *Parama* will raise women's consciousness to becoming more attentive about how to "build family" rather than to "break it" (Meenakshi Sinha 1985, 41). Drawn from an array of urban backgrounds (educator, student, journalist, and homemaker), these women's voices certainly demonstrate that a feminist film could spawn female audiences and viewing positions that are heterogeneous to patriarchal liberal mores. Less obvious is the sensuous infrastructure of these viewing positions—that is, how they might have been conditioned by sensoriums of the Bengali contemporary associated with the star persona of Aparna Sen.

Crucial here are impassioned observations about Aparna's orientative influence on her fans made by the late gender-queer director and performer Rituparno Ghosh. In his view, Sen's famous personifications of agential and wayward women in widely consumed Bengali cinema had already prepared audiences for the feminism in *Parama* (Ghosh 2008). Her stardom had been intimately influential on a whole generation of Bengali female and queer male fans who sought to participate in her generic waywardness by trying to "be Aparna Sen 'in the look and feel.'" Elsewhere, Rituparno named himself as one such queerly oriented mimic of the female idol (Ghosh, qtd. in Bakshi and Dasgupta 2017, 201). Exploring the complex negotiations of cinematic meaning between the processes of production and consumption, Christine Gledhill argues that "whereas the culture industries must look for exchange-value as a source of profit, audiences look for use-value" (1994, 120). Rituparno Ghosh's insightful comment suggests that Aparna Sen's famous norm-bending roles in the Bengali social film genres evolving through the 1960s and 1970s had already made transgression of heteronormative and patriarchal respectability into a tangible value useful for fans of family melodramas. Scholars often point out that nation-scale feminist debates and a state-supported wave of good cinema joined with transnational feminist media to provide the context for the unorthodox works of women directors like Aparna Sen (S. Sen 2000, 24–27; Sawhney 2015). The previously unnoticed reception archive of *Parama* discussed above illuminates another, closer-in level of authorial activity. We find that an infrastructure of expectation and potential revenue for her dissident social cinema was being successfully authored on a small scale by Aparna Sen herself, a star persona familiar to the gendered shifts in the Bengali social genre. The next Bengali-language fiction directed and scripted by Aparna Sen seems to have followed the same aesthetic trajectory. While it comes on the heels of the filmmaker's explicit support of sapphic love in the diasporic feminist filmmaker Deepa Mehta's *Fire* (1996), *Paromitar Ek Din* weaves a fiction of intergenerational same-sex desire similar to *Fire* into the genre of social film with which the star-author is identified. In this vein, Aparna's Bangla-language productivity is not unlike that of the other regionally routed female star-authors studied in this book. She regularly avails of regional linguistic infrastructures that are specific to her stardom and takes up opportunities for transborder mediation of the values she personifies.

From the mid-1980s through the 1990s, Aparna Sen was extending the home entertainment space of magazines to reach out to Bengali-literate metropolitan and provincial urban women through her editorship of the foremost women's magazine, *Sananda*. This relatively large-scale platform for public mediation was offered to her by the leading Bengali newspaper conglomerate, Anandabazar Patrika, after her success with *Parama*. In the words of avid women consumers and Aparna fans, *Sananda* combined pieces on "politics, education, and lifestyle choices" to raise taboo topics of sexuality and *samakāmi* (same-sex) orientation hand in hand with the non-normative familial choices of single motherhood, abortion, and living together (qtd. in Bakshi and Dasgupta 2017, 193). In effect, editor Aparna Sen was moving across different scales of mediation. She was relating with her female readership at the intensively localized level of a familiar female persona to inculcate large-scale change in gender perspectives. Noteworthy is one *Sananda* editorial written in 1993. In the short piece, Aparna evokes motherliness and domesticity as interpersonal affect rather than as the constative norms assumed by the avant-garde male film discourse discussed above. Characterizing the "language of touch" to be the most "suggestive" (*ingitbāhi*) of all communication, she writes that this language is born with both a mother's tactile care of her baby and the care-giver's comforting hand on a shriveled elderly face (1993). The point is that domestic relations are forged through a corporeal language of care—through a feminine form of intimacy "that amounts to cutaneous contact" (Sedgwick 2003, 17). Such evocations of feminized and maternal intimacy are what prepare a pathway of expectations for the social realist drama *Paromitar Ek Din*. The work performs Bengali motherly intimacies in a way that supersedes the constative norms of heterosexual family relations.

Aparna Sen's screenplay revolves around a day in the life of the title character, Paromita (Rituparna Sengupta), on which she attends the last rites of her former mother-in-law and, sitting in the "house of memories" (the English title of the work), recalls her life as a mother and housewife in this joint family, prior to divorce by her own choice. We learn through flashback of the unlikely friendship she had forged with her matriarchal mother-in-law, Sanaka (Aparna Sen). The intimacy is conditioned not by hierarchal family norms but by a process of mutual individuation well described as "appreciation . . . and practical love" (Lugones 1995, 136, 142).[4] This friendship solidifies in the course of mother work for each other's disabled offspring. The key struggle in which the matriarch joins hands with Paromita is against the patriarchal demand for an able progeny befitting a high-caste Hindu patriline. Sanaka herself has a grown-up schizophrenic daughter. When it turns out that the baby boy Paromita has birthed—thus far cherished as the male heir—suffers from cerebral palsy, Paromita's alcoholic husband grows brutal. He alleges that her possible debased background has produced an unfit child. The narrative moves on to depict the two mothers, Paromita and Sanaka, developing same-sex intimacy through their tactile nurturance of needy offspring. Images of Bengali middle-class interiors familiar to patriarchal social films are inhabited anew by a feminist camera to frame the mutually erotic orientation of the mother workers. Although love between the same-sex couple is temporarily ruptured by heteronormative privilege—the educated young Paromita having found a job and a companionate man divorces Sanaka's abusive son and leaves (after they lose the child to cerebral palsy)—the intimacy is rekindled in yet another episode of tactile care work. Putting on hold the demands of her career and new conjugal life, Paromita returns to tend Sanaka on her deathbed, staying on with untiring tenacity till the passing.

The intense effect born of Paromita's contact with Sanaka's shriveling body on the deathbed is staged through a memorable episode of her canny perception of the dying women's inarticulate feelings. When none of the women present in the sickroom (including a hired nurse) is able to perceive why for days Sanaka refuses to urinate, Paromita understands. She saves Sanaka's life by creating a secluded space (a makeshift toilet by the bed) where Sanaka can urinate in private and maintain dignity while she performs bodily functions.

Fig. 5: Aparna Sen as Sanaka facing Paromita (Source: *Paromitar Ek Din*)

Vision and sound take on the attributes of what Eve Sedgwick calls "touchy-feely" perception in a series of tight close-ups that create a self-sustained space of cutaneous comfort (2003, 16–18). The two faces come close—Paromita holds Sanaka steady, the latter strokes Paromita's face with a wordless gratitude (fig. 5)—and the faint sound of urination is heard in the background. What has evolved into this intensely feminine language of touch is a visual telos of same-sex desire that, early in the narrative, had sidelined heterosexual couple formation. An early mise-en-scène saturated with the fertility-coded colors of vermilion and yellow, not unlike the early scenes of *Parama*, had staged the Hindu rite of *badhubaran* (bride-and-groom ushering) being performed by mother-in-law Sanaka. Only, in that instance, close-ups fired with key and fill lighting are focused on the mutually admiring faces of mother-in-law and daughter-in-law, peripheralizing the husband and momentarily decoupling the women. We see a restaging in the sickroom of a similar mutuality of female faces and maternal care work sans men.

It is arguable, nonetheless, that the narrative resolution reinstates mother Paromita in companionate conjugality. The last frontal shot shows her guiding her new husband's hands on her body to feel the movements of their unborn child within the expectant mother. The conceptual linkage of maternity with heterosexual conjugality, being a core preoccupation of the Bengali modern, is frequently dealt with in Aparna Sen's works. The concepts are negotiated from a transborder perspective, dutifully inhabited and yet interrogated from within. Along these lines, the narrative as a whole explores themes of heterosexual companionship both in and outside marriage. The matriarch Sanaka herself is shown to defiantly maintain her friendship with a childhood sweetheart. Still, Paromita's "day" in the mnemonic "house" she shared with her mother-in-law suggests a disconnect of same-sex maternal intimacies from the narrative flow of modern heterosexual space and conjugal time. Paromita's husband has an only passing question about how her day went at the funeral service and why she had suddenly phoned him from there (in the midst of his busy workday schedule) and broken down in tears.

Motherhood and Maleness in Brand Scale Kolkata Cinema (2000s): A Concluding Word

Thus far, this chapter has followed women's transborder negotiations of the tropes of motherhood and conjugality, key to West Bengali modernity, through two different structural formations that enabled female stars to become film authors in earlier decades. Clearly, the cases of Kanan Devi and Aparna Sen differ in the structures of opportunity as well as in the scales at which the respective women negotiated creative authority. Nonetheless, the cases reveal how female authors working at the spatial levels of star body appeal or family-like businesses are able to accrue resources or orient large-scale consumption practices in ways such that male-centric divisions of labor and convention are unsettled. To end this chapter, I briefly touch on how these tropes might evolve in productions of the 2000s.

Among the evolving complexities, two are germane. On the one hand, the urban Bangla media environment over recent decades has been shifting under global and pan-national influences. It has been aggregating mainly with brand concepts found from the towering Hindi-language cinema and television of post-liberalized India. Abhijit Roy (2000) argues in this vein that the assumed division between a Bengali city gentry and working-class/village audiences must be rethought in the terms of a more flexible televisual consumer culture stratified largely by access to globally privileged forms and technologies, notably satellite television.[5] On the other hand, precisely the liberalizing urban landscape allows women unprecedented access to production roles. We see this momentum both in Kolkata and elsewhere in India. Sudeshna Roy, Kolkata-based actress-director and editor of the popular magazine *Suvidha* (funded by a contraceptive company by the same name), said much the same to me in a personal conversation. She emphasized that nowadays we find women in all kinds of production roles, save the most technical (such as sound design) (personal interview, 2014). This spate of women in filmmaking in India and across South Asia intersects with a new transnational generation reaping the benefits of feminism (White 2015, 18). In the West Bengali case at hand, exhibition venues crisscross between festivals and urban theaters.

Curious in the light of this liberalizing contemporary, however, is a peculiarly recursive aesthetic trend. It seems that urban Bengali cinema is reverting to the tradition of hero-centric narratives, although at the same time, it deploys familiar women's cinema tropes. The latter function as complementary attractions, composing an appropriately gender-diverse cinematic address to liberal urban audiences. Noteworthy for the topic of this chapter is a recent maternal melodrama titled *Mayer Biye* (Mother's Marriage; 2015) codirected by Sudeshna Roy and produced by Eskay Movies, a company also known for its cross-border entrepreneurship in collaborating with Bangladeshi production houses. Sudeshna is prominent in the regional middle-class market for codirecting urban comedies and romances such as *Teen Yaari Katha* (Three Male Friends' Tale; 2012) and *Benche Thakar Gaan* (Song of Survival; 2016). Her works often focus on the travails of debilitated men (lower-middle-class; aged). By contrast, *Mayer Biye* is a maternal social film revolving around a mother-daughter relationship. In a promotional column, Sudeshna writes that she had been inspired to take up the female theme of single motherhood by the life of Aparna Sen, the one she knows as "the filmmaker with a difference" who takes up "contemporary subjects" and questions beliefs (S. Roy 2017). Having watched Aparna's daughter Konkona arranging the entire ceremony of her mother's remarriage, she felt compelled to make a film out of this admirable slice of life.

Mayer Biye tells the story of a young medical student trying to make a match for her lonely single mother, who had conceived out of wedlock and waited in vain for the boyfriend to return. Yet the seemingly radical narrative takes a sharp heteronormative turn when the sensitive and handsome medical professor the daughter had picked out for her mother proves to be none other than the errant boyfriend and her own birth father. The role of the father is played by Sabyasachi Chakraborty, a new-era Bengali hero towering over the space of global Kolkata cinema. We learn that for reasons beyond his control, this morally upright man failed to fulfill paternal responsibility and has since lived in solitary grief. The mother's initial resistance to the match on account of what she calls his act of betrayal, while staging the notion of independent motherhood found in the promotional citation, is constructed in this narrative as a form of intransigence at odds with the brands at once of heroic paternalism and of soft masculinity.

What strikes me about this deployment of the radical meanings associated with Aparna Sen's star-director persona—in this instance, the meanings of independent motherhood and older women's sexual desire—is the aspect of pastiche. It seems that in the flexible formation of brand capital, a feminist persona and related female-focused Bangla genre turn into what Fredric Jameson terms "badge[s] of affirmation" for liberal cinema (1991, 65). In other words, they repeatedly appear as politically innocuous attractions, in this case, as complement to a new hero brand. The male brand signifier aggregating the "visual field" of post-liberalized India has been best described by Mary E. John. He is the "anti-macho, vulnerable" man who fully reciprocates women's familial and conjugal feelings (1998, 378). Then do the transborder practices of women's cinema and star-authorship recede in the face of male brand formation, or might they intersect and partially transmute the latter? I take up this question in the concluding chapter of this book by returning to the case of star-author Aparna Sen, who remains active till this day.

2

Public Maternities

Women's Companies and a Sororal Production Mode, Dhaka

The previous chapter illuminated the transborder complexity in women's ways of inhabiting female genres produced of patriarchal nationalism. We saw that in West Bengal, maternal filmic genres constitute a gateway for women to access creative and entrepreneurial opportunities. Yet, if women laboriously perform the generic concepts in both diegetic and extradiegetic spaces, they could unsettle or rework underlying assumptions. Following these transborder paradoxes of female authorship to Bangladesh, which shares fictions of womanliness with West Bengal, this chapter delves further into the maternal politics of film entrepreneurship. An emphasis on how female entrepreneurial history becomes mixed with the authorship of genre is apt for Bangladesh. Women's leadership in setting up small film companies to release theatrical cinema has a far longer genealogy in Dhaka than in Kolkata.

My comparative research in film archives of the Bengal region suggests that this difference in women's entrepreneurial histories bears the trace of a shift in the cultural referents of respectable womanhood. The Indian Bengali concept of the respectable woman as a domesticated mother-goddess, studied in relation to women's history in chapter 1, refers to a Hindu nationalist framework. The concept transmutes into a relatively ambiguous "public mother" in Bangla Muslim-majority frameworks of nationalist activism (in 1960s East Pakistan) and state development (in Bangladesh after 1971). My point in this chapter is to demonstrate that ambiguities of the public mother genre loop through the diegetic field to the many production roles women from the respectable classes have taken in what is called in Bangladeshi film discourse *muldhārār/bāṇijyik dhārār chabi* (Md. Fokrul Alam, WhatsApp 2023)—that is, mainstream/commercial stream cinema.

Femaleness, Genre Mixing, and National Cinema in Dhaka: Contexts

In illuminating historical difference between concepts of respectable woman-hood in the two Bengals, my female-focused lens inflects a prevailing scholarly position on film history in Bangladesh. The position is that the West Bengali filmic space was a key referent for developing the industry of a "cultured" Bangla cinema for the vernacular elite in Dhaka (Hoek 2014, 18–19). There is little doubt that a shared heritage of Bangla traditions was key to the forma-tion of national culture industries in Dhaka prior to the birth of Bangladesh because linguistic nationalism constituted the popular appeal of the movement for regional political autonomy among the elite classes of East Pakistan.[1] West Bengali heritage was normative for the fledgling film industry, set up in 1958, with the inaugural director of the Dhaka Film Development Corporation willing to admit personnel only if they "had some filmic background from Calcutta" (Kabir 1979, 25). Moreover, specific gender influence was percolating not only through the import of West Bengali films, up until the India-Pakistan War of 1965, but also through Dhaka-based film periodicals such as *Rupchaya* and *Udayan* showcasing West Bengali icons of refined domestic femininity (Suchitra Sen, for example; Khandakar 2011, 50, 59). As recently as 2002, Sheikh Mahmuda Sultana describes the ideal woman of the Bangla screen in similar terms as a deified maternal figure (*pūjonīya mātrisvarup*), respectably bound to the home (qtd. in Hayat 2013b, 64).

What Sheikh Mahmuda also reflects on, however, are gender-mixed female forms. In her view, these configure an "artificial manly nature" (*krittim purushali svabhāb*), by implication unhousing the woman from her natural domestic place. In the only comprehensive survey to date of women and femininity in the commercial media spaces of Bangladesh, *Ganamadhyam O Nari* (Mass Media and Women; 2013b), Anupam Hayat aptly illustrates the mixing of modality. He notes that women on the commercial Bangla screen are "connected" at once to familial relations—mothers, stepmothers, sisters, aunts, sororal friends—*and* to public or professional positions such as female leader (*sardārni*), physician, nurse, policewoman, agent, actress, singer, servant woman, and prostitute, among others (2013b, 56). I maintain that the various mixed-mode figurations of familial public women found in Hayat's list are best understood in relation not to influential heritage but to dynamic differ-ence. It is arguable that although the contours of public maternity shift over time, the ambiguous genre itself has been ubiquitous to Bangla commercial stream cinema since the 1960s. The generic form carries indexical traces of the substantial roles that Bengali Muslim women have taken in the public arenas of cultural nationalism and socioeconomic development.

Feminist historiographers of Bangla Muslim culture adequately delineate these historical roles. Through the course of the Bangla Language Movement in East Pakistan leading up to the Liberation War in 1971, for example, educated upper-class Muslim women performed publicly in order to enact "political dissent [contravening] . . . official Islam" (Kabeer 1991, 121). Beyond this, the very seeds of the Bangla linguistic sphere, eventually to spawn Bangla cinema in Dhaka, had been sown in the nineteenth century by educated Muslim women who chose to publish in the everyday language of Bangla rather than in the Arabic or Urdu cultivated by their elite male counterparts (Shehabuddin 2014, 54; Azim and Hasan 2014, 30–31).[2] Following the assassination in 1975 of Prime Minister Sheikh Mujibur Rahman, the leader of the liberation movement, the nascent nation-state of Bangladesh went through two consecutive regimes of Islamizing martial bureaucracy (1977–1990). During this period, structural adjustment initiatives brought large numbers of villagers, lower-middle class, and working-class women into public and professional domains (Feldman 2001, 1098–1099). At the same time, policies of Islamization tacitly strengthened the patriarchal fundamentalism of the right-wing Jamaat-e-Islami party and related violence against working women and women visible in public spaces. In this shifting context, argues Shelley Feldman, patriarchal relations came to constitute "mediated processes of negotiation" involving complex practices of femininity within and outside the home (2001, 1101). The mixed-genre familial women represented in Anupam Hayat's list of cinematic roles are best understood in relation to these negotiations and the longer history of Muslim women's mutating roles in the public sphere.

Examining genre formation in Indian social films, Madhava Prasad observes that in parts of the world where "affect remains entangled in the realm of necessity," genre mixing or bricolage—the aesthetic process of introducing or eliminating attractions of "contemporaneity"—is best understood in terms of "film-as-performance": a contingent practice wherein imaginative energies are tangled with the necessities of societies and the functioning of community (2011, 71–72). Through the eras of mainstream Bangla cinema, the mixed-genre practice of depicting women as mobile outside domestic interiors and secure patriarchies has been enmeshed with the political and economic necessities outlined above. Accordingly, filmic practice has been shifted by the authors both on screen and in extra-cinematic spaces. Focusing on performances of public maternity, I argue that while the genre enables and, indeed, invites women's labors on both sides of the camera, female filmmakers transact the appeals in ways that unsettle male-dominant concepts of socially needed motherliness. Women's negotiations of the sexual ambiguities underlying public mother genres are well understood in relation to the role female film entrepreneurs from the respectable classes have taken in the mainstream commercial media of Bangladesh. Honing in on two moments of heightened female activity in mainstream cinema, I examine how women reuse the mother concept in both diegetic and production spaces and what differs with the scale at which the opportunity structures women rely on are controlled from elsewhere (by financiers, the state).

My first case in point is a female star-studded motion picture from the 1980s celebrated by Dhaka cinephiles as a male-independent, *sororal mode* production. The action-heroine film *Tin Konna* (Three Sisters; 1985) was written by Kohinoor Akhter Shuchanda and produced from her small-scale company in collaboration with performer sisters Farida Akhtar Babita and Gulshan Ara Akhter Champa. Babita ran a parallel star-name production house with support from older sibling Shuchanda (to be discussed in chapter 5). The disaggregated star-value of the sororal ensemble drama *Tin Konna* magnifies the social contradictions of 1980s Bangladesh (described above). Proceeding to the 2000s, an era blossoming with women directors in Bangladesh and across South Asia, I examine the entrepreneurial politics of director-producer Nargis Akhter. This non-star filmmaker heads an all-women's media company in Dhaka by the name of FemCom. My lens is an AIDS-awareness education-entertainment fiction feature sequence directed by Nargis titled *Meghla Akash* and its sequel, *Megher Koley Rod*. I show that the complexities of a relatively small-scale, NGO-sponsored production house—specializing in educational "feminism," as claimed by Nargis—must be seen in relation to the emerging state-supported corporate infrastructure wherein signifiers of public maternity aggregate with appropriate brands.

In focusing on the role taken in mainstream cinema by female author-entrepreneurs from the respectable classes, this study bridges a gap in the scholarship on Bangladeshi cinema and gender. Important historiographies by Zakir Hussain Raju and Alamgir Kabir, among others, note that women's involvement with public culture germinated in early 1950s East Pakistan within a Bangla Language Movement that embodied the struggle of the modern middle classes to "create a distinct cultural identity" (Raju 2015, 126). Many university-going "Moslem girls" began by participating in theater that broke "social taboos" (Kabir 1979, 20). From the mid-'50s, nationalist theater was intersecting with a middle-class mainstream cinema. This aimed to develop a vernacular modernity through portrayals of "social life" (Abdul Jabbar Khan, qtd. in Raju 2015, 133) replete with rural women and village settings. Out of this pastoral social genre branched another "folk fantasy" tradition of film targeting rural Muslim audiences (Kabir 1979; Ziad 2010). Raju goes on to discuss how the liberal middle-class filmic space underwent a dramatic shift after 1976. While film production and exhibition expanded at an exponential rate under the developmental drive of Islamizing martial bureaucracies (see above), they were circulating a new "national popular cinema" fraught with spectacular excess. The new film form was "negated" by the middle-class intelligentsia (Raju 2015, 143–152). Examining Bangla media of this period through a sexual lens, Lotte Hoek persuasively demonstrates that the norm of female respectability came to be entangled with the vicissitudes of Islamized development, which was bringing women of all classes into the workforce while it heightened patriarchal anxieties (2014, 17–22). Urban publics were deeply divided: on one side, brimming with lifestyle choices (appearing even in Islamic novels) and consumerist youth events, and on another, torn by youth, workers, and women's movements against the injustices of structural adjustment and Islamizing patriarchy. If rebellious images of working women crowded commercial screens, these were typically associated with undesirable forms of boundary crossing. Seen by the respectable classes as the harbor of transgressions, the commercial film industry itself carried a stigma of obscenity, reinforced by illegal traffic in the porn-heroine genre of *nashtā* (despoiled) womanhood (Hoek 2014, 22–24).

To further explain women's cinema in Bangladesh, historians turn to an alternative repertoire of film and documentary known in local film discourse as the *bikalpa dhārā*, or alternative film stream (Tanvir Mokammel, personal interview, 2014). In a book subtitled "Representing Women by Women in Bangladesh Cinema," published by the Bangladesh Film Archive and supervised by progressive female filmmaker Shameem Akhtar, Bikash Chandra Bhowmick lists a relatively large number of educated middle-class women making issues-centered fiction and documentary films in the alternative film stream (2009, 61–79). Independent filmmaker and media activist Shameem Akhtar herself has directed three women's issues–based fiction films in the serious, alternative film mode—titled *Itihaas Konna* (Daughter of History; 2000), *Shilalipi* (2004), and *Rina Brown* (2017). In a personal interview (2014), Shameem described to me that the bikalpa dhārā was an artisanal production mode (short fictions and documentaries, to begin with) that arose in the late 1970s from international art-house-inspired film clubs. The effort was to mobilize aesthetically against the "*kālā kānūn*" (black laws) of the Islamizing martial regime. The Euro-American and Indian embassies in Dhaka gave support to the movement by screening imported art films for the cineastes. While alternative stream filmmakers historically eschewed the "profit-making motives of cinema halls" (Raju 2015, 185)—screening their work at libraries or makeshift open-air venues (Shameem Akhtar, Tanvir Mokammel, personal interviews, 2014)—this mode of avant-garde film has since evolved into a new "global Bangladeshi cinema" poised for the diasporic and festival circuits of the 2000s (Raju 2015, 172–198). Elora Halim Chowdhury, a leading scholar of Bangladeshi film feminism, discusses selected fiction films made in this mode by and about women. In her words, Bangla works like these "push against masculinist visions of national cinema and open the door to a more diverse scope for the genre as part of a larger movement . . . for human rights advocacy and political justice" (2020, 289).

Overall, historiographies of cinema and gender in Bangladesh take two broad approaches. Scholars of the commercial stream situate female roles and women participants—actresses and entrepreneurs—within patriarchal national formations of film and media (Kabir 1979; Zaid 2010; Hayat 2013b; Hoek 2014; Raju 2015). Feminist readings illuminate the nuanced counternarratives in women's alternative stream productions, in the artisanal mode as well as the globalized mode, while pointing to the persistence of patriarchal nationalism even in the more progressive works by male directors (E. Chowdhury 2020; 2022; Gayen 2012). What has been left out of studies to date is a reckoning with the remarkable role played by middle-class female film entrepreneurs in the evolving *conceptual* history of mainstream commercial cinema in Dhaka. My point, as noted above, is to delineate how the ambiguous necessities for the formation of the nation and its genres provide women with the resources for entrepreneurial authorship. Across the eras I consider, women-made mainstream productions of maternal fiction riddle the borders of female respectability and otherness, although the traversals are also constrained by the scales at which social fictions of femaleness become aggregated.

Kohinoor Akhter Shuchanda and *Tin Konna*: Motherliness and a Sororal Fiction

Kohinoor Akhter Shuchanda belongs to the first generation of actress-entrepreneurs. Having begun her film career in East Pakistan alongside her liberation activist husband, Zahir Raihan, she rose to fame by starring in political cinema and politicized social films and folk fantasies made for theatrical release by Raihan. Through the 1960s, she also collaborated in the family film business as a producer (of fiction films such as *Taka Ana Pai*; 1970) and sometimes as a gender concept developer for films directed by Zahir Raihan (more on this below). Figure 6 is a rare early photograph of the small-scale familial film business. We see actress-entrepreneur Shuchanda with her husband, director Zahir Raihan, by her side and what looks like a close-knit familial crew (all men).

In the years after the demise (possible assassination) of Zahir Raihan in 1972, Shuchanda went on to write and enact scripts while running her own starname company, Shuchanda Cholochitra. Released under this banner in 1985, *Tin Konna* was prominently showcased as being produced and distributed by Shuchanda Cholochitra (fig. 7). The 1980s saw a rush of actresses turning to production, scenario or scriptwriting, and direction (Hayat 2013b, 68; Ziad 2010, 274–275). Periodicals of the time report that "one frequently sees the names of *mahilā prayojak* [women producers] on film posters and billboards

Fig. 6: Shuchanda, Zahir Raihan (holding cigarette), and a familial crew (Courtesy: Md. Fokrul Alam)

these days" ("*Mukhomukhi*" 1988, 41). While it is likely that the number of women in film production kept pace with an overall rise in women's urban workforce participation under structural adjustment, the momentum must also be seen as specific to transformations in the film industry. Mainstream filmmaking was being fostered by an industrial climate of entrepreneurship and team financing (Raju 2015, 160), which spawned small-scale production houses. In this climate of disaggregated entrepreneurship exhibitors, the principal financiers and controllers of the box office under a state-protected exhibition sector (156) may well have been inclined to provide infrastructural support to the fame and fandom of star-name companies and productions.

Still, in thinking regionally about a women-led company such as Shuchanda Cholochitra, I am drawn to a commonality in mode of access. Not unlike in the industries of Kolkata and Lahore, in Dhaka, too, female entrepreneur-authors step forward as middle-class male-led infrastructures weaken. At this time, the middle-class film business in Dhaka felt the loss not only of the leading male director and entrepreneur Zahir Raihan but also the wave of Liberation War filmmaking that had been led by activist male directors in the wake of 1971 (Awwal 2018, 37). The moment was opportune for female stars from the respectable activist lineage to take up female fiction filmmaking and to address the necessities and anxieties of an expanding urban middle class, which now encompassed the non-elite (as noted earlier). Crucial as well was the role being played by new media formation—specifically, by video networks that rapidly increased domestic consumption by female and middle-class audiences. Cinema halls, by contrast, were becoming populated by men and the working classes (Hoek 2014, 24).

Announcing the premier of the motion picture *Tin Konna*, a poster published in the periodical *Chitrali* in December 1985 (not the poster in fig. 7) deploys action-adventure vocabulary to whet audience appetites for the

Fig. 7: Poster for *Tin Konna* (Source: Md. Fokrul Alam. Private Collection)

spectacle. We read that it is a tale of the three sisters Shuchanda, Babita, and Champa out on a *duḥsāhasik abhiyān* (daring expedition) against *samājbirodhī* (antisocial) elements. By mixing an authentic family narrative of real-life sisters with the promise of proactive mobility outside the home, the posters for the premier begin to cultivate a pathway of audience desire to what is best described, in terms of the local genres evolving in this period (Awwal 2018), as a social action film. In this case of a social action–heroine film, the poster offers diverse female poses intermixing an ensemble of appeals befitting the needs of the times. The premier poster shows a close-up of the maternal sari-clad propriety of elder sister Shuchanda juxtaposed, on one side, with the respectable muscularity of policewoman Champa, and on another, with the transgressive irreverence of a cigarette-waving, Western-clothed Babita. We see a similar juxtaposition in figure 7, except that Babita's pose has been transmuted to a solemnly aggressive martial arts heroine. The hybrid array of female deportments and lifestyle choices on the posters poses the mixed-genre heroine film for a range of metropolitan and provincial audiences across middle-class strata. We learn that *Tin Konna* is to be exhibited in theaters in Dhaka, Chittagong, Khulna, and elsewhere. The widespread appeal to both male and female cinemagoers is vindicated, in fact, by a fan letter written to the periodical *Purbani* from Narsingdi, a provincial town outside the capital city of Dhaka. Bearing the names of two men and a woman, the letter states that having gone together to the theater to watch *Tin Konna* and "really liked it" (*satti bhālo legeche*), they request that Shuchanda, Babita, and Champa be given more opportunities for performance (*Prasanga: Tin Konna* 1986, 15).

Written soon after the premier, the accolade takes the three women to be only actresses, dependent for opportunities presumably on male authority figures, neglecting the autonomy of the female film company Shuchanda Cholochitra, save a passing reference. However, the film poster line shapes the attractions of the work in a way that counteracts such gendered neglect. As the production ascends in mass appeal and at the box office, we see a new line of Golden Jubilee posters appearing in *Chitrali* (January 1987). The new line showcases the three star sisters and the star-name company while side-lining male contributions. Male star images are altogether disappeared, with their names appearing in only one corner parallel to the naming in another corner of the male director Shibli Sadiq. The sidelining of the male director's name could well be part of a business arrangement controlled by the female star-producer, a point to which I will return in the next section. For now, let me add that the Golden Jubilee poster line announces as well that the sisters are now in "everyone's home" (*sabār ghare ghare*), implying that the film has been released in video format for home entertainment. Perhaps an expansion of target middle-class female audiences via video explains, at least in part, the ambiguous marginality of male participants in the cultural address of the Golden Jubilee posters.

There is little doubt that the evolving artistry of the posters for *Tin Konna* brings contradictory feminine appeals into an acceptable, and increasingly foregrounded, sororal ensemble of production and performance. This evolving configuration calls my attention to reports I find in Bangla periodicals about the way the star-owners Shuchanda and Babita ran their small-scale businesses. An article in *Saptahik Purnima* (January 1986), for example, describes the women's intensive involvement in day-to-day production work, as well as a sororal mutuality in the practice. The article is accompanied by a photo of the two sisters making banners and posters for a film release (see chapter 5 for a discussion). In connection with these reports, I understand how the evolving posters for *Tin Konna* as authorial cine-objects laboriously created by these star bricoleurs perform female filmic value. For one thing, the poster arts gradually foreground the female star-name company as one that is relatively independent of male support on both sides of the camera. Moreover, the sororal personas being mutually juxtaposed present a complicated ensemble of female star texts and related ambiguities, rendering them equally legible and necessary to the context. The implication is that a film business managed by women at a small scale of collaboration could provide a space for authoring heterogeneous incarnations of famous women, to "reflect the public's interest in changing views of the [female] self" (Hallet 2013, 28). The specialized labor of each sister is assembled—and chaperoned by respectability—to sustain an irreducibly ambiguous range of "public mothers" who stage the mixed demands on middle-class women in a time of change. In this vein, the mixed-genre maternal personas of Shuchanda and Babita, who had earned fame in earlier Bangla works by male film directors, are reused from a female-focused perspective for the turbulent '80s. To shed light on the re-authorship, let me briefly contextualize the available personas.

Shuchanda had catapulted to fame after being cast as Behula in a politicized folk fantasy by the same name directed by Zahir Raihan in the wake of the Bangla Language Movement. *Behula* (1966) is based on a Hindu puranic legend that deifies a self-sacrificing maternal wife. The significance of the folk ideal of self-sacrificing womanhood, drawn from a syncretic culture of village *jatra* (musical theater) shared by Muslims and Hindus of the Bengal region, is that it had widespread audience outreach in 1960s East Pakistan. Transported to the screen in the form of a jatra-style "folk-musical film," the ideal had served to sanctify and popularize the very medium of cinema among rural Muslims, who otherwise ascribed the "Islamic" sin of idolatry to visual figuration (Kabir, qtd. in Raju 2015, 86).[3] While Raihan possibly sought to draw rural audiences into the orbit of the Bangla Language Movement by making a folk fantasy film, in his hands, Behula transmutes, in my view, into a gendered metaphor for revolutionary struggle against political travails. The first frame of *Behula*, showcasing a text and a voiceover, says as much by stating the legend together with the *Padma Purana*, from where it is drawn, is "*mānusheri kabya*" (an epic of humans only). As such, Raihan's *Behula* is open to reading as a folk-façade sociopolitical allegory that mines folklore as, in Dipesh Chakrabarty's words, "a special [romantic] kind of archival resource . . . [in order to accrue] a political yield" (2004, 677, 682). In this instance, the political humanist yield is a gendered melodrama of female domination and resistance wherein female-ness is desacralized and subjected to performative scrutiny (at odds with the Hindu mother-goddess trope). The opposition of sanctified and desacralized (demoniac) femininity found in *Behula* was soon to be remixed in Raihan's renowned nationalist allegory of an *unmaternal* woman qua Pakistani state, *Jibon Theke Neya* (Taken from Life; 1970; dir. Zahir Raihan), staged on the emotional grid of a domestic social film. Identified to this day as *prānabanta Behula* (lively/active Behula; Hasan et al. 2020, 79), the persona of Shuchanda incarnates an ambiguous maternal concept of cross-breeding self-sacrifice with the intrepidity of a woman who had headed out for an actual face-off with a demoniacal goddess. As far as *Jibon Theke Neya* goes, Shuchanda not only had a leading role but also a claim to the authorship of the concept, an important point to which I will return in the next section.

In the subsequent decade, we find a widely popular female destitution melodrama titled *Golapi Ekhon Traine* (The Endless Trail; 1978) studded with unsacred maternal protectors and daughters. Directed from a left-leaning perspective by Amjad Hossain, the work casts sister Babita in the title role of a *sramajibi* (laborer) peddler, and displaced village woman with a good dose of sex appeal (Raju 2013, 132). Babita's personification of the maternal daughter Golapi layers the energies of the worker/youth protests of the time with neo-liberal lifestyle choices, performing the stark contradictions of developmental-ism in late '70s Bangladesh. *Tin Konna* enters the same field of genre-mixing activity and sociopolitical contradictions and draws on the already familiar personas of the two lead heroines, birthed in the works of male directors like Raihan and Hossain. However, the women's work inhabits and remixes the conventions into a memorably irreducible mixture of pure and impure motherliness that magnifies the gendered inequities of the 1980s. Not to be forgotten is the hand of scriptwriter Shuchanda, who once had collaborated with her activist husband, Zahir Raihan, in the latter's experimentation with mainstream genres in his endeavor at democratic outreach. That being said, the work is *obviously transborder* in the appeal to middle-class tastes. It dutifully dwells within a conservative social fiction that closes by reinstating family and state patriarchies. According to the scriptwriter's own testimony to periodicals (Hasan et al. 2020, 79), this three-daughter fiction was created by Kohinoor Akhter Shuchanda upon her father's suggestion that she write a story of her family. The complexity lies with the layering of female personifications and performative excess, which refuse to cohere with the closure.

The narrative depicts three sisters—named eponymously Chanda, Champa, and "Bobi"—displaced from their loving patriarchal home by smugglers who were chased by the girls' police officer father. The father disappeared and presumably has been slaughtered, and the now-deranged mother roams the streets of Dhaka in search of her lost daughters. The foundling daughters themselves come to be adopted, separately, by a businessman, a Catholic priest, and a *mostān*. (In urban Bangladesh of the time, a mostān, a figure "akin to a gangster," acted as the officious leader of a locality [Jackman 2017, 16; Van Schendel 2009, 252–253]). Doubling as a care worker for the urban *kāngāli* (destitute), the mostān in question finds and trains street children to become thieves. The respective daughters grow up to be the photojournalist Chanda (Shuchanda), who voluntarily mothers the son of her widowed boss (Prabir Mitra); the righteous police inspector Rosie Rozario (Champa), who cleanses the streets of gang activity while indulging in romantic interludes (with the youth hero Ilyas Kanchan); and the female mostān and thief Bichchu

(Babita), who fulfills obligatory mother work for her adoptive father's destitute wards. All three, along their own paths, are looking for their long-lost family members and seeking justice against the gangster who destroyed their blissful home. An episodic plotline of chance encounters and misrecognitions peppered with kung fu–style street fights and romantic dances leads up to a last melodramatic fight resulting in the reunion of the respectable biological family and the pairing off of all three daughters. This happy patriarchal ending rounds out what is revealed to be a corrective plan orchestrated by the paternalistic superintendent of the Dhaka police and his worthy police officer son. Unsurprisingly, the latter (played by Sohel Rana) is the reformist romancer of Bichchu. Her name not only means "the naughty one," but off and on she is called a nashtā woman. The reformist couple's romance implies a cultural rescue narrative of a fallen woman, identified in contemporary middle-class discourse with pornographic obscenity (Hoek 2014; see my discussion above).

If we read the filmic text with an eye to the narrative resolution, we easily settle for a melodramatic spectacle conflating respectable private patriarchy with a state-governed order that both reforms and polices the criminalized poor, coterminous with the perilous urban landscape of Dhaka. This social action film appears to be little other than a heroine version of the action-hero genres dominating the new media field. Arpana Awwal argues that in the video age of the 1980s, a transnationally influenced urban action-hero genre, replete with *mardānga* "heavy-duty action" spectacularized by color, was "colonizing" Bangla social and family genres (2018, 30). According to film periodicals of the time, such films were consumed both in theatrical and video format largely by audiences in provincial towns and by teenagers in Dhaka ("Video" 1990, 43). The masculinist Bangla aesthetic was populated by working-class action heroes like Joshim, personifying for youth audiences the "militarized-cum-democratic" modernity being promoted by the developmental military regime of the time (Awwal 2018, 35–37). Notable among regional video influences was the Amitabh Bachchan–led Indian action-hero genre—the ensemble hero film *Amar Akbar Anthony* (1977; dir. Manmohan Desai) being especially telling in this instance.

There is indeed little doubt that *Tin Konna* mimics these action-hero genres in the arcs of both the narrative and the fight choreography. The Indian action-hero drama of disassembled families, maternal distress, and youthful couple-mode patriarchy seems to be reproduced, together with the sanctification of the biological bond of offspring with the body of the mother/land. In the vein of *Amar Akbar Anthony*, *Tin Konna* shows three unrecognized offspring donating blood to the injured birth mother so as eventually to be reclaimed as truly her own. Likewise, the arc of the fights is that of a robotic mardānga action found from Bangla action heroes like Joshim. Although action heroines Babita and Champa do fight, musclemen most often gain the upper hand. Key fight scenes are narratively put together to allow for the self-assured policeman protagonist and reformist hero Sohel Rana to suddenly appear and take over as the rescuer of abruptly weakened fighter heroines. Then the question is, Does an aesthetic that obviously mimics male action genres allow for the ambiguities of female personification suggested by the evolving poster artistry, described earlier, or does it reduce the ambivalence and underlying social conflict? I maintain that the ambiguous appeals of motherly public selves are indeed staged by the heroines in a way that magnifies rather than suppresses contemporary sociosexual inequities. To pry out the multiple layers and attractions of female personification in *Tin Konna*, we need to be attentive to the diverse ways in which the action film form itself is deployed. In plotting the diverse commodity lives of the three personas from the poster pose to the filmic text, I seem to see the posters orienting viewers toward scenes in which publicly active women "command the narrative" (Tasker 1993, 132) and away from scenes that center on men and masculine stardom.

In this video age, the Bangla action-heroine aesthetic must be situated in a worldwide gendering of the spectacular new cinema of effects whose primary appeal and meaning are "rooted in stimulus" rather than in the narrative (Tom Gunning, qtd. in Tasker 2004, 7). Examining the gender language of stimuli in early Hollywood action heroines, Ben Singer discerns an artistry he calls "eustress," a euphoric form of "sensory excitation" that prepares the female body to keep pace with the rapid and "inviting" stimuli of urban change (2001, 114, 124). Considering more recent Hong Kong and American action heroines, which were flowing into Bangladesh through video and cable television, both Leon Hunt and Yvonne Tasker argue that spectacles of female excitation typically transgress proper feminine space and behavior (Hunt 2007, 152; Tasker 1993, 148). The provocative historical difference of the action-heroine spectacle at hand is that the eustressful transgression of propriety does not dramatize women stepping out of the private sphere into the public. Women's public participation was already deemed socially necessary across class strata. Instead, transgression is stimulated in the heroines by the "proprieties" of resource allocation and consumption dividing the urban landscape of Dhaka and being controlled by a respectable patriarchy and state institutions. Thus, the sensory excitation in the *Tin Konna* aesthetic is mixed with the conflicting energies born from structural adjustment, on the one hand, from youth-oriented consumerism (found in Bangla action films starring hero Joshim, for example [Awwal 2018]), and on the other, from the oppositional momentum of protest movements by students, workers, and women against the inequities of the developmental Islamizing regime.[4] The meanings of maternal, aspirational, and radical femininity attached to the star personas acquire *fresh use value* for these irreducibly contradictory stimuli of 1980s Bangladesh. Babita's appeal as the displaced sexy maternal laborer

Golapi certainly comes to mind, as does Shuchanda's sanctified image of the proactive maternal wife Behula fighting against despotic power. The evolving film poster authorship discussed earlier guides the eye precisely to the heterogeneous, female-focused stimuli—eustressful attractions that partially upend the teleology of the respectable patriarchal family and its maternal ideal through implicitly interrogating privilege.

Let us start with an early scene that brings to the moving frame the juxtaposition of bodies and attitudes in the poster for the premier of *Tin Konna* discussed earlier. A close-up of a clicking camera held by photojournalist Chanda (Shuchanda) is joined with a medium shot that "tutors" the viewer's eye on Babita/Bichchu's irreverent posture (Dayan 1976, 438–450). She is caught on camera leaning against a pillar, clad in a snug T-shirt, jeans, and beret, puffing away at a cigarette. Far from being evenly paced, the shot jerkily cuts to another close-up of the startled Bichchu jumping forward to angrily demand of Chanda why she is being photographed. As a fashionable woman on city streets leisurely holding the cigarette, Babita/Bichchu dramatizes for the urban youth of the time what Ranjani Mazumdar describes as a "novel experience of flânerie," that of drifting along with the sexy "activity of consumption" (2007, 91). The cinematic urban street itself is not unlike many others in depicting the meeting place of strangers from unequal walks of life, the classy respectability of Shuchanda's expensive *shalwar kameez*–costumed figure being juxtaposed with Babita's, clad in cheap imitations of Western fashion. The female encounter is clearly unequal to begin with. The urban street is constructed as a space of transgressive consumption in which the Westernized *flaneuse*, a potential streetwalker, is to be "patrolled through surveillance" by the respectable nationalist woman (80–81, 204). In response to Bichchu's aggressive question, Chanda replies with judgmental derision that she took the shot because she has never seen a *bangali meye* (Bengali girl) smoking, especially on the open street. With her urban slang and swagger, Bichchu is also an androgynous version of the city boy of Hollywood urban cinema, infused with the regional figures of the Bangla filmic *mostān* as well as the Hindi filmic *tapori*, or vagabond (51, 41), most clearly Amitabh Bachchan in the latter case. Rebellion against urban inequities is the key characteristic of the convention-mixing performance by the two stars, for Bichchu's rebelliousness is soon to generate contradictory outcomes.

On the one hand, we see the disparate female personas being pulled together in a familial configuration. Asserting with heady youthfulness that she smokes because she feels like being intoxicated, Babita/Bichchu goes on to add with a conspiratorial wink that the photo of her smoking should not be published in any newspaper, as she has to maintain her "prestige in the *mohallāh*" (locality). This comedy of tomboyish irreverence transforms Chanda's judgmental derision into an indulgent maternal smile, tracked through a medium close-up of her eyes following Bichchu's moves. In effect, the respectable Shuchanda's maternal eye opens cinematic space for performing new female roles and contested body politics that reflect change in middle-class public interest. The indulgent maternal eye of Shuchanda chaperones, so to speak, the sexually ambivalent star persona of her sister Babita. Shuchanda's role as the maternal older sibling chaperoning her star sisters' access to mainstream filmic space and diverse personas—in other words, her gender activity as a casting producer— will be taken up in the next section. In the scenic construction in question, on the other hand, Babita/Bichchu's actions grow to be irreducibly heterogeneous to respectability. Her momentary comic posture of (respectable) "prestige" is little less than a caricature of the socioeconomic privilege commanded by the elite respectable woman she confronts. Moreover, the irreverent pose is soon linked to criminality as close-ups track Bichchu's prowling eyes on Chanda's purse, which she eventually picks through. Moreover, the juxtaposing of the rebellious criminal poor with a consumerist flaneuse is soon to be ironically magnified through a spectacular sequence of episodes. Stimulating much of the sequence is the drama of Bichchu's serial thefts of sports cars, which ornament Dhaka city and waylay the urban experience of destitution with incorrigible excitation. What this sequence tests are patriarchal boundaries of resource and consumption shown to also divide women and classify maternal genres.

A most inviting audiovisual spectacle suffuses the frame. A long take shows a glistening yellow European car cruise forward and park in front of a Pepsi advertisement as its exceptionally melodious horn engulfs the soundtrack. We see this pointedly eroticized spectacle, set against a globalized cityscape filled with imported commodities such as Pepsi vending machines, as connected to Bichchu's characteristically heightened gaze (Mazumdar 2007, 91). Performing an ecstatic song and dance and blowing kisses to what she calls her "darling," Babita/Bichchu dashes forward to physically hug the automobile and then turns to pick the lock, although forestalled by the owner's return. This overt performance of eustress, excitation responding to the inviting stimuli of urban change (Singer 2001), soon mutates into a specific pleasure of action-heroine power found in Hollywood films—that of a speedy woman controlling cars and other technologies (Tasker 1993, 152). Note that the indomitable physicality of Bichchu the action heroine is far more consistent in her agile acts of chasing and stealing than it is in the fight scenes borrowed from the contemporary hero aesthetic. Nonetheless, the provocative blurring of boundaries between heroism and villainy we find in the destitute protagonist's technological prowess participates in the Bangla action film's generic response to contemporary inequities (Awwal 2018). Action heroine Bichchu's outlaw technological power is pleasurably stimulated by the technological objects owned and consumed by the pillars of public and state legality, respectable patriarchs who tower over the city and effectively normalize its uneven resource allocation. The two yellow automobiles she steals, drives, and tries to illegally traffic belong, respectively, to the owner of a newspaper trying to investigate the true face of crime in Dhaka and to the superintendent of police leading punitive measures against criminals. All in all, this audiovisual melodrama pitting globalized development against criminalized dispossession is a compelling case of what Moinak Biswas characterizes, with reference to West Bengali cinema, as a staging of "the more democratic . . . and nuanced aspects of its audience's desires" (2000, 131).

Specific to *Tin Konna* are the democratic nuances of gender desire in the staging of the motherly concept in female-focused scenes—to be precise, in scenes that depict interactions between the women characters. On one side, we have Bichchu shown as prone to stealing cars and picking pockets in order to earn the daily keep of the destitute children she "mothers" (we see the children cry in hunger and clamor for rice when she fails). On another, we have respectable motherly women, the seemingly sympathetic journalist Chanda indulging the urchin-like pickpocket as well as the innately driven birth mother who madly wanders the streets of Dhaka in search of her lost daughters. These class-coded personas are soon pitted in opposition such that the concepts of femininity and maternity become fraught with conflict.

After Bichchu is recognized as the thief/outlaw, the once-maternal journalist Chanda aids ruthless policewoman Rosie to fight and punish the criminal. The punitive duo also succeeds in antagonizing the birth mother. Having been struck by a car, the birth mother recovers only after receiving blood from her three unknown daughters. The rejuvenated mother's tender welcome to Bichchu, in the recovery room, is interrupted by violent aggression when the other two recognize the car thief and leap to the latter's pursuit. When she next sees Bichchu, the mother reproduces precisely the aggression learned from her respectable progeny (albeit still unknown). As we see Bichchu run forward with the spontaneous cry of "Mother," the camera cuts to a close-up of the righteously aggressive old woman refusing the name. She avers that a nashtā woman could never be a "daughter" to her. We also see *Tin Konna* doubling on the narrative of the Hindi film *Amar Akbar Anthony* to wrest away the Hindu nationalist concept of deified motherhood, laying the supposition of innate maternal purity open to conflict. The Raihan legacy of scrutinizing the concept of the maternal nation-state seems relevant instead, for we see the loyal, albeit unknown, offspring talking back. Bichchu repeatedly entreats the old woman to explain why she is not to be considered blood-related even though she has given blood to the body of the one she has called Mother. The mise-en-scène is the den of an arch criminal who holds both women in captivity. The birth mother appears spectacularly chained in a symbolic configuration of the pure maternal body as national land/state becoming shackled by masculinist crime. While the destitute Bichchu is easily misrecognized by the respectable women as yet another criminal, her claim in this scene is to be re-recognized as an integral part of the maternal/national body because she has taken the agentive filial decision to sustain maternal life—in effect, to actively forge kinship. Overall, we see a democratic layering of female personifications. By interrogating concepts of nation and inclusion, this layered drama allows transborder performances of motherliness that crisscross the limits of legality and privilege. As such, Bichchu's performance of the activist kin-maker in this scene is intratextual with others in which the sororal stars bond together to command the narrative of maternity rather than being pitted in opposition to one another by the teleology of patriarchal respectability.

These female-focused scenes include not only the fleeting verisimilar images of Bichchu's daily maternal (di)stress in trying to provide for her destitute wards but also a heroic street fight that positions the three protagonists against masculinist invasion of family life. The episode begins with the young son of the newspaper magnate for whom journalist Chanda works being kidnapped from outside his posh school. Chanda has been acting as a maternal figure for the motherless young boy while developing a romance with his widower father. When the boy is kidnapped, Bichchu, in the role of the protective female gangster of the locality, takes justice into her own hands. She dashes forward to stop what in her words is "*polāpān* [child] hijack in Dhaka city." She is joined in the chase by Chanda and then police inspector Rosie Rozario riding up on her official motorbike. In this transborder traversal of legality, the lawless and the lawful are seen to come together in a collective motherly crusade to protect and nurture the children of the city. This is the one fight in which the team of women actually triumph, with lead heroine Babita/Bichchu turning into a "masculine" action figure with the "developed musculature" needed for a hard-fought kung fu battle (Tasker 1993, 3). The simultaneity of heroine performances, crossing the borders of both the legal city and urban privilege, could be plotted to the juxtaposition of female poses and meanings we find on the Golden Jubilee poster of *Tin Konna*, discussed above. Recall that the same poster disappears men and, implicitly, sidelines the attraction of the male-dominant and pro-state closure.

Generally speaking, in *Tin Konna*, heterogeneous contents of economic inequality and moral anxiety, riddling an era of transformations, navigate the concepts of family and womanhood that are conventional to the urban Bangla social films. What evolves is a contradictory drama of maternal actions and feminine attractions. Following the three performer sisters to the production space, I find that attaching heterogeneous concepts of maternity and respectability to their personas gives the women access. They come to be accepted as female entrepreneurs befitting the times. In effect, the conceptual ambiguities they personify enable the women to negotiate authority as independent film producers working in a female family mode and to shift the infrastructure of patriarchal acceptance as needed. This means their claims to entrepreneurial and creative authority remain related to a business discourse that is sexually divided by labor and propriety. Nonetheless, a female-focused transborder analytic that digs for traces of women's authorial decision work in the folds of the dominant familial narrative of male control is bound to find clues in Bangla press accounts of the era. Clues of Shuchanda's creative roles in script-writing, casting, and sororal production work that possibly rolls into direction appear repeatedly while being entwined in a transborder rhetoric of mother work. The following section begins by examining how the three sisters mediate their disaggregated specializations in feminine performance and focuses on Shuchanda's.

Producing in a Small-Scale Mode: Sororal Paradoxes of Authority and Creativity

In the months directly preceding the premier of *Tin Konna*, we find film periodicals such as *Chitrali* and *Purbani* buzzing with what they claim is a tumultuous event of the film industry in Bangladesh. The event is a parallel inauguration of two star-name film companies headed by women in adjacent offices of the Rajmoni Film Complex in Dhaka: Shuchanda Cholochitra and Babita Movies. A report titled "Dui Bon Shuchanda O Babita" (Two Sisters: Shuchanda and Babita)" published by the periodical *Chitrali* on this occasion notes that even though involvement with production is hardly new to male and female stars of Dhaka, what is causing *āloṛan* (commotion) in the cinema world is the news of two women becoming *karnadhār* (helmspersons) of production-distribution organizations. The report goes on to emphasize the remarkable independence characterizing the business model of the two women-owned companies, by contrast to prior cases of women taking *gauṇa*, or secondary, production roles under their husbands or being labeled producers for the sake of paperwork only (*kāgoche kalame*) (*Chitrali* 1985, 4).

This master narrative of the family mode of production being male-dominant, with women taking on peripheral laborious roles while being familiar with the Dhaka film environment is inaccurate. Historian Anupam Hayat endorses the narrative by noting that while no less than twenty-two women were listed as "voting members" of the Bangladesh Producers and Distributors Association till 2008, and that many more unnamed participants had worked from that or a similar *nepathya* (background), most had come to the film business through the "*sahāyata* [help] of husbands or close relatives" (2013b, 70–72). Yet Hayat's own book as well as Md. Fokrul Alam's *Amader Chalachit-tra* partially discount their own discourse of female dependence by describing prominent cases of women taking up film directorship, acting, and production after divorce or separation—noteworthy being the first Bangla female film director-actress of Dhaka, Rebecca, as well as female star-producer Sumita Devi (Hayat 2013b, 50, 54, 56; Alam 2011, 6–7). Such consistent records as these of the participatory and leadership roles taken in the Bangla film industry by educated Muslim women from the respectable classes stem from women's agency in the national public arenas of Bengali Muslim modernity, discussed earlier in this chapter. Note that the sororal trio under discussion—Shuchanda, Babita, and Champa—are daughters of a college-educated woman.

What we find in the sororal case at hand is a seeming shift in the narrative of production modes. The *Chitrali* columns, as well as those from other periodicals reporting on this new female family mode, apparently celebrate the women as independent owners of a film business, embrace a sororal rather than spousal support system, and recognize a matrilineal way of inducting female talent into the world of cinema. No doubt, this acceptance of women's independent professional status in mainstream production intersects with structural changes in film entrepreneurship and in women's workplace participation in 1980s Bangladesh (discussed earlier). At the same time, the enabling concept of female empowerment is implicitly bounded by patriarchal questions about the obligatory duties of respectable women—all the more so in relation to a film world increasingly identified with low-class taste, obscenity, and violence (Hoek 2014). These questions loop around the sisters in the extracinematic sphere just as they do in the text of *Tin Konna*. In the extra-cinematic workplace, the normative concerns are more systematically managed through celebrity rituals performed by the star-entrepreneurs. In a sense, the sexual contradictions of the turbulent 1980s are staged by the respective personas and negotiated through mutually sororal body work (relating siblings in an appropriate hierarchy).[5] Crucial to the mutuality is the small-scale bricolage of contradictory female values undertaken by the sister entrepreneurs in their interactions with public discourse.

The reporter for *Chitrali* (1985) goes on to depict in colorful detail the inauguration of the two women's companies. We learn that the inaugural event for Shuchanda's company was a relatively humble affair, one that at the same time staked a matrilineal heritage. With just a few invitees around, the ribbon was cut by Begum Subhash Dutta, wife of the director Subhash Dutta, who had cast Shuchanda in her debut feature. We also get a sense of how Shuchanda might have used her physicality to incarnate her company and control its public image from a detail about the props supporting her deportment on the first day of work. She is described as using a relatively modest, low-back chair in her office because no woman could sit for long in a large, high-back one that might mess up her neatly tied bun. A bun at the back of the head is traditional for appropriately long-haired women in the Bengal region and elsewhere in South Asia. We learn, too, that in conflict with Shuchanda's look and behavior are those of Babita in the adjacent office. We learn that Babita not only cut the inaugural ribbon herself but that she also procured a huge, high-backed owner's chair—suggestive of an unfeminine self-assertion, identified in this instance with Babita's Westernized short hair. In brief, the look and feel of entrepreneur Babita is implicitly characterized as more sexually ambivalent and aggressively independent. Yet what mediates Babita's transgressive persona of star-entrepreneur is additional information about the respectable matrilineal guidance being provided by her forbear Shuchanda. Both Babita and youngest sister, Champa, are repeatedly portrayed by the Bangla press in a tactile configuration of innate obedience to elders familiar to Bengali family discourse, that of being inducted in "holding the hands" of elder sister Shuchanda (*hāta dhore*). Moreover, this public discourse of a sororal collectivity and the exemplary elder chaperone—a discourse reprocessed both on the film posters and in the filmic text, discussed earlier—is intertextually modulated and partially authored by star interviews. The female stars, as "negotiating historical subjects" (Wang 2011, 22), interact with the public discourse of family proprieties while positing their ambiguous identities and specialized labors.

Shuchanda's interview tempers her status as an independent film entrepreneur by performing the core value of a self-sacrificing maternal Bengali woman. In a subsequent interview on the success of her film company, given to the periodical *Saptahik Purnima* in 1988 ("*Mukhomukhi*" 41), she is meticulous about the labor she puts into fulfilling her motherly and domestic duties before coming to work. Newcomer sibling Champa holds the "hand" of her respectable elder by publicly reinforcing her own commitment to motherly duty. At the same time, Champa enacts a new-generation public mother for the youthful modernity of developmental Bangladesh by posing as a Western-clothed *adhunik* (contemporary) woman attractive to *taruṇa-taruṇī* (male and female youth) audiences ("*Champa: Bhetare O Bāire*" 1988, 35–36). Whereas Babita, too, performs youthful *adhunikatā* (modernity) for the times—reportedly appearing with hand-held video game devices and Lady Diana hairdos ("Uro Katha" 1982, 47)—she comes to incarnate a sexually complex fame. The contradictions depicted by her role in *Tin Konna* are most germane. In a written interview given to *Saptahik Purnima* in 1989, Babita responds to a male reporter's trenchant questions by defending her transgressive "sex appeal" with a voice of rebellion "juxtapolitical" (Berlant 2008, 8) to the turbulence of worker and urban women's movements against the military rule of this period. She explicitly celebrates the *jāgoraṇa* (awakening) of women and the underprivileged from within a *purush-śasita o śreni-bibhakta samāj* (patriarchal and class-stratified society) ("*Babitār Ekānto Shākhātkār* [Babita's Exclusive Interview]" 1989, 41). At the same time, Babita is quick to contain her rebellious autonomy within the bounds of respectable family discourse. She proclaims herself to be no other than an "ordinary pleasant Bengali woman [*sadhāraṇa ramani*] from a traditional happy family," one who is committed to developing for her people a "socially healthy canvas" (*sāmājik sustha prekkhāpat*).

The transborder paradox of these celebrity politics of personification lies in the fact that precisely obedience to the prevalent proprieties of family value and social status permit women access to both production infrastructures and creative decision work. The complexity, on the other hand, is that women's family-mode work could easily be pushed under the master narrative of male filmic agency—in the words of the reporters and historians quoted above, to be seen as household-type labor in the background, remaining secondary to male innovation. Thus, my argument is for a female-focused analytic that looks for women's decision work around commercially made and released films that bear women's names in some production capacity, assuming that female claims to innovation are interminably transborder and bounded by paradoxes. If we then plot the path of these claims to filmic texts and orbital objects with which women's names are associated, considering which signifiers pull together, we might find traces of sexual innovation and difference (from male-dominant genres and conventions).

The interview about her successful film company quoted above does not terminate with Shuchanda's list of the maternal duties she completes before coming to work. Having responded obediently to the reporter's query about domestic obligations, she grows far more eloquent in response to a new question about how she likes her profession of production and distribution. Emphasizing that this "interesting" work provides much "food for thought" (*cintā-bhābnā*), she breaks the point down by elaborating on another list of jobs. She maintains that as the producer, she has to decide which form of story would appeal to common viewers, how to structure that storyline, which actor would fit in what role, who could best direct and delineate the story, which costumes to choose, and, finally, how to steer the production to the final print (*"Mukhomukhi"* 1988, 42). Far from being uncommon, the role she depicts of the producer as a hands-on decision worker involved at all stages of the production had been traditional to the relatively low-budget celluloid industry of Dhaka, according to Anupam Hayat's archival study (2013b, 70). In the producer/exhibitor–dominated financial landscape of the 1980s, the director functioned as a subordinate, contracted employee. Periodicals of the time note that many directors earned monthly wages like the other temporary workers on the set (Bhuyian 1981, 27). What nuances Shuchanda's account of the producer-director relationship in the case of her own company is a story of matriarchal authority that personifies her as towering, as the conceptual life force of the production, over the male directors she has employed: Shibli Sadiq and Chasi Nazrul Islam. She describes the male directors in elder-matron parlance as "good *technicians*" (italics mine) behaving toward her in a bhadra (respectable/respectful) way (*"Mukhomukhi"* 1988, 42).

It seems to me that Shuchanda's excited claim about her hands-on engagement with film production work, and how it has given her much food for thought, combines with her passing remark about male directors being good technicians (only) to push back the prevalent master narrative about women producers doing household management–type duties. As a matter of fact, the same narrative frames this Shuchanda interview. While acknowledging that many female names appear as producers on film posters in the 1980s, the reporter overtly feminizes production work as a form of hassle-filled mechanical labor that is implicitly backgrounded, in sexual terms, to creative agency: he asserts that while women manage the *jhakki jhāmelā* (hassle and trouble) of keeping accounts and coordinating bookings, very few come to the "unit" ("*Mukhomukhi*" 1988, 41). Despite the large number of women in the production profession at the time, the more innovative components of production work and decision making appear to be temporally "unthinkable" (Gaines 2018, 67) within the prevalent sexual division of labor. Could it be that Shuchanda, riding on her legitimacy as an independent female star-entrepreneur befitting the times, was trying to shift the divisive assumption and make her innovative hand thinkable? One is able to arrive at this conjecture only by doing the fugitive work of gender research across Bangla media platforms, for Shuchanda's stories about her innovative work, including her account of writing the story of *Tin Konna*, lie buried in Bangla periodicals. Shibli Sadiq is named as the writer and director of the film both in the more visible records found in Bangladesh and on the Internet Movie Database (IMDb).

As I argue throughout this book, excavating such neglected records of "unthinkable" creative work by women means we plot histories of female innovation intertextually: as encrypted both in extra-cinematic discourse (such as interviews) and in particular diegeses in whose production the women were involved. Noteworthy in this light is another neglected history of Shuchanda's hand in story and scenario development. In at least two interviews, Shuchanda tells how, in the lobby of a cinema hall in what was then West Pakistan, she and her spouse, Zahir Raihan, together began imagining the scenario of Raihan's renowned production *Jibon Theke Neya*, the filmic allegory depicting unmaternal (Pakistani) statist domination. Story and script credits for this work everywhere are given to Raihan alone (Hayat 2013a, 108; Kabir 1979, 44–45). The scenario she had suggested was of "two sisters," "a bunch of keys," and a "family feud" over control (Shuchanda, qtd. in Hayat 2013a, 109–111). It began turning into a script that very night in their hotel room when Raihan asked her to pull out a notebook and write together with him. These tidbits make me think of the inexplicably radical episode in *Tin Konna* that goes against the grain of the pro-nation-state resolution. I refer to the episode of unmaternal femininity that includes a "family feud" between the (nation-as-) mother and the destitute daughter (described above). Perhaps the episode carries a cryptic trace of innovations in which Shuchanda had collaborated with Zahir Raihan.[6]

Any such analysis of unthinkable female innovation necessarily begs another. What do we make of times when women's creative agency as film director and screenplay writer grows socially *thinkable* and rewardable—in contexts aware of women's voices in a way that opens up structural opportunities at national and global levels? And how might gender proprieties inflect to the change? I attempt a response to these questions by turning to female author-directors in relation to the large-scale infrastructures of Bangla cinema in the 2000s Bangladesh.

Female Author-Directors and the National-Global Scale: Proprieties in the 2000s

Although Shuchanda had directed and produced one fiction feature in the 1990s (print unavailable), the relatively recent production for which she received the national awards of Best Director and Best Producer is *Hajaar Bachhar Dhorey* (Symphony of Agony; 2005), a close filmic version of an early novel also written by her renowned late spouse, Zahir Raihan. Enhanced by visually compelling shots of riverine villages and a well-edited screenplay (written by Shuchanda), this lyrical work reveals Shuchanda's thoughtful command of the craft of filmmaking. We know from her own testimony, quoted previously, that the craft was cultivated through years of hands-on experience in all aspects of film production as well as in story and scenario development. In the national award-winning and state-of-the-art Dolby-enhanced production, Shuchanda's authorial craft has been developed in collaboration with a professional crew.

The teleology of this rural drama is driven by a reformist young male villager who seeks but largely fails to break the unjust patriarchal religious norms internalized by both men and women of the village. These norms uphold women's lack of freedom to choose partners and the oppressive use of *talak* (divorce) by feudal Muslim men. A full analysis of the hero fiction lies outside the scope of the female-centric textualities with which this book is concerned. Still, relevant for my study are two contradictory aspects of gender depiction in what appears to be an overtly faithful literary film following the original novel chapter by chapter. On the one hand, the narrative arc foregrounds the "agonizing" subordination of female desires under stagnant Muslim patriarchy, highlighted in the non-literal English translation of the Bengali title as "Symphony of Agony," albeit the precise episodes about the women are lifted from the novel. Further, this arc is clarified in relation to a male-centric plot that reduces the ambiguities of male character interiority and action in Raihan's story in favor of a progress-oriented young romantic hero, staging an emergent citizen-subject. On the other hand, the young female protagonists, especially the heroine involved in an extramarital romantic relationship with the youthful hero, are portrayed in a contradictory vein. Subordinated by religious-patriarchal norms, they still are subjects of desire and choice in their own right. This dichotomous depiction of female selves illuminates a new trend of Bangladeshi "world cinema." According to Zakir Hossain Raju (2015, 195–197), the new cinema falls in line with a "global nativism" found in similar formations of Asian art cinema. The cinematic arts reproduce for "global as well as modern, national audiences" the uniqueness of local culture and village customs that at the same time are replete with pro-Islamic backwardness. Variations on the theme incorporate narratives of women's independence and thwarted progress.

Produced by Shuchanda Cholochitra and partially funded by a government grant for "*śilpamān sammata*" (artistically tasteful) films (Ziad 2010, 347), this work is important for the comparative scalar approach of this book. It marks the intersection of small-scale star-name companies with state and corporate infrastructures in the 2000s. These infrastructures support a new crop of Bangladeshi author-directors coming from both the mainstream and the independent film clubs movement. The rise of the author-director paradigm accompanies a shift from the relations of the state to the film industry found in the 1980s. In the later 1970s through the '80s, film and media infrastructures were loosely state-governed. The producer-exhibitor networks were disaggregated in a way that enabled small-scale entrepreneurship and collaborative authorship. Further, the networks were destabilized by video trade and piracy routes. Evolving in the scale of capital through the 1990s, infrastructures in 2000s Dhaka combine state support with corporate conglomeration in film and television productions. The rise of a new author-director paradigm in this context is well registered in the comment made by non-star director Nargis Akhter to the fortnightly periodical *Binodon* in 2010. In her words, "Ours is a Director's Media rather than the Producers' Media it had become" in Bangladesh ("*Shilper Sathe Mitali*" 2010, 33).

Once we situate the Shuchanda-directed literary film in the new Bangla media space, we see a large-scale manufacturing of production value through which the modern woman director is aligned with a heritage text. Opening shots of the filmic text make heritage tangible through signs such as the late Zahir Raihan's photograph and the physical book, whereas the DVD of *Hajaar Bachhar Dhorey*, released by the upmarket film and music corporation G-Series, showcases the female author. The jacket artistry includes a close-up photo of Shuchanda in a modern directorial pose, wearing a baseball cap and with her eyes glued to a cine-camera. The look and feel of the filmic text taken together with cine-objects in its multimedia orbit (the DVD jacket for one) embody a new Bangladeshi brand of world cinema. This cinema is best characterized in the words of Scott Lash and Celia Lury (2007, 4–6) as having the "sign-value" of a national-global identity. This value system flexibly assembles diverse authorial voices and genres while polarizing the preferences. Along these lines, signifiers placed in the filmic text and across orbital objects encompass progress and pro-Islamic backwardness, exotic village patriarchy, and women's autonomy (on and off the screen). Noteworthy is the contrast of this large-scale, systematic valuation of the filmic product with the commodity value mutating through the poster artistry of *Tin Konna*. In the latter case, the value of heterogeneous femaleness evolving through the poster arts came from the participatory desires of the female star-producers and their diverse fans. Although the new media space clearly assigns values to the woman author-director and her product, these values are flexibly aggregated by a large-scale brand logic. The capital logic of brands operates at a higher level of abstraction than filmic commodities that inflect to the needs of multiple makers and users.

Infrastructure for the new Bangla brand cinema has been greatly strengthened through the conglomeration of selected television corporations with motion picture production. According to Bangladesh Film Archive official Md. Fokrul Alam, feature film production has grown exponentially since 2001, reaching an all-time high of 104/105 releases in 2004/2005 (WhatsApp message, July 2023). Upheld by both corporate and state finance, film capital today is transnational. It moves across nation-state borders to forge coproductions with the West Bengali industry and supports international location shoots. In the introduction to this book, I discussed my conversation about the new Bangla filmic space with Faridur Reza Sagar, the CEO of the foremost conglomerate, Impress Telefilms. Here, I briefly recapitulate. Faridur Sagar explained to me what he also writes in his preface to the expensively produced *Impress Telefilm's Movie Album 2000–2010*. The success of the company's new (high-value) production model lies in supporting "good and quality feature-film" intended at once for a range of international events including the "exalted Oscar" and Asian talent competitions and for Bangladeshi people living abroad (Sagar 2011, 3). What researchers Gitiara Nasreen and Fahmidul Haq (2008, 78–81) and Abdullah Ziad (2010, 346–347) unanimously observe is that the new line of "quality" productions fails to reach audiences in Bangladesh—that is, to appeal widely and be successful in the country. Nasreen and Haq's study shows that the role taken by media corporations and the state in supporting author-directors nonetheless lends momentum to the wave of liberal middle-class and issues-based mainstream cinema moving along the multiple urban consumer circuits of select exhibition venues (cineplexes mostly), DVD, and television. The same study adds that this drive for a socially uplifting national and world cinema, appealing to the gentrified classes in Bangladesh and across diasporas, has been accompanied by a state-led initiative to morally cleanse mass film culture. The early 2000s saw paramilitary action against obscene cinema and video piracy—seen as coterminous (a point to which I turn in chapter 5)—and an accompanying restructuring of the Bangladesh Film Censor Board (Nasreen and Haq 2008, 81–83).

In this new liberal mediascape, more and more women take up roles of author-directors and writers of fiction films centering on women and issues related to gender and sociosexual inequities. Thus, the periodical *Bangladesh Pratidin* reported in 2013 that the government itself taking notice of women's success in making fiction cinema resolved to allocate special opportunities to women filmmakers (Majeed 2013, 10). Through these conjoined support structures of the state and media conglomerates, we see women becoming directors of uplifting narrative features about women, family, or rural Bengal. The cohort includes not only Shuchanda but other female stars and media personalities as well, such as teen idol Moushumi, activist Kabori Sarwar, and news/talk-show anchor and television CEO Samia Zaman. Trendy sex symbol Moushumi, for one, was invited by Impress to direct and star in the salutary literary film about a self-sacrificing yet reluctant female public performer *Kakhano Megh Kakhano Brishti* (Sometimes Clouds, Sometimes Rains; 2003) (Sagar, personal interview, 2014). This respectably reformist trend of New Women's cinema intersects with what Elora Halim Chowdhury characterizes as "linear progress narratives of development and global feminism" to yield a local version of an "education-entertainment" genre (2010, 302). Spawned and supported by liberal-nationalist state programs and international NGO-led development initiatives, the education-entertainment melodramas posit new Bangladeshi women either as victims of local oppressive conditions or as liberated elite activist-saviors (302). In this light, I end the chapter by turning to the case of Nargis Akhter.

Nargis Akhter began her career as a fiction filmmaker on the same track as a director and producer of educational-entertainment cinema in the main commercial stream. With a degree in social welfare from Dhaka University and a declared commitment to women's issues, Nargis is the founder and managing director of an all-women media group named FemCom. The company could be seen as carrying the sororal production mode of yesteryear into the globalized national media space of Dhaka. At least in the early years of fiction filmmaking, Nargis built infrastructure at a somewhat small and disaggregated spatial level by drawing support from diverse sources of the state and of international NGOs. Relevant here is a point made about NGO activity by Elora Shehabuddin. Shehabuddin argues that although NGO projects for Muslim women's reform and modernization have a long history in the Bengal delta region, women across urban and rural strata have been active in "provoking changes in the different organizations that target them" (2014, 58–61; 2008, 4). Seen in relation to the transformative role taken by women in the history of NGOs in Bangladesh, Nargis Akhter's early authorial practice is noteworthy. Prevalent concepts of maternal guidance, sexual dis-ease,

Fig. 8: Nargis Akhter celebrated at the Bangladesh Film Archive (2023; photograph by Md. Fokrul Alam)

and patriarchal culpability are traversed in contradictory ways in the AIDS-awareness education-entertainment film sequences of the films *Meghla Akash* and *Megher Koley Rod*. Since then, Nargis Akhter has expanded her repertoire by directing literary and social films, with support from Impress, among other producers, and become the most prolific woman fiction film director of the 2000s in Bangladesh. Her repertoire was recently acquired with public fanfare by the Bangladesh Film Archive (fig. 8).

Through the lens of the early AIDS movie series, I examine the complex cross-scalar route of Nargis Akhter as a director-entrepreneur. Both of the fiction films in the series question the typical victim-savior binarism found in the dominant educational-entertainment genre. However, the productions move sequentially toward a maternal savior identity that grows increasingly inhospitable to stigmatized motherhood. As expressed by Jacques Derrida, "The secret of the duty of hospitality or of hospitality as the essence of culture . . . is to pay attention . . . and to pay homage . . . to difference" (1993, 8). The extent of attention to the different and sexually marginalized given by the filmic texts must be seen in continuity with the traversals of Nargis as a female author through mainstream cinema. The point to consider is what changes as her work rises in Bangladeshi "world cinema" value.

Female Authorship and the Maternal AIDS Movie: Nargis Akhter's Cross-Scalar Route

Nargis Akhter began by directing development documentaries on topics such as fisheries in tribal lands and soon moved to her aim of "feminine communication" (condensed in the acronym FemCom) by taking up issues of HIV/AIDS in relation to sex traffic. In the mid-1990s, FemCom produced the made-for-television AIDS-awareness documentary *Ajana Ghatak* (Unknown Predator; 1995), in parallel with government policies attempting to curb the rapid spread of HIV and sexually transmitted diseases among the highly mobile low-income demographic of the country (Hawkes and Azim 2000, 10–11). Nargis Akhter's unexpected transition from the genre of advocacy documentary to the fiction feature was fraught with tensions. These tensions are provocative for my postcolonial reading of the female author as a negotiating historical subject—a subject who continuously interacts with force fields of neocolonial and statist modernity. As she explained in an interview with the *Star Weekend Magazine* in 2010, Akhter turned to the thought of educating through entertainment, making cinema "with all the necessary elements of a commercial or regular film . . . plus a development message," because her made-for-television documentary on AIDS was heavily censored and cut before television channels would air it (T. Khan 2010, 24). The medium of television in Bangladesh indeed is strictly governed by rules upholding the "purity" of the establishments of family and domesticity and a concomitant prohibition of distasteful, "low-class" sexual relations (qtd. in Ziad 2010, 425). The commercial film medium, although governed by a not dissimilar set of codes (412), has been far less consistent and successful in upholding the codes. Nargis Akhter made the ambiguous decision of negotiating censorial anxieties by making fiction feature films with sexually sensitive messages in the commercially viable medium.

When Nargis narrated to me her journey from the educational documentary to mainstream fiction filmmaking (personal interview, 2014), she repeated practically the same story of television censorship quoted above except that she added an emotionally charged aside. With a touch of rebellion, she noted that the censor cuts to her AIDS documentary having made her "feel stubborn" (*rokh cepe gyalo*) had led her to a commercial medium that would allow her to convey what she wanted to with "open and uninhibited expression" (*kholāmyalā bhābe*). Press interviews about a crucial scenic construction of lovemaking in *Meghla Akash* reveal that the relative "openness" was criticized and implicitly censored by middle-class publics (Choudhury 2013; Khalid-Bin-Habib 2006, n.p.), even though it had passed through official censorship. I turn to this scene below. For now, the point is that Nargis Akhter remains invested in the open and malleable expressive forms available to commercial-stream cinema in Bangladesh, to use her own words, in her taste for "gorgeous *nāndanikata*" (aesthetics) ("Cover Story" 2009, 1). These gorgeous objects include the glamour idols of mainstream fiction film she consistently casts as protagonists of "movies for a cause" (T. Khan 2010, 24). We find here a sustained engagement with what Purnima Mankekar characterizes as "the relationship of mass media, fantasy, and the erotic . . . [that is, of] sexualized longings" (2004, 403–404) brought on by a transnational commodity sphere, being shaped in Bangladesh since the 1980s by neoliberal policies of structural adjustment. What Nargis asserts, however, is her inclination to "play" with the erotic surfaces of color, location, and costume ("*Shilper Sathe Mitali*" 2010, 32). This could mean, as we see below, the inclination to re-mediatize fantasies and longings in a subversive way. It is the tendency to take up available forms of erotic fantasy in a female-prone mode that makes the aesthetic of *Meghla Akash* potentially hospitable to the marginal.

Such transborder travels are necessarily constrained and enabled by the reformist maternal subject position that Nargis, as a woman director from a respectable background, assumes in relation to the disreputable commercial film space. For one, she poises herself as an elite "high-profile" person who is difficult for industry people to "interact with" (*calāpherā karā*), being that she is a "bluntly outspoken . . . danger" (*thomṭakata . . . bipod*) maintaining a "vegetarian" workplace (E. Choudhury 2013, 69). As explained to me by Nargis Akhter herself, her "vegetarian" space means that she refuses to serve alcohol on the set and that she actively protects actresses from sexual harassment by male coworkers (both events being common to the ways of the film industry, according to Nargis Akhter). In short, Nargis positions herself as a matriarchal director-activist who saves and protects young actresses. She is also recognized in Bangladeshi urban publics as upholding through cinema the national liberal vision of Islam, that the religion grants "equal dignity" (*samaryādā*) to women and men ("Nari Dibose Protyaśa" 2007, 16). She is described as holding a spiritual belief in equal dignity that motivates her to take up "hard-hitting issues" related to women, the underprivileged, and "gender-based violence" (Khalid-Bin-Habib 2006, n.p.). Her national awards, as well as increasing support from media conglomerates, reveal that, despite the hard-hitting gender politics associated with her name, Nargis Akhter's works are carving out a niche within the new brand environment of Bangla cinema. How does the brand evolve through the tensions of censorship and respectability, and which concepts of female body might it enable or occlude along the way? Let me turn to a few details of the AIDS movie series for a possible answer.

Meghla Akash is very much a stock education-entertainment melodrama. It pairs an underprivileged female victim against the maternal savior figure of a female physician blazing the trail of HIV/AIDS education at Dhaka Medical College. The latter role was performed by Shabana Azmi, the leading Indian actress of serious-issues cinema, an AIDS activist in her own right, and at the time a nominated member of the upper house of the Indian Parliament. Shabana doubtless adds a respectable, transnational layer of activism to the crossover film. The plot narrates how innocent village girl Meghla (Moushumi) is trafficked by a pimp under the pretense of marriage and sold to a brothel in the city. When her bid to escape lands her in a car accident, she is rescued and her life is saved by a transfusion of blood donated by the car owner himself, a handsome young businessman named Javed Ahmed (played by Indian television and Bollywood film actor Ayub Khan). Although Javed takes on the benevolent responsibility of giving succor and protection to Meghla's innocence, going to the extent of paying for her seclusion in the brothel once she is recaptured, it is he who ultimately betrays her trust in the most damaging of ways. Taking advantage of a moment of mutual unrestrained desire, he leads her to unprotected sexual intercourse and thereby infects her with HIV, which his well-nourished asymptomatic body is then revealed to carry. Unbeknownst to himself, he is HIV-positive from the unprotected sexual relations he has had with a woman abroad. The narrative ends on a satisfactory marital note upon the matronly savior figure of the female physician, in the role of Javed's older sister, stepping in to rehabilitate the HIV-positive couple by socially chaperoning their marriage while temporarily healing Meghla of her mild symptoms.

This matriarchal educational fiction, punctuated with medical messages, is filled with a female-prone subversive strand. The troubling gender- and class-coding is that of the untrustworthy patriarchal savior, always and already a potential violator of vulnerable female bodies. Put differently, the figuration of the savior common to the education-entertainment genre is melodramatically engendered and polarized: the true and trustworthy female savior-nurturer is pitted irreducibly against the culpable male rescuer. The latter point is clearest through a "play" (to use Nargis Akhter's own word) with the expressive forms of lighting and color in relation to song lyrics in the construction of the fateful scene of intercourse between Meghla and Javed. Dimly illuminated with low-key blue lighting and shadows, the male body and hands move insistently around the clothed female form facing the camera as she submits to him taking off her earrings and anklets piece by piece. Shot mostly at medium length with an occasional close-up of her feet with anklets, the shots conform to Bangladeshi censor codes. These codes prohibit the display of "actual intercourse" and "unbridled excitation" (*indriyo uttejak abastha*; qtd. in Ziad 2010, 412). In her personal interview with me, Nargis Akhter passionately recounted her memory of the stubborn labor that had gone into the lighting of this "bed scene." She said she had personally spent a whole day arranging the lights of this one scene; all the while, she was hearing male industry veterans ridicule her waste of time and resource while at the same time categorizing her as an innately hypersexual specialist of the bed scene. I am persuaded to see a cryptic historical trace of Nargis's rebellious labor in the complex play with erotic fantasies upending masculinist assumptions in the aesthetic arrangement of the lovemaking scene in question. Let me explain.

The camera repeatedly interrupts the scene of lovemaking to cut to a duet dance being performed by Javed and Meghla in exotic costumes, choreographed by the director herself (Sakhatkar 2003, 31). The soundtrack is belting out a song and refrain: "One-time union is so very needed" (*ekbār milan baṛo prayōjan*). This interruptive song and dance would have been peculiarly helpful for bypassing codes because the Bangladesh Film Censor Board typically assumes that fantastical costume dramas are less impactful on viewers because they have "little to do with reality" (Awwal 2018, 41). The costumes switch from erotic mythological outfits, of the bare-bodied Javed in a dhoti and the bare-armed flower girl Meghla clad in a short sari, to tight-fitting Western attire for a couple dance. Meanwhile, the viewer's eye is being trained on a point-of-view spectacle of predatory fantasy: the man's clandestine longing for seduction is taking tangible form through close-ups of his voyeuristic gaze pursuing the erotically appearing Meghla. While these fantastic spectacles cutting in and out of the lovemaking scene certainly constitute an instance of the technique of coitus interruptus noted by Lalitha Gopalan in classic Indian cinema (2002, 21), this female-prone Bangladeshi aesthetic disrupts the alignment of the male national subject with the film spectator common to the technique. In brief, a play with the audiovisual techniques of fantasy and interruption found from both local and regional (Indian) cinema displaces the respectable savior-patriarch on the screen and as a viewer. Instead, the nurturant agency of women as savior-protectors is valorized as the learning outcome (of this educative-entertainment feature) on both sides of the screen.

This same female-centric trajectory comes to be interwoven with a more sustained critique of patriarchal saviorism in the sequel, *Megher Koley Rod*, once again directed and scripted by Nargis Akhter. Yet the sequel at the same time grows curiously less tensile in terms of social class and female publicness. What has changed as well is production value. Whereas *Meghla Akash* was shot in Bangladesh and supported by a disaggregated range of donors and crowd-sourcing, *Megher Koley Rod* was partially shot on location in Malaysia. Riding on the commercial success of *Meghla Akash*, the scale of the sequel production had substantially expanded into a new filmic arrangement with partner economies. It was poised, at least in part, for the high-end consumption network targeting diasporic and local cineplex audiences. The DVD jacket markets this global brand value of location spectacle by naming this as the first Bangladeshi film to be "picturized abroad."

The narrative opens with the late Meghla and Javed's daughter, Rodela (literally, "touched by sunlight"; performed by glamour idol Poppy), pursuing a successful university student life in Kuala Lumpur, unaware that both of her parents have died from AIDS. She is soon caught in a love triangle between her college mate Nijhum (Tony Diaz) and the latter's barrister buddy from London, Udoy (Riaz). This drama of erotic longings is accompanied by fantastic flânerie across upscale Malaysian locations. The narrative takes a subversive turn when Rodela's emotions are shown to become a pawn in the fraternal bond between Nijhum and Udoy, with the latter heroically stepping aside for his friend's sake. Thereafter, it is coincidentally revealed on the very night of Rodela's wedding to Nijhum that her parents passed away from AIDS. She is rejected by her in-laws, who assume she, too, is HIV-positive and also fear the social stigma attached to sexually transmitted disease. The narrative evolves to a courtroom drama. Rodela, having tested HIV-negative, is the plaintiff charging her husband with the violation of her human rights, and barrister Udoy is her litigator (on behalf of his law firm) without her active consent. This courtroom drama is the pretext for the central education/advocacy message—that an AIDS-afflicted mother is capable of birthing a healthy child through proper treatment and medication. The message is given by yet another maternal-savior professional (Kabori Sarwar), the obstetrician who had cared for Meghla and now narrates her story with a tearful plea for the care work deserved by sickened and afflicted family members.

Yet the didactic courtroom at the same time is the stage for a melodramatic confrontation pitting the woman's autonomy against patriarchal saviorism. Whereas Udoy thinks he has fought and won the case to reinstate Rodela in his friend's family and Nijhum wants to step aside for Udoy to reclaim his romance, Rodela pronounces her desire to divorce her husband with the court and judge as witnesses (fig. 9), ignores Udoy, and chooses to live alone running a shelter for socially stigmatized and underprivileged women in Bangladesh. Depicting the woman as the agent of divorce in itself is a radical stride for women's rights in Bangladesh, since neither the Muslim *sharia* law nor local statutory laws permit this agency to women without a court ruling (Patwari and Ali 2020, 50). Although the staging of the divorce in court abides by the letter of these patriarchal laws, the accompanying melodrama challenges legal boundaries. Depicted through a sequence of tight medium shots and close-ups, plaintiff wife and defendant husband face each other as the latter is shown to cringe in humble guilt at this failure to protect his wife against unjust allegation. The patronizing barrister Udoy is left nonplussed by the failure of his heroically patriarchal plan to rehabilitate Rodela in her marital home.

However, there is a remnant—an important *conceptual* border within a resolution that actively celebrates gender equality and women's rights. The

Fig. 9: Rodela hands divorce papers to Nijhum (Source: *Megher Koley Rod*)

progress narrative seeks to occlude a stigmatized national past through uplifting the "innocent" body of the healthy and respectable female citizen-activist. She is tangibly separated from an unhealthy and potentially culpable family line. Neither visual nor extended narrative space is allowed for the agency of the AIDS-stricken birth mother. Instead, an elite female physician-savior implicitly steps into the place of the mother, dead upon giving birth, by depicting how tenderly she had nurtured the newborn and medicated the baby for health and well-being. Although the configuration of sick and healthy bodies and sexualities in the Bangladeshi genre at first glance seems to be at odds with the Hollywood AIDS movies of the 1990s, an implicit resemblance and possible influence is noteworthy. In his study of family imagery in AIDS movies such as *Philadelphia* (1993; dir. Jonathan Demme), David Caron remarks that since mainstream AIDS movies appeared when AIDS "began to be perceived as a threat to the family" (1998, 64), the genre tends to expel and delegitimize certain identities and bodies from its typical rhetoric of familial "connectedness." In the case at hand of women's AIDS-awareness cinema in Bangladesh, the endeavors for familial and national connectedness implicitly expel stigmatized maternity from the rhetoric of respectable citizenry. The women displaced or disconnected from secure respectability are either *occluded* in favor of the healthy elite women's bodies, or they are *dependent* on the latter. The final shots pay homage to the concept of the respectable female savior situated above the marginalized. Long takes stably place Rodela at her shelter. She is configured as a strong and well-clad maternal advisor and patron towering over shriveled, sick, and indigent women.

This chapter has explored how the genre of public motherhood becomes a crucible of film entrepreneurship for consecutive generations of women from respectable backgrounds working in the commercial cinema space in Bangladesh. Evoking maternal stereotypes on both sides of the camera enables women to access infrastructures and engage aesthetically in social debates. Following the mutating history of women's film companies in Dhaka from the 1980s to the 2000s, we see that a new "woman director's" mode of film entrepreneurship enabled by national and corporate capital has come to displace an earlier modality of "producer's" cinema reliant on star personas and disaggregated capital. The study above suggests that the small, female-centric producers' film is comparatively more open to paying homage to maternal difference and harbor generic collisions than the director's mode, for the small-scale practice is irreducibly collaborative in value production. It involves maker-performers and fans who are diversely entangled with the necessities of the times. The journey of a small director-entrepreneur like Nargis Akhter through the large-scale structures of censorship and resource demonstrates the complex possibilities and limits of the director's mode by contrast. The next part of this book delves more extensively into the relation of women's cinema to industrial scale and state support.

PART II

Corporeal Modes and Scales of National Labor

3

Performing Bodies

Entertainer Authors and Small-Scale Urdu Cinema in Lahore Studios

This chapter is the first in a sequence of chapters in part 2. The point of part 2 is to examine more closely how women's ways into genres of femaleness differ with the spatial scale of filmic capital. To highlight the argument about scalar difference I am developing in this book, the part counterposes two globalizing cultures that, at first glance, appear to be spatiotemporally at odds. Whereas chapter 3 explores 1980s Urdu cinema made by women at localized spatial levels, chapter 4 turns to how women's Hindi cinema transforms under large-scale state and industry initiatives. Beginning with a look at women's fiction film production in relation to the Indian women's movement of the early 1980s, chapter 4 focuses on the complex role being taken by women directors in the production of an Indian "nation brand" in 2000s Bollywood. What these chapters share is a comparative focus on female body politics in two national language cinemas mediatizing under global flows. Thus, part 2 shines light on filmic contestations that are specific to a fraught moment in the politics of the domestic that undergirds social film histories shaping women's participation in postcolonial culture production. This historical moment demands the nation's women to become working women, self-gratifying consumers, and earners of their keep rather than dependents domesticated by providers. The question is, How do we situate fictions of public femininity made by women in relation to differing scales of production, audience address, and underlying activities of globalizing nation-states? This chapter attempts one answer by focusing on a remarkable efflorescence of female star-made Urdu cinema in the small-scale production environment of the Lahore studios. The growth of women's cinema began in the mid-1970s and continued through the 1990s. It spans the decades in Pakistan of uneven transformation and Islamizing state development conditioned by cold war flows.

Two female star-authors of this period are renowned for their prolific directorial repertoires. Sangeeta (aka Parveen Rizvi) started her filmmaking career in mid-1970 in her family's film company, where she collaborated with her screenwriter mother, Mehtab Bano. Still active today, Sangeeta is said to have directed around one hundred motion pictures (the exact count varies in the available records). The late Shamim Ara, illustrious star of 1960s "golden era" Urdu cinema, headed her own star-name company, beginning production in the late 1960s and, subsequently, as director and producer collaborated with female film and media entrepreneurs in both South Asia and Southeast Asia. These leading female star-filmmakers came from hereditary entertainer backgrounds. They may well have developed for the Lahore studios an infrastructure of specialized arts to which women's labors were perceived as organic in terms of both creativity and audience desire. In the 1980s through the 1990s, we find some of the same tropes being reused and newly positioned for Urdu bourgeois couple-form social fiction film by the elite feminist star-director and producer Samina Peerzada. The sections of this chapter plot the tropes of mobile and public femininity through their commodity lives in works by these three star-authors. Urdu fiction films directed by and starring Sangeeta depict working women in Western clothes and those who perform the erotic body in both their public and private lives in order to support their families (*Society Girl*; *Mutthi Bhar Chawal*). Shamim Ara–directed and produced films stage Pakistani action heroines who fight on behalf of their families, including an expatriate who blazes the screen as Hong Kong's kung fu champion (*Miss Hong Kong*). In the upscale bourgeois social films directed or crafted (as costume designer) by Samina Peerzada, we find fashionable "New Women" going to college, careening in couple form on bicycles, and claiming their sexual rights in defiance of violent patriarchy (*Nazdeekiyan*, 1986; *Inteha*, 1999). I attempt to plot how the contentious concept of female publicness is reused in the productions named above. The plot evolves across media platforms as the respective star-authors negotiate spaces of diegeses, production, and publicity. This chapter discusses what histories these aesthetic traversals might encrypt about how women worked around the camera and with audiences in a drastically transforming Pakistan.

Female Mobility, the Urdu Social Film, and Women's Cinema in Lahore: Contexts

Far from being unique to women filmmakers' repertoires, images of mobile women map a transition in Urdu film history from the mid-1970s onward. Elements of the transition are discernible both in visual and narratives codes as well as in infrastructures of production and exhibition. My argument is that precisely the transitions in genre and infrastructure are what opened a niche of opportunity for women to make middle-class cinema with a pronounced female address and thereby participate in remaking generic Urdu femaleness. It is significant that this women's cinema burgeoned in the late 1970s. The period is noted by Mushtaq Gazdar, in his magisterial chronicle of Pakistani cinema (1997, 175), to be one in which the number of films made in the national language of Urdu was in decline. To consider why the moment was, conversely, opportune for *women's* Urdu social films, let me begin with a look at available historiographies of Urdu social films and Pakistani cinema.

Ethnographer Wajiha Raza Rizvi (2014) observes that the Western-clothed working women, motorbikers, and fighter heroines one finds in 1970s Pakistani cinema are at odds with Urdu heroines of the 1960s, who related primarily to domesticity. Star-heroines of the '60s, Shamim Ara being a foremost, encode a body language that domesticates "Islamic values" in a modern domain; their "trendy wardrobes" invite bourgeois consumerism in modest ways (Rizvi 2014, 88) (see the '60s heroine Shamim Ara in fig. 12). The domesticity typifying the ideal female body is illuminated by film scholar Iftikhar Dadi's meticulous delineation of the Urdu social films of the "long sixties," the period from 1956 to 1969 (2022; 2016b). Dadi demonstrates that the melodramatic realism of Urdu social films from this period enacted "modernization in the very temporal structure of the film" and, at least for a short time, "became aligned with elite normalization of the Pakistani national imaginary" (2022, 5; 2016b, 85). The long sixties were conditioned by rapid industrial and urban development in the nation-state governed by General Ayub Khan (Dadi 2022, 5, 21–22). Hand in hand, infrastructures of film production and exhibition expanded in both East and West Pakistan. The "well-equipped" Eastern Film Studios and an English-language periodical titled *Eastern Film* were established in Karachi, and film awards were instituted as well (Dadi 2022, 5; Gazdar 1997, 60–102). These infrastructures enabled a good number of educated young male directors in Urdu filmmaking. Nonetheless, the Urdu social film, not unlike its counterparts elsewhere in South Asia, grew as a form of mass entertainment inflecting to the sociopolitical fissures of modernity (Dadi 2022, 14–18). At least in some cases, '60s Urdu fictions are less reducible, in my view, to nationalist boundary narratives than the Indian Hindi or Bengali fiction films of the time. Gender scholars Kamran Asdar Ali and Nasreen Rehman discuss how elements of the perverse or the uncontainable question Urdu heroine figurations in the 1950s and early 1960s (Ali 2020; Rehman 2020). These sexual complexities stored in the genre were to be repurposed for the corporeal politics we find in the cinema of the 1970s onward.

By the 1970s, infrastructures of Urdu film production and exhibition were being impacted by new media networks. For one thing, educated Urdu talent and audiences had begun to gravitate to television (from the mid-'60s). The medium of Urdu television came to be perceived as the domain of college graduates cultivating refined and realistic tastes as against the "lower income group" space of a Lahore studio cinema replete with (presumably) tasteless fantasies (Gazdar 1997, 116–117). With the globalizing network of video trade in the mid-decade, urban middle-class audiences began consuming entertainment in another familiar tongue that shares the linguistic register with Urdu—namely, Indian Hindi cinema and television serials (the latter beamed from Indian Punjab) (175). Moreover, the networks of video piracy brought in attractions not only from India but also Hong Kong, Taiwan, and the United States. The disintegration of the human infrastructure of Urdu cinema—wherein I include artists, experts, and audiences—was accompanied by depletion of physical and economic resources.[1] The process was further compounded by a pall of obscenity coming to hang over cinemagoing with the escalation of right-wing Islamist politics from the late 1970s.

Cinema halls frequented by the middle classes were growing poorer in condition and, subsequently, under the cold war–aided economic boom during the Zia-ul-Haq regime (1977–1988), being replaced by shopping plazas. Meanwhile, "low-cost and hastily put together" productions became the order of the day in the Lahore studios (Gazdar 1997, 176). While the number of Urdu productions declined, the count of low-budget Punjabi and Pashto productions was on the rise. These repertoires of action/horror films were made in the mother tongue of *altaf* working-class audiences rather than in the national language of Urdu spoken by the *ashraf* elite (Tariq Rahman, qtd. in A. Ahmad 2016b, 16). Scholars of Punjabi cinema such as Gwendolyn Sarah Kirk (2016; 2020), Ali Khan and Ali Nobil Ahmad (2016), and Iqbal Singh Sevea (2014) delineate the aesthetic of a violent vigilante Punjabi hero oriented toward working-class and rural male audiences. Needless to say, these lowbrow entertainment films reinforced the stigma of tastelessness attached to studio film culture. Meanwhile, Islamist censorship rolled into brutal censorial measures targeting the sphere of public visibility during the Zia regime (Toor 2011). The regime had taken shape through superpower maneuvers around the anti-Soviet War in Afghanistan and an accompanying radicalization of Islam in the region. A stringent new Motion Picture Ordinance was promulgated in 1979, with bans being imposed on no less than three hundred Pakistani films from earlier decades (Gazdar 1997, 167).

Although my understanding of Pakistani cinema is deeply indebted to the studies cited above, my attempt to look for women's cinema in the Lahore studio culture fills a gap by complicating available histories. My research on women-made films of this period shows that a transitional and globalizing Pakistani cinema produced the tensile field on which women's Urdu cinema could flourish at the very moment of decline in Urdu productions. First, an Urdu tradition historically identified in Pakistan with middle-class propriety and cultural value likely had an appeal for women and the middle classes in a climate rife with obscenity. Well into the 1980s, Urdu cinema was being publicized by the state and Urdu journalism as being regulated by censorship and national goals.[2] In this light, the very depletion of an Urdu cinema dominated by educated male directors may well have opened an opportune yet labor-intensive space for women from entertainment backgrounds to take up film direction and infrastructure building. Second, the spread of pirate networks meant that films reached middle-class urban homes and secluded women's spaces at this time of public policing. A report by the censor bureau chief, Abdur Rashid, contradicts a general perception that only imported videos were being pirated. Published in *From Colourless to Colourful: Platinum Jubilee Film Directory 1913–1987*, the report states that by then all domestic productions were also being pirated to *inexpensive* video (suggesting distribution networks across urban class divides) (Rashid 1987, 61). Third, the pirate networks for home entertainment contributed to an expanding female consumer culture, which went hand in hand with an increase in women's access to the public domain of education and salaried work (through cold war–fueled state development).[3] In the women's sphere of work and leisure, according to both Nighat Said Khan and Kamran Asdar Ali, principles and obligations of Islamic spirituality "interrelate" to a modern Muslim way of life (N. Khan 1992, ix): liberal modern forms of "individualized agency" are tempered with "other visions of the self . . . [such as] the desire to be modest" (Ali 2004, 140). In this era of transformation, however, women's modest modern habits of flourishing in urban settings were embattled by right-wing Islamist discourse against immodest public visibility and working/consuming women.

The moment was peculiarly apropos for a women-made Urdu cinema oriented to the entertainment needs of middle- and lower-middle-class Pakistani women living lives of contradiction.[4] My position is that a specific transborder modality of women's cinema, focusing on *corporeal arts*, took shape at the interface of female desires and entertainer authorship. Renowned art historian Salima Hashmi, eldest daughter of Pakistan's national poet, Faiz Ahmed Faiz, made the spontaneous assertion to me that films by Sangeeta and by Shamim Ara always drew women audiences (personal interview, 2013), while her daughter Mira Hashmi recalled in a flash that she had gone with her *khala* (aunt) to a movie theater in Lahore to see Shamim Ara's *Miss Hong Kong* (personal interview, 2013). Both Mira's recollection and a published ethnography confirm that middle-class women from different age groups were going to select Lahore movie theaters and showtimes not only through the late 1970s but well into the 1980s (Murtaza, qtd. in Nabi 2017, 272). Moreover, Salima Hashmi's spontaneous conviction leads me to conjecture that many more urban women beyond the actual cinemagoers were also watching these women's films on inexpensive pirate copies at this time of parallel media economy. The candid performance of fan subjectivity I encountered in these oral testimonials itself is analyzable for the historical trace of a women's cinema in all the classic senses of the term: a cinema made by, about, and for women. Even though, like all mainstream South Asian motion pictures, they were made for general audiences, the films not only evoke female fandom till today, but they were also promoted in their day as being made for women (at least in some cases). Further, the aesthetics provocatively spectacularize female-oriented contents. They clearly name women as directors and producers. And they populate the filmic texts and orbital objects—notably, posters—with female bodies that perform gender in modestly ambiguous or agonistic modes.

The sections below trace the referents of these polyvalent contents to both sides of the camera. On one side we have modest middle-class women across urban strata finding meaningful entertainment in the artistry of Sangeeta's and Shamim Ara's works. On the other side, we have female entertainer authors socially authorized as productive and timely entrepreneurs of interventionist performances. The genealogy of the aforementioned entertainer authors/ entrepreneurs requires an interdisciplinary detour to how popular film arts developed in relation to the richly ambiguous practices of hereditary entertainers in Pakistan. I get to the cases of Sangeeta and Shamim Ara through a brief look at the pioneering female entertainer entrepreneur Noorjehan. Following the mutations of the female-focused Urdu social film, the chapter closes with a discussion of the bourgeois television-inflected productions of Samina Peerzada.

Entertainer Authors and Interventionist Arts

Mushtaq Gazdar names Madam Noorjehan as both the "earliest female director" of the nation of Pakistan and the only reigning star who returned from Bombay (now Mumbai) to Lahore after the partition of India and Pakistan in 1947. Arriving in Lahore with her director/editor husband, Shaukat Hussain Rizvi, she persuaded him to purchase the remains of Shorey Studio (instead of the lightbulb factory he had planned) (Gul 2008, 50), which, like many other studios in Lahore, had been "licked by the flames" of partition violence (A. Said 1962, 792). Together, the couple built on those grounds the Shahnoor Studio, which in 1951 released the Punjabi-language feature *Chanway* (O, Moon), starring Noorjehan and naming her in the credits as the *hidāyat kār* (director). Whereas we hear that Pakistani audiences were eager for a "Noorjahan [*sic*] starrer" (Gazdar 1997, 38), we find accounts of her authority as director to be more conflicted. Dismissive assessments by Gazdar himself and biographer Aijaz Gul are at odds with a rare interview published by the pro-woman magazine *SHE* showcasing the star-author's photo with the caption "Directing herself in *Chanway*" ("Malika- e-Tarrannum" 1985,

71). Many biographical accounts of Noorjehan's career draw on *Noorjehan ki Kahānī Meri Zubānī* (Noorjehan's Story, My Words; qtd. in Gul 2008, 77), a narrative characterized by Noorjehan in the same interview as a "defamatory" tale published by her ex-husband, Shaukat Hussain Rizvi, after their bitter divorce and a custody battle embroiling over her ownership of Shahnoor Studio ("Malika- e-Tarrannum" 1985, 71). Yet what does emerge out of these conflicted narratives is the social authority of a creative entrepreneur with multiple specializations.

Aijaz Gul foregrounds Noorjehan's entrepreneurial identity as that of a "working woman." She is acknowledged as having envisioned, established, and managed the family studio and "acted in films" while fulfilling maternal duties on the side (Gul 2008, 61). Further, biographical narratives complicate their skepticism about Noorjehan as the director of *Chanway* by celebrating her knowledge of the vernacular and its arts. They tacitly accept her authorial role by noting that her elite Urdu- and English-speaking husband depended on her command of the Punjabi language to make a film appealing to regional audiences (Gul 2008, 18–19, 52). Following her career through the rise of talkie cinema to television in Pakistan, we find her being recognized as both a pioneer of the generic film song (Sarwat Ali, qtd. in Gul 2008, 55), which is integral to the narrative code of the South Asian social film (Anna Morcom, qtd. in Dadi 2022, 9–10), and an authority on song picturization and sound recording.[5] In sum, Noorjehan commands in Pakistan an authoritative social role in two primary capacities: as a productive film worker and entrepreneur and as a dynamic bricoleur of vernacular arts who transformed familiar appeals into the new cinematic medium. The mother work she fulfilled is a sideline.

Thinking about Noorjehan's authority from a regional perspective, we find a female film history that is at once shared and not. Clearly, Noorjehan is one among a female generation that came into production roles in the wake of the devastations and displacements wrought by the partitions of the northern region of South Asia and consequent shifts in male control over resources. Her entrepreneurship parallels Kanan Devi's in 1940s Kolkata and Kohinoor Akhter Shuchanda's in 1980s Dhaka. Where Noorjehan differs from her counterparts is in her public identity as a film worker and entrepreneur. In the elite male-dominant film cultures of Kolkata and Dhaka, the concept of reproductive body work anchors the discourse of small-scale female film entrepreneurship. Female star-entrepreneurs accrue capital in those bourgeois masculine contexts through an "aesthetic of frontality" (N. Majumdar 2009, 142–143) that is morally coded as respectable domestic work—in other words, as *not* productive work nor generative of sovereign creativity. In such contexts, women's creative labors are put aside in favor of production labor, which in turn is understood in terms of household management or feminine care work. In this vein, Kanan Devi's innovations in camera work, costume and set design, or Shuchanda's in scriptwriting are ignored by standard film histories even though clues are visible in the visual and print materials in the orbits of filmic texts. Although we see Noorjehan being positioned as working through familial networks, she is visible as the productive worker on whom her society depended for steering the growth of the vernacular arts and their mediatization in new technologies.

The collective dependency on the authoritative skills of Noorjehan is best understood in relation to a longer legacy of hereditary performers leading the growth of talkie culture in Lahore. Noorjehan as an entertainer persona stands at the forefront. Born to a family of hereditary performers of the *kanjar* caste, who viewed female offspring trainable as singers and dancers as "asset[s]) (Gul 2008, 2), as a child Noorjehan performed with her sisters in local theaters and fairs. They soon found their way to the Lahore entertainers' market Bazaar Sheikhupurian and by the early 1930s were staging "*zinda nach gana*" (live song and dance) at the intervals of silent film screenings (9). Thereafter, she was to be recruited for theater and film performance in Calcutta ("Malika- e-Tarrannum" 1985, 72) and, eventually, to ascend to gramophone and film stardom in Bombay and Lahore. The trajectory of Noorjehan's fame demonstrates that by weaving regionally attractive artistic repertoires into new media, the talkie studio culture of Lahore gave a new and lasting lease on life to preexisting infrastructures of hereditary specialization led by women. The historical implication is that the social authority granted in Pakistan to Noorjehan's productive identity as author of cinema or film song arts is legibly framed by her background in hereditary entertainment. Therein lies the complex specificity of the Pakistani entertainer authorship being studied in this chapter. Noorjehan's journey from an entertainers' market to film and gramophone stardom is hardly uncommon to hereditary female entertainers in early twentieth-century South Asia. What stands out in the Lahore case is the legibility of entertainer backgrounds in the frontal aesthetic of female star fame. We find a similar clarity of entertainer background in the star personas of Shamim Ara and Sangeeta.

To examine the distinctiveness of the female star history of Lahore, let me briefly detour to Indian cities. Kaushik Bhaumik's archival study of Bombay cinema shows that the coming of the talkies gave renowned live performers from entertainer (courtesan) backgrounds, such as Kajjan Begum and Jaddan Bai, opportunity to dominate talkie cinema (K. Bhaumik 2001, 137). However, the *longue durée* of performers from the entertainer classes diverges from Lahore's. The dominance of the Indian educated elite in the production of talkie social films from the 1930s introduced reformist national concepts of respectability and publicness in the genres of film fiction and female stardom (146–152; Gooptu 2010, 65–114). Neepa Majumdar persuasively studies how Indian modes of female stardom collapsed the "metaphoric foreground and background" to produce ideal figurations of national identity (2009, 143, 53). This aesthetic front obviated the "social stigma against [public] female performance" by implying the woman's essential location in the respectable family (127).[6] We see Kanan Devi in Kolkata striving from both sides of the camera to achieve a teleological collapse of identities. Both in her productions and in meta-cinematic space, she spectacularly steps from her socially stigmatized performer background into a respectable and essentially domesticated foreground, even though she stakes ambivalent claims to her identity as a productive and innovative film worker (chapter 1). The stigma against public female performers goes back to the nineteenth century, with Indian nationalist reformers joining hands with the colonial state and missionaries to sexually cleanse the performing arts of the "nautch-girl" or dancing/courtesan women influences and to stigmatize hereditary female performers as prostitutes (Morcom 2013). Anna Morcom observes that although a few female performers from entertainer backgrounds, by way of gaining respectable status through marriage, did manage to contribute to nationalist "classical traditions," by and large, performance and cinema in India came to be dominated by women from the respectable classes. The majority of performing-class women have been driven into a vulnerable "illicit realm" of practice (2013, 41).

In Lahore, by contrast, the entertainer communities, far from being relegated to illicit publicness, flourished from the early twentieth century through subsequent decades. With the coming of talkie cinema, the entertainment markets became informal schools "for performing arts particularly for female artistes" (Gazdar 1997, 13–14). They were soon to grow into hubs of economic activity linked not only with the mainstream of Lahore city but also with other small-scale entertainer networks strewn across the common linguistic region of Undivided North India. While Noorjehan herself, Shamim Ara, and a good number of other prominent female performers and filmmakers of Lahore did gain respectability through marriage, their marital status tended to remain at the background of their productive worker identities (as explained above). Beyond that, they differed from their counterparts in India in that their status was never exclusive or hierarchal. Both Shamim Ara and Noorjehan thrived through small-scale collaborations with communities of entertainers and creative businesspeople (more on this later and in chapter 5). All in all, the specialized labors of women from the hereditary performer communities that foreground women film workers and their small-scale familial networks came to be a locus of artistic and infrastructural sovereignty in the talkie studio culture of Lahore.

The predictable complexity lay in the fact that this empowering locus here, as elsewhere in postcolonial South Asia, was pitted against that of honorable, respectable domestic womanhood. Even the male musician-teachers, or *ustads*, who train performing women to sing and dance typically refuse to impart the same skills to the women in their family (Saeed 2002, 133; Ali, personal interview, 2013). Further, in this Muslim-majority context, the cultural border against entertainers could well have been hardened through the inimical relation of female public visibility with male piety, conceived from an orthodox perspective. The typically postcolonial concept of respectable women acting as cultural "safe guards" (Batool 2004, 58), shared across South Asian national cinemas, grew in Pakistan in complement to the values of manly piety and honor. Early on in the life of the nation-state, filmmaking was officially labelled as a "work of lust and lure" opposed to the principles of Muslimness on which the country had been founded (qtd. in Gazdar 1997, 24). Even though this declaration in 1949 by the Ministry of Industries, being driven by a Pakistani lobby of distributors for Indian films, had limited impact on the growth of the film industry in those pioneering days, the stigma of lust-provoking publicness adhered to the cinema. The stigma is rooted in what Hamid Naficy characterizes, in reference to Islam in Iranian cinema, as a concept of the masochistic male gaze (2012, 106–107). The incorrigible gaze of the man on the visible body of a non-family woman is tantamount to committing the sin of illicit intercourse, or *zina*, and losing pious manhood. In this vein, sexual censorship of the visible evolved in Pakistan along with right-wing orthodoxy about the pious Muslim man being the ideal citizen of the Islamic nation (Toor 2011, 134). It is arguable that the provocative staging of relationships that appear to be between a male and a female in Urdu social films in the eras of heightening censorship carry historical traces of these politics. To get there, let me stay a bit longer with Noorjehan's famous persona. As in the case of other female stars studied in this book, the performance of the persona aesthetic is managed by the star herself, at a small-scale bodily level, with intimate participation from numerous fans and observers.

Noorjehan's performance of persona, as narrated and as reported to have been staged by her, gives aesthetic valence to diametrically opposite selves. On the one hand, she is culturally centralized as Pakistan's authentic voice—the national singing star (fig. 10) and charitable cultural "ambassador" who once was blessed for her divine song by a Sufi *peer* (spiritual guide) (Gul 2008, 143, 134). On the other, she is positioned and (self-)marginalized as a "vulgar" and "hot-headed" public woman born to an unruly family from the red-light area (Shaukat Rizvi, qtd. in Gul 2008, 78–83). In gossip circuits, she is famous for having said, when asked how many songs she had recorded in her prolific career, "I don't keep a count of my songs or of my sins" (Kirk, personal interview, 2021). Locking pure and impure bodies in an inextricable tangle, Noorjehan personifies a polyvalent aesthetic of the entertainer as *marginal insider*. This paradoxical insider claims social value from the margins through performative interventions in the status hierarchy within which she dwells. Her persona forcefully evokes for me premodern modes of performing the body

Fig. 10: Noorjehan, singing star (Source: *Eastern Film*, December 1965)

that undermine social hierarchy in hereditary traditions of entertainment in Pakistan.

Claire Pamment's pioneering scholarship reveals a living tradition in Pakistan of hereditary performing arts that stake deeply ambiguous relations with the hierarchies of the times. Pamment discusses how performers of irreverent "current events" comedy and trickster-esque gender-fluid identities appear in rural and urban festive gatherings and public spaces as well as in "new fora and media" (2017, 5–9). Traditional *bhānḍ*, or comedy troupes, for example, could enter wedding parties in a disruptive manner, comparable to Western guerilla theater, to engage in conventional "status intervention" acts that "promote social identities just as much as they can diminish them" (9). Likewise, female performances in the post-partition traditions of Punjabi *nautanki* and variety theater evolved in an interventionist vein. Under the Islamizing regime, from the late '70s onward, actresses improvised on comedy and dance in ways that "tease[d] at the increasingly rigid gender control" (Pamment 2015, 202–205). In this field of corporeal intervention, the titillating courtesan dance, or *mujrā*, developed a "confrontational gaze . . . [replete with] vigorous and raunchy sequences" to stage an agonistic "burlesque" of dominant norms (221, 213).

As such, the Pakistani celluloid mujrā—coupling "fierce and sustained eye contact" with belligerent *jhatkās*, or jerks of the upstanding upper body (A. Ahmad 2016b, 12)—is strikingly at odds with the more refined sitting-posture courtesan dance, or *baiṭhakī mahfil*, we encounter in Indian films.[7]

Turning to posters of women-made Urdu films studied in this chapter, I find in all of them upstanding female figures looking back at the viewer with an uncompromising, confrontational gaze (figs. 11, 13, 14). Small-scale production networks of Lahore historically included poster and billboard painters housed in workshops, often attached to inexpensive single-screen cinema halls (Batool 2004, 54–64). An artisanal trade handed down from specialists to familial pupils (Kazi 2006; A. Khan 2016), poster painting thrived on physicalizing poses to heighten the stylistic drama of the composition (Batool 2004, 59). Thus, the localized orbit of filmic and poster arts illuminates a dynamic infrastructure of corporeal conventions and resources. Considering the studio-based women's Urdu cinema flourishing from the mid-1970s, I see a plot of how the body artistry evolves: it is reused, in appropriately modest or censored forms, for transborder interactions with statist and global masculine hierarchies. In Sangeeta's productions, it is framed in a complex, left-leaning realism. In Shamim Ara's social-action fantasies, it is couched in obliquely agonistic codes. In Samina Peerzada's repertoire, it is repositioned for bourgeois taste and feminist melodrama. What also seem woven into the female aesthetic trajectory are mimetic traces of workplace practice and how the latter shifts with the authorship. The surfaces of works by the entertainer authors Sangeeta and Shamim suggest a predominantly female-led familial production mode, whereas those of Samina Peerzada gesture at a heterosocial mode of production as well as of audience address.

Working Women and Erotic Performers: Sangeeta's Social Melodrama

Born of parents with a "long-term relationship with the film industry" ("Revival of the 'Society Girl'" 2014), Parveen Rizvi (aka Sangeeta; she was given this screen name by the first director she worked with) began her career in the late 1960s as a twelve-year-old child actor, and she stepped into the role of director only about seven years later (Sangeeta interview by Hina Altaf Khan, 2016). She directed and acted as the heroine of *Society Girl*, the motion picture widely acknowledged by reviewers to have "changed her career" and "made her live forever" in Pakistani memory ("Revival" 2014; Kanpuri 2012, 132). In its day, the family-based production—according to the credits, "presented" by Sangeeta's actress mother and screenwriter, Mehtab Bano—won a number of prestigious Nigar Film Public Awards, including a special award for Sangeeta and the Best Supporting Actress prize for sister Kaveeta (aka Nasreen Rizvi).

The accolades, argues film journalist Zakhmi Kanpuri (aka Jameel Ahmed) in his collection of reviews titled *Yaadgar Filmen*, were more than deserving for a "talented personality" like Sangeeta, who "showed a major evil in society through this film" (*mu'āshre kī ek burā'ī ko dikhāyā thā*) and, in general, took up "themes" (*mauzū'āt*) others in her line would "tremble [with fear] to touch" (*jhijhakte haiñ*) (Kanpuri 2012, 132). At the same time, Kanpuri complicates his praise of the reformist narrative by suggestively noting that "even without relying on the story" the film was inestimable in worth (*kahānī ke a'itbār se yih ek lājavāb film thī*).[8] Although he differs from Kanpuri's unequivocal assessment of worth, reviewer Omar Ali Khan (2020) concurs on the lasting impression made by the hyperbolic "show" compared to the narrative per se. Khan concedes that despite the excesses of a "doomed Society Girl" melodrama, the work is "somewhat of a convention breaker," eschewing the "obligatory romantic formula" and instead offering a "woman dominated movie all the way with a potent message for a society riddled with double standards." The Urdu script for *Society Girl* was prepared by the educated male screenwriter Syed Noor, also listed in the credits as the associate director, whereas the construction of spectacle was attributed to Sangeeta herself. Implying that *Society Girl* constituted the crucible for her simultaneous rise as female director and as star, Mushtaq Gazdar observes, "Sangeeta surprised many with her knowledge of shot composition, lighting and camera movement," such that the production won over many who at first were skeptical of a woman as the filmmaker (1997, 145). These reviews relate intertextually to the melodramatic pushes and pulls of a reformist teleology and an agonistic female spectacle. The incoherence characteristic of mid-1970s Urdu social films takes a female turn (Dadi 2016b, 90–91).

The narrative of *Society Girl* revolves around a young Christian Pakistani working woman by the name of Juliana Wilson (Sangeeta). In the daytime, she holds a secretarial job in modest clothing, and at night she turns into a dancer with a garish Western look (cheap blonde wig and glitzy miniskirts), executing overtly erotic moves while also doing sex work at a nightclub. Other than leading this sinful nightlife, she has no recourse for the extra income she needs to support her dependents: an ailing mother (Bahar Begum) and a younger school-age sister, Moona (played by sibling Kaveeta). From early on in the narrative, we see Juliana drowning her sorrows in glasses of whiskey that spell the doom of sobriety and health. We also learn from the mother's laments that Juliana's path to this life of alcoholic abjection began with her rape by the owner of a warehouse where she had gone to fulfill the family duty of buying rice for her mother. When her father subsequently hangs himself for failing to protect the *izzat* (honor) of his daughter, Juliana, becoming the sole breadwinner, has no alternative other than to take up the profession of a dancer and prostitute. The plot unfolds through Juliana's relationships at work and at home. At the nightclub, she shunts between her exploitative encounters with a villainous businessman (Aslam Pervaiz) and her friendship with a soft-spoken, grieving young man (Ghulam Mohiuddin) who comes to the club to forget the untimely death of his wife. At home, she at first faces the moral opprobrium of her church-going younger sister and, thereafter, the latter's unstinting support. Moona's attitude transforms to devoted solidarity upon coming to know of the loyal sacrifices for the family made by her doomed sister, Juliana. Soon enough, Juliana is on her deathbed from an incurable liver disease brought on by alcoholism. The attending physician maintains that nothing, other than the whiskey that is killing her, can relieve her physical agony. Nonetheless, when Moona wants to replace Juliana at her nightclub job to sustain the family, Juliana rises from her deathbed to return to the nightclub and demand that the vile businessman who had consistently used her sexual and emotional services now marry and give her (and her family) a home. Throughout, enhanced audiovisual spectacles of physicality and clothing pit the longings of a female breadwinner and protective older sibling against social brutality leveled at the public woman.

Society Girl made Golden Jubilee in cinema halls across Pakistan, with ticket queues for morning shows forming in Karachi as early as 2 a.m. (by the director's own testimony; Sangeeta interview with Khan, 2016). The appeal of the formal incoherence may well have been timely as well as specific to a lower-middle class and women-centric address. Reviewer Omar Khan (2020) points out that the aesthetics are "sorta *Roti, Kapda*, and *Makaan* inspired." Meaning "bread, clothes, and abode," the slogan originated in the anti–Ayub Khan movement of the late 1960s that brought Zulfikar Ali Bhutto's populist party to power in the 1970s. At the time, the movement itself and its symbolic slogan, seeming to represent common mass interests, had garnered the support of "socialist intellectuals" (Toor 2011, 98). As more and more women entered the urban job market in the 1970s, the equalizing slogan likely gained emotional heft with "women from the lower strata of society" even though concomitant state reforms were based on issues of class rather than gender (Jalal 1991, 98). In this light, it is arguable that *Society Girl* had a gendered appeal for urban publics across class strata. For a number of reasons beyond the present discussion, a globalizing momentum of Saudi-informed right-wing Islam was also on the upswing. Facing allegations of religious transgression, by the mid-1970s the Bhutto state had banned nightclubs and alcohol consumption (Toor 2011, 124). In this context of heightening radicalism, the stigmatized body of the alcoholic nightclub worker metaphorically magnifies contestations around the public mobility of lower-middle-class women who worked to earn the keep of the family. Scenic compositions pit against the inexorable teleology of the public woman's doom a multilayered spectacle of the intransigent working woman and her struggle to survive. Juliana materializes onscreen both as a modest feminine identity committed to family values and as a professional of the erotic arts advocating from the social margins for her prerogatives. Thus, a melodrama touched by 1960s socialism seems to be blended with the interventionist logic of entertainer arts discussed in the previous section.

For example, a Manichean allegory of female piety and depravity, framed by the angst of paternal honor, is staged in the bedroom of the ailing Juliana. As Juliana writhes on her bed, her ill-fated agony being exteriorized with the shock effects of thunder and lightning, we see a medium high-angle camera bearing down on her sister, Moona. Moona looks up with ardent supplication at the apparition of a crucifix that has magically appeared in the bedroom, until the moment when the camera jerks and pans. In a trice we see, instead, the corpse of their father dangling from a chain. If this implicit flashback to the father's suicide turns attention to the failure of paternal honor, the focus on patriarchy and, indeed, on male characters is only short-lived. The aesthetic structure, indeed dominated by women (as noted by Omar Khan), foregrounds the female leads, a women-only household, and the dancing women at the nightclub. It is arguable that the dominance of women onscreen is the sentient emissary of a production process controlled by female homosocial relations and by the skills and habits familiar to the women professionals involved. Mother Mehtab Bano is known to have supported Sangeeta's project and her debut endeavor as director, whereas her producer father, Tayyab Ali Rizvi, at first had been opposed ("Revival" 2014). This bit of information about female-helmed production could also be traced to the poster art of their next release, *Mutthi Bhar Chawal*. We see that the names and production roles of the two women—director Sangeeta and production house owner Mehtab Bano—are displayed far more prominently than any male name (fig. 11). Returning to the diegesis of *Society Girl*, I find that the dominance of women onscreen is put to spectacularly rebellious use.

The most riveting of shows to engulf the screen of *Society Girl* is that of the sequence depicting Juliana's return to the nightclub. She arrives to demand her rightful sustenance from the businessman, who thus far has consumed, at a pittance, her erotic dance numbers as well as her sexual services. A compelling use of close-ups begins by showing a sober and plain-faced Juliana in a simple black dress, the color of which reproduces the look of her pious sister, Moona. Moona's well-covered dresses switch between the purity of Christian white and the modesty of Muslim black as if to visually metaphorize religious syncretism. As the black-clothed Juliana confronts the businessman at the club to voice her demand for a respectable marital home, the soundtrack suddenly falls silent before we hear the laughter of men. A Hollywood-style camera, which no doubt catches the influence of the video age, has begun to roll in a way that produces a horrific special effect. What the camera work also evokes is a logic of shape-shifting that is common to regional theatrical arts. A long take moves across and monstrously distorts the faces of the male customers who stand around, guffawing with hysterical brutality. The camera then pulls back to reveal the sniggering businessman, exploiter of Juliana's services, callously joining other available erotic dancers on the floor. However, we also see Juliana resolutely standing her ground.

The dance floor is framed as a polyvalent spectacle. It juxtaposes the dancing women who are ready and available for sexual service with the one who becomes an advocate for the right to modest and respectable domesticity of all female service workers and of entertainers and sexual professionals. In effect, these scenes dramatize the emotions of female-focused socialist mobilization, an effective impetus that derived from the 1960s social movement and still appealed to lower-income women at the time *Society Girl* was released (as explained above). Moreover, by staging the social mobilizer as a professional entertainer, the scenic construction of advocacy focuses on women of that specific service background. This advocacy for erotic performance as a woman's way to finding sustenance for herself and her dependents was soon reclaimed in an even more paradoxical form by director-heroine Sangeeta in the widely acclaimed literary film *Mutthi Bhar Chawal*.

In *Cinema of Pakistan 1970–1980*, the official publication of the National Film Development Corporation (NAFDEC), established in 1973, *Mutthi Bhar Chawal* is described as a "film with a touch of harsh realism," one among the dozen or so "which qualify as [Pakistan's] distinguished contributions" to the category of "art films" (1981, 37). It is also a rare instance in Pakistan of the literary film (Gul 2016). The work is adapted from the renowned Urdu novel *Ek Chadar Maili Si* (*I Take This Woman*; 1967) by the Sikh Indian writer Rajinder Singh Bedi. Sangeeta is said to have met Bedi on one of her trips across the Punjab border between India and Pakistan and expressed so much liking for the story that Bedi "gave it to her as a present" (Hameed 2021). Having preceded the Hindi film version of the same novel,[9] *Mutthi Bhar Chawal* is known to have been screened and well-received in India (Hameed 2021), although exact details of distribution and exhibition are not on record.

This border-crossing history of travels and networking by both Sangeeta and her cinema is all the more compelling because it came at a particularly fraught moment of Pakistan-India relations, the period following a military confrontation between the two states around the Liberation War of Bangladesh (1971). Sangeeta's village-style Urdu-Punjabi motion picture *Mutthi Bhar Chawal*, which was born of her face-to-face contact with Rajinder Singh Bedi, is an important instantiation of how small-scale connectivity could bridge rifts in the once "indivisible" linguistic culture of the Punjab (Jalal 2017). Such bridgework also demonstrates the cultural potential of the contingent practices of networking that are historical to the women-led entertainer communities of the South Asian subcontinent. (Chapter 5 explores at length these small-scale filmic infrastructures made and sustained by women in the late 1970s and 1980s.) What must await a future venue is a detailed reading of how this literary film made by a woman in the Lahore studio tradition enters the sexual politics of a novel about women's bodies and habits written by an Indian man. The film was shot with available resources and personnel at the Evernew Studios and Bari Studios of Lahore (Hameed 2021). For now, I stay with one aspect of the sexual politics of Sangeeta's production: that of interpolating an erotically belligerent mujrā dance performance into a domestic marital narrative.

In a nutshell, *Mutthi Bhar Chawal* narrates the story of a Sikh woman named Rano (Sangeeta) living in an East Punjabi village. She is persuaded by female neighbors and coworkers (in the cornfields) to marry a much younger brother-in-law by the name of Mangal (Nadeem Baig) after the sudden death of her husband. The goal of the remarriage into her marital family is to hold onto a roof and sustenance for her children and herself, as they have nowhere else to go. If Rano is reluctant to marry Mangal, whom she once had treated as a son, Mangal, for his part, has to be literally chained down to be brought to his wedding because he is already in a romantic relationship with another village girl. The episode I examine here depicts how Rano catalyzes desire in Mangal so that this marriage is consummated and made credible in the eyes of her mother-in-law and the villagers. The episode opens on a night when Rano and Mangal are locked in a physical struggle in their bedroom. She is attempting to prevent Mangal from leaving home to see his girlfriend. When Mangal, in the heat of the scuffle, inadvertently tears open Rano's blouse, she is finally reduced to immobility. We see her close up, frozen with the shock of exposure, attempting with furtive modesty to cover her breasts with her hands. At a stroke, this realistic mise-en-scène filled with natural light is interrupted with exotically lit frames of the finely decorated bed on which Mangal sits.

A tracking camera dynamizes Rano, now clad in a *cholī* (revealing blouse), *ghāgrā* (skirt), and veil. She is performing the defiant upper-body jerks and gyrations of the Pakistani-style celluloid mujrā while she meets the viewer's eye with an uncompromising confrontational gaze (reproduced on the poster; fig. 11). We see the execution of an overtly erotic *kathak* dance performance that exposes the full body while showing the dancer using her legs and arms to boldly beckon the patron/customer to come closer. The full-bodied, upstanding dance, or *khaṛī mahfil*, contrasts with the more covertly erotic sitting-posture dance, or *baithakī mahfil*, found in Indian courtesan films, as noted earlier. Mangal sits still and devours Rano's every move with calculating eyes, as if he is a patron/customer who has contracted the performance. The matching song lyric is replete with typical titillating phrases that invite him to know the intoxicating "language of [her] red and pink eyes" (*lāl gulābī nainoṅ kī tū kab samjhegā bolī*), her insatiable desire to "jingle her anklets," and her vow that he must awaken her "sleeping destiny" (*so 'e bhāg*).[10] Subsequent episodes reveal that the performance has stood in for a happy consummation of the marriage that has kindled mutual desire.

There is little doubt that the interruption of sexual intimacy by a non-illusionist dance number is similar to censoring strategies found on the Indian screens of the 1970s (Gopalan 2002, 36–40). The interruption may well have reinforced the censored tastes of middle-class Urdu audiences in Pakistan consuming the Sangeeta film. The scenic construction itself of the mujrā dancer vis-à-vis a male customer/patron is common to many South Asian screens. Nonetheless, the underlying marital relationship particularizes the presentation in *Mutthi Bhar Chawal*, making this use of the erotic dance historically specific. In Indian features of this decade, non-illusionist techniques of interruption, what Lalitha Gopalan has called "*coitus interruptus*," allows for sexualized images of the female body that provoke "surplus pleasure" and imply the liberation of clandestine longings (39–40). Where Sangeeta's robust performance of the erotically present female body departs from the Indian framework is that it enables a *legitimate* form of pleasure for audiences. The diegesis works to integrate the premodern erotic arts of femininity, embodied by the mujrā, into a woman's obligatory duty—that is, into modern work that is necessary for making a family and supporting dependents.

Equally compelling is the implicit positioning of the performing body in extradiegetic space. In effect, such specialists of the celluloid mujrā as Sangeeta come to be mimetically included as necessary workers for the affective lives of people and, as such, as deserving of social and economic sustenance on par with other social members. This means that in the artistry of *Mutthi Bhar Chawal*, once again, we find an ambivalent realism that places a marginalized performing body *inside* middle-class genres of domesticity and propriety, making the entertainer's heredity visible and required for the cultural foreground. The commodity field of these figurative details can be plotted to the extratextual poster art in figure 11. Sangeeta's generic figure of the wife and homemaker—coupled with her first and her second husband—is partially decentered by the gyrating pose of the mujrā dancer occupying the core of stylistic drama within the composition of the poster. The decorous clothing of the gyrating figure on the poster may have been aimed at intensifying the address to middle-class literary/art film interests, supported by the recent establishment of the NAFDEC.

Sangeeta is known in present-day Pakistan as a "spokesperson, advocating positions of the old industry" ("Revival" 2014). Publicly mobilizing her status of a marginal insider from the professional entertainer classes, she is articulate on television talk shows about the treatment both she and her family members have faced. She speaks of how acquaintances "abandoned their company" (*milnā hī chhoṛ diyā*) once their professions were known,[11] and at the same

Fig. 11: Poster for film *Mutthi Bhar Chawal*

time, she makes her way into sitcom performances on gentrified Pakistani television. It is arguable that the frontal aesthetic of an advocate star-director persona took shape decades ago in the course of Sangeeta's work as an actress and director of a waning socialist politics in the 1970s.

Dance-Fight, Comedy, and Elusive Censorship: Shamim Ara and *Miss Hong Kong*

As someone who rose to fame in that transitional phase of the bourgeois social film when working womanhood was at issue, Sangeeta clearly identifies with the entertainer-worker background for which she advocates. By contrast,

Shamim Ara's heroine persona rode the crest of an earlier phase of the Urdu social melodrama. At the moment of her growth to towering stardom, the decorous patriarchal home was the space where female and family matters were being deployed to debate cultural modernity and expose fault lines. Yet Shamim Ara would rise in the late 1970s as the star-director of a hybrid form of Urdu heroine cinema that reinvented the family social film in a public action mode. To get there, she performed small-scale interactions with the femaleness she herself had personified. The transmedial plot of her performative labor looped from extradiegetic platforms of celebrity rituals and film publicity to the texts of the action-heroine films she directed and produced. It appears that Shamim's widespread "intimacy" with an Urdu fandom from the respectable classes had poised her well for reauthoring genre. The genres of gender created by Shamim Ara, off and on the diegetic screen, exteriorized the conflicts of urban Pakistani female life while enabling new filmic bodies. These screen bodies entwine hereditary regional artistry with global influences.

Taking a brief detour to accounts of her celebrity rituals in the 1960s, we see Shamim Ara cultivating a persona that addresses the urban elite classes in an intelligible form. Various star poses and star interviews appearing in the English-language periodical *Eastern Film* portray a decorously consumerist shalwar suit–clad Shamim Ara (fig. 12). Reported to have a weakness for expensive cars while also being a "voracious reader" and a practitioner of the Islamic virtue of *Niāz* (ritual giving), she is celebrated as commanding a leading position in the Pakistani film world ("Shamim Ara: Scanning New Horizons" 1963, 9; Asif 1964, 10–11; Jaffery 1965, 8–11). As she gives body and voice to a respectable national community, Shamim Ara's public persona to a certain extent is pried apart from the entertainer classes. She becomes something of a national "touchstone" (N. Majumdar 2009, 10), making cinema acceptable to respectable Pakistani families in the 1960s. For instance, another *Eastern Film* issue reporting on the state visit of Chinese prime minister Chou En Lai in 1964 features Shamim Ara delivering the welcome address to the dignitary. The reporter writes that Shamim "made a big impression on the Elites [*sic*] who otherwise have a vague and confused opinion about stars" ("Chinese Premier," 6). By invoking elitist "confusion" about star-entertainers, the ambivalent report remembers Shamim's background even as it wants this foremost female star to move away. Two photographs accompanying the report are laid out, as with all press photographs, to connote a similar message (Barthes 1982, 199). One showcases Shamim delivering the welcome address, becoming the symbolic linchpin of the national order, while other women form a blurry line in the background. The parallel photograph reveals the latter to be the entertainers slated only for song and dance. Turning to Shamim Ara as the Urdu star-filmmaker of a fresh decade, however, I find her celebrity rituals striking an agonistic stance toward established symbolism.

Fig. 12: Shamim Ara, '60s star (Source: *Eastern Film*, June 1965)

Let us take a televised interview given by Shamim Ara to the BBC Urdu Channel (c. 1993). This celebrity interview typifies the claim she routinely made to authoring new entertainment that was meaningful and appropriate for the times. Here, as on similar celebrity platforms of television and magazine interviews in Pakistan, we hear Shamim rebut a widespread allegation that her Urdu action-adventure film is escapist (Gazdar 1997, 42). Having introduced Shamim Ara by naming her famous heroine roles, the female host of the BBC interview implies this allegation, and adds a sexual innuendo, by way of a derisive query. She asks why Shamim creates wayward heroines who roam "here and there" (*idhar udhar*), getting into fights and "throwing punches" (*mār-dhār*), in place of the nice "family" roles she herself had played in "golden era" Pakistani cinema. The host invokes imagery that overruns the action films being released by Shamim Ara. Shamim's action-heroine repertoire twines trendy international spectacles with cross-dressed female martial arts that are inextricable from the gender-ambiguous fluidity of mujrā dance and emasculating bhānd comedy. The interviewer seems inclined to complain that the contents of the films she makes are both sexually helter-skelter and inappropriately public by comparison to the familial orderliness characterizing Shamim's golden-era star persona. Shamim Ara is quick to retort by maintaining that she is configuring action heroines for the Pakistani women of the *nayā daur* (new age) who fight for their *haq* (prerogatives, rights). Proceeding to stage an aesthetic choice, Shamim says that in her own works she has resolved to change what she disliked about her own domestic roles of tearful women facing *zulm* (tyranny) while singing "sad songs." Her statement is sensationally accompanied by a distasteful collocation of wailing voices and "sad" tunes clipped from soundtracks of her '60s roles.

If Shamim's nayā daur heroine evokes the classic liberal concept of a New Woman striving for "emancipation from domestic constraints" (Sarah Grand, qtd. in Anwer and Arora 2021, 2), a following comment reins in the liberal individualism with the claim that hers are all "family subject" films. In exploring popular cinema in Pakistan, I encountered the descriptor "family subject" being associated with two overlapping functions. The broad assumption is that the film is functional for "all members of the family," being that the "morals and principles" of an Islamic country are observed (Inam 2009). More specific to the time when Shamim Ara worked was the assumption that the production functioned for the legal codes—in other words, that it had been submitted to and passed by the censor board; the classification was important for a time of video piracy, when many directors, producers, and productions could not be traced by the state systems of registration and censorship (Rashid 1987, 62–68). The connection of "family subject" with censorship came to me from a comment made by the late Shamim's brother. Irshad Ahmed Khan noted that his sister's productions always passed censorship, even during the Zia regime, because she made only "family films" in which the women were "covered" (personal interview, 2014). In this light, I see Shamim Ara's performative interactions with genre as a way of authoring her action heroine as the legatee of her own modest family heroine persona rather than as a radical departure. This also means that Shamim's generic voice—to which the talk host herself and so many other bourgeois Pakistani fans clung with nostalgia—ended up inhabiting the cultural capital of her earlier roles and reorienting the effect. Celebrity rituals and platforms already available to this influential female star were being deployed anew to produce a different infrastructure of middle-class desires and distastes and potential revenue channels. The emergent infrastructure of female-focused Urdu cinema mines the resources and pleasures at hand to address the "real [entertainment] needs created by real inadequacies" (Dyer 2002, 26) in 1980s Pakistan.

Particularly timely for middle-class urban female entertainment during the brutally censorious regime of Zia-ul-Haq is Shamim Ara's ambivalent positioning of the Urdu action heroine against masculinist tyranny. The ever-increasing public presence of "working and professional women," stemming from the macro-economic boom fueled by cold war aids was being policed at the time by the Zia state's idealistic slogan of the woman's rightful place within the *chādar aur chār-divārī* (covering and the four walls of the home). The point was to protect the pious male citizen from obscene provocations to *zina* (illicit intercourse) (Toor 2011, 131, 154, 134). The modern concept of zina, mentioned earlier, deploys a premodern Islamic idea about the male gaze being tactile rather than voyeuristic (Mottahedeh 2008, 9). The brutal policing of "obscene" exposure during the Zia regime was driven by the fear of the pious male gaze committing zina if non-familial women appeared in public without the proper visual cover. Note also that a (elite) women's move-ment was burgeoning against the oppressive regime. Shamim's naming of masculine tyranny could be seen as "juxtapolitical" to the aggressive energies of the movement.[12]

I have already discussed that in Muslim societies like the Pakistani, Islamic familial principles of spirituality and modesty are deeply entangled in modern female ways of life. Likewise, they are inextricable from feminism in ways that make the liberal discourse of individual rights debatable in the Pakistani women's movement (Weiss 2012, 52). In this context, Shamim's ambiguous promise of the new female fighter of family subject films seems to unleash the contradictory energies of middle-class female life in contemporary Pakistan. It stages a female cry to be emancipated from the brutal masculinist contesta-tions of the time while living the pleasures of modern life in a modest way. The body politics in Shamim Ara's action-heroine repertoire bear the histori-cal trace of these ambiguous longings, working intertextually with Shamim's authorial claims on celebrity platforms. In the diegeses, we also catch the Urdu social form at a new moment of hybridization. As already noted, video trade was training urban Pakistani tastes on a global action film boom that brought along aggressive heroines and publicly mobile action women. In this context, films like *Miss Hong Kong* inflect to the spectacular stresses of global action films whose appeal and meaning are "rooted in stimulus" rather than in the narrative (Tom Gunning, qtd. in Tasker 2004, 7). At the same time, they catch the momentum of the localized culture of Punjabi film and per-formance dramatizing the purity of violence against a "monstrously impure" society and state (Khan and Ahmad 2016, 124–126). Vigilante heroes of the contemporary Punjabi action/horror repertoire were being complemented by hereditary female practitioners of *mahi munda*, or tomboy theater and dance, who crisscrossed the stage and screen (Pamment 2015). These local energies are both adapted to the stimuli of international action-heroine imagery and, simultaneously, equalized to modest modern body politics in Shamim Ara's debut action-heroine feature, *Miss Hong Kong*.

The thin narrative, penned once again by Syed Noor, depicts Hong Kong's reigning martial arts champion, a young expatriate Pakistani woman named Tina (Babra Sharif) dutifully taking on the mission of rescuing her scientist father from the clutches of an international Pakistani gang of drug dealers. Headed by the self-anointed "Black Business" magnate Black Jack, the gang has imprisoned the scientist at their den in Hong Kong and forced him to deviate from his honorable pursuit of science into manufacturing heroin. The narrative refers to the (state-supported) illegal traffic in drugs and arms surrounding the Afghan War. Tina is soon joined in her rescue mission by Bina (Babra in a double role), who arrives from Pakistan in search of her long-lost sister and father, whom we see through a flashback being abducted by the drug dealers from the family home in Lahore. The two sisters develop romantic relationships with traveling Pakistanis, honorable men who also join the action and eventually marry the sisters.

The heteronormative narrative teleology is soon offset, however. Ludic queerness takes over as the romantic heroes, under various narrative pretexts, are mistakenly thrashed and hurled around by martial arts heroine Tina. In this way, the principal hero aesthetic is crossbred with status-interventionist bhāṇḍ comedy that is typical to hereditary male entertainers. Following convention, the comedy both promotes and diminishes bourgeois heterosexual manhood (Pamment 2017, 7–9). In terms of the action aesthetic, heroes are pushed to secondary and weak roles, leaving the foreground to Tina's evolving prowess. Turning to the poster of *Miss Hong Kong*, we see this sidelining of male heroism flagrantly dramatized in the two puny figures with revolvers placed between the legs of the flamboyant figure of the fighter/dancer heroine (fig. 13). Occupying the center of the poster, once again, is a defiantly moving female body who meets the eye of the offscreen viewer with an unrelenting look. This fighter/dancer loops into the filmic text, evolving through kinetic interaction with codes of censorship and male/female-appearing relations.

As the opening credits roll, we see a montage of city lights by night crosscut with tight and medium close-ups of the heroine's face as she sits at the wheel of a car, cruising along with a girlfriend by her side. The frames showcase a luminous-skinned beauty with trendy bobbed hair while the soundtrack plays a tribute to Miss Hong Kong's *pankh bina* (wingless) flights. Camera angles, color, and lighting combine to produce a sensation well described in the words of William Mazzarella as a "haptic eye," getting stuck on an image that is erotic not because it is explicitly sexual but because it forges a tactile relationship with the beholder (2013, 210). Here, an implicitly modest camera avoids sexualizing the female body by focusing on the face rather than on fragmented body parts. Yet the viewer's eyes and ears are seized with a euphoric longing for the woman's freedom of mobility and self-fashioning. Shamim Ara's heroine carries a material trace of the longings of Pakistani audiences across urban strata experiencing the stimuli of global commodity flows through both legal and parallel routes. Magazines from the era report a flood of "imported and local consumer goods . . . at astonishingly low prices" even at the "cave-like shops" of inexpensive wholesale markets of Lahore ("Marriot Road Whole-Sale Market" 1983, 57).

Made in this sensory climate, the Shamim Ara production similarly trains the haptic eye on self-propelling and technologically savvy consumerist New Women like Tina. Subsequent episodes construct Tina's mobile body as a site of *covert* longings that conjoin, in Purnima Mankekar's words, "erotic desire and the desire to consume" through staging "forms of imaginative travel" into unreachable terrains (2004, 408). We see her walking through fashionable parks and malls clad in shorts and sleeveless blouses (see the fan-waving Tina on the film poster, fig. 13), although these scenes being modestly shot at medium-long range avoid seizing on the exposed body parts. Meanwhile, censor codes fitting for the time are built into more *overt* conventions. Returning to the opening episode, we find Tina's freewheeling mobility becoming vulnerable to the masochistic eyes of predatory men. Medium shots track several drunken young men looking and immediately moving in to touch her (as she sits in her parked car awaiting her girlfriend's return). Their aggression implicitly censors Tina's public mobility in the way that censorship, as argued by Annette Kuhn, can become a "productive capacity . . . activated . . . in the interrelations of various practices," including filmic narration (1998, 6). If this Pakistani heroine's individualized self-propulsion is laid open to sexual aggression, it is soon revealed to be angrily cross-gender. A series of rapid cuts at medium to long range capture the woman, now seen as wearing unglamorous white slacks, leaping out of her car, and overpowering the sexual harassers in a dexterous martial arts battle. Thus, phallic tyranny against the woman's freedom of mobility is ferociously confronted and reversed, as if to mime Pakistani women's collective anger at the systemic masculinist tyranny of the Zia state and followers. From this moment on, we see Tina engage in street fights with predatory gangs that waylay her euphoric movements across the city alone or with girlfriends.

As I have argued at length elsewhere (De 2021), these fight scenes, while they find visual codes from Hollywood action and horror traditions to weaponize the body of the fighter female, tend to depart from the appealing sexploitation of female action-avenger imagery common to prominent filmic traditions worldwide. In the fight scene in question and in later episodes,

Fig. 13: Poster for film *Miss Hong Kong*

scenic constructions use not only loose-fitting clothing that shields the curves but also camera angles that refrain from chopping up the female body and peering at parts. Instead, the women's I-camera viewpoint, shot from the woman's POV, is spliced with the weapon-like moves so that an unremitting ferocity stands out as the primary appeal. As fighter Tina mauls droves of marauders and reduces them to a state of emasculated abjection, we see what is well described in Carol Clover's words as a "spectacular gender play" with "bodily sensations" that invites "cross-gender identification" from both male and female audiences (1987, 215–216). At the same time, the appeal of this Hollywood style of equalizing gender play is limited, for it soon morphs into a more female-focused and regionally familiar corporeal play with gender hier-archy—that of the mujrā crossbred with combat. A further complexity of the female-oriented non-liberal pleasures in *Miss Hong Kong*, and other Shamim Ara action films, makes them quintessentially ambivalent and transborder. This complexity arises from the fact that patriarchal honor and heterosexual family life stand as the norms that the heroines want to defend rather than transgress. As such, the heroine's fights for her individualized prerogatives of mobility and consumerist selfhood are soon forsaken in favor of her obligatory prerogatives toward her father, family honor, and society. She raids the space of social villainy in order to rescue her honorable scientist father, arriving in the torture cell where he is being brutalized by the drug lord and kung fu master Rocky (the arch villain).

Tina's body is now fully covered—from neck to toe—in a military green suit. As suggested earlier, the visual art of covering the publicly visible female body meets the codes of censorship and propriety under the Islamized regime. Moreover, the use of military colors like green could well be reinforcing the disciplined legality of the fighter heroine at a time when militarized nationalism was intersecting with the discourse of censorship. The censor bureau chief, Abdur Rashid, was to report in 1987 his provocative exchange with film producers on how shining historical examples of "military nations" should constitute the models of discipline for contemporary Pakistani cinema and society (68). Yet if the deportment of the fighter heroine meets official codes, her figuration as a warrior against social evils powerfully parallels the interventionist righteousness of the Punjabi action aesthetic—that of a hero uprising "against an oppressive state . . . [and a] monstrously impure society" (Khan and Ahmad 2016, 128–130). Tina the female fighter is similarly visualized as a righteous warrior corporeally purified to take on the fight against impure social elements. What also purifies the public female body is an artful shielding of the body from an invasive viewer eye through the use of screen choreography and rapid edits. We see unfold onscreen a female form that defers the tactile eye and inverts phallic aggression through a polyvalent combination of mujrā dance, kung fu moves, and bhānd-style antics.

My female-focused quest for bodies and hands of women behind the scenes draws me to connect the screen performance to tidbits about the specialists working at small scale with hereditary resources and cultivated skills. Daughter of a dancer and actress who had performed theater with Noorjehan (Jaffrey 1965, 8–9), Shamim Ara had been trained from childhood to dance (I. Khan, personal interview, 2014). Both she and her lead heroine, Babra Sharif—named her "lucky star" by Shamim (Shamim Ara interview, *Film Asia* 1987)—were virtuosos of the celluloid mujrā. Babra is reputed to have taken up commissions for live performance at the homes of elite male clients in Lahore alongside her film career (Jevanjee, personal interview, 2019). On the set, they worked with the skilled "dance master" Qaisar Mastana. Filmmaking is reported to have been an arduously involved skill for the late Shamim Ara. I cannot help but couple the dance-fight edits in *Miss Hong Kong*, described next, with an unhesitant comment made to me by her associate director, Syed Hafeez Ahmed. He noted with clarity that although Shamim could not do the editing herself, she sat with the editor throughout the entire process.

Tracing these glimpses about production on *Miss Hong Kong*, I see a complex choreography of corporeal mobility. On the one hand, we see what Aaron Anderson describes as a "soft" kung fu style of dance-fight being used to showcase Tina's multiplanar agility as she bypasses brutal contact through a series of slides, loops, and scurries (2009, 194). Fast edits fudge the human form rather than make it legible. On the other, we find the heroine's ludic acrobatics and facial contortions morphing into an erotic mujrā number performed on an elevated platform. The jhatkās, or jerks, of breasts coupled with a fierce eye meeting the viewer's on screen and off screen typify the *overt eroticism* of the specialized, Pakistani-style screen mujrā (we saw another intertextual instance of this specialized art in Sangeeta's *Mutthi Bhar Chawal*, above). These movements are fittingly accompanied by a lyric that goes "Tina is my name / I will make you go crazy [*deewana*] for me / with my mannerisms." Following the convention of the mujrā, the erotic body of the dancer, in the words of Anna Morcom, is being made theoretically available to the viewer (2009, 129). At least so it seems until the moment the song turns into a threat. Tina is singing that she will teach a lesson to one and all if they come close: the dancer is morphing back to the martial artist, who loops down to attack.

The entire dance sequence being shot at a medium to long range not only refrains from chopping up the female body, but it also places the public dancer/body artist at an unreachable height that further forecloses voyeuristic control. As such, Tina's defiantly titillating agility mocks Rocky's static tension and renders him all the more immobile while also diminishing his erect musculature. Even though sadomasochistic combat does follow, the heroine's euphoric agility endures as a primary appeal. These movement arts showcase to a context of escalating violence on women how palpable contact with invasive male bodies and eyes could be *deferred rather than suffered*. In an Islamizing context, where the male gaze is assumed to be tactile rather than voyeuristic, the female form's fugitive fudginess and untouchable titillation combined seem even more potent as an agonistic way of human flourishing addressed to women. What adds to the familial female-focused appeal is that Tina both fights for the cause of her father and under his proper paternal eye. The camera repeatedly cuts to the protective eye of the father, albeit he is hostage to a circle of men.

Discussing the use of heightened style and outlandish imagery, Durriya Kazi argues that since the Zia regime, popular Pakistani filmic and poster arts have been negotiating Islamist censorship by portraying a "supramundane space [in which] religious sermons" can be ignored; even the Islamic clerics do not consider the space of popular entertainment to be "a part of society" (2006, 4, 9). As detailed here, implausible bodily arts and outlandish locations overrun the screen of *Miss Hong Kong* too. What my reading should reveal is that I find in this, and other Shamim Ara productions, not a suspension of social politics but rather an oblique and *transborder* engagement with the gendered situation in which they were produced. The aesthetic of *Miss Hong Kong* is transborder insofar as it inhabits oppressive codes of sexual censorship and male anxiety and defers the violence.

I round out the chapter by turning to a slimmer strand of conventional cinema that was also produced from the Lahore studios in the 1980s through the 1990s. These productions replace the aesthetic of the supramundane familiar to entertainer authorship with a verisimilar Urdu social film form that draws personnel and audiences from the infrastructure of bourgeois Urdu television. The gentrified strand of verisimilar Urdu cinema, location-shot in the country, claims a gendered space for (elite) Pakistani modernity within the nation-state rather than from an obliquely politicized outland. My case in point is the work titled *Inteha*, directed, cowritten, and produced by Samina Peerzada in 1999. With emphasis on the feminist melodrama, the story is about domestic violence and marital rape. In the introduction to this book, I wrote at length on Samina Peerzada's star persona, examining how useful her star-body work proved to be in building a small-scale infrastructure of desire and opportunity for *Inteha* at the time. The 1990s carried the "long shadow" of Zia's Islamist policies, with honor-related brutality escalating hand in hand with feminist legal battles (Toor 2011, 162–178). Here, I look more closely at how Samina's creative output relates to the female-focused Urdu social films being developed by her female forerunners in the studio production culture (i.e., Shamim Ara and Sangeeta). I show that key tropes reappear and are repurposed for a pro-woman bourgeois audience and, in *Inteha*, for the framework of political, counternarrative film. Once again, we find virtuous family women, belligerent mobilizers against male violence, as well as pure and impure patriarchs pitted against one another. What differs is that Samina Peerzada's *Inteha* is clearer in resolving ambiguities than any of the works by Sangeeta or Shamim Ara that I have come across. In this respect, Samina Peerzada's negotiations of image and persona diverge from the perpetually ambivalent interventions from margins suggested by the female-oriented practices of the entertainer authors.

Samina Peerzada in the Studios: Arts of Respectability, Consumption, and Feminist Rage

Ethnographer Fouzia Saeed situates Samina Peerzada in a "minority subculture" of female professionals within the traditional Lahore studio culture (2002, 143): that of educated women from the respectable classes rising to film stardom. This small cohort includes Nayyar Sultana (a close colleague of Shamim Ara), Shabnam (aka Jharna Basak, who began her career acting in Urdu and Bengali films in East Pakistan), and a few others. In the respectful words of a scriptwriter on a set at the Shahnoor Studio, "Very few women are like Samina Peerzada, who came from outside these circles, who are beautiful, talented and brave enough to maintain their high acting quality and make it in the industry, without giving in to the pressure of vulgarity" (qtd. in F. Saeed 2002, 146). These words from an obvious fan not only draw an isomorphic relationship between Samina's eminent social background and her frontal aesthetic; they also demonstrate an emergent need for entertainment film associated with respectable sexuality. No doubt, the need was spawned by new media such as television and by select video trade. The fact that Samina had entered the film profession in respectable couple mode—together with her actor-director husband, Usman Peerzada, son of the eminent pioneer of Pakistani art theater Rafi Peerzada (rafipeer.com)—poised her for fulfilling this need from both sides of the camera. Among her small cohort of respectable female stars, invariably working in respectable couple mode with their husbands, Samina was the only star who took up filmmaking. As she discusses in a rare interview given in 1986 to the pro-woman magazine *SHE* (Peerzada 1986, 50–53), she began her production career with costume designing and couple choreography along with acting in their family produced Urdu romance, *Nazdeekiyan*.

The fragments of footage I was able to access reveal a way of placing bodies and costumes in locations that claim acceptable social space for teen movie–style pleasures in everyday Pakistan. They also set up figuration that reappears in *Inteha*. Staying with Samina's claim about her production roles in *Nazdeekiyan*—hidden as these are from the credits widely available on the Internet Movie Database—let me attempt to conjecture her creative labor in the picturization of the theme song. Seen throughout the song with her partner, played by husband Usman, Samina appears in a loose-fitting and long-sleeve decorative red blouse and white slacks that paradoxically eroticize her looks by covering her curves. Her partner's casual white suit is coded to match hers in style and color. Shot and edited in the Hindi film style of speedy "cinematic flânerie" (Mazumdar 2007, 94), the song sequence depicts the couple riding bicycles and a motorboat or dancing through verdant parks and imposing cityscapes. The stylish shapes of female and couple-form clothing, to use the words of Giuliana Bruno (2011, 87), are "enveloped in the city's fabric" rather than estranged from modern Pakistani life and its morality.

Noteworthy is the way the scenes stage socially acceptable space for public female mobility and couple romance in verisimilar terms. The urban male public appears onscreen to routinize couple romance. Many men on motorcycles (most familiar to Lahore streets and traffic jams) are seen riding past the freewheeling bicyclists, and a working-class shalwar kurta–clad boatman likewise sits with no demur at the helm of the motorboat they have hired. In effect, the shots mimetically glamorize everyday negotiations of modern space in contemporary Pakistan. Cinemagoer Murtaza Kamran notes that during the Zia era, select film theaters and showtimes drew couples on dates and newlyweds; if they came, "others in the audience would sit some rows or seats away, giving them some privacy . . . [turning the darkened hall into] a strange kind of fraternal space" (qtd. in Nabi 2017, 272). Such contingent productions of protective fraternity in the interstices of brutally phallic censorship seem to be animated in the motorcyclists who defer to the privacy of the romantic couple on the open street by refusing to turn the phallic eye (be that censorious, invasively tactile, or voyeuristic). In these mise-en-scènes, I am inclined to see the hand of Samina as designer/choreographer of appropriately consumerist youth identities and couple space, for the three tropes—the publicly visible and consuming modern girl, couple romance, and fraternal social responsibility—reappear in *Inteha*, only to be subversively crossed and pierced by an intense counternarrative of domestic violence and rape.

Directed, cowritten, and produced by Samina, *Inteha* is labeled in the credits as "A Film by Samina Peerzada." In other words, the production is discursively framed with the marks of the author's "recognizable vision . . . [and] singular choices" (McHugh 2009a, 142–143), setting it apart from that of the director–production house framework suggestive of a more collective production mode to be found in the promotional discourse of works by Shamim Ara and other studio directors. The production undoubtedly caught the attention of the urban elite, once she had succeeded in reversing a ban by the censor board for depicting marital rape in violation of Pakistani "social values" (Inam 2009, 15; see my discussion of the ban in the introduction). *Inteha* is reported to have been a "sensational success at the major urban centers of Pakistan" and to have made a record run at the Nishat Cinema in Karachi (en-academic.com), at the time, an "up-to-date cinema that attracted the popular and the fashionable" (Jamil and Tayyebi 2015). While reviews were mixed, with some critics finding a lack of tasteful "aesthetic novelty and sensitivity," the filmmaker rebutted the criticism by staking the position that she was introducing "bold initiatives" into industrial Pakistani cinema: she had wanted to make *Inteha* a visceral experience of emotional, mental, and physical thrills through which society at large and, especially, her target viewers would see "their real faces" (Inam 2009, 15–17). As noted to me in a personal conversation, her attempt had been to give popular filmic conventions a "feministic [*sic*]" turn (Peerzada, personal interview, 2013). Cowritten by Samina with the Peshawar-based Canadian writer Dennis Isaak, the plot was seen by reviewers (qtd. in Inam 2009, 16) as being influenced by the Hollywood domestic violence thriller *Sleeping with the Enemy* (1991; dir. Joseph Reuben). The resemblance is thin at best. By Samina's own testimony to me, her key ideas were developed at a workshop with activist theater performers and writers (personal interview, 2013).

Inteha tells the story of the free-spirited, upper-middle-class college girl Sara (Meera) finding her dream romance with fellow college student Farrukh

Fig. 14: Poster for film *Inteha*

(Zeeshan Sikander). Farrukh is an orphaned artist living in his humble studio close to a shantytown. Despite her liberal-minded father's (Arshad Mahmood) support of the unequal match, compared to the mother's disapproval of Far-rukh's social status, Sara is tricked into marriage by an obsessively enamored Zafar (Humayun Saeed), the son of a wealthy friend of her father's (the film poster depicts the love triangle; fig. 14). Soon turning into a compulsively jealous husband, Zafar subjects Sara to violent physical abuse and marital rape. When the violence being perpetrated on Sara is finally discovered by her parents, her mother is reduced to distraught guilt (for her status-complicit support of Sara's wealthy match), whereas her father takes action. He chal-lenges Zafar's father, Murad Ali (Nadeem Baig), to rise to honorable pater-nity by interceding in the cycle of domestic violence he himself had begun. A flashback recalls the latter's past of abusive violence on his wife (Samina Peerzada in a cameo), whose influence his emotionally disturbed son Zafar had imbibed. Amid high melodrama—replete with thunder, lightning, and fires—Murad Ali is shown to enter his son's home to control Zafar's monstrosity at the same time that Farrukh appears on the scene to rescue Sara. We soon see the gun-wielding Zafar in pursuit of the fleeing couple. At the climax, Zafar, having overpowered Farrukh, is about to lay hands on Sara again when he is gunned down from offscreen by his own father. The final medium close-up shots show Murad Ali appear to take his son's bleeding corpse on his lap and crumble in helpless grief with a shocked Sara sitting beside him with tender humility, extending solace to her honorable "papa" (by marriage).

It is arguable that the widespread success of *Inteha* in urban Pakistan, suggestive of appeal both to the educated classes and beyond, arose from the powerful way it revivified the Urdu social film tradition of internalizing contemporary conflicts of society and the state (Dadi 2016b). Saadia Toor sees the 1990s as the period when private patriarchy, already strengthened by Zia's policies, further evolved through tacit support from the legal system. The laws made "familial violence on women . . . [into] a crime against persons instead of the state" such that it could be settled between (typically male) individuals or "forgiven by the women's next of kin" (2011, 162–163). In *Inteha*, domestic violence indeed becomes a matter to be dealt with by individuals but one that refuses both settlement and compromise between men and forgiveness by the woman. Samina Peerzada described the narrative as working through two popular conventions of the time (the possible reference being to both cinema and television serials), that of the "forgiving wife" and the infallible patriarch (personal interview, 2013). Providing a heady pretext to both of these conventions is the trope of the Pakistani Modern Girl/New Woman, glimpsed also in *Nazdeekiyan*.

Considering the genealogy of the New Woman and her "alter ego," the Modern Girl, Baidurya Chakrabarti calls this familiar figure a "specifically capitalist and global phenomenon": across liberal capitalist contexts, she appears as a "working and [/or] consuming woman" whose relations with the "familial-social" are tensile (2021, 54–55). Staged for the globalizing non-liberal culture of Pakistan, the self-propelling and technology-consuming New Woman comes to be supported by (rather than exist in tension with) progressive family men and virtuous sociality. As such, Sara is another incarnation of the modern heroine we meet not only in *Nazdeekiyan* but also in *Miss Hong Kong*. In *Inteha*, Sara's liberal and wealthy father likewise empowers her consumerist individualism by purchasing her a trendy automobile. However, a feminist hand turns the car into an image of mobilization. Now Sara independently chooses her paths across the city and, thereby, moves against social hierarchy. Verisimilar shot compositions of the city and typical domestic interiors constitute an aesthetic device for claiming familiar Pakistani space to inhabit and to interrogate—in physical and generic terms at once.

The political heft of the gender drama lies in a two-pronged attack on systemic violence. On the one hand, the patriarchal perpetrator of brutality is made to see his fallible "real" face and that of his monstrous progeny (to rephrase the director's own words) in the mirror of opprobrium held up by a fraternal man—none other than his longtime familial companion. Sara's father stands in for an imagined fraternity of viewers who are being called on to take similar virtuous action. On the other hand, Sara transforms into an enraged New Woman, dramatizing a form of systemic anger against structural injustice known to stem from women's movements. Naomi Scheman notes, with reference to Euro-American contexts, that feminist movements and related practices of consciousness-raising typically interpret women's indignant feelings systemically, in a way that is "intimately linked to certain controversial political views" (1980, 86). In a similar vein of conscious-raising through emotional drama, *Inteha* stages systemic rage against male violence that is entwined with consumerist bourgeois patriarchy—on whose privileges and attractions insider men and women rely (not the least, Sara herself).

Crucial to the consumerist New Woman's politics of revolt are Sara's actions following her rape by her husband, Zafar. The rape itself is suggestively portrayed using a medium-close tracking camera that shows Zafar zipping up as his body towers over Sara's; it then moves on to show the woman's bruised thighs and her trendily clothed upper body. Subsequent medium-long and high-angle shots find Sara abandoned in the room, realizing rage. As she begins to shatter and wreck the expensive décor, tall mirrors, and a clock in the upscale bedroom, she is tearing down her sexy clothes and letting out wordless yells. In one fell swoop, New Woman Sara is reflexively mobilized against the erotic trappings of consumption—found both on her body and in her familial-social milieu—that hide or normalize systemic male violence. The final, high-angle shots of the bedroom show Sara's *desexualized* disrobed body in a neutral blouse and a petticoat. It is compelling as well to consider this scene intertextually, in relation to the stylistic drama on the film poster. While the poster hypersexualizes Sara's consumerist body (selecting an image that appears only fleetingly in the motion picture), it superimposes on her demeanor the familiar frontal look of uncompromising belligerence and places a pistol in her hand. The poster seems to be playing with provocative ambiguity on the duality of consumer erotics and angry rejection. The gendered turn of melodrama in *Inteha* is that it resolves social disorder by reinstating a heterosocial sphere of reformed fraternity. The pure patriarch redeems the impure one. Murad Ali finally fulfills his honorable paternal duty of protecting his daughter-in-law Sara and, in turn, elicits the virtuous woman's humble respect. From this angle, the bourgeois feminist social film stands apart from the women-suffused diegeses directed by Sangeeta and Shamim Ara. The ambiguities surrounding female bodies and status relations remain irreducible in the latter.

Despite the difference, what threads these Urdu women's productions through an era of flagrant contradictions is a two-pronged, transborder drama of gender. We encounter ambivalent figurations of women who perform anger or resistance against systemic wrongs while holding on to patriarchal family values. In addition, we find male characters who are subjected to normative scrutiny. Borders are repeatedly drawn and interspersed between the weak and the strong, the pure and the impure patriarch—seen in social, moral, and physical terms. Precisely the duality of gender appeal seems to have been intelligibly entertaining as a women-centric cinema to largely non-liberal audiences living through turbulent times of state-led violence. As such, a collective female-focused address identifying with diverse "intimate publics" of Pakistani desires arose from these filmic texts together with the extratextual star personas of the female authors studied here (Berlant 2008, viii). It is important to note that these female-focused intimate publics included numerous men, as all the productions discussed above were made for general audiences and successful at the box office (even as they drew women audiences). These previously ignored histories from the traditional Lahore studios are compelling for my study of women as small-scale specialists of female-focused cinematic meaning: those in a position to stake authorial control because familial collaborators depend on them for gender artistry. Beyond that, the prolific success as creative entrepreneurs of entertainer professionals such as Sangeeta, Shamim Ara, and Noorjehan reveals another transborder layer of public intimacies. These intimacies have been forged by mainstream Pakistani audiences with the interventionist arts inherent to the regional entertainers who populate film studios in Lahore.

In staying focused on these submerged histories of women, this book largely brackets discussion of a new Pakistani cinema that has emerged over the last two decades. Even though "old cinema" personalities like Sangeeta do cross over, the new cinema and media in Pakistan have been characterized as a formation that is discontinuous from studio culture. To recapitulate, the Lahore studios function through small-scale familial networks. Moreover, since the mid-1970s, they have come to be led by entertainment professionals who are adept at weaving into new media technologies agonistic and irreverent traditions of performing arts that address contemporary tensions. With the expansion of a common middle-class media culture in the 1970s, we do see towering entertainer filmmakers such as Sangeeta and Shamim Ara taking up cinema that spoke to women's concerns in the middle-class language of Urdu. Nonetheless, the Lahore studios continue to carry the stigma of being an undeveloped, local industry of public entertainment.

By contrast, New Pakistani Cinema, according to Zebunnisa Hamid, is gentrified and state-governed. It was born of the large-scale neoliberal policies of a frontline state involved in the post-9/11 global War on Terror. The formation has nurtured transnational flows of people and finance, rapid urbanization, and a multiplex culture. Multiplexes flourish through the deregulated import of Bollywood and Hollywood films while providing an exhibition venue for high-tech and big-budget Pakistani productions as well (Hamid 2020b, 216–217; 2020a, 20–23). The new cohort of Pakistani motion picture directors and producers include a good number of Western-trained or diasporic women such as Sabiha Sumar, Meenu Gaur, Mehreen Jabbar, Iram Parveen Bilal, Afia Nathaniel, and more. Their productions, informed by "liberal thought," work in complex ways through globally legible aspirational genres of "strong, independent women, often working and, like their male counterparts, dreaming of a better life" (Hamid 2020b, 217, 223). Like elsewhere in South Asia, large-scale pathways of resource (institutionalized education, financial capital, technology) and emotion (aspirations and issues) uphold the new cinema and media formation in Pakistan. Such large-scale infrastructures can also bring along brand economies and global imperialist attitudes. Within the limited scope of this book, I look more closely at questions of scale, brand, and empire in relation to Hindi "Bollywood" film culture (chapter 4) and to transnational Bengali cinemas (chapter 6).

4

Timing Bodies

Hindi Cinema and a
Female Brand Author
at Bollywood Scale

The previous chapter examined how women's mainstream cinema made in the national language of Urdu flourished in an urban Pakistan mediatizing under cold war globalization in the late 1970s through the 1990s. Women professionals of the Lahore studios took up filmmaking in Urdu at a time when Urdu cinema was a waning tradition, with Urdu being cultivated and performed in the more respectable middle-class space of television. Flourishing through the creative and entrepreneurial labors of star-authors from hereditary performer backgrounds, Urdu studio cinema opened a performative space for intense contestations over the gendered demands of a globalizing military state. Although this space was "proximal" to the energies of the organized resistance to Islamist policies being mounted in the same period by middle-class Pakistani women (Berlant 2008), it diverged in the way it was working hereditary practices of agonistic arts into the cinematic global. In other words, the *excessive nation work* done by women on a small-scale rode on the failure of the Pakistan state to *annex intransigent media labor*. This chapter explores a very different South Asian genealogy of women's national cinema work. This history evolves in close relation to film nationalism and respectability politics, state-sponsored media, and globalization.

As previously noted, this part (part 2) of the book examines how fictions of female bodies and gender relations become especially acute sites of contestation in globalizing nation spaces where middle-class women grow mobile as income earners and consumers. The present chapter plots the path of women-made body fictions to an environment of globalizing national cinema that shares industrial and geopolitical histories not only with Pakistan but also West Bengal, India (studied in chapters 1 and 6). I explore female authorship of Hindi fiction films that tangle with nationalist concerns over middle-class women's mobility in public spaces as workers and consumers. Looking for women makers of globalizing Hindi cinema, I easily find an expanding cohort of women directors in the new Bollywood space of Hindi cinema in the 2000s. The "Bollywoodization" of Hindi cinema began on a large scale with the liberalizing of the Indian economy in 1991 and the subsequent recognition by the state in 1998 of cinema as a leading Indian industry. Starting as a "diffuse cultural conglomeration . . . of distribution and consumption activities," Bollywood has since grown with international and expatriate Indian support into the figurehead of a "global 'Indian' culture industry" that defines the "brand" of the modern nation on conglomerated media platforms (Rajadhyaksha 2003, 28–32). However, the history of women directors of Hindi cinema remains incomplete unless we look, at least briefly, at another generation spawned in the late 1970s and 1980s *also* by large-scale infrastructural support—in this case, support given by the nation-state for the "mediatization of the women's movement" (Gopal 2019, 40). In both of these eras, we see Indian nationalist film politics depending on women's cinema as a key transformative site for debating cultural modernities and sexual reform. In the time of social movements, the dependency is on the *voice* of the woman filmmaker, whereas in the era of neoliberal conglomeration, it seems to be more on female *fictions* made with the right mix of elements (by women or men). To examine how women's authorial claims alter between these periods, I take up the cases of two social comedy films made for theatrical release in the respective eras: *Chasme Buddoor*, written and directed in 1981 by Sai Paranjpye, and *English Vinglish*, written and directed in 2012 by Gauri Shinde.

Although the cases are located in two different socioeconomic contexts, before and after the liberalization of the Indian economy, they share a similar spatial interest in the mobility acquired by middle-class women through independent work and participation in urban or global consumerism. A comparative reading is helpful for clarifying what mutates in women's labor of authoring national body fictions as Hindi cinema enters the temporality of Indian nation-brand production. As Keith Dinnie writes, marketing scholarship defines the "nation-brand . . . as *the unique, multidimensional blend of elements*" that culturally differentiates (and implicitly aggregates) the country and its people with reference to conceptual "attributes" that already exist in the minds of target consumers (2008, 15; italics in original). I ask, What recurs or changes in the way multiple bodies and geographies are *blended or not* in the two fiction films under consideration, and how might these shifts relate the respective women directors to infrastructures?

This chapter's focus on large-scale film production is indispensable to my attempt at thickening the texture of South Asian women's cinema studies by relating female authorial claims to infrastructural politics. It helps me to explore how women's production work being a gendered web of social relations forges "multi-scalar connections" with the enabling yet regulatory frameworks of the nation-state and the global brand economy (McDowell 2001, 238), and how social movements might function therein. At the same time, the scope of the discussion is necessarily limited because this book mainly excavates previously neglected histories of creative and infrastructural work in sound cinema managed by women, mostly female stars, at a closer-in scale (through familial and body work). What we see instead in the Hindi filmic space of Bombay (now Mumbai) is a gradual disappearance of female star-author entrepreneurs in the years following the silent and early sound eras. These were also the years immediately preceding and following the partition of India and Pakistan—the same period when female author entrepreneurs were growing prominent in the industries that shared the consequences of partition with Bombay—namely, Lahore, Calcutta, and Dhaka (East Pakistan).[1] As the previous three chapters have argued, an early cohort of star-producer/authors working in the small-scale familial mode blazed the trail of female star-authorship in the latter contexts soon after the 1947 partition. Although this gendered difference between the interlinked industrial histories awaits much more research, it is noteworthy for my comparative regional approach. To get to the case studies, I begin with a look at the shifts in women's production roles and female authorship in Bombay/Bollywood. My point is to consider how these shifts might relate to the development of the Hindi as the national cinema industry of India. The extensive scholarship in the field is illuminating.

Women's Production Roles and Female Authorship in Hindi Cinema: Contexts

Scholars shine light on the gendered phases of production history in the Hindi film field. Important feminist historiographies by both Neepa Majumdar and Debashree Mukherjee find in the first decades of the twentieth century a significant presence of female stars, with nearly all top-billed actresses drawing salaries through the 1940s that superseded those of male stars (N. Majumdar 2009; D. Mukherjee 2015, 38). The same decades saw leading actresses such as Bai Jaddan Bai (aka Jaddanbai Hussain), Devika Rani, and Gohar Mamajiwala run family-mode or partner-mode film businesses. Out of these, only Jaddanbai has been studied by Mukherjee as an author-producer known to have run a matrilineal production house while she wrote scripts that debated contemporary women's issues, such as "stigmatized [filmic] female labor" (D. Mukherjee 2020a, 178). Jaddanbai, a hereditary entertainer professional was not unlike the publicly famed female author entrepreneur of Lahore, where she was once based as a gramophone artist.[2] Debashree Mukherjee argues that the coming of synchronized sound in the early 1930s, having produced a "visual of the voicing body," had opened a space in Bombay as well for such singing stars as Jaddanbai from Muslim entertainer backgrounds to claim the right to author entrepreneurship. Mukherjee goes on to add that the early Hindi filmic space was still gendered in a way that makes it "historiographically difficult to pull out" traces of authorial decision work by female star-entrepreneurs. A case in point is the entrepreneurial history of female star Gohar, who ran a partner-mode business with Chandulal Shah and is known to have "participated in the creative and business decisions of the studio" (D. Mukherjee 2020a, 74–78).

Neepa Majumdar's (2009) meticulous analysis of female stardom in the early Bombay space of Hindi cinema is illuminating here. Majumdar argues that with the growth of the Indian nationalist movement in the 1930s, cinematic discourse was reshaped. The female star was discursively vested with the class-coded labor of becoming a "touchstone" through which the disreputable culture of entertainment cinema could be made worthy of the "attention" of the nationalist elite. Where needed, the disreputable entertainer background of actresses had to be morally "repaired" in the course of personification (as in the case of the illustrious '50s icon Nargis, daughter of Jaddanbai). As such, stardom itself was "feminized in relation to the production studios" (9–14). The implication I draw from Majumdar's argument is that as the Hindi film field developed in relation to the politics of nationalism and respectability in the 1930s through the 1950s, female star labor came to be bounded by the role of performer, whereas production and creative decision work was gendered male. Thus, the borders of labor and capital in this filmic environment were rigidly sexualized. Female star identities were constructed as doing reformist-performer labor, or ancillary gender-production labor (such as costume designing by Devika Rani), under male nationalist structural control. Their public personas might not have been readily available to make authorial claims on their own creative labor. Tejaswini Ganti's (2012) feminist reading of the Bollywood Hindi production culture of the 1990s and early 2000s reveals that the entrenchment of patriarchal control not only has endured but also grown considerably stronger through the presence of top-billed male stars who now regularly supersede the female in net worth and prominence. Sharmistha Gooptu (2010) and Sumita S. Chakravarty (1993) situate the rise of the male Hindi star of Bombay in the first decade after Indian independence, when a youthful male persona grew to be the key site for staging the "popular issues of the new nation" (Gooptu 2010, 128–129). By 1981, government publications on Hindi cinema report that "most stars in India are male . . . with commercial filmmakers mak[ing] no bones about the fact that it is a male-dominant industry" (*Film India: The New Generation* 28). As shown by Valentina Vitali, a higher-end exhibition sector had also gained ground through the 1970s to showcase the narrative ingredients of the leading male star of the time, Amitabh Bachchan (Vitali 2008, 202–203). Although she affirms the assessment of persistent male dominance in Bollywood, Ganti points to a significant influx of women into production roles in the early 2000s, a key point to which I return below.

Staying for a moment with my region-think on industrial linkage, let me ask, How do we account for the prominent women in production roles in other fields of nationalist cinema, notably Calcutta, which could hardly be said to fall outside the sexual politics of Indian nationalism and respectability? Sharmistha Gooptu's comparative study of two parallel formations of "national cinema"—respectively, in Bombay and Calcutta—in the post-partition years is particularly illuminating. Gooptu observes that in both cities the salaried studio system was giving way to a rush of producers and contracted stars under the shifts of wartime economy, with the Bombay film industry benefiting far more from speculative finance than the Calcutta industry (2010, 115–124). Nonetheless, well into the 1940s, the Calcutta studios fought to hold on to an all-India market by releasing a substantial number of Hindi, as well as Bengali, productions. The Calcutta studios, by producing Hindi/Urdu motion pictures, had begun to compete with Bombay for the all-India market in the 1930s. What dealt the decisive blow to both the stability and the scale of fiction film production in Calcutta was the partition of India and Pakistan in 1947, leading to the loss of the market in East Bengal (which became East Pakistan). Writing for the *Silver Jubilee Souvenir* of Indian talkie cinema in 1956, Kanan Devi, the pioneering female star-producer and author of '50s Bengali cinema and the leading persona of Calcutta-based '30s Hindi cinema, says as much. She maintains that the dual losses of the Hindi market and the home Bengali market through partition makes the Bengal industry the "greatest sufferer" of changes in the Indian cinema economy (Devi 1956, 135). What this short article by Kanan illuminates, however, is that a systemic discourse had emerged, implicitly calling on energetic Bengali film workers to resuscitate what she describes as the "vitals" of production (machinery, technicians). Chapter 1 discussed the creative and entrepreneurial work being done and managed at a small matriarchal scale by Kanan Devi at the precise moment she wrote this piece. As also demonstrated, the female-centric maternal social films produced by Kanan carry a cryptic history of her authorial entrepreneurship. Let me add that Bengali periodicals like *Chitrabani* were abuzz at the time with coverage of her leadership role in a flagging industry.

My point is that partition experience co-constituted the interlinked fields of filmmaking across the northern subcontinent—Bombay, Calcutta, Lahore, Dhaka—in a way that altered the gendered frameworks of production to opposite ends. The drastic infrastructural shifts in Calcutta and Lahore after 1947, by way of partition-related migration and violence in the latter case,[3] produced both the need and a discourse enabling female stars and women to own their creative and entrepreneurial labor. The same argument can be extended to Dhaka cinema in the decades between the two "partitions" of the northern region (1947, 1971).[4] By contrast, resources and market opportunities came together in the late '40s and early '50s Bombay to strengthen an already male-dominant nationalist framework that might have constrained women's scope for doing and claiming agentive film work. The large-scale nationalization of Bombay productions in this same era (Rajadhyaksha 2003), which evolved into state-supported Bollywood, was only expedited by Hindi becoming the state language in 1950 and bringing along a bulwark of linguistic nationalism that had been gaining strength since the anticolonial movement of the late nineteenth and early twentieth centuries (Orsini 2002; Sadana 2012). For female-authorial agency to become publicly ownable and talkable, an institutional shift had to happen at the level of patriarchal national structures.

The shift came in two phases of "director's cinema" led by men but with an important difference. A state-supported "new cinema" movement that had gained ground through the 1970s along with the new media networks of television and video brought in a small female cohort of Hindi fiction filmmakers in the 1980s through 1990s. These women directors were relatively independent professionals enabled by a state-level attempt to promote socially uplifting media by institutionalizing the contemporary women's movement. As female authors of the contemporary, they produced fictions that were variously intertextual with the debates on structural inequalities born of organized feminist resistance. Even though state-level film initiatives were dwindling by the '80s, they had birthed both "director-producers" and a "small band of producers . . . [wanting to] support the production of good quality low or medium budget films."[5] Sai Paranjpye's *Chasme Buddoor* was funded by one such producer (more on this below). The next female cohort, which populates positions of director and production personnel today, began expanding from the first decade of the 2000s by taking advantage of familial and social contacts with the patriarchal networks of production and stardom already in place in the Bollywood/Bombay industry. The existing networks of dominance were only being strengthened in post-liberalization India through multi-scalar conglomeration. Nonetheless, these two generations of female authors have in common a production identity with a specific aesthetic telos. They emerge at two moments when Indian cinema was being constituted by state-industry infrastructures as the authorial medium of realistic national cinema, a medium where directors explore Indian realities through an ethnographic use of local people and geographies. What grew in proportion at these moments was the implicit dependency on women's cinema, a cinema by real Indian women or about real Indian women, as a key site for debating Indian modernity.

In 1980, official sources described the nation's "new cinema," influenced by international avant-garde forms, as a mirror in which "the reality of India assails us at every flick of a frame," by contrast to the mass-oriented "dream-world" of commercial Bombay cinema (Dutt 1981, 33). Seen another way, the publicly understood goal of the new cinema author-directors was to produce "cultural and political literacy" about authentic Indian realities through images and storytelling.[6] Precisely this national literacy initiative was to be reclaimed, with a global inflection, by the gentrified Bollywood author discourse in the first decade of the 2000s.[7] Leading male directors had begun to discuss how the "escapist fare" of mass Hindi cinema was finally giving way to box-office "acclaimed" Indian stories told in a way that "Indians enjoy and so does the world."[8] The trade press noted that the increasingly urban consumers of Bollywood films sought a "cool barometer" cinema offering stories "that match up to current Indian situations" ("What College Students Want" 2007, 96). Between these generations, however, there is a significant shift in the politics of infrastructural "address" (Larkin 2013, 329). The change occurs in how the infrastructural components of physical/financial resource and fantasy come together to produce a public address enabling filmmakers in their India literacy work.

In the 1980s, infrastructural support was partly being claimed and oriented by the women's movement; in other words, questions of women and structural inequality were being inserted into the fantasy realm of educated publics. By contrast, the infrastructure of resources and fantasies characterizing 2000s Bollywood has a class-coded "multiplex" address, which interlinks an exhibition sector born of "urban redevelopment" in metropolitan India with international venues and capital (Athique and Hill 2007, 112–117). A journalist writing for *Filmfare* in 2007 nicely characterizes this infrastructural address and what form of Indian storytelling it requires. He celebrates the fact that the multiplex "revolution" has given rise to a new cohort of "niche" directors of offbeat cinema who target only the discerning viewer "empowered with purchasing power and the right to choose cinema that reflects his taste and individuality" (T. Amin 2007, 69–70). We find here the description of a neoliberal universalist address to the structurally empowered individual-as-consumer of various real Indian situations, implicitly calling for suppression of structural details and differences that refuse to "match up" to trending tastes (to restate the pithy words of the urban Bollywood consumer, quoted above). What we find, then, is a literacy infrastructure for processing India as a nation-brand. While the offbeat, or *hatke*, multiplex wave promotes the "use of real locations in India" (Dwyer 2011, 198), bodies and geographies need to be aggregated to match attributes already trending in some measure in the minds of target consumers.

What evolves between these generations in the way female authors of Hindi fiction films work? What does the change tell us about the woman's labor of *becoming the author* of a "current Indian" woman's situation in 2000s Bollywood, a space at once gender-inclusive yet regulated by the spatiotemporal drive of a structurally determinate "India" brand? By rigorously contextualizing women's cinema and female fictions in the respective eras, feminist studies help to approach these questions.

Sai Paranjpye and *Chasme Buddoor* have been situated by scholars in a temporal context wherein women's filmmaking emerged as an "identifiable trope" of "oppositional" work (Sawhney 2015, 152, 162) because the 1970s women's movement had put the "woman question" into the statist "discourse" on modernization (Gopal 2019, 43).[9] This national discursive framework brought a good number of women into filmmaking via state-supported media infrastructures—of television, video, radio, and film institute training. Although many in this cohort made fiction films in regional Indian languages (to wit, Aparna Sen's Bengali cinema), Sai Paranjpye is one of three who made Hindi fiction films (Aruna Raje and Kalpana Lajmi being the others) and the only one to work in the mainstream "middle cinema" genre of social comedy with backing from an established film distributor. Sangita Gopal insightfully theorizes Sai as a "nomadic" gender media worker who crisscrossed the infrastructures of television, feminism, and film. Along the way, she wove a "televisual aesthetic" of quotidian desires and community interests into her fiction films (2019, 54–59). By contrast, works with "vernacular" and "local" accents, such as Gauri Shinde's *English Vinglish*, are positioned by scholars in a particular Bollywood niche of the "*hatke* [offbeat] impulse to intersect the global with the local and create new ways of articulating female sexual desire" (Ram 2021, 135; Madhavi Biswas, qtd. in Anwer and Arora 2021, 18). The "addressee" of niche Bollywood's offbeat universalism—of the impulse to confer agency to all women and minorities—is noted by Megha Anwer and Anupama Arora to be new patriarchal structures that keep up with Indian "liberalization's imperatives" (1). While these imperatives allow for national literacy in diverse female realities, at the same time, they seek the female body as a stage for "new age fears over indiscriminately open economic and national borders" (6). Focusing on women filmmakers, other scholars complicate the picture by arguing for an "emergent women's cinema" that poses spatiotemporal challenges to mainstream techniques of Bollywood production (N. Majumdar 2017, 45). Such fiction films by women could also take a feminist counternarrative approach to "perfervid social concerns" (Viswamohan 2023, 11).

This fast-expanding feminist debate on female fictions and women filmmakers in globalized Bollywood stays largely with form- and text-based criticism. We await more research on how the many women directors producing niche cinema work behind the camera or negotiate resource structures for authoring images and stories.[10] Later in this chapter, I take a small step in that direction by examining the production of *English Vinglish* in relation to orbital materials and an oral history given to me by director and scriptwriter Gauri Shinde the year after the film's release (2013). To arrive there, let me speak in the light of the scholarly perspectives cited above to the questions I posed earlier about Hindi female authorship and film work.

My argument through the rest of this chapter is that as we turn from Sai Paranjpye to Gauri Shinde, we find that the modality of female filmic authorship constitutively changes even though both women forge multi-scalar connections with large structures whose locus of decision work supersedes their own. Extending Gopal's formulation of the meddlesome gender media worker to a consideration of generic social film, I position Sai Paranjpye's authorship of *Chasme Buddoor* as a transmedial traversal of the fantasies permeating the infrastructure of patriarchal middle cinema (primary to this work). The seemingly lighthearted narrative, embedding a sexually conscious televisual aesthetic of changing urban lives, makes the realistic content unblendable into a coherent temporal concept of modern India. By contrast, I find Gauri Shinde leveraging multi-scalar connections with brand-partner economies and liberal patriarchal networks to develop a niche female brand by way of reblending the spatiotemporal elements of what began as an *untimely* mother's story. In this light, I understand the female author-entrepreneur of present-day Bollywood as a compliant historical subject who laboriously negotiates available familial and patriarchal networks in order to become a signatory author of an already trending brand identity. Her aesthetic work is readable as an archive of brand authorship that addresses and negotiates cultural borders but also resolves difference and subsumes the local. Yet, my ethnographic approach to this archive of process, which entwines an oral history, suggests another transborder way to read the female authorial trace in 2000s Bollywood productions. This way is to look for the spatiotemporal "shibboleth effect" (Derrida 1993, 10) for episodes or images that fall behind or hover on the edge of the narrative teleology of globalizing Indian womanhood. Let me get there through a comparative look at the more meddlesome counter-telling of gendered bodies and geographies in Sai Paranjpye's authorial practice.

Hindi Female Authorship and an Incoherent Gender Geography: *Chasme Buddoor*

Sai Paranjpye's media career includes the roles of an announcer at All India Radio, a theater director, a television serial producer at the state-sponsored channel Doordarshan, a lecturer at the state-funded Film and Television Institute, a documentary filmmaker, and the director and scriptwriter of a handful of Hindi fiction films. The first motion picture she made, titled *Sparsh* (The Touch; 1980), is a serious romantic drama depicting tensions within a premarital romance between a blind man and a seeing woman and quietly displacing the taboo against Hindu widow remarriage found on the mainstream Hindi screen of the time. Although the film went on to win a number of prestigious awards at the national level, Sai had struggled to gather funds for it and to get it released. Nonetheless, the awards paved the way to her next motion picture, *Chasme Buddoor* (Far Be the Evil Eye), a social comedy that turned out to be a major theatrical hit. At a time when established distributors were refusing to buy works made in the new cinema mode,[11] she was invited to script and direct this fiction film by a well-known distributor by the name of Gul Anand who had recently entered the production field. He had coproduced in 1978 the comedic social film *Khatta Meetha*, directed by Basu Chatterji, a leading author of what is called "middle cinema" (Gokulsing and Dissanayake 2004), or "middle-class cinema" by scholars (Prasad 1998a). By the time her second comedy film, *Katha* (1982), was making the exhibition routes, Sai Paranjpye herself was being celebrated by the press as a new voice in the middle-cinema genre rather than as the maker of women's art cinema of the vein of *Sparsh* for a narrow viewership. Announcing the theatrical release of *Katha* at the Metro Cinema in Kolkata, for example, *The Telegraph* applauds the fact that "Sai's simplicity of approach hasn't changed to artiness despite the critical appreciation *Sparsh* received." And even as it generically aligns her work with that of the male "middle" Hindi directors Basu Chatterji and Hrishikesh Mukherjee, the article finds in her comedies a "freshness" missing in the "formula" films being made by her male predecessors ("Katha" 1984, 10).

Clearly, a resourceful discursive space was opening up at the moment in both production and reception circuits for the female author of mainstream middle cinema—that is, parallel cinema in generic form. The opportunity did come with many gendered stipulations from the producer Gul Anand about how to wrap the script of *Chasme Buddoor* in the generic fabric. Still, thanks to a large-scale mediatizing of the woman's "voice," the time may well have been ripe for the woman scriptwriter and director to claim some degree of creative freedom. Looking back today at the legendary success of *Chasme Buddoor*, Sai maintains that she had later been "thankful" for a number of Gul Anand's suggestions but grown "tired" of others (2021). It is arguable that the "freshness" found by a hospitable press in the authorial mode of middle-cinema comedy she had cultivated has something to do with both the use of given conventions and growing tired thereof. As a transborder female author, in the sense in which I am developing the idea in this book, Sai availed herself of dominant infrastructures while partially undoing their cultural address. *Chasme Buddoor* unsettles key gender tropes of middle cinema by deploying a televisual aesthetic of quotidian habitations and desires. Moreover, the film pushes against the prevailing tendency to reduce woman-made cinema to the "woman question" only by inserting contemporary feminist concerns (women's self-reliance, sexual divisions of propriety and desire) into a male buddy movie about expanding consumerism.[12] The sexually nuanced aesthetic portrays the self-reliant female body in relation to an uneven web of gender and class formations within a fast-transforming urban Indian geography. The aesthetic is suggestive of Sai Paranjpye's declared resistance to institutional categories of the time, such as the "woman filmmaker" and "middle cinema" (Gopal 2019).

On Sai Paranjpye's own testimony, *Chasme Buddoor* was based on a telefilm she had made called *Dhuan Dhuan* (Smoke, Smoke, c. 1980). She describes the latter as depicting three "good-for-nothing" young men who develop a "crush for the same girl" and spin many fantasies. They end up hating her, reclaiming their friendship, and going back to being the non-aspirational losers they always were, forever passing around the same cigarette (Rangayan and Gupta 2013, 162). When Sai narrated the story to producer Gul Anand, he immediately wanted one of the three young men to be turned into a "serious" romantic hero and kept returning with suggestions for additional family-type characters (Paranjpye 2021). Despite tiring of the numerous suggestions, Sai eventually scripted one of his ideas in a meddlesome mode into the widely applauded character of a paternalistic Muslim tobacco and *pan* (betel-leaf roll) stall owner located in the same neighborhood as the young men (Paranjpye 2021). In this light, it is noteworthy that the producer's suggestions had fallen in with key conventions of the familial middle-cinema genre cresting at the time. Madhava Prasad argues that Indian state-level initiatives for developing quality cinema were being "transferred" by directors such as Hrishikesh Mukherjee and Basu Chatterji into a "realist sub-sector of the commercial cinema" (1998a, 160–181). Addressed to the aspirations of an upper-caste Hindu middle class that carries on its shoulders the "burden of national identity," this aesthetic sought to produce the "nuclear couple" in relation to "extended familial networks." As practiced by the male directors named above, the middle-cinema genre dramatizes the quotidian look and feel of modernizing Indian patriarchy. The upright and hardworking young heroes are typically lacking in metropolitan glamour (sexy grooming, trendy motor-bikes, professional track records). They end up achieving metropolitan status and upper-middle-class coupledom not only by getting jobs or promotions but also by learning to man up with tutelage or protection from professional or otherwise working father figures. For their part, the female leads, although independent working women or students, are relatively passive counterparts of romantic duos, often falling prey as well to consumerism, until they are domesticated. These conventions appear in various configurations not only in *Khatta Meetha*, produced by Gul Anand, but other highly successful motion pictures such as *Rajnigandha* (1974) and *Choti Si Baat* (1976), directed as well by Basu Chatterji, and *Guddi* (1971), directed by Hrishikesh Mukherjee. A number of these conventions are taken up in *Chasme Buddoor* and reworked with an uncompromising satirical eye on transforming womanhood in relation to the gender inequalities dividing Indian middle-class reality. The fabric of patriarchal nationalism in the available middle-cinema genre, in other words, is inhabited and ripped.

Not unlike the original telefilm, *Chasme Buddoor* portrays three male college buddies from village backgrounds living in a familiar New Delhi neighborhood. Whereas the "serious" romantic-hero-to-be, Sidharth (Farooq Sheikh), an ace student of economics, is preparing to pursue a doctoral degree, his loser buddies Omi (Rakesh Bedi) and Jomo (Ravi Baswani) are trying to chase girls. Or at least they gaze with sex-starved eyes at the bikini-clad pin-up girls and film stars plastering "their" walls of the apartment. Nonetheless, all three hang out together smoking the same cigarette butts or chitchatting with Lallan Miyan (Saeed Jaffrey), the indulgently paternalistic tobacco vendor around the corner, whose debt they can never repay. Deploying televisual scenic constructions of the local (Gopal 2019, 53–56), these episodes evoke spaces of male homosocial bonding typical to middle- and lower-middle-class neighborhoods in urban India of the time. But this is only so until their relationships—to each other and to the locality—are forever transformed through attraction to the cutely independent upper-middle-class saleswoman who happens to cross their path. First spotted in attractive attire from afar by Omi and Jomo, the door-to-door saleswoman Neha (Deepti Naval) arrives at the apartment for a sales pitch and, having met Sidharth face-to-face, initiates a romance with him that ends in wedlock. Sidharth is motivated by his reciprocal attraction to improve his looks and climb the urban social ladder by taking a lucrative job (at Neha's father's office, no less). Although the romance is temporarily scuttled by the jealous maneuvers of Omi and Jomo, who have also tried in vain to approach Neha, the rupture is healed through community endeavor: the bumbling efforts of Sidharth's compunctious buddies and Neha's Dadi Amma (grandmother; Leela Mishra) as well as crucial intervention by the protective neighborhood father figure, Lallan Miyan.

A number of middle-cinema conventions are invaded in this work. Foremost is the displacement of relatively dependent female figures into the agentive identity of the female lead. Moreover, heroine Neha materializes as a proactive agent not solely by herself but rather in relation to similar female personifications. We find onscreen a transforming geography of middle-class Indian female bodies. Neha herself is an independent, successful income-earning woman by her own choice and quite ready to own her sexuality by initiating the relationship with Sidharth (she leaves him with a word about where and when to find her and later candidly tells him that she had purposely done so). Yet, in exerting her sexual independence and standing up to her benignly patriarchal father, Neha is not alone. She is robustly supported by the dynamic figure of Dadi Amma, whose movements render fluid the border between respectable domesticity and the public world (fig. 15). Dadi Amma shows up to look for Sidharth in the men's apartment and awaits his return perched resolutely in the midst of blow-ups of bikini-clad women and *Playboy* magazines (at which she even takes an unwitting peek). Beyond this, Neha is shown to be one among an upper-class generation of independent young women who, when faced with sexual harassment on the streets, fight back. Neha herself is stalked by both Omi and Jomo, who separately end up on her doorstep once they have figured out where she lives. Not only does she remain unperturbed, but she also leads Jomo to her karate expert brother and visibly enjoys watching Jomo getting beaten up. In a similar vein, Omi and Jomo get upended time and again by the women they chase and tease on the street. One young woman snatches away the kerchief being used to attract her attention, and another hitches a motorbike ride with Jomo simply in order to meet up with her boyfriend (the only time Jomo can get the rickety motorbike to start). However, there is satirical nuance to this drama of female empowerment. This lies in the conflicting sexual meanings staged around the upper-class female body, mainly protagonist Neha's.

In an ambivalent urban regime in which door-to-door saleswomen were at once "harbingers of the consumer revolution" and testimony to the increase in female mobility (Gopal 2019, 55–56), Neha becomes an erotic embodiment of the commodity she sells. Entering the space of the simply clothed overachieving young man from a village background, she in effect entices Sidharth to climb into the urban time of professionalization and consumption. We see a tongue-in-cheek drama of Sidharth embracing *his* sexuality by immediately going shopping so that he can turn out with a well-groomed look for his tryst with Neha. The wry sexual critique lies in the conflicted staging of mutual desire—as being involved in consumption and spontaneously innocent at the same time. Such scenes are suggestive of how mutual consumption is the natural path to becoming the ideal progress-oriented couple in India. The scenic construction of Neha's pitch to Sidharth for the detergent she sells is particularly telling. A rare sequence of tight and medium close-ups of Neha's

Fig. 15: Dadi Amma and Neha (Source: *Chasme Buddoor*)

face begins, advertisement-style, by framing her next to the detergent box as she recites her sales pitch. However, the camera shots are quickly melded together to show the growth of romantic desire as she stoops over a bucket with Sidharth (for a washing "demonstration" that is a part of the pitch). Soon we see Sidharth with childlike spontaneity offering her a sweetmeat sent by his mother, implicitly bringing her into his respectable domestic circle. The contradiction surrounding the respectably sexualized body of the upper-class Indian woman, though, lies in the way it provokes sexual stratification between middle-class masculinities and metropolitan access. Jomo and Omi remain the forever emasculated underachievers loitering on neighborhood streets and chasing expensively clothed girls who ignore or take advantage of them. By contrast, high-achiever Sidharth not only gains access by way of the woman to upper-middle-class urban geography (home, office, high-end cafés and stores) but also has sexual potency inscribed in his bourgeois persona from the outset. He is the only one who can get the rickety motorbike they share to run at first crank and carry along his inept buddies (who can seldom get the bike going).

All in all, we find in Sai Paranjpye's *Chasme Buddoor* a transborder meddling in the sexually coherent identities found in middle-cinema nationalism—notably those of the passively mobile modern woman and of the middle-class man who invariably climbs the socioeconomic ladder. In the gender landscape of this work, only a few chosen men from less-privileged backgrounds can climb in society, whereas many others simply hang out and get by. We find here a feminist aesthetic of the incoherent nation-space of modernizing India, which typifies women's cinema of the '80s. Most helpful here is Sangita Gopal's argument about Sai's transmedial aesthetic, the use of narrative and visual sources from television (documentary, teleplay) to evoke "human interest" in particular neighborhoods and communities (2019, 54). Along these lines, we find human interest being stimulated in bodies and communities not only in *Chasme Buddoor* but also in Sai Paranjpye's next social comedy, *Katha* (Gopal 2019). The point to note in our case at hand is that the human form and place are being shown as both coterminous and structurally unequal. Jomo and Omi not only occupy the same neighborhood as Sidharth and Neha, but they also have their own loving father figure in parallel to the romantic couple's professional patriarch. The neighborhood merchant Lallan Miyan is always indulging their manhood by encouraging Jomo and Omi to pursue the female *shikār* (hunt), despite their invariable lack of success. That character, spun by Sai from a suggestion made by producer Gul Anand (see above), seems to be another meddlesome doubling on the patriarchs who tend to populate middle-cinema works by male directors of the period. The discursive momentum of the women's movement—a mediatizing of the woman's voice on a national scale—allows resources for female authorial claim on mainstream Hindi cinema.

As I turn from the quotidian realism in 1980s women's cinema to that in women's productions of the 2000s, I find instead a distinct push for temporal coherence, a collapse of difference, in the depiction of Indian bodies and spaces. The reason is certainly *not* because feminist movements disappear from India. Rather, it has to do with the multinational structural formations outlined earlier in this chapter: the formation of a conglomerate production-circulation economy for developing the country and its people as a nation-brand; the official support given to that formative process by the right-leaning liberalized nation-state of India; and a concomitant reinforcement of the historically entrenched patriarchal networks of Mumbai/Bombay cinema. Female filmic authorship of personal realities must negotiate these formations on a multiple scale. Let me elaborate by looking closely at the case of Gauri Shinde and *English Vinglish*.

Timing Female Bodies, Blending Indian Geographies: *English Vinglish*

A blog posted in May 2018 by the Box Office India Trade Network describes the "Top Fifteen" motion pictures "driven by the female lead." The list itself and an accompanying commentary suggest at least two ways in which Indian women's cinema discourse has changed between the 1980s and the 2000s. On the one hand, productions directed by women are revealed to be few in number and only fleetingly gendered. Trade press coverage does not appear to be hospitable to the woman director and her voice in the way it was in the 1980s. Although the Top Fifteen list shows that only two of the successful productions were directed by women, there is no mention of the small representation. The blog does recognize in passing that Gauri Shinde's *English Vinglish* is the first successful "female lead" film by a woman director. The discourse focuses, on the other hand, on female-lead fictions and their success rate. The commentator is clear about the fact that "films driven by the female faces . . . that actually work are very [few]." I must add that the Top Fifteen Box Office list demonstrates that female-lead fiction films still rise in national visibility through a discursive push from organized feminist resistance, exactly as they did in the 1970s and '80s. The relevant discursive background for the expanding list of female-lead productions found in the 2018 trade blog is the widespread mobilization against the Nirbhaya gang rape in New Delhi in December 2012.[13] What the trade commentator argues for, however, is *not* any connection with social debates or current events but rather with production value. Assessing how the success rate of female-lead productions has been and can be improved, the commentator categorically states that "with brand value they can get a huge push" ("Top Fifteen" 2018). The list indeed does illuminate how heroine fiction films have burgeoned with the multiplex director's niche brand value, Gauri Shinde's success being the first female case in point (the production was released in October 2012, before the Nirbhaya gang rape case).

Promoted as based on the story of the director-writer's own mother, the production was launched with the trending niche touch of a real-life Indian situation with a cool local accent (Ram 2021). Trade reports from the time note that extensive publicity, well-received teasers, and rave reviews made *English Vinglish* one of the "most anticipated films" of 2012. Yet, box-office collections on the opening day were disappointing (Kulkarni 2012; IANS 2012). By the very next day, however, the tide had turned through word-of-mouth publicity. The production was not simply holding on to but actually expanding its brand value. Sarah Banet-Weiser (2016, 24–25) reminds us that brands sold in advanced capitalist economies are unlike tangible commodities in that they sell immaterial social expectations and values by coordinating sets of interactions between target ranges of consumers and the objects being marketed. *English Vinglish* proved more than capable of expanding brand value by coordinating the immaterial experiences it offered to different ranges of viewer/consumers.

By the end of the first weekend, the success reports for *English Vinglish* poured in not only from the marketing department of the high-end Cinemax multiplex chain, located across posh malls in metropolitan Indian cities (Ganti 2012, 329–330), but also from single-screen urban theaters that offer a spectrum of ticket prices and draw audiences from different class backgrounds (the Regal in Mumbai, for example, started canceling other shows in order to schedule more showtimes for *English Vinglish*). The fact that the film was released simultaneously at multiplexes and at single-screen theaters suggests a push beyond niche marketing, since urban films often are released first at multiplex venues and only upon success at single-screen theaters (Mirchandani, qtd. in T. Amin 2007, 70). The irony lay in the fact that at the promotional stage, the brand value instead appeared to have been too narrowly defined, in the words of a trade analyst, to have come across as that of a "film made for a niche audience [of] ladies only" (Amod Mehra, qtd. in Kulkarni 2012). The reference is to an audience of older women, who would relate to the middle-age mother/housewife heroine, compared to youthful "girls," who would not. While "senior citizens" were indeed reported as being drawn to the theaters, in part to see the return to the silver screen of the '80s era superstar Sridevi, theaters began overflowing with audiences from all age groups and walks of life (IANS 2012). *English Vinglish* was soon being valued by "Gen Next" consumers who look for real Indian stories that have undergone a cool "style check" (i.e., of eroticism). This consumer group is the principal target of an increasingly "youth-oriented" Bollywood ("What College Students Want" 2007, 96;

Ganti 2012, 110–118). In this vein, twenty-five-year-old female cinemagoer Kavya Mishra hailed *English Vinglish* as a "movie that transcends the taboos of this aspirational Indian society" by showing that taking the right "actions" allows an individual to overcome the tabooed "bars" of "language" and "age" (qtd. in IANS 2012). Clearly, the work was passing the "style check" required by the Indian youth market: it was making aspirations and values of locally grounded older women and quotidian issues tangible in a way that believably blended into an Indian-brand concept of transformative action.

In the personal conversation I had with her, Gauri Shinde indeed did dwell at length on the laborious style work she had done through a costume brand partnership on heroine Sridevi's film costumes. Into her story of costume design, Gauri wove details about location choice and shot styling that appeared to have become integral to the final presentation of the niche-brand heroine's look and feel. Trade commentators measuring *English Vinglish* on the sexy style check of "Bollywood chic" applauded the subtle eroticism of Sridevi's "sensible" wardrobe, made up of traditional daily wear of handwoven saris and long-sleeve blouses chosen from classic "Indian palette colours." They pitted it favorably against the typically extravagant "sensuality" of female costumes found in many mainstream Bollywood films (Speaking Chic 2012). Clearly, the everyday female look and feel had successfully carved for itself a niche in a multiplex infrastructure that inflects to different forms of Indianness, including the ordinary shapes that were previously marginal in the erotic fantasy realm of Bollywood cinema. In light of the insistence on *corporeal style* I find in its production and reception circuits, I submit that *English Vinglish* invites being read as a globalized-nationalist fashion film. It follows the generic "makeover" narrative arc—transforming the "fashion-challenged girl into a fashion-insider" (Munich 2011, 268)—sans a literal sartorial makeover. The cameo appearance of the male megastar Amitabh Bachchan, also in traditional wear, inserts another crucial nationalist element. The Indian palette color sense of an older, familiar female body—taken together with her cameo hero—are made into a stage on which the spatiotemporal borders of globalizing middle-class life are staged *and* partially critiqued. This reading leads into the text as an archive of the making-over process, yet one that can also read for disjunctive traces.

English Vinglish, the fiction of an affluent housewife and small business-woman lacking in cosmopolitan skills, begins in the quotidian spaces of Pune (the western Indian city that is home to the director) and leads to New York City. Sashi Godbole (Sridevi) leads parallel lives. On one side, she is a thorough homemaker and a loving mother who bonds deeply, especially with the little son who is devoted to her. On another side, she is a small business-woman making and selling *laddoos* (a traditional South Asian sweetmeat) to a loyal customer base of families located around town. Inept at cosmopolitan skills, such as English speech or formal behavior at parent-teacher meetings at her daughter's upscale high school, Sashi faces humiliation by her corporate executive husband, Satish (Adil Hussain), and by their insolent, miniskirt- and slacks-wearing teenage daughter, who has imbibed patriarchal elitism. While he complacently consumes the fruits of her care work, especially the delectable food she prepares, Satish devalues Sashi's home-based business in favor of his own financialized professional work (Banerjee and Desai 2021, 32–34). The hierarchy dividing this working couple dramatizes the spatio-temporal borders troubling middle-class family life in an India where English speech and cosmopolitan skills have become "indispensable to the clamoring for respectability" (S. Chatterjee 2016, 1186–1187). The couple form is all the more dysfunctional because Satish fails to reciprocate Sashi's companionate gestures and takes her sexuality for granted. However, a transcendence narrative soon begins to wrest Sashi away from the gendered inequities, posing a challenge to the "denial of coevalness" found in mainstream Bollywood techniques (N. Majumdar 2017, 46–47). The transcendence arc works on multiple fronts—turning Sashi's small business earnings into capital for self-profit and social mobility; allowing space to posit the worth of her skillful care work in its own right (rather than as devalued reproductive labor); and permitting the middle-age woman to explore her sexual self-worth and make choices. Further, the narrative arc is provocatively driven by another Indian woman whose financialized identity and global access supersede the subject-hood of the local patriarchal professional—namely, husband Satish. He gets turned into the symbol of a stagnated and somewhat atavistic form of Indian masculinity needing reform.

A phone call comes from Sashi's expatriate sister and working professional, Manu (Sujata Kumar), inviting the whole family to her older daughter's wedding in New Jersey and offering plane tickets, with the request that Sashi travel earlier to help out with arrangements. Manu's financialized status in the global North immediately tames Satish's patriarchal bravado. Now dependent on his sister-in-law for the coveted international trip, he attempts halfheartedly to prepare Sashi for the trip and give her the confidence she lacks to travel on her own. Finally, Sashi agrees with much trepidation to travel alone to New Jersey and have the rest of the family follow later. The confidence she needs for her lone journey actually begins to be breathed into Sashi by another man. She receives benign guidance in cosmopolitan skills from an elderly man (Amitabh Bachchan) who fortuitously appears on the plane and helps her throughout the flight. Thereafter, Sashi progressively transforms into an aspirational flâneuse in New York City, who does not simply tour as a foreigner consuming the spectacles but also mines the opportunities for self-care. Using money saved up from her laddoo business, she enrolls in an English-speaking course and secretly attends from New Jersey while her sister is at work. There, she cultivates friendship with her multiethnic class peers and the gay instructor and forms the beginnings of a romantic relationship with a French chef named Laurent (Mehdi Nebbou). Meanwhile, her older niece's wedding day draws near; Satish and the children arrive in New Jersey. Eventually, by her own choice, Sashi withdraws from the budding transgressive relationship with Laurent and instead commits to her family. Moreover, she makes another complicated turn in the narrative by choosing to withdraw from her aspiration of earning the English-speech certificate and instead remaking laddoos on the eve of the wedding (the original batch having been destroyed by a prank her little son has played). All ends well and she does earn the English certificate because her supportive younger niece invites the teacher and class to the wedding. There, with her entire family present, Sashi unveils a newfound confidence in her cosmopolitan Indian feminine self by giving a speech in English about family values and companionate respect. Both her domineering husband and the overbearing daughter are reduced to compunction.

English Vinglish stands at the head of a niche Bollywood trend of the female confidence fiction. It was followed by a range of such fiction films directed by women and men including *Queen* (2013; dir. Vikas Bahl), *Margarita with a Straw* (2014; dir. Shonali Bose), *Dil Dhadakane Do* (2015; dir. Zoya Akhtar), and Gauri Shinde's own *Dear Zindagi* (2016), among others. These works are nuanced portrayals of the Indian "new woman figure as a sympathetic/intriguing/contentious one" wrestling with the dynamics of sociocultural transformation (Anwer and Arora 2021, 18). However, they typically reinforce a global North/South divide (18). Seen another way, they are prone to blend in local elements with global/developed images of bodies and geographies in order to achieve the right brand of the globalizing Indian woman for target markets (i.e., high-end multiplex in India and international/diasporic markets). In this stylistic blending, the local could get to be constituted as sexually regressive, unaware, or undeveloped in a way such that female protagonists develop confidence only by entering globalized spaces (outside India and also within). As such, the Bollywood female-confidence fiction is a subset of the corporeal modality of neoliberal feminism in which "the *body* figures as central in the struggle for confidence . . . and a panacea" (italics in original; Banet-Weiser 2018, 92) for social and historical tensions. In the instance of *English Vinglish*, however, the mode of branding the confidence teleology corporeally had to be more complex than any of the other female-lead fiction films named above, for across the board of the aforementioned works, the confidence-begetting heroine body is young and most often Western-clothed. In our case at hand, the elemental form of a commonplace, sari-wearing older female body had to be made over spatiotemporally to be adequate to the "chic" brand identity of a globalized yet authentic Indian woman. It had to be made to fit, as it successfully did in the chic style commentator's estimation, with certain attributes of the national female brand in which the minds of target consumers were already literate. As discussed earlier, the targeting of existing consumer knowledge is essential for the successful production of the nation as a brand (Dinnie 2008).

The visual metaphors at play in making over Sashi's timidly local demeanor into a sexily confident Indian female look begin appearing in the global setting of her flight to New York. The supportive older man who appears by her side exuding self-assurance and ready to train her in cosmopolitan skills is dressed traditionally, like Sashi, in a complementary "Indian palette" color. Clothed in a white *dhoti*, *kurta*, and shawl, the male figure is reminiscent of the anticolonial Hindu activists from British India. Speaking fluent English and commanding the technological know-how for international travel and consumerism, he teaches Sashi to use headphones and sip a glass of wine. He lives up to his aspect by going on to stage the phallic excitement of nationalist machismo against waning Western domination both on the plane and upon landing in the United States. He seizes opportunities to flex the "soft power" (Dwyer 2021) of Indian economic muscle over white labor sectors. He construes the white female flight attendant as the "*maya devi*" (magical goddess) whose servitude is at the beck and call of the Indian passengers who now control the button. Aggressively talking down as well to the American man at the immigration desk in New York, he leaves Sashi with the parting wisdom that she should no longer be afraid of these "*engrez*," or English speakers, because these days they are instead learning to fear the Indians (i.e., as rivals in the global field). Both the sartorial appearance of this older Indian man and his protective emotions toward the non-cosmopolitan Indian woman Sashi highlight the paternal role the globalized Indian man must take in authenticating the nationalist element in the confident self of a mobile Indian woman. Indeed, it makes soft masculinity—with a muscular male Hindu accent[14]—into an indispensable supportive element of the Bollywood brand of Indian womanhood. Moreover, target consumers are highly literate in this masculine element of the Bollywood nation-brand, being that it is the male megastar Amitabh Bachchan who pitches it, and composes a total gender brand value of authentic Indians with a global sensation (women plus men). Needless to say, the drama of Bachchan's paternalism as the go-between for Sashi's cosmopolitan ways gradually breeds confident independence in the provincial Indian woman. A series of long takes at medium close-up, highlighting Sridevi's expertly realistic method acting, shows Sashi overcoming bouts of awkwardness in the course of the plane journey. As she journeys through New York City on her own, we see the public environment of the global city itself taking on the role of another phallic actor in the melodrama of the woman's transformation. Mutating shapes and feels of the city begin to texture the older female body with visual metaphors of progress and to cathect her "authentic" Indian saris with global aspirational shapes.

What begins as a pleasant experience of flânerie—with Sashi strolling across a park in New York City consuming the sights and sounds of performers and musicians while picking up a compliment for her (presumably exotic) raw silk sari—turns into a nightmare of surveillance for ineptitude. Unprepared for the speed and protocols of ordering lunch at a Manhattan café, the confused Sashi creates a mess and then flees in terror from the impatient antagonism displayed by customers and café staff alike. Rack focus shots stage her agitation as buildings and streets appear helter-skelter around the moving sari-clad form, pointedly unsettling the body from the setting. The visual texture of relating the body with architectural space quickly shifts, however, from antagonism to permeable juxtapositions. Shot compositions begin to put the costumed body and the Manhattan skyline into a fluid "dialogue" (Bruno 2011, 87). The cinematic style evokes the gender metaphors of American "skyscraper cinema," wherein mammoth buildings could become suggestively phallic by being invested with meanings such as upward mobility and the entrepreneurial spirit (Schleier 2008, vii–xiii).

Whereas at first Sashi is dependent on her cosmopolitan sister and younger niece for every step she takes through the awe-inspiring landscape of global desires, the mode of her physical interaction with the setting becomes aggressively confident after Sashi enrolls in the English class. Noteworthy is a scenic construction in which frontal shots depict Sashi in the same pink silk sari worn on her disastrous sightseeing tour striding confidently at the forefront of her class peers. With her rhythmic forward movement enveloped by urban sights, woman and clothing alike are metaphorically made over from an outsider consumer of unattainable global sites to a trendily erotic yet authentic Indian insider of the aspirational framework. Similar aspirational body imagery wraps a range of brightly colored handloomed saris, representing various regional Indian crafts, on Sashi/Sridevi's body. Repeated juxtapositions of the sari-clad body with mammoth buildings invite pan-Indian consumption of the made-over global attributes of the local heroine look. A spatiotemporal conundrum complicating this globalization narrative surfaces, however, in the latter half of the film when Sashi suddenly decides to withdraw from her aspirational path and, effectively, divert the location of the story from the global city back to her home. The momentary narrative diversion generates a different kind of literacy about the woman in relation to space and labor.

Earlier, Sashi had volunteered to add a caring domestic touch to her niece's wedding menu by making the laddoos in which she takes so much pride (despite being indulgently laughed at by her callous husband as the woman "born to make laddoos"). Although it turns out that her final English speech exam clashes with the wedding date, Sashi still is expert enough to complete making the promised laddoos in time. What offsets the plan, as already noted, is an innocent prank by her little son that destroys all the laddoos. Forsaking the exam that would legalize her cosmopolitan identity as an English-speaking woman, Sashi adamantly takes on the intense labor of quickly producing a fresh batch. We see Sashi through a long take in fading light working at the laddoos with steadfast hands late into the evening (having refused the help her family has offered). In this interior mise-en-scène strewn with everyday objects, Sridevi wears a simple cotton sari that stimulates for the viewer/fan another order of "style consciousness" (Gaines 1990, 18)—one that is *disjoined* from the stylish sexiness of the regional sari-wearing Indian flâneuse. Seen another way, the referent of these aesthetic contents is an entirely different concept of female agency familiar to the Indian consumer. The episode momentarily re-roots Sashi in a space of corporeal care work that is irreducible to transactional value—whether this is the value of reproductive labor for the family or the aspirational labor of making over into a confident public self. We find here a concern with the uncompromising value of care work similar to Indian feminist cinema of the earlier era, such as Aparna Sen's *Paromitar Ek Din* (discussed in chapter 1).

Even though the episodic moment is soon passed over by the brand narrative arc—which closes on the cosmopolitan wedding scene into which Sashi fits in and speaks about authentic family values—it has an intertext. It recalls an early scene sequence from a different urban setting depicting the vernacular lifeworld of laddoo-maker Sashi in Pune. Those early scenes stimulating a similarly disjunctive style consciousness show Sashi dressed in a modest white cotton sari that works well for navigating the streets in a hired auto-rickshaw. She is seen going from home to home distributing laddoo orders to an established circle of kin-like customers devoted to her unparalleled expertise in this culinary skill. These scenes of routine belonging stimulate literacy about women engaged in home-based wage work and exerting some control over public spaces, especially in the absence of domineering men (such as husband Satish, in our case at hand) (Raju and Paul 2016–2017, 130–131). Although these visual moments are left behind in *English Vinglish* by the literacy drive of the globalizing India female brand, they jostle against the latter and perhaps account in part for the diverse audience appeal and exhibition venues of the production.

What compels my attention to these disjunctive details of the realism in *English Vinglish* is that they are curiously intertextual with the stories about the production process I heard from the director. In light of the oral history and other orbital material, I discuss the production as an archive of the contradictory labor of a female author entrepreneur of brand-realist female fiction in present-day Bollywood. Her labor, on the one hand, goes into finding the right elements and brand partners for blending together a "real" story of globalizing India, thereby placing her signature on trending gender brands. On the other, her labor might involve negotiating what could be left as unblended or, perhaps, as a discordant remainder of the real.

Female Brand Authorship and the Remainder of Production: Gauri Shinde

Sitting in late 2013 with Gauri Shinde in a Mumbai office of the Lowe Lintas Advertising Corporation—at the time, owned and run by Gauri and her husband, R. Balki—I heard about her film education at the New York Film Academy and her eclectic tastes in cinema (fig. 16). Her tastes range from the new wave of niche Bollywood films such as *Dil Chahta Hai* (2001; dir. Farhan Akhtar) to the extravagant blockbusters released from Yash Raj Films as well as the directors' cinema of Satyajit Ray and Aparna Sen. Soon, I broached the question I always want to ask women directing motion pictures for mainstream circuits: Did she face hurdles as a woman filmmaker? Gauri responded with alacrity that she had faced no discrimination whatsoever on the basis of her gender. She went on to volunteer the equally categorical statements that the film she has made is "not feminist" and that "cinema is magic" that must "make money" (personal interview, 2013). She is far from alone in taking this position. The well-known Bollywood woman director Zoya Akhtar, for example, takes the same approach to infrastructure by stating that "no one in the industry cares about gender" and that "change" is already under way with a "few men being really involved in the process." As such, what the industry needs is not "a woman tag on everything" but rather the identity of a director or producer of "commercially viable" cinema (qtd. in Farzeen 2019).

As our conversation proceeded, I brought up another aspect of women's cinema. I noted with approval the fact that Gauri had made a female-lead film

Fig. 16: Gauri Shinde, film director and film firm co-owner

with no hero and that the only male megastar in her film, Amitabh Bachchan, departs from the narrative so quickly. Gauri Shinde seemed pleased with my praise of her female-lead production. However, she resisted my tendency to dismiss the Bachchan presence and averred that he had offered "crucial help" to her production and done so "free of cost." It did seem that Bachchan had brought needful industrial capital to the female-lead work (despite the fact it had female star Sridevi in the main role). As noted by Tejaswini Ganti (2012, 364–365), male megastars of Bollywood constitute crucial infrastructural support for women's cinema on both sides of the camera. Even low-budget productions directed by women without a star cast become commercially viable through the heft of male star-producer capital, namely *Peepli Live* (2010) directed by Anusha Rizvi and produced by Aamir Khan. Gauri Shinde's male-driven networks of opportunity included not only creative and financial support from her familial contact, Amitabh Bachchan, but also the couple-mode family firm she established in partnership with her husband, film director R. Balki. His contact with the Indian billionaire Rakesh Jhunjhunwala brought in outside finance (Balki 2018). The stories about infrastructure I was hearing affirmed that even though the 2000s Bollywood industry diversifies its contents at an exponential rate, enabling many niche directors and small firms, control stays historically entrenched in male relations. The contradiction is quite typical of expanding global economies. Multi-scalar decision work frequently remains "grounded" within nation-states and local regulatory practices even though organizations propagate at the multinational level (McDowell 2001). As such, entrepreneurial and creative labor by women in Bollywood has to be a continuous working through of scalar connections.

As the conversation turned to aesthetic concerns, Gauri Shinde grew more animated to talk about hurdles, raising some of the points that had been at issue in the initial reception of *English Vinglish*. She described how her biggest hurdle had been finding a producer for her script. All the major production houses of Mumbai refused support for some of the same reasons: it was a female-lead script; it was about an older woman wearing a traditional sari rather than a young heroine in Westernized, skimpy attire; it was about a housewife rather than a working woman or professional. The details shared with me by Gauri Shinde were not really new, for she repeats this account about her debut feature on public platforms (she did so recently, for example, at the *Algebra Conversation* show on which she appeared with R. Balki; Balki 2018). However, the plot of our conversation and the emphases on additional tidbits exceeded the main narrative.

The success story I heard of Gauri Shinde's growth as a director flowed with a larger plotline, that of shaping popular cinema anew as an author/niche director's medium rather than one controlled by big production houses and preexisting star texts. She went on to note, for instance, that even though the script had not been written for Sridevi, who had indeed not been on the scene, the actress refrained from bringing with her the "baggage of a superstar" and instead entered the script with cooperative eagerness. In Gauri's words, Sridevi became a "director's actor." Beyond this was the key narrative of how Gauri Shinde had made and produced the work she had scripted by setting up with R. Balki a new couple-mode film company called Hope Productions, whose only release at the time (October 2013) was *English Vinglish*. The website of Hope Productions reiterates the story Gauri had detailed for me. It describes the company as being "officially created in 2011 with the film *English Vinglish*," with Gauri Shinde and R. Balki having started the firm with the goal "to control production of their own films, besides providing a platform to create and shape original content." The author identity of the firm as a whole keeps pace with the niche-brand interest in distinctive directorial visions of life that offer a "kernel of truth" notwithstanding "so-called commercial compromises" (Pillaai 2007). Yet, the plot of Gauri Shinde's story about her own signatory claim on the family film identity was drifting in conflicted directions. The primary production narrative had to do with investing her initial concept of telling a real story of her mother with a "thoroughly discursive" meaning—namely, that of a timely sexy heroine. But the narrative came with "pragmatic . . . shibboleth effects," tidbits of contextual pragma estranged from the key storyline (Derrida 1993, 10–11).

Gauri was mainly focused on narrating that the principal production value she had rooted for was the transformation of the regional sari and its older female wearer into a "sexy" look. It seemed that the challenge had to do with how to effectively inhabit the cool, erotic "style check" ubiquitous to the Bollywood heroine brand by way of infusing it with a realistic touch of difference (of the older, sari-wearing heroine). Since then, I have gathered that the fashion designer Sabyasachi Mukherjee came to be the brand partner in producing Sridevi's sari-clad look. In his own words, the look could not be a luxurious "Sabya look per se" but rather an "authentic and effortless" getup that nonetheless was "sexy" (S. Mukherjee 2012). Indian palette colors and regional handcrafted saris were key elements of the final branded blend. The discursive premise of this drive to turn the regional/local body into a sexy brand keeps pace with a post-liberalized Indian culture of visibility that conjoins a gazing upon commodities with "the yearning for erotic pleasure" (Mankekar 2004, 403–408). Along these lines, Gauri Shinde's narrative of costume design evolved into choosing New York City for location shoots. She went on to clarify that while the location choice had doubled on a family precedent, it had also changed the latter. In effect, she was narrating how she had placed her signature on the evolving brand of a family-mode partnership.

Gauri referred to the production *Cheeni Kum* (2007), directed by her husband, R. Balki. Another food and travel movie with an older male protagonist—Amitabh Bachchan as a sexually diffident master chef led into a January–May romance by an agential young Indian woman—*Cheeni Kum* was location-shot in London. Gauri had picked up some of the same narrative elements: an older protagonist, sexual agency, culinary acumen, mobility in the metropolitan North. However, she brought up the family precedent only to point out what differed, especially in the location choice. She maintained that she had wanted to film in a "tall city" rather than in "flat" London so that she would be able to maximize the display of the human form through heightening and diminishment. As discussed in the previous section, an urban aesthetic of phallic corporeality is used to eroticize the identity of an older, sari-wearing heroine capitalizing on home-based culinary work. The same trendy heroine brand diverges as well from the family precedent by signing in resistance to the sexual divisions of labor and desire inherent to middle-class domesticity in transforming urban India (despite the female author's refusal of the feminist label, common to Bollywood today).

Other accounts of the choice of New York City are found on public platforms, in fact, all kinds of reasons could have driven the location choice. But what caught my ear was the disconnected information Gauri Shinde added onto the location story. She volunteered that she was imagining how small her mother would have looked *had she gone* to New York City, as compared to *how she did look* when she visited London. In other words, her choice of location in the global North was presented to me as being driven by an additional curious tendency—that of *disjoining* it from her mother's bodily reality. In the course of our relaxed chat that afternoon in an empty office in Mumbai, Gauri's concept story drifted onto another contextual detail. I heard of her mother's struggle over English speech but also that (said more than once with emphatic gestures) her mother "did *not* learn English." From the stories and her body language, I somehow came away questioning if her mother, who indeed did run a home-based pickle business, had really *wanted* to master English. These details were unexpected for me, as I had gone to the interview armed with another assumption about her mother's story based on press coverage.

Changing real-life stories for screenplays is far from new. In this case, however, I was compelled to think not simply about what details got taken out of the original idea but also what remain in the aesthetic compass of the production but are sidelined by the narrative flow. The push and pull of details in Gauri Shinde's narrative drew me with some libidinal force to the scenes left behind by the teleological drive of *English Vinglish*. As discussed above, early episodes depict Sashi as a middle-age woman in daily cotton wear being independently mobile and entrepreneurial in her own locality, prior to becoming blended into a brand definition of Indian female progress. Staged on and around the body of female star Sridevi, these contextual details acquire their own stylish exhibition of female competence. Do we see here conflicting ways in which the realistic arts of portraying localities and female life-space evolve in niche Bollywood fiction films? Should these be read, then, for a deeply multilayered practice of *transborder realism*—on the one hand, for the way women directors laboriously negotiate brands of gender fiction and resolve spatiotemporal contradictions as needed; on the other, for those ethnographic bits that by exhibiting familiar femaleness and community space as fields of action *remain apart* from the coherent geography of the nation-brand narrative?[15]

Detailed research on how diverse women laboriously negotiate creative and entrepreneurial opportunities within the quickly expanding scale of the Bollywood cinema lies much beyond the scope of this book. My modest attempt in this chapter has been to situate two generations of Hindi female authorship in relation to infrastructures of support. I have noted that a large-scale nationalization of the Bombay-based Hindi film industry, expedited by the mobility of resources and personnel brought about by the India-Pakistan partition, has evolved into a state-supported Bollywood that entrenches patriarchal privilege. In this context, female authors (including directors and scriptwriters) emerge through forging multi-scalar connections with new state-sponsored and global/multinational media networks, being especially enabled by waves of realistic cinema that call voices or fictions of "real" Indian women into national discourse. I have argued that the two prominent cohorts of Hindi filmmakers—in the 1980s and the 2000s—constitutively differ in the modes of female authorship. Born of a discursive context of feminist debates, female authorship of mainstream filmic realism in the 1980s exposes the gendered divisions between bodies and spaces and yet renders them coeval in Indian filmic fantasy. By contrast, women's realistic fictions of femaleness and gender in the 2000s, aiming to create niche brands of Indianness, tend to aggregate details and suppress spatiotemporal difference. Still, dissident female perspectives might be found in the disjunctive details of Bollywood brand authorship. Since women's participation in the Hindi filmic field has been historically conditioned by patriarchal national and multinational infrastructures, however, the locus of decisions and resources tends to always supersede female creative entrepreneurship.

The next chapter turns to a collaborative female practice of small-scale cinema that moved *transnationally* for resources—crossing statist borders of geography, ethnicity, religion, and legality (even though they were legally registered productions). This history of pirate mode authorship shows how a women's cinema driven by the losses and rifts caused in this postcolonial region through partitions—the 1971 devastation birthing Bangladesh in this case—could thrive on bridging borders.

PART III

Familial Modes and Scales of Transnational Crossing

5

Families Out of Bounds

The Pirate Mode and
Women's Coproductions
across Pakistan and Bangladesh

The previous parts of this book have examined women-made social films in reference to national frameworks of politics and media. The concluding part explores how infrastructures of media relate to transnational cinema made by women in the region of northern South Asia. The "transnational" is understood as cinema whose scope of imagery and resource crosses territories and unsettles boundary formation. All case studies in this part demonstrate that global networks of media enable deterritorial movements of imagination and resource. A deterritorial dynamic of comprehending the divided region through filmmaking seems to give new life to the family-centric social film. In women's cinema, female-centered family drama becomes the emotional grid on which collective social experiences of dismemberment, displacement, and cross-border kinship are configured in generic forms. Likewise, the transnational mode of production seeks resources and audiences across state borders and normative nationalisms—whether these are legal, linguistic, religious, or geographic. However, deterritorial processes invariably run up against the borderly limits that are innate to postcolonial conflict in the region. As such, mediatized pathways to filmmaking constitute the paradoxical transborder grounds on which female authors negotiate creative claims. The chapters in this concluding part combine to further examine the somewhat counterintuitive argument being developed by this book: that the extent of heterogeneity in women's transnational cinema is complexly related to the scale at which the production is resourced, exhibited, and legitimized on media platforms.

This chapter studies selected works from a previously neglected archive of small-scale coproductions led by female film performers and entrepreneurs in the 1980s and 1990s. My cases in point are two Urdu action-heroine melodramas and a Bangla version of the same: *Miss Colombo*, an Urdu work directed by Pakistani star Shamim Ara and coproduced with star-producer Sabita from Sri Lanka in 1984; *Lady Smuggler*, another Urdu work directed by Shamim Ara, coproduced with the Bangladeshi star Babita, and released in Pakistan in 1987; and a print of *Lady Smuggler* dubbed in Bangla, released in Bangladesh in 1990 by coproducer Babita. These transnational productions are compelling for the traces they carry of a sexually paradoxical practice of filmmaking helmed by the star-authors Shamim Ara and Babita. The practice unfolds in contradictory ways in the filmic texts and across extratextual spaces of (cross-border) production and (domestic) publicity. It is irreducibly transborder in the spatial ambiguities it deploys and inhabits.

On the one hand, we find hybrid movements of images and people that breach borderly concepts of territory and gender on both sides of the camera. Multiple regional sites and performing arts—shot on location—are dynamically mixed with female and gender-queered action pitted against masculinist violence and statist injustice. Further, aggression is inexplicably tempered in these women-made action films with an expressive aura of female kin-making that bridges national divides or heals violence against minorities. Behind-the-scenes photographs found from private archives complement oral accounts given to me by crew members and industry observers to illuminate a production process that routinely crossed national borders. It thrived through familial collaborations contingent on commonalities of habits, languages, and small-scale business interests. On the other hand, we find the star-authors engaging in ambivalent performances of persona to promote desire for the films themselves as well as for the concept of women's companies moving beyond national culture. As discussed in previous chapters (2 and 3), both Babita and Shamim Ara personified bourgeois national values to mediatized publics in Bangladesh and Pakistan, respectively. As star-filmmakers of coproductions, we find both women attempting to generate infrastructures of desire (and potential revenue) by performatively quelling middle-class nationalist anxieties around the particular mode of filmmaking in which they were engaged. The transnational mode was parasitic on the new media field of video trade and, hence, stigmatized by association with the illicit surge of piracy. As explained by Brian Larkin, infrastructures of media piracy are inexorably deterritorial. They generate a "mode of spatiality" that, by linking diverse social imaginations, fosters persistently hybrid spatial practice (2008, 240). This chapter demonstrates that such female star-practitioners as Shamim Ara and Babita inhabited the spatial ambiguities in middle-class public yearnings for entertainment in this video age by engaging in a transborder mode of pirate cinema. While the mode of production dwelled and innovated within pirate infrastructures, star-authors at the helm took on dutiful promotional roles as national border guards of their products. Yet, the duty-bound performances were far from teleological. They were, in fact, legitimizing desire for a collaborative women's cinema that roved "out of bounds," encompassing the labors of different hands and bodies.

Later sections of this chapter plot the traces of this pirate mode of collaborative cinema as they loop through filmic conventions to extratextual practices of production and publicity. To get there, I contextualize the way I pieced together the archive explored in this chapter and my challenges in doing so. No available account of cross-regional collaborations pays serious attention to the repertoire of border-crossing cinema that accompanied video piracy in 1980s South Asia. Thus, I was driven to read women's productions for how they remain inadequate to the available accounts. My attempt was to consider which historical presuppositions about regional borders or film production might account for the "disjointed . . . remainders" (Derrida and Prenowitz 1995, 24, 45). The importance of reading aesthetic conventions intersubjectively, as an assemblage of disjointed contents that push back readings or impel me to make extratextual connections, came home to me in the process. As I pieced together degraded quality images from pirated VCDs (Video CDs, similar to DVDs) as well as fugitive sources from digitized ephemera (e.g., YouTube) and periodical gossip columns, I also learned to think about the disjointed parts that did not to fit into any neat explanation. I began to consider how such tidbits could rupture the archives we assemble and also lead us to ask where else we could find clues.

Coproductions and a Pirate Mode of Women's Cinema: Contexts

Historians of small industries in South Asia do note a rush of low-budget multi-star coproductions crossing borders from the late 1970s through the 1990s. Abdullah Ziad and Mushtaq Gazdar, studying Bangladesh and Pakistan, respectively, concur that artists and production companies moved beyond national borders to collaborate and shoot on multiple locations, working across religious, linguistic, and ethnic differences. Coproductions by multi-sited entrepreneurs also meant that the films dubbed in local languages were released to audiences across countries (Ziad 2010, 261; Gazdar 1997, 205–218), even though their primary frame of reference tended to be that of the countries where the principal producers and directors were located. Recurrent in these descriptions of coproduction are stories of the leading roles taken by women, including female stars, production company owners, and tour entrepreneurs. Discussing the spate of cross-regional stars and multilocation shoots in the Pakistani culture, for example, Mushtaq Gazdar points to Shamim Ara's heroine fiction films *Playboy* (1978; coproduced and shot in London) and *Miss Hong Kong* (shot in Hong Kong) as early successes (1997, 162, 178). Laleen Jayamanne points out that the multi-sited infrastructures for filmmaking were supported by female stars from Sri Lanka. Jayamanne discusses the agency of Anoja Weerasinghe, who acted in Pakistani commercial cinema while striving to preserve the local Sri Lankan film industry (2001, 124). We find another Sri Lankan female star by the name of Sabita growing to be a steady collaborator of Shamim Ara's Pakistan-based company. Even more significant for the scope of this book is Abdullah Ziad's account of how Bangladeshi star-producer Babita flourished as a star in Pakistan to the extent of winning a national award in the late 1980s (2010, 260). We learn that she not only coproduced and starred in the Urdu film *Lady Smuggler* but that she also led the release of the dubbed Bangla version of the film in Bangladesh through her own company. Note that this coproduction followed the bloodbathed war leading to the birth of Bangladesh out of East Pakistan in 1971.

Accounts of these transnational successes of artists, entrepreneurs, and film prints agree on at least two counts. They detect an instrumental and expedient attitude in the efforts to reach across borders for finding new sensations or "plagiarizing" attractions (Kabir 1979). Gazdar argues that film entrepreneurs from Lahore were "compelled" to seek beyond national borders for geographic and star glamour in order to stem a decline in the film business and manage rising production costs through incorporating the "freshness . . . of new locations and faces" (1997, 205). Likewise, Abdullah Ziad avers that Bangladeshi film producers were driven to collaboration by a poor market and the dearth of stars (2010, 260). The point is well taken, no doubt. Small-scale companies in both Pakistan and Bangladesh were attempting to build infrastructures for production and exhibition by reclaiming markets lost through the genocidal partition of Pakistan and Bangladesh and by finding new markets (in Sri Lanka and Nepal, for example). The geopolitical division of markets and resources was further compounded, as we know, by illegal trade in pirated videos of popular films flowing in from India and elsewhere. Thus, the attempt to develop new infrastructures through coproduction was instrumental to the need felt by small-scale entrepreneurs to compete with the regional video piracy market. What characterizes the aforementioned narratives about this small-scale transnational wave, however, is a reductive assumption of territorial closure. The narratives ride on the concept of expedient native capital out to exploit the exotic freshness of regional resources. Presupposing a "borderly limit" in the very system of collaborative productions, they foreclose a reading for codes and practices that disjoin from borders or forge solidarity in the breach (Derrida 1993, 18). The foreclosure is especially blinding for an excavation of small-scale transnationalism *within* South Asia, a region fraught with postcolonial upheavals and nationalist divides. It precludes, for example, serious analysis of how coproductions like *Lady Smuggler* were bridging the partitions of a once-indivisible artistic region (Jalal 2017) or what role creative entrepreneurs took in revivifying commonalities. The Urdu production was born of active collaboration between Bangladeshi and Pakistani cast and crew after the partition of 1971, and the version dubbed in Bangla was exhibited in a post–Liberation War Bangladesh wherein Urdu/Pakistan functioned as an "undisputable symbol of alterity" (Hoek 2015, 144). Since the independence of Bangladesh in 1971, the domestic Bangla film market had been protected by a law banning theatrical exhibition of all regional cinemas, especially Urdu and Hindi (Raju 2015, 154–155).

Recent film scholarship takes important strides in critiquing impulses to territorialize archives and exclude difference. Salma Siddique, in her exploration of archiving practices in Pakistan, studies the fact that the partition of Bangladesh and Pakistan is typically perceived by unofficial archivists as having a "lacerating effect" on the film industry (2019, 203). Examining the official Bangladesh Film Archive, Lotte Hoek similarly notes that the "political watershed of 1971 limits the possibilities of excavating the past of Bangladeshi cinema" (2015, 101). Emphasizing the leaks in archival amnesia, Hoek goes on to explore cross-lingual collaboration in the making of Urdu cinema by Bengalis in East Pakistan both before and after 1971 in Lahore (2016).[1] This chapter is indebted to these critical explorations of archival exclusion and forgotten traces of regional collaboration. However, no approach at hand offers a way into archives of popular *post-partition* cinema in South Asia, which might function in a deterritorial mode or even heal regional lacerations through familial business practice.

Certain aspects of Abdullah Ziad's description of Bangladeshi coproductions were the first to clue me in on the specific mode of transnational cinema I was looking at. Ziad emphasizes that these productions were prone to "*āin ke langhan*" (law violations) (2010, 260–261). He is referring to violations of the culture protectionist law of 1984 that required coproducers to deploy significant numbers of Bangladeshi locations, artists, and resources from the state-backed Film Development Corporation of Dhaka. The goal, overall, was to ensure that the *bhābmurti* (essential form) of the nation is projected onscreen. Coproductions had burgeoned in Bangladesh with the expansion of private entrepreneurship and small film business under the bureaucratic-military regime of General Ziaur Rahman (Raju 2015, 152–160). They shared entrepreneurial space with small-scale local productions such as *Tin Konna* (studied in chapter 2). However, multilocation productions drew additional support from state-sanctioned structures for international video trade, in place from 1979 and 1980 (Raju 2015, 156, 148). By the early 1980s, respectable Bangla film periodicals like *Chitrali* report that the glamour of "color films picturized on foreign locations" was captivating urban audiences in Dhaka (H. De 1982, 57). Since they belonged to the state-sanctioned realm of globalizing media, coproductions were subjected to the measures for Bangla culture protection noted above. Yet coproductions, according to Ziad, typically transgressed codes and dwelled in the *abaidha* breach (2010, 261–262). The Bengali word "abaidha" means illicit in both legal and sexual senses. Most revealing is the fact that the same two accusations—transgression of nation space and of licit entertainment—appear in the strident tone of yellow journalism in Urdu film periodicals published in Pakistan in the 1980s. An article in *Film Asia* titled "Why Don't Our Film Heroes Have a Goal?" alleges that these days (Urdu) cinema fails to recognize "which world does it belong to, and which characters are the sons of its own soil [*kaun sī duniyā us kī apnī duniyā hai aur kaun se kirdār us kī apnī dhartī ke beṭe haiñ*]" (1989, 1). This uprooting from native locales and traditions means that makers of coproductions "lose sight of any political responsibility [*kisī siyāsī zimmedārī ke pāband nahīñ*]." Irresponsible political behavior seems to be understood in this article as a forsaking not only of geographic boundaries and national roots but also of authentic moral roots. For, the author soon proceeds to deplore, in colorful terms, a "lecherous new culture" (*lachariyat kā nayā kalchar*) that pervades the songs and music of contemporary Pakistani cinema (2). Sexually paradoxical negotiations of aesthetic practice and publicity discourse to be found in the transnational work of Babita and Shamim Ara must be situated in these contexts of masculine territorial anxiety.

A precise picture of the spatial logic of transnational coproductions from this era finally came to me from a less deprecating report on coproductions published in 1987 by the state-sponsored volume *From Colourless to Colourful: Platinum Jubilee Film Directory 1913–1987* (discussed also in chapter 3; henceforth, *Film Directory*). This article and others in the *Film Directory* reveal that conditions for coproduction in the globalizing state of Zia-ul-Haq differed from Bangladesh. No Pakistani law governed coproductions per se nor explicitly protected national culture. According to the unnamed author of the report, coproductions had risen in Pakistan because "with the wild expansion of video piracy, the cinemagoers wanted extraordinary gimmicks, new exotic locations, fresh faces and high adventures on the wide screen . . . [so that] the filmmakers had little choice but to go [on similar routes]" (1987, 42). Although this account pits "wide screen" Pakistani cinema against video piracy of imported films, the "Censor Bureau Chief's Report on Film," written by Chairman Abdur Rashid in the same *Film Directory*, clarifies that at least by the 1980s all Pakistani films and imported videos were being speedily pirated and exhibited via uncontrollable routes. Pirate infrastructures of low-cost reproduction were, of course, widespread across South Asia by the 1980s. Kuhu Tanvir (2013) and Ravi Sundaram (2009) have studied the Indian context. In both Pakistan and Bangladesh, infrastructures of national cinema at this time were turning into transnational media economies far less officially organized than illegal in the routes. Video and satellite networks, having arrived in both countries in the 1970s, had produced a layering of media routes best characterized as the official "structural conditions" setting in motion an infrastructure of piracy (Larkin 2008, 210–220). In Pakistan, the infrastructure included reproduction and exhibition. According to Abdur Rashid, the Islamabad Censor Board's very structure of processing Pakistani films, through the submission of a video copy, had been accused of "leaking videos," some of which were being exhibited uncensored at wayside teahouses at very low rates (1987, 61). Abdullah Ziad's description of abaidha traffic in transnational media possibly refers to similar practices in Bangladesh. Note, however, that the *Film Directory* report on coproductions in Pakistan is saying not merely that these films proliferate along the infrastructures of video piracy. The main import I take from the report is that piracy had given birth to a *mode* of filmmaking that adapted the "wild" pirate logic of mobility beyond national and normative bounds. In other words, the pirate mode of filmmaking is best thought of as sprouting within a larger media ecology of film piracy.

Debashree Mukherjee explains that media ecology "is an organic, dynamic assemblage with permeable boundaries, dependent on the continuous exchange of energies between its constituents" (2020a, 19). In this relational environment, rational and adaptive choices are inextricable. Mukherjee's formulation of commercial filmmaking in South Asia as a dynamic ecology of exchanges between constituent bodies is more or less apropos of all the cases studied in this book. It shines light on the various ways women's cinema is spawned from existing social film genres and resource structures. Especially helpful for thinking of the pirate mode of cinema, in my view, is Mukherjee's argument that the fluidity of media ecologies could exceed the capitalist "systematization of bodies" (19). In this light, scholarship on the under-capitalized business of film piracy run by specialists in South Asia becomes relevant. Exploring the "black market archive" in Pakistan, for example, Timothy Cooper points to the many innovative personnel who specialize in the globally poised media work of film piracy. These specialists thrive with a quite unsystematic "spirit of self-determination . . . [on] the margins of technological legality" (2015, 207). Although Cooper speaks of illegal video trade rather than filmmaking, this study of video piracy in Pakistan reveals an incompletely capitalized infrastructure of deterritorial media held in place by many specialized hands. It seems to me that the report on coproductions published by the 1987 *Film Directory* points to piracy infrastructures as constituting a permeable environment within which small-scale film specialists *as well* were innovating their transnational motion pictures with a similarly unsystematic energy of self-determination.

Taking my cue from this insightful report, I turn to the filmic contents of *Miss Colombo* and *Lady Smuggler* for traces of a pirate mode creativity. I first saw these works on low-quality, hand-labeled VCDs given to me by Syed Hafeez Ahmed, associate director of *Lady Smuggler* and a close colleague of the late director and producer Shamim Ara. Since then, I have found similar degraded-quality copies streaming on YouTube, including a Bangla version of *Lady Smuggler* that is identical to the Urdu print whose copy I possess (an important point to which I return later in this chapter). I anchor my reading on filmic contents and referents while attempting to also account for related objects (film posters, press reports and photographs, archival photographs and oral accounts, online databases), some of which are contradictory and fugitive. Then what traces do these contents suggest of what I call a pirate mode creativity?

At a glance, *Miss Colombo* and *Lady Smuggler* look like pirate texts in the visible marks they carry of a hybrid spatiality linking social and physical geographies. These textual assemblages clearly have been worked on in different locations by many hands and bodies. The spectacular locations range from tropical forests and Catholic monasteries in Sri Lanka to verdant riverbanks and ominous prison gates in the Philippines. The skills of a Pakistani *mujrā* (courtesan) dancer and a gender-queering comedian (*bhānd*) alternate with the specialized moves and costumes of Philippine "tribal" dancers. In these aesthetic contents, I find the traces of a pirate mode authorship that fosters exchange between different regional artists and repertoires, suggesting that reciprocal business relations were being forged by creative entrepreneurs. I elaborate later that the pirate mode of production had given a new lease on transnational life to the South Asian business practice of forging familial networks among heterogeneous specialists, typical to undercapitalized film-making in South Asia. However, the complication in these aesthetic traces of spatial migration is that they are ambiguous, for the hybridity is *not* additive. Instead, the expressive codes in particular seem historically dynamic insofar as they mobilize against separatist violence or forge female-prone kinship across differences. The codes could be seen to comprise what Priya Jaikumar terms a "second act" of hybridity, a transnational reckoning with the gendered horrors of South Asian history (2017, 239). I maintain that the inexplicable historical dynamism in these hybrid conventions is traceable to permeation through the environment of video piracy. These archival traces of a female-focused practice suggest which infrastructures of piracy the works have moved through and displaced and which they have inhabited and more fully flourished within.

Take, for example, *Miss Colombo*, coproduced and directed by Shamim Ara from Pakistan and pronounced to have been a "success" on local grounds (Film Directory 1987, 42). The spectacles of tropical forests, performing animals, or ethnic song and dance call out tropes from Indian, American, and Hong Kong screens as well as Sri Lankan advertisements from their various commodity lines of cinema and tourism into timely history. These are turned into "sociocultural trigger points" (Jaikumar 2017, 226) for emotional interaction with an Islamizing Pakistan state caught in the grips of violence on minorities (Toor 2011). In addition, the profuse imagery of female homosocial interdependencies in *Lady Smuggler* makes me attentive to how patriarchal narrative and visual devices at the same time are borrowed *and* expressively displaced. A number of these devices are reproduced from contemporary Indian action-hero films starring Amitabh Bachchan or from action-heroine imagery found on Hollywood film and American television screens (as well as Hong Kong martial arts films, as discussed in chapter 3). Clearly, the women-made images were thriving on the infrastructure of *reproduction,* the key to piracy. The doubling on the Indian action-hero genre, for one, reveals that Shamim Ara's Urdu productions sought to claim the same middle-class audiences in urban Pakistan who consumed pirated videos of Hindi films. The Urdu practice of doubling on Hindi film tropes itself has a complex genealogy, rooted in the "affect of truncation in the psyche of the generation of filmmakers" creating Urdu cinema in the decade after the India-Pakistan partition (Dadi 2022, 17). The Shamim Ara Urdu social films were engendered in hybrid form under new conditions of state development in Pakistan. What gets displaced in this repertoire counts as a trace of female-prone pirate creativity. Codes of patriarchy and nationalism found from the Hindi action-hero genre, for example, are refused reproduction. Another set of negotiations surround the reproducibility of neoliberal Western action-heroine imagery in relation to non-liberal modernity. The ambivalent refusals suggest to me that the Shamim Ara action-heroine films were flourishing along another infrastructure of piracy replete with desires and distastes that partially clashed with the borrowed attractions, albeit calling for innovations around the same familiar conventions. This piracy infrastructure of video *circulation* was inhabited by female and middle-class consumers across urban strata, now able to access inexpensive entertainment in the seclusion of homes or women-only spaces.

I have discussed at length in chapters 2 and 3 that while in the 1980s women's work and consumer cultures expanded apace in both Pakistan and Bangladesh, the expansion brought with it sexual tensions and censorial brutalities. In Pakistan we find the brutally Islamizing military dictatorship of Zia-ul-Haq accompanying the Afghan War and illegal traffic of war and drugs in the region (Gazdar 1997, 152–156). In Bangladesh we find an Islamizing military bureaucracy dense with everyday insecurities being run by generals Ziaur Rahman and, subsequently, Hussain Muhammad Ershad (Van Schendel 2009, 193, 252). Under these conditions, domestic or secluded circuits of film exhibition enabled by video trade and piracy were especially inviting to women and, indeed, middle-class consumers in general. The second-order hybridity found in the heroine texts in question make sense if seen in mimetic relation to the energies and contradictions being experienced by the target consumers. Overall, the historical dynamism in the filmic conventions to be discussed next is best situated at a particular site of media permeation. At this site, pirate infrastructures of reproduction and consumption crosshatch a pirate mode of female-oriented authorship helmed by self-determining women entrepreneurs. The small-scale female authors, through bodily and familial work, collaborate across different geographies and skillful performer pools, assembling innovative energies.

Multireligious Families, Phallic Violence, and the Caring Touch: *Miss Colombo*

Miss Colombo begins with the death of the birth father and the destruction of an ideal Pakistani family living in Sri Lanka at the hands of a Pakistani drug lord by the name of Black Eagle. After managing to escape from the clutches of the villainous drug lord, the orphaned children find nurturance from a strikingly heterogeneous cast of other parents. Son Salman is adopted by a bumbling restaurant owner who is a traditional turban-wearing Sikh man speaking largely in rustic Punjabi. The young daughter, on the other hand, is raised as "Bela" by the Mother Superior and inhabitants of a Catholic convent. There, she finds a parental companion in the shape of a gigantic elephant named Sabu. Location shoots and screen arts tracing the fluid migration of the product across geographic and ethnic boundaries seem at first glance to erase borders and difference. The assessment by historians that these transnational productions were out to exoticize the freshness of regional locations seems apropos. Salman lapses into either slapstick imitations of his adoptive Sikh father, invoking tropes from a Punjabi Sikh comedy common to Pakistani television and theater, or song-and-dance performances down picturesque Sri Lankan landscapes in the company of girlfriend Rosie (played by the Sri Lankan star-producer Sabita). Once she acquires her own boyfriend, we see heroine Bela (Babra Sharif) also lapsing into couple or group dances in exotic Sri Lankan costumes. Probably encoding the hands of local tour operators and animal trainers, the spectacles include lush forests and a she-Tarzan-like Bela riding on elephant Sabu. These hybrid spectacles, calling out local and global repertoires of cinema and tourism, clearly attempt to reproduce pirated video attractions. The agential decision seems to be to turn the screen into a site for advertising action-adventure films and tourism. In this vein, glamorous Bela guides the viewer's eye by operating a tour business to support the Catholic convent through performing elephant shows in front of camera-clicking travelers. However, a closer look at the codes, seen as an archive of practice, suggests that the journey down the pirate path of film reproduction is more complexly agentive. It is, in fact, replete with refusals and innovative negotiations.

Scripted by the veteran Urdu screenwriter Syed Noor in collaboration with Shamim Ara, the thin narrative of *Miss Colombo* obviously borrows devices from the Hindi action-hero genre being widely marketed at the time. The resemblance with *Amar Akbar Anthony*, starring Amitabh Bachchan, is clear. Tropes such as "the dismemberment of the family" (Vitali 2008, 208), villainous drug dealers, and adoptions cutting across religious lines are visibly reproduced. What is *refused*, though, is the teleology of a Bachchan-style family drama that ends with the restoration of couple-form patriarchy, "calling women back to the house" (211), and of Hindu motherhood qua nation. Another familial form of social film takes shape in which female heroes take action in the absence or debilitation of honorable patriarchs while parental protectors reach across religious borders to nurture and sustain the orphaned. Action-heroine imagery begins to double on Western codes pirated from American television serials and Hollywood cinema. Even though the Western imagery of self-propelling attractive women offers an eminently habitable infrastructure of reproduction for regional makers of action-heroine cinema, neoliberal contradictions in the available codes are innovatively reused and blocked.

As noted in chapter 2, early Hollywood action heroines display a euphoric and "curiosity-inducing" excitation that prepares the female body to keep pace with the stimuli of urban change (Singer 2001, 124). Readings of more recent action-heroine genres, such as Yvonne Tasker's (1993, 18–19) and Leon Hunt's (2007, 152), demonstrate that across historical contexts these gender-reversed demonstrations of female action present responses to women's aspirations for independent agency and accompanying contestations over the female body. Feminist scholars go on to emphasize what, in effect, is the neoliberal ambivalence at the heart of female action-avenger films—the phallic appeal of sexploitation. In both Hollywood film and American television, as elsewhere, the pleasures of gender role transgression are contained or inverted by traits of female weakening and vulnerability. Phallic excitement is stimulated through shot compositions of "the body [being] fatally penetrated" (Tasker 1993, 17–20) or through female pain being spectacularized in graphic rape scenes (Schubart 2007, 47). Images of successful working women and female technological prowess appear in a similar euphoric vein in the Pakistani and Bangladeshi action-heroine films studied in this chapter and elsewhere in this book (chapters 2 and 3). In *Miss Colombo*, for example, we find the she-Tarzan image of tour operator Bela, whereas in *Lady Smuggler* we encounter motorbike drivers and gun swingers evoking the stimuli of women's adaptation to change. Not unlike its Western precedents, the freewheeling body of the Pakistani action heroine is invaded by phallic aggression and violently weakened. The ambivalent innovation in the Shamim Ara action-heroine films, at odds with the global influences of this video age, is that they also appear to stem the stimuli of gender violence through tactile codes of feminine and parental care work. The phallic appeal of action heroism is concurrently inhabited and paradoxically refused.

In *Miss Colombo*, the physical freedom generic to Bela as a Western cross-dressed action heroine is relatively short-lived. Soon she is severely punished, implicitly censored, for her self-propulsion in public space. In her attempt to save the convent, her adoptive home, from the clutches of drug dealer Black Eagle, Bela locks in singlehanded battle against five or six of his hulky henchmen. Her body becomes flagrantly vulnerable to attack by a drove of men who deploy phallic whips to almost fatally penetrate her form, repeatedly flogging and maligning it to near death, only to be melodramatically counteracted by "other-parental" care surging in to rescue orphaned Bela. The mission's elephant, Sabu, leads the intervention. Embodying an androgynous parental force, Sabu crashes into the scene of flogging to rescue Bela and then to tenderly carry her limp body to a haven of tranquil rehabilitation deep in the heart of the forest. Soon a medium to close-range camera is tracking the elephant's legs and trunk as it hastens back and forth to tend to Bela's wounds and bring in therapeutic fruits and twigs. We see the static exoticism of tropical flora and fauna becoming an emotional trigger for the touch and feel of female pain and healing. Slowly, Bela revives and begins to await the return of Sabu's unfailing maternal touch. This reciprocal motion—of a nurturing touch and the clinging dependent—is best described as a fetish: a volatile image corresponding to "the materiality of its original scene" of maternal care work (Marks 2000, 92). A colorfully telling codification of this fetish is a close-up of a comfortably smiling Bela clad in red resting her cheek against the dark stability of Sabu's trunk.

What we are soon to realize is that Sabu's protective volatility is divinely motivated insofar as it responds to supplication by pious maternity. Sabu reappears at the head of a herd of warring elephants to break into the enclosure of gallows where action-heroine Bela and hero Salman as well as girlfriend Rosie and the Mother Superior of the convent are strung up. The action leads up to a final fight against Black Eagle and his gang. This Manichean melodrama pitting the virtuous Pakistani action figures against predatory Pakistani masculinity is catalyzed by a desperate prayer to Jesus Christ by the Mother Superior (Nayyar Sultana). Once more evoking the "close-up's fetish-like ability" to enliven face and voice (Marks 2000, 93), the camera zooms in on the nun in prayer (fig. 17). With desperate ardor, she is calling on Christ to "save the children"—that is, the youths Bela, Salman, and Rosie. The palpable quality of this supplication evokes many material scenes of Christian missionaries working as caregivers and educators of children and orphans in both Pakistan and Sri Lanka (the coproducing countries). In this vein, trading in the architecture of a Sri Lankan convent seems to stage a Pakistani way of striking what could be seen as "sentient reciprocations" (Taussig 1992, 72) with the topography of missionary work and religious life in Sri Lanka (the South Asian country with the highest number of Catholics and Protestants).

Fig. 17: Nayyar Sultana performing the Mother Superior's prayer (Source: *Miss Colombo*)

The series of close-ups depicting the gallows scene jump-cuts to a rapid montage of objects and icons in and around the mission's church. We see these coming to violent life and whirling around onscreen. Crucifixes fall from walls, a Virgin Mary figurine slides from the pedestal, and a cacophonic church bell refuses to come to rest. The tension building up through this montage of supernatural motion peaks as a bolt of lightning strikes Black Eagle, leaving him momentarily blind. The camera once again jump-cuts to Sabu at the head of a warring herd of elephants. As Sabu crashes into Black Eagle's enclosure, we see Bela turn toward her parental protector with utter childlike dependency. Soon thereafter it is Bela's turn to fulfill her filial obligation by tending to her wounded elephant parent and crying over the gigantic suffering body. The resolution of the melodramatic conflict, marked by the defeat of evil forces, is preceded, moreover, by one more intervention tellingly spearheaded by yet another pious parental figure. The bumbling Sikh man who had adopted Salman appears with the police at the scene of battle and then runs to grab his *kirpan* (dagger) and join the fray.[2] It is arguable that these minority stereotypes—caregiving missionary, comedic Sikh—have dual appeal for viewers. They function both as reproducible commodities, recycling through pirated and legal media, and as dynamic emissaries of emotional knowledge about the familial multireligious community. The knowledge, in effect, is being exchanged between filmmakers and audiences in Pakistan and across the bordered region. If we take what Jaikumar terms a "circuitous route" to these identities and hybrid locations through the changing formations of gender and religion in Pakistan (2017, 226), we are able to approach the forms and topoi as emotional trigger points for target audiences (for the scope of this book, I bracket discussion of audience address in Sri Lanka, where *Miss Colombo* was also exhibited). As noted earlier, the pirate infrastructure of video circulation, reaching middle-class homes and women consumers in urban Pakistan, must be seen to permeate the infrastructures of both reproduction and transnational collaboration in the media environment at hand.

The audiovisual performance of Bela's brutal humiliation at the hands of phallic men has dynamic historical immediacy, for the relentless lash of whips mimics the sonic agitation being experienced by Pakistani women in this context. It evokes women's fears about the Zia state-sanctioned practice of flogging and publicly degrading the female body for alleged sexual offenses ("On Flogging" 1984, 11). Such anxieties would have been acute for the many women consuming vernacular Urdu entertainment in this period because the cold war–backed economic boom was bringing more and more urban women from the middle to lower-middle classes into the workforce. While non-liberal pieties of the modest self and familial obligations had been voluntary to women's somatic practices and to the vernacular cultures of the middle classes in Pakistan, Zia's Islamization program had imposed a new set of borders around the female body. (These conditions have been discussed at length in chapter 3.) The codification of masculinist oppression is further compounded in *Miss Colombo* by the emotions it triggers against the rising violence against minorities, especially Christians, which were accompanying measures against blasphemy in the Zia state (Toor 2011, 157). By the time *Miss Colombo* was released, masculinist ideals of the pious (Sunni) Muslim family had come to mark the standard of a morally elevated Islamic civilization against which the putative licentiousness of Westernized consumerism was measured. Previously, religious minorities, including Western-clothed Christians, had coexisted with Muslims (Rouse 2004, 98). Now they began to be increasingly separated and policed, with blasphemy-related violence growing apace (Toor 2011, 157, 180–181).

The codes of melodramatic action animating *Miss Colombo* were shaped in the aesthetic field of an Urdu social genre that typically internalizes the "psychic costs" of institutional measures (Dadi 2016a, 487). In this video age, they comprehend minority violence in spatially hybrid ways. While the Manichean imagery stages the righteous anger of bodies and topoi surging against violence that scatters family and community life, it simultaneously tempers angry action. Customary feminine pleasures of reassembling the patriarchal family—conceived not as a dominant form but as weakened or comical—become the way to caring for the orphaned and vulnerable across religious and ethnic divides. In the process, seemingly marketable attractions found from Indian and American action-film piracy—respectively, the angry young patriarch and the sexually exploited action-heroine body—are refused a market. The refusals seem to speak to middle-class women consumers' non-liberal emotions in a violence-torn context like 1980s Pakistan, where both sexual censorship and brutality were widespread.[3] Tracing the expressive melodrama in *Miss Colombo* to extratextual processes, I am drawn to the possibility that infrastructures of female consumption and female-led transnational production permeate through both sides of the camera to produce aesthetic choices.

The ensemble-heroine Urdu film *Lady Smuggler*, coproduced by female stars from three South Asian countries, offers an even richer archive of how a pirate-mode textuality helmed by women produces female-friendly cinema in a hybrid form. Women performers overrun a text that queers the pleasures of outlaw action against patriarchal injustice while foregrounding female homosocial nurturance. Moreover, the production and publicity materials I was able to gather help me to plot the transmedial continuity of female authorship both within filmic significations and across extratextual spaces. The remaining sections of this chapter plot the paths of female authorship on and off the screen of *Lady Smuggler*.

Queer Action, Outlaw Justice, and Female-Friendly Desires: *Lady Smuggler*

The poster-booklet of the ensemble-heroine film *Lady Smuggler*, while it lists participants from three countries, emblazons Shamim Ara as the producer and director. Foregrounding the busy hybridity of the poster-booklet cover are faces of the three female stars from different countries, of whom Babita and Sabita were also coproducers (see fig. 18). The poster art clarifies the infrastructure of reproduction the work inhabits. By pirating the logo, the film explicitly doubles on the attractive female buddy action genre found in the American television serial *Charlie's Angels*. The text doubles on the male buddy genre typical to the Indian Hindi screen, borrowing many narrative devices and a few visual ones from the Hindi action-hero blockbuster *Sholay* (1975; dir. Ramesh Sippy). Even though *Lady Smuggler* reproduces these devices in the form of an Urdu *masala*/mixed-mode social action film, it is adamant in displacing a key aspect of the influential models: the centrality of male action and masculine command in the pursuit of justice. Not only are the righteous outlaw heroes of the Hindi genre rejected, but so is the disembodied mastermind Charlie directing his "angels."

All three heroine narratives in *Lady Smuggler* begin with standard patriarchal dramas of couple romance and paternal nurturance. However, they evolve into male violence and injustice. The three angry heroines finally meet in a Philippine prison cell because they were framed or misrecognized as drug smugglers. Claiming righteous indignation as a women's prerogative, the women strike a friendly pact to share their obligatory missions of vengeance and of rescue (of an abducted sister) by escaping from prison. Their anger is leveled not only against illegal but also lawful patriarchies, for the injustices inflicted by blindly righteous state representatives are shown to complement the terrorizing acts being committed by impure social entities such as international drug lords.

Fig. 18: Poster-booklet for the Urdu film *Lady Smuggler* featuring, on the right, bottom to top: Babita, Babra Sharif, Sabita, and comedian Rangila (Courtesy: Salman Carim)

What complicates the spectacular codes of female action against masculinist aggression is that they play not only on sadomasochistic appeal (to be expected in action films) but also on a ludic queerness replete with the mutuality of dancing and touching female and male bodies. Choreographed on the screen as an assembly of diverse regional arts and artists, the mutuality reveals traces of collaborative authorship.

Let us take as an example the narrative of the lead action heroine Momie, played by the Pakistani star Babra Sharif. It opens with medium-long takes tracking the mobility of yet another strong working woman along the line of Bela in *Miss Colombo*. We see snake farmer Momie in a white sleeveless blouse cruising in her motorboat. With a smile of confident freedom, colored by a montage of the blue lagoon against lush greenery, she effortlessly swoops her hand into the waters to grab up snakes for her pail. The liberal imagery of independent mobility and deportment is soon to be comically contained by her boyfriend's (Nepalese actor Shiva) head bobbing up next to the boat to remind her of the tryst she failed to keep. The frame is set for a narrative of bourgeois heterosexual coupling common to South Asian screens. In this instance, the couple romance is deferred not only by Momie's predictable refusal of the kiss, classic to the negotiation of companionate coupling on Hindi and other South Asian screens (Prasad 1998a, 88–104), but also by her non-liberal assertion of family commitment (she must stand by her elderly father and help to marry off her younger sister). Found notions of individual and companionate agency are deferred. Nonetheless, the scene is the pretext for a male-dominant companionate relationship leading to a typical couple-forming dance, influential from the Hindi genre for one. Yet, precisely the performance starts to dismantle the coherent masculine form.

The performance begins with panoramic long shots of an asynchronous ensemble of female and male figures in myriad colorful costumes and headgear presenting folk-dance moves from the Philippines and neighboring regions. If we follow the making of these shots behind the camera, we likely find the heterogeneous resources of Mary, the Filipina tour operator, who became a local coproducer of *Lady Smuggler* in the Philippines (more on this in the next section). What we find here, however, is not simply an addition of transnational gender color instrumental to competition with pirate media hybridity in this video age. The events come to be internalized by the semiotic form and inflected by gender. The community performance in a substantial sense is also a performance of a female-focused community. For one thing, it limits the form of heterosexualized couple dancing that is common to the Hindi screen, including to the blockbuster *Sholay*, upon which the narrative of *Lady Smuggler* doubled. Couple dancing on Hindi screens in that era, and in the present, invokes metaphors of male-dominant coital intimacy. For another thing, the juxtaposition of dancing bodies in the performance under discussion begins to comically unwind the coherent male form through contagious correspondences with feminizing moves.

Panoramic shots of ensemble folk dancing cut to medium range, showing a romantic couple performance of synchronous hand and leg movements. In this first frame and subsequent ones, Momie's skillful boldness and titillating curvature prevails over the movements of her partner. Performed by the talented mujrā dance virtuoso Babra Sharif, Momie executes the defiant hip and breast jiggles and writhes typical of the Pakistani version of the celluloid mujrā, or courtesan dance (A. Ahmad 2016b, 11). (Chapter 3 discusses at length the politics of the celluloid dance.) Provocative in this screen choreography is the mimicry by her male partner of Momie's hip and shoulder jiggles. The man's movements are repeatedly led by Momie/Babra Sharif's superior dancing skills into reproducing these feminine sexual motions together with her hand and leg loops. Beyond this, the euphoric femininizing of his movements comes to be accented time and again by decoupled formations. In more than one shot, we see the gyrating man performing at the forefront of female Filipina folk dancers rather than the few male folk dancers who also appear onscreen. There is little doubt that heterosexually arousing spectacles do appear, accompanying a wedding song playing on the soundtrack. For example, a momentary odalisque pose is struck by Momie and felt over by her partner. We catch a fleeting glimpse, shot at medium-long range, of his hands moving along her inclined form. However, these occasional shots pale in impact by comparison to the man's comically emasculating moves. What these provoke is the consumption of cinema as a physical experience—an experience driven by what Jennifer Bean characterizes, building on Walter Benjamin, as a "contagious movement that renders . . . porous the boundaries between inside and outside," subject and object (2002, 436). In this case, contagious cinema becomes the aesthetic way in to the mutual relations of a group in which women decide the moves and contain phallic dominance. This inexplicable inversion of found conventions of the heteromasculine couple dance creates a happy spectacle of *female-prone sociability*. This curiously sociable spectacle calls on me to look more closely at the energies and voices behind the camera.

Being choreographed through a reflexive juxtaposition of male with sexy female moves is a softening down of erect phallic musculature in favor of the physical dexterity of the dancing woman to turn action heroine. The viewer is being affectively conditioned to expect the narrative role of this hero as a secondary action figure—one who will fail to control and conquer the phallic prowess of the arch villain so that the battle has to be taken over by the action heroine. Soon enough, a dwindling of bourgeois domestic patriarchy begins entwining with that of state patriarchy. While her father is killed and sister abducted by the arch villain/drug lord of the narrative, Momie is mistaken by an unrelenting police force to be a smuggler and hurled into prison. Thereafter, the plot arrests Momie's heterosexual romance. Her boyfriend, himself a policeman, embarks on his righteous pursuit of the unruly woman (despite initial doubt) when Momie escapes from prison. This temporality of law and order is only a minor strand, however, subordinated to that of escape and female ensemble vengeance. Leading up to the escape is another euphoric performance that turns vicious in its ludic inversion of gender behavior.

Wide-angle frames capture a women-only prison yard where Momie frolics with newfound female friends, the other two heroines also betrayed and set up as smugglers. We now see the other two female star-coproducers of *Lady Smuggler*—Babita and Sabita—showcased alongside Babra Sharif, Shamim Ara's lead heroine and "lucky star" (as phrased by the director-producer herself; see below). In this powerful evocation of female interdependency, I see a trace of the production practice of women's collaborations that lay behind the small-scale transnational wave in 1980s South Asia. Note that a still from the prison yard scene showcasing the three friendly heroines appears in a Bangla periodical to promote the release of *Lady Smuggler* in Bangladesh in 1990.

The still lends sentient support to a photograph of coproducer Babita busily collaborating with elder sister Shuchanda in preparing banners for the release. Returning to the prison yard, the three smiling women are taking exhilarated turns and twists as they lip-sync a song of *dosti* (friendship). They sing of how *terā dushman* has become *merā dushman* (your villainous enemy has become my enemy); of being together in life and death; of the *va 'ada* (promise) never to be forgotten. Medium long shots cut to medium close-ups as the camera follows the euphoric abandon of interdependent homosocial desire and as it lingers on the female bodies moving together and caressing one another.

Then the camera has pulled back to frame a field full of women prisoners moving and circling in synergy around the three friends. This harmonious collective of women, enervated by the jubilation of female dosti, has displaced earlier scenes in which the inmates of this women's prison randomly attacked one another in frustration. The montage is dialectically juxtaposed, however. Menacing images of rifle-bearing guards, dark phallic shapes that stand tall upon the prison walls, frame the dance of female friendship and bear down upon its bright feminine spaces—but only so to be rendered inert. The heroines are shown at medium close-up intermixing with careless mockery between the erect guns and hardened musculature. Look and frame are consistently frontal, with the three dancers breaking the invisible fourth wall to evoke a female address.

The camera pans to show the prison gate being held open. Enter the prison warden, Rangila Jailer, played by the eponymous comedian. The trailblazer of gender-queer artistry drawing on the regional tradition of bhānd comedy, Rangila was a "polysexual" male comic performer who had directed a drag comedy titled *Aurat Raj* (Women's Rule) in 1979 (A. Ahmad 2016a, 472; chapter 3 discusses at length the arts of bhānd comedy current in Pakistan). In this instance, the stocky bhānd in uniform is hurrying and tripping, Charlie Chaplin–style, until he arrives center-frame. He whips out a phallic cigarette and turns an exaggerated glare upon the dancing heroines. Then shot-reverse-shot shows him at close range looking and beginning to twitch in uncontrollable mimicry, breaking and curving up his militarized musculature. A montage contraposes his curvy jerks with the sightless immobility of the uniformed prison guards. We view a compelling adaptation of mimetic reflexivity from Chaplin-style early comic cinema, the staging of what Bean describes as a "tactile, performative, sensuous form of perception" bringing the viewer into intimate contact with his object (Bean 2002, 436). The implication of performing tactile perception in this context is profoundly unsettling, however. It undoes the proprieties of pious-looking relations, propagating in contemporary Pakistan through Zia-ul-Haq's measures against obscene propensities that putatively violated modesty (discussed earlier in this chapter and in chapter 3). Since from this perspective the male gaze is understood as tactile rather than voyeuristic (Mottahedeh 2008, 9), men are seen as prone to be "masochistic" (Naficy 2012, 106–107) in looking and effectively engaging in illicit intercourse (*zina*) if they look at non-family women without a proper "visual shield" (Mottahedeh 2008, 9). Rangila's performance of tactile perception is playing precisely upon these masochistic anxieties. He performs the masochistic man prone to gaze into a secluded female homosocial space (in this instance, the women's prison yard) such that he implicitly touches the frolicking women and loses his militarized masculine resolve. Soon enough, he is surrounded by the three dancing heroines, who further entice his body to catch the contagion of jiggly moves.

Having let down his sexual guard, Rangila Jailer visibly unravels phallic identity. In this way, he has forfeited his symbolic guardianship of (unjust) state discipline and paved the women's way to a lawless fight for justice. Taking Rangila Jailer as hostage, the three women prisoners steal a truck and escape. As the stolen truck pulls away from the prison gate, we hear Rangila's enamored voice asking in a self-indulgent tone, "Where do you take me, my pretty ones [*hasīna*]?" The episode leads up to Rangila Jailer being brought by the women to a deserted field, where he is to be abandoned. With a ridicule turned vicious, the cross-gendered action heroines stand firm and erect in their masculine clothing, framed as towering over the stooping form of the elderly man. They compel him to pull a heavy cart in place of the horse. For a while, Rangila evasively bumbles around. With a snatch of song and an emasculated grin of supplication, he is improvising as the typically gender-fluid bhānd (Pamment 2017, 5–9). We hear him plead with the heroines to stop their tyranny upon his *nāzuk* (fragile) body. In this ludic vein, the action heroines confront the violence of an unjust patriarchal legal system, of policing and incarceration, and turn the tables on the militarized state representative, a prison warden in uniform.

The ludic performance of cross-gender play soon transforms into a violent one. The heroines' anger against systemic tyranny leads into intense confrontations as the three exact revenge on the enemies who have destroyed their families and lives. The climax is a prolonged slasher sequence that locks heroine Momie in mortal combat with arch opponent Mashiyar—played by the leading villain of Urdu and Punjabi screens, Humayun Qureshi. Shot in Hollywood-style slow motion, this sequence is overrun with what Carol Clover characterizes as sadomasochistic "bodily sensations . . . [that invite] cross-gender identification" through a sharing of masculine aggression and the reducing of male bodies to abject emasculation (1987, 215); see also my discussion of *Miss Hong Kong* in chapter 3. In these hybrid performances by male and female specialists (such as Rangila, Babra, and others), we see how local (bhānd) and global (Hollywood) genres entwine in an innovative play with hierarchies of gender and state in the transnational action-heroine films generated by a piracy environment.

Along these lines, affect has shifted again in the closing shots of *Lady Smuggler*. The soundtrack picks up the song of dosti as we see the prostrated and blood-bathed bodies of the three heroines, who have triumphed over Mashiyar and his gang at the cost of their own lives. High-angle shots cut to long takes at close-up as the camera hovers over each woman's face. These separated takes seem oriented to the multiple audiences of this coproduction—in Pakistan, Bangladesh, and Sri Lanka—and to the desires to gaze upon the local star. However, long takes are soon replaced by tracking shots. We see the three female friends inching closer together with gentle hints of smiles. Their extended hands begin to touch and caress one another in a quintessentially loving union as their bodies sink into death.

Tropes of female homosocial friendship, as Kamran Asdar Ali demonstrates (2020), are hardly anomalous to an Urdu cinema legacy that has tended to internalize fissures in bourgeois Pakistani nation formation. Yet, if we examine the politics of the Urdu action film form in the light of a mobile infrastructure of production, we must also acknowledge sentient correspondences between the desire for female friendship among *hybrid strangers*, cultivated by the imagery of *Lady Smuggler* and the female-led heterogeneity of the production mode. As demonstrated through this chapter and elsewhere in this book, by stimulating desire, the cinema produces virtual infrastructures for circulating and commodifying the contemporary—in other words, "emergent forms of value" (Larkin 2013, 339). It is provocative that the attractions of female friendship among strangers and gender-queering stimuli emerge as the valuable commodities being traded by the transnational cinema at hand. Such appealing image commodities as these stimulate audience desire for women-centered transnational films that breach phallic borders by performing the value of female-friendly sociability. And they do so precisely by immersing in the pirate logic of wild mobility, which linked diverse creative geographies and self-determining innovators at this time. The following sections explore the story of this pirate mode of transnational cinema from the other side of the camera.

A Pirate Familial Mode and the Transnational Life of Social Aesthetics

As this book demonstrates, small-scale familial networks involving heterogeneous specialists are hardly momentary in South Asian film business practice. To this day, the undercapitalized Lahore industry survives on kin relations, whether they are based on blood ties or on cultivated "fictive kinship ties" (Kirk 2016, 91). What changes with the video age and its pirate logic of "wild" spatial linkage is that kinship practices of the film business begin to migrate beyond geopolitical and cultural borders. That the burgeoning of a transnational familial mode was being managed at the small scale of tactile relations is well illustrated by a captivating bit of information published in 1987 in the Urdu periodical *Film Asia*. The piece colorfully describes the Islamic ritual of giving gifts of sacrificial meat on the occasion of Eid-al-Adha in order to cement family ties and kin-like relations with close friends. We learn that by this time Shamim Ara and other industry stalwarts had begun to distribute packets of sacrificial meat to film personalities located not only in Lahore or Karachi but also in neighboring countries such as Nepal ("Eid Mubarak" 1987, 25). These active "investment[s] into sociality" cultivated a sentient web of economic and artistic interdependence across national borders (Larkin 2013, 338). The business practice of assembling hybrid talents and inspirations from across divided territories also seems to have paved a robustly *sociable* way in to the family-centered social film, traceable to the images previously discussed. Curiously suggestive of the value of cinema in South Asia as a form of sociable performance that bridges sociopolitical divides is an interview given by star-filmmaker Shamim Ara in 1993. While her vision is apparently unrelated to the transnational business practice described above, it cannot be disconnected from context. To get there, I turn first to the production archive of *Lady Smuggler*.

Parallel stories of the familial route along which *Lady Smuggler* came to be coproduced in the Philippines were told to me at different moments by the late Shamim Ara's associate director Syed Hafeez Ahmed (personal interviews, 2015; 2018; 2019) and by the local facilitator, Raja Riaz Khan (personal interview, 2016). Khan, a Pakistani Muslim, described how he had been running a small tour company in the Philippines in partnership with a Filipina Catholic woman named Mary and an Indian Sikh man named Mohan Singh Makkar when word came to him that a Pakistani company wanted to shoot a film in that country. For his part, Syed Hafeez Ahmed elaborated on this linkage process by telling me that Shamim Ara Productions frequently made word-of-mouth contacts based on familiarity and trust, even though contracts were later signed for "tax purposes" (phone interview, 2018). Noting that tour operator Mary had become a coproducer of *Lady Smuggler*, the elderly Ahmed broke into a smile as he meandered into quite unrelated stories of how Mary grew to be a "sister" to him (I heard that to this day they exchange letters and greeting cards on birthdays and celebrations) (Skype interview, 2015). Photographs shared by Ahmed from his personal archive suggest that the familial commitment may well have been deepened at a bodily level through the sparse conditions under which the filmmakers collaborated, exchanging skills and resources. One such photograph shows Shamim Ara flanked by Mary and Syed Hafeez Ahmed seated in close proximity in a cramped and sweaty studio space poring over what appears to be a script (fig. 19). Another outdoor photo depicts a smiling Mary posing behind a camera on a tripod with Shamim Ara seated next to her, indexing perhaps a role of elder sister and maternal guide on how to shoot film. Known in the Lahore context to have

Fig. 19: In a Philippine studio, from left to right: Mary, Shamim Ara, Syed Hafeez Ahmed (Courtesy Salman Carim)

been a mother figure to women in the industry (S. Khan 2014), Shamim Ara seems to have been forging similar collaborations with female entrepreneurs of entertainment across her mobile production route.

Such archival photographs as these, gathered from the private collections of Syed Hafeez Ahmed and Raja Riaz Khan, also serve as clues to how these interpersonal business relations might have been sustained across geographic distance through an evocation of sensory memory. Whereas I learned from Ahmed that a still photographer would accompany the company on its production routes (phone interview 2019), I did not hear of any clear destination for these photographs. Pakistani periodicals and government reports publish occasional stills from coproductions of this era, but none that I have seen carry such behind-the-camera photographs of a collaborative production unit. Where these photos from Shamim Ara Productions reside today is as private treasures of the late star-director and producer's crew members, helping them to remember the familial ties and retain contact with erstwhile colleagues. In this light, I take a "conjectural . . . [approach to] methodological *bricolage*" (Kuhn 2007, 283), imagining what practical scenes might have grown tangible through photographs like these taken on the sets of an itinerant film company of the video piracy age. At least one reason these photos could have been taken and circulated was to sustain a sentient web of business relations for a small-scale production mode following the pirate logic of migrations. Shamim Ara Productions planned to return to the Philippines in 1990 to shoot their next action-heroine film, *Lady Commando*. Still, archival traces also alert me to what distinguishes the transnational film production and illegal video trade of the time. Sources show that the productions by and large were *formal and legitimate* (at least in the cases I found). As already mentioned, Syed Hafeez Ahmed categorically stated that contracts for collaboration were signed and requisite taxes paid, even though the linkages may not have been anchored in the assumptions of contractual individualism. Speaking of coproductions from the Dhaka end, Md. Fokrul Alam, research officer at the Bangladesh Film Archive and a film producer in his own right, reiterated the formal nature of the business arrangement by stating that bringing in (*nite hoto*) "local talent" and resources was a requirement (personal interview, 2014). In a similar vein, poster-booklets of the transnational coproductions formalize participation by country. For instance, the poster-booklet advertising *Lady Smuggler* calls it a "Pakistan, Bangladesh, and Sari [*sic*] Lanka Combined Venture" and offers a meticulous participants list. The point is that coproductions permeated through the deterritorial logic of the piracy environment rather than imbibed unlawful conduct per se. The inexorable deterritoriality of coproductions is what bred male nationalist anxieties about illicit entertainment, quoted earlier and further discussed below.

Fig. 20: Cast and crew of *Lady Smuggler*, extreme left, Shamim Ara; third, fourth, fifth from left, Mohan Singh Makkar, Syed Hafeez Ahmed, Raja Riaz Khan, respectively; three heroines in costume; extreme right, fight master Qaisar Mastana (Courtesy: Salman Carim)

Clearly, the deterritorial momentum of coproductions not only bridged national divides, but in small ways it also healed the lacerating effects of partitions in South Asia. The "combined venture" credits list on the poster-booklet of *Lady Smuggler*, for example, indicates that a significant number of Bangladeshi cast and crew were working alongside Pakistanis on location in the Philippines. Archival photographs and oral accounts show, too, that the Sikh Indian tour operator Mohan Singh Makkar was involved in the production along with the Pakistani crew (see fig. 20). Further, women's coproductions clearly thrived on female collaborations, which produce the profusion of female bodies and gender artistry we find in the texts. In this respect, Shamim Ara's coproductions stand apart from other Pakistani coproductions directed and steered by men.[4] Both behind-the-scenes records and the mise-en-scène of *Lady Smuggler* reveal just how many women entrepreneurs and performers were assembled from across countries. It also appears that gender-queering male performers such as Rangila (Pakistan) and Shiva (Nepal) came to be aptly paired with the skilled women in lead roles. Thus, there is little doubt that a gender-hybrid production process is what corresponds mimetically to the pirate ambiance of the diegetic text, detailed earlier. Less transparent is the *authorial* process through which a seeming mish-mash of transnational gender attractions acquires second-order life in such collaboratively made conventional films as *Lady Smuggler* and *Miss Colombo*. How do we account for the innovative expressions of transnational female friendship and kin-making that emasculate territorial guardians or rise up against masculinist oppression on religious minorities in these works? I have already attempted one account of aesthetic dynamism in relation to audience address in a transforming Pakistan. However, the dissident aesthetic remains underexplored unless we turn to the other side of the camera, where female authors make art and negotiate referents.

A televised interview given by Shamim Ara in 1993 sheds light on authorship. We hear her responding to a question from the host on how she (as a Pakistani Muslim) was able to represent a Hindu girl and perform the requisite religious rites in the Pakistani partition narrative *Lakhon mein ek* (One among a Million; dir. Raza Mir; 1967). Shamim Ara replies with conviction that the part came easily to her because she had learned to carry out *pujāpāth* (Hindu religious rites) from living with Hindus in a close-knit neighborhood in pre-partition India. She goes on to add with some force that she could demonstrate her knowledge of the rites to her interlocutor by carrying out puja/*puja kar ke* right there and then. In sum, Shamim implies that her skill in performing religious difference on film comes through the *knowledge she carries in her body* of being with other (Hindu) women. We find here a notion of cinematic performance imbued with the immediacy of bodily cognition. Her words stage an understanding of aesthetic performance as a way to know the other and feel sociable through the "corporeal sensorium"—the sensorium that wants to preserve and nourish both oneself and one's lifeworld (Buck-Morss 1992, 6). Susan Buck-Morss explains that the word "aesthetics" derives from a Greek original that means "perceptive by feeling," a form of sensory cognition exceeding acculturation (6).[5] Situated in a post-partition South Asia widely acculturated within borders, Shamim Ara similarly evokes the cinematic aesthetic as a perceptive way to feel sociable by performing the once-indivisible lifeworld. She speaks in 1993 not as an actress but as the director and producer of a social action film that not only crosses geopolitical borders but also yields fictions about nourishing hybrid sociality. In Shamim's evocation of a practice that invests artistic value to indivisible neighborliness, we get a glimpse of the sensory logic that possibly animates the collaborative images of kin-making discussed above. These women-led transnational films, permeating through a piracy environment, might well have been striving against territorial culture in both business and aesthetic practice.

The complexity of the context in which these women's coproductions were released lies in the fact that the sensibilities of target consumers were thoroughly acculturated in the politics of borders. As previously explained, the inexorable deterritoriality of coproductions, exacerbated by association with pirate media, provoked acutely anxious questions about the national and licit contents of these works. The very concept of women's companies roving beyond national bounds was also at issue. Under these conditions, Shamim Ara's performance in her celebrity interview of an erstwhile hybrid religious persona and the imaginal neighborhood are necessarily marked with a strain of defensive ambiguity. Precisely the alertness to the borderly limits of nation and legality complicates the publicity discourse for *Lady Smuggler* produced by both Shamim Ara and Babita on the respective domestic platforms of Pakistan and Bangladesh in 1987. In both cases, I find the star-filmmakers engaging in dutiful performances of national and legal subjecthood. Yet, this publicity discourse is irreducibly transborder in its referents, for it simultaneously promotes and legitimizes desire, among video-trained consumers, for a cinema engaging diverse performers and women entrepreneurs. Thus, the transmedial plot of female authorship in this piracy era must include the paradoxes of publicity.

Publicity Authorship in Pakistan and Bangladesh: Coproducers Shamim Ara and Babita

A few weeks before the release of *Lady Smuggler* in Pakistan, on the occasion of Baqr Eid in 1987, the Urdu periodical *Film Asia* published a promotional interview of the director and producer Shamim Ara (Shamim Ara 1987). The reporter writes that he found her busily preparing to take *Lady Smuggler* to the Moscow Film Festival. The occasion provides the reporter with pretext for narrating the formative role Shamim Ara had taken in developing and promoting national Urdu cinema by setting it apart from foreign traditions. We read that she had entered the fledgling Pakistani industry at a time when Indian (Hindi) films were being imported—in other words, when a budding local cinema faced competition from films flowing in from across the border (not unlike during the video age when the *Film Asia* article is situated). At that embattled moment, Shamim Ara's "high quality" debut performance in the Urdu social film *Kunwari Bewa* (1956; dir. Najam Naqvi) had captivated Pakistani cinemagoers, paving the way to her ambassadorship at international film festivals. The report avers that Shamim has had the "honor" of representing Pakistan in foreign film festivals most often. The heritage narrative effectively revives bourgeois Pakistani memories of Shamim Ara's star-publicist persona from the 1960s—a persona writ large, for example, on the pages of the English-language film magazine *Eastern Film*. As discussed in chapter 3, 1960s Urdu film culture in mid-decade embodied an elite nationalist inclination. At that moment, Shamim Ara was being showcased by *Eastern Film* as a "roving ambassador" ("Shamim Ara" 1964, 37), taking Pakistani films to many international festivals to promote export. The August 1964 issue, for example, carries an article titled "Shamim Ara: Pages from My Diary" detailing her representative role at international film festivals in Jakarta, Hong Kong, and Tokyo (38–39), whereas the July 1966 issue offers an emblematic photograph of the ambassadorial star posing in front of a gigantic globe (Jaffrey 1966, 18).

Returning to the 1987 *Film Asia* interview, meant to promote *Lady Smuggler*'s journey to the international film festival at Moscow, we find Shamim Ara stepping into her ambassadorial part—and not. While she does hold on to her role as Pakistani film industry leader, she alters the teleology. On the one hand, her reported words cooperate with the reporter's framing narrative about her star-ambassadorship by depicting both the look and the rivalrous goal of an ideal Pakistani delegation. According to Shamim Ara, the delegation should include a screenwriter, a journalist, and a lineup of at least "four girls" (female stars) who will add the necessary factor of "glamour" to make the country (*mulk*) look striking (*numāʾindagī*). The goal of female glamour is to make the delegation shine in rivalry with parallel nationalist formations made up of Indian, Bangladeshi, and other Asian country girls (*hamārī film inḍasṭrī meñ bahut laṛkiyāñ haiñ jo glaimar ke lihāz se Bhāratī, Bangladeshī, yā dūsre aishiyāʾī mumālik kī laṛkiyoñ ke muqāble meñ kam kashish nahīñ rakhtiñ*). These words tangibly present to readers the classic film festival concept of delegates serving as keepers of a national cinematic spectacle oriented to an "implicitly masculine connoisseurship" of the global culture market (White 2015, 15). The obvious irony here is that the rivalrous nationalist image of an all-Pakistani delegation occludes precisely the transnational multiplicity to be found in the coproduced film (*Lady Smuggler*) this interview is meant to promote. The occlusion of transnational difference seems to be keeping the gate of bourgeois territorial nostalgia for the golden days of national cinema in Urdu—implicitly managing anxieties about the pirate media environment through which coproductions like *Lady Smuggler* permeated.

The transborder ambivalence in Shamim Ara's star-author interview lies, on the other hand, in the fact that it displaces the territorial concept of cinema, found in the reporter's heritage narrative, and instead breeds curiosity about a female-led cinema. She effectively inhabits and re-authors the concepts of national purity and otherness in their "very processes of binding" by dislocating her female star-performer community from the nation (Meyer 2009, 7). She asserts that any such ideal festival delegation is impossible today. Due to a lack of state support, festival delegations must come together in a haphazard manner through the initiative of individuals like herself. The article dwells on the scene of Shamim Ara scurrying around to do everything herself, checking the print for exhibition while she runs errands for her journey to Moscow. As the drama of the female star's self-sacrificing labor for the nation does take over—with the article capitalizing on the star-filmmaker's body as "human infrastructure" (D. Mukherjee 2020b, 44)—prior narratives about Shamim Ara's heritage role are suspended in a time warp. Instead, what grows tangible and attractive is another contingent infrastructure taking shape through the resourceful efforts of a female director-producer. Stepping into the breach of official masculine machinery, Shamim orients toward female film workers. For one thing, she names and promotes one by one the women who would be in her imaginary lineup of industry delegates, dwelling with loving adoration on their "glamorous" bodies, but refrains from mentioning any male names (the screenwriter and journalist remain necessary but faceless identities). For another, she stages a magical mutuality with the female lead of all her heroine films by stating cryptically, "Babra Sharif has been a lucky star for me."

As illustrated by other Urdu magazine tidbits on the film industry, such interdependent relationships among women upheld a cross-border infrastructure for the flow of valued people and commodities. A 1987 issue of *Weekly Akhbar-e-Jehan* showcases Shamim Ara's transnational collaborator from Sri Lanka, Sabita, who coproduced and starred in both *Lady Smuggler* and *Miss Colombo*. We see Sabita depicted as relaxing in Karachi as a local celebrity ("Sabita" 56). Noteworthy as well is the Urdu magazine as an extra-cinematic media platform for altering urban middle-class tastes, combined with Urdu television channels (on which Shamim Ara also promoted her productions). Urdu magazine tidbits, in Kamran Asdar Ali's words, tended to be "polyphonic" in addressing the "social and ethnic heterogeneity" of Pakistani urban spaces (2004, 124). Women-oriented magazine materials reached out to a wide spectrum of urban middle- and lower-middle-class literate women (130), the spectrum who also consumed Shamim's Urdu films in this piracy age. Shamim Ara's transborder performance of publicity seems to have been a way of flourishing as a female Urdu filmmaker in a media environment like this, rife with the possibilities and anxieties of hybrid flows. By materializing as a national persona on Urdu media platforms, she was binding and securing one pole of Urdu public desire, that of an embattled nostalgia for a cinema proximal to the state and bourgeois patriarchal proprieties. Deploying her authority as a heritage persona, she was, at the same time, generating attraction for a women-populated transnational production mode that was adequate for the hybrid contemporary.

Following the coproduction of *Lady Smuggler* to its release in Bangladesh, I find another way women materialize as transnational entrepreneurs on publicity platforms. In this context, the authorship of a female transnational-producer identity is more paradoxical. Traversals of legal and sexual boundaries are interminable. These transborder complexities must be situated in relation to a number of contextual factors—the strict laws governing coproductions in Bangladesh, the specter of pornography permeating film piracy, and the respectable heterosocial class position of the two female stars involved in the release of the dubbed Bangla version. In 1990 we find Bangla periodicals reporting on the imminent release of *Lady Smuggler* in Bangladesh. They identify Babita Movies as the coproducer, together with an unnamed Pakistani production house, and they name Bangladeshi male filmmaker Chasi Nazrul Islam as the director. Chasi Nazrul was known and respected in Bangladesh as a director of Liberation War art film as well as mainstream Bangla cinema. Two details are noteworthy. First, the Pakistani poster-booklet of *Lady Smuggler*, put out in 1987 by Shamim Ara Productions, does list Chasi Nazrul as one among the Bangladeshi "cast" while naming Shamim Ara as the director. And second, the print of *Lady Smuggler* dubbed in Bangla, currently uploaded on YouTube, is exactly the same as the Urdu film (in the VCD copy I possess, for one). Only the credits have been altered in the Bangla version, naming Shamim Ara in the category of "*jugma parichālana*" (codirection). The Bangla film poster for *Lady Smuggler* describes the work as being "directed by Chasi Nazrul Islam" (see fig. 21).

A full account of this striking discrepancy in identifying the director must await further research on the representation and publicity of coproduced films in their various national-linguistic routes of exhibition. A fuller account of *Lady Smuggler* calls for sources from Sri Lanka, the third country named in the "combined venture" credits. We could well be looking at the material trace of a heterogeneous directorial team at work behind small-scale ensemble-heroine films like *Lady Smuggler*, which reappeared in local-language versions for different audiences across the region. For the purposes of the present study, I bracket the discrepancy in the identification of the director. Instead, I turn to

Fig. 21: Poster for the Bangla film *Lady Smuggler* naming Chasi Nazrul Islam as the director

an anxiety-ridden narrative about the imminent release serialized in four issues of the weekly periodical *Saptahik Purnima*. This narrative describes director Chasi Nazrul's elite paternalistic role in legitimizing the coproduction and establishing its respectable origin. This paternalistic narrative constitutes the aesthetic platform on which the respectable woman producer Babita and her sister/collaborator Shuchanda appear to national public view. Babita emerges as both a legal subject of the nation and a respectable female *authorial* entrepreneur—the one who is able to maintain control over her cultural product. What we see, in other words, is the staging of an appropriate woman-run business model. The performance is best understood in relation to a piracy environment rife with allegations of "law violations/*āin ke langhan*" (Ziad 2010, 261).

Dramatizing how the pathway of this multilocation coproduction intersects with that of media piracy, the narrative serializes how the intervention by an upright male director like Chasi Nazrul Islam rescues and legitimizes the film. Journalist Robi Armaan has reported on the theft of reel 16 of *Lady Smuggler* from the studio laboratory of the state-sponsored Film Development Corporation in Dhaka (FDC). The reel is to be returned only for a ransom. The theft of a film reel would be especially threatening in a piracy environment where "cut pieces" of porn reels were spliced into film prints (Hoek 2014). In fact, *Saptahik Purnima* surrounds the *Lady Smuggler* report with the specter of illicit fragmentation by running (unrelated) parallel articles on pornographic cut-piece exhibition. In this discursive space, reporter Armaan proceeds to frame the theft of reel 16 in relation to the "*durnīti*" (corruption) rampant in the studio economy. Armaan maintains that the corruption is driven by the grandiose aspirations of "*sādhāran karmachāri*" (common workers) seeking to become film producers through illegal means (Armaan 1990, 45). Bourgeois patriarchal morality is reinforced, by contrast, through another narrative published a week earlier about a press conference in which director Chasi Nazrul Islam recounts the initiatives he took ("Abosheshe" 1990, 47). He claims that while he was guiding the police on how to retrieve the stolen reel from the petty technician who turned out to have stolen it, he had made a backup plan. He was prepared to procure the "dup negative" (i.e., duplicate negative) from Pakistan were he to fail in the retrieval. One nationalist implication of the latter claim—going to Pakistan for the duplicate negative—is that the original negative resides in Bangladesh and deploys local resources, as required by the local law governing coproductions.

Chasi Nazrul's account at the press conference is accompanied by a "press photograph," framed and laid out in the typical way to connote a message (Barthes 1982, 199). Chasi Nazrul is shown sitting center-front, using hand gestures as he speaks. Dependently huddled at the back of the legitimate male director and moral agent are star-coproducer Babita and her mentor and elder sister Shuchanda. In a sexually charged environment of reel piracy, this press photograph and the surrounding reportage could be seen as connoting to middle-class readers an emotionally comforting message about a *porda* (covering/screen) practice by the two women film workers. As Lotte Hoek argues, in the liberal middle-class Muslim context of Bangladesh, porda practice should be understood not as "female seclusion or veiling . . . [but] as a set of community-based aesthetic demands on female public presence" (2009, 78). By fulfilling the aesthetic demands of respectable female publicness, the performance of diffident dependence makes the female star-producers intimately acceptable to target middle-class audiences. Drawing visibly on patriarchal moral support, the female entrepreneurs in effect legitimize their authorial control over the transnationally made object. In other words, they become legitimate producer-guards of an object tainted by the environment of piracy—perceived to be prone to migrations and duplications at a rate that confounds the distinction between the national original and the many copies. The complexity in this staging of dependent female entrepreneurs, however, lies in the fact that it is disjointed from the remainder of the serialized narrative even though it constitutes the latter's emotional pretext.

A week or two later, the same periodical depicts Babita as busy with the release of *Lady Smuggler*. She is portrayed as laboring away in her office at the Rajmoni Film Complex on such details as the photo set, poster and banner designs, and trailer materials ("Ekhan Babita" 1990, 45–46). We also learn that Babita, having morally cleansed her own film business—by divorcing an embezzler husband and business partner—has found her biggest collaborator and advisor in older sister Kohinoor Akhter Shuchanda. Note that as older sibling, Shuchanda had led the family in setting up her star-name company, Shuchanda Cholochitra, in a small-scale sororal mode and forging ahead as an independent woman producer (detailed in chapter 2). The press photograph accompanying the climactic report on the release of *Lady Smuggler* in Bangladesh—published January 28, 1990—looks rather like a family album. A close-up shows the two sisters examining a banner with mutually supportive attention. As such, the photograph brings readers tangibly close to a *male-independent* infrastructure for film circulation, built through the collaborative labor of two self-determining female stars. Showcased alongside is a still from the prison yard episode of *Lady Smuggler*. Carrying a trace of transnational female collaboration in the form of tactile sociability, the still similarly depicts the three heroines touching one another with purposefully happy smiles.

This chapter has sought to demonstrate that an ecology of video piracy in the 1980s and '90s bred across Pakistan and Bangladesh (and interlinked media spaces) a coproductive mode of women-led cinema best characterized as piratical and heterodox. Even if coproductions in this filmic mode were legally registered—as Shamim Ara's and Babita's were—they were permeated by the contemporary pirate logic of unregulated transnational mobility and susceptible to nationalist stigma by association. As such, the history of pirate mode filmmaking helmed by star-authors such as Shamim and Babita reveals a sexually paradoxical practice of transborder cinema. On domestic platforms of promotion and publicity, respectively in Pakistan and Bangladesh, these women were putting their bourgeois star personas to ambivalent use—acting as national/legal border guards for the productions while generating desire for images and enterprises that move out of national boundaries. On the transnational routes of production and distribution, the collaborative mode was breaching borders of geography, ethnicity, and religion. Reading from both sides of the camera, I have shown that the filmic images comprise an archive of female authorial practice permeating through the migratory logic of piracy. They not only look like pirate texts (i.e., migratory objects worked on by many hands), but they also bridge sociopolitical divides and unsettle statist manhood, producing a curiously sociable aesthetic of female-targeted fiction. As I have also sought to demonstrate, clues to such neglected archives of border-breaching women's work as this must be pieced together from the remainders of visual and print material: bits that are inadequate to narratives of boundary, propriety, or taste.

6

Families Torn and Found

Feminist Modes and Transnational Bangla Media

The previous chapter argues that women's pirate mode collaborations, managed on both sides of the camera at the "closest-in" spatial scales of sociality and female (star-)body work (McDowell 2001, 229), engendered a provocatively sociable form of transnational film in the 1980s. The female-focused family and action dramas implicitly referred to historical trauma in postcolonial South Asia through unsettling or transcending masculine territorial forms. This chapter turns to a well-recognized repertoire of regional transnational cinema directed by women. To reiterate, I understand the transnational as cinema that not only fictionalizes geosocial boundary formation but also crosses territories in search of stories and resources. The feminist directors' cinema evolves in the large-scale media spaces of the 2000s. Keeping with the focus of part 3 of the book, I examine how women-directed social films made for theatrical release comprehend in feminist terms the conventions of broken and remade family typical to regional trauma film in South Asia. The cases in point are star-author Aparna Sen's Bangla horror comedy *Goynar Baksho* (The Jewelry Box; 2013) and independent author Rubaiyat Hossain's Bangla war film *Meherjaan* (2011). The first of these films inhabits the field of Bengali displacement/resettlement genres. These genres of cinema and literature deal with collective experiences of displacement, urbanization, and linguistic gentrification in post-partition West Bengal. The second film reworks the sexual tropes of wartime genocide and rape found in the patriarchal nationalist *Muktijuddho* (Liberation War) genre in Bangladesh.

To plot a shared practice of feminist genre-making to both sides of national borders, I have chosen to limit the scope of this chapter to the Bengal region. This scope helps to focus on how the spatial conventions of kinship and community typical to Bangla genres (joint family homes, villages, riverine landscapes) materialize in parallel ways in these feminist social films. In the hands of female authors Aparna Sen and Rubaiyat Hossain the conventions become metaphoric "trigger points" for interacting with the socio-sexual exclusions immanent to battles over language, land, ethnicity, and religion in the region (Jaikumar 2017, 226). For another, I am able to compare how women's border-conscious cinema conjures the region through the lens of the *two* major events that consecutively devastated and reconstituted lands and lives in the northern subcontinent—namely, the partition of India and Pakistan (1947) and the Bangladesh Liberation War (1971). This interlinked history of upheavals, which happened on Bengali grounds, is generally left out of the Hindi and Urdu repertoires of cinema studied elsewhere in this book.

This chapter demonstrates that transnational female authorship in the 2000s is not unlike the pirate mode found in the 1980s in the way fictions of female kinship are used as the emotional grid on which to process regional historical experiences of conflict or healing. If the female focus on postcolonial trauma remains steady, what obviously shift are the formal contents. As feminist counternarratives, the works studied below generically subvert the "masculinist contours" of national and neocolonial historiographies (Shohat 1997, 183–209). Counter-telling of familial activities—care work, child-rearing, female bonding—becomes a working through of collective memories of trauma. However, what reappears in the feminist production modes studied below is another aspect of women's film work that is immanent to the context. We find individual women endeavoring at a small scale to generate resources and desire for their own debates with nationalist norms. Intensively localized practices of star-body performance and familial networking, habitual to female film work in South Asia, come alive in productions by the feminist bricoleurs of heritage and nation.

Thus, the studies in this concluding chapter further complicate my analysis of female authorship in relation to large-scale infrastructures in South Asia. Noteworthy is the difference with the Hindi female authorial modes unfolding in Mumbai with support from state-sponsored national and multinational media networks (examined in chapter 4). The cases studied below show, by contrast, that multi-scalar networks of production and circulation, far from being monolithic, inflect to localized habits of labor and connectivity. However, these cases also shine light on the complexity of sustaining small-scale female authorial practice in the new media spaces of the 2000s, specifically in reference to the logics of state formation and brand marketing relevant to these spaces. We see that feminist creative decisions as easily could become connected to those overarching concepts of legitimacy and timeliness. By flexibly interpermeating small- and large-scale media geographies, the new filmic environment moves toward trending criteria. This environment is constitutively at odds with the disaggregated transnationalism of piracy examined in chapter 5. It seems that authors and imaginations today are able to develop and flourish only by aggregating with concepts legitimized by statist and imperial trends. In other words, an enabling transborder momentum of inclusion and aggregation tends to prevail. I develop this argument below by looking at the aforementioned texts from both sides of the camera. My attempt is to understand how aesthetic codes might carry material traces of dissident or aggregate practice whose stories unfold in the production contexts within which the respective authors work. The pathway of Rubaiyat Hossain, a transnational filmmaker of the non-star generation, leads me, in closing, to the racially ambivalent infrastructure of funding and exhibition in the global North, including international film festivals. While keeping the lens mainly on works made in the region, I round out the chapter by briefly considering films made about the region for international film festivals. My point is to consider if some such large-scale infrastructures of transnational connection whose locus of control lies in the global North might come with their own limited concepts about "other" regions. These concepts might stem from imperial patriarchal histories of Orientalism, Islamophobia, and developmental aid.

The productions to be discussed below participate in a transnational feminist practice of border and trauma films and documentaries. My analysis is indebted to the extensive scholarship in the field. Studies reveal that transnational feminist critiques of borders are both historically specific and shared across progressive filmic spaces. I draw on, for example, textual scholars of South Asian feminist cinema who examine how women's counternarratives "dislodge" hierarchies binding subjects to nation-states,[1] and instead illuminate the persistent trauma of bodies maintained "out of place" by borders of nation, language, religion, and development in the partitioned region.[2] As other scholars note, images of female intimacy become an affective grid to "engender a conversation about nation, history, identity, healing" (E. Chowdhury 2020; 2022). Production scholars remind us that in the 2000s, modes of making feminist film and documentary range widely across parallel and mainstream platforms as well as digital networks.[3] What the rest of this chapter attempts is to add questions of limit to the important scholarship on transnational feminist productions. How do female counternarrative authors of the present day negotiate the "interminable" experiences of conceptual borders and occluded others (Derrida 1993, 16)? What of the political-economic value assigned to trending concepts and transmitted across mediatized spaces?

Authoring *Goynar Baksho*: Heritage Brand and Feminist Haunting

In a personal interview granted to me in 2012, Aparna Sen responded to my admitted interest in women's border cinema by noting that her next production was to be a feminist narrative about borders. *Goynar Baksho* was in preproduction. She went on to explain that the multigenerational story, set against the backdrop of the two partitions of the Bengal region, was feminist, being that the narrative centered on women. The essentialist idea that women-centric fiction films made by women are feminist, which I have found to be quite common in Indian film circles, derives from an association of those works with women's parallel cinema, led in the waning days of the Indian New Wave by filmmakers like Aparna (Sawhney 2015, 152–153). Today, Aparna Sen positions herself in the way she did at the interview with me, as an only occasional feminist filmmaker. Hardly irrelevant to this subject position is the fact that typically serious realist social films of the feminist parallel tradition have been difficult to fund and market since the demise of the '80s wave. Nonetheless, Aparna's conviction in the feminism of *Goynar Baksho* is analyzable in terms of the legacy to which it points. Her words drew me close to how the work weaves together two signatory characteristics of Aparna Sen's parallel repertoire: feminist cinema and border cinema. For one thing, we find key tropes of such Bangla feminist counternarratives directed by Sen as *Parama* and *Paromitar Ek Din*. Not unlike those works, which were spawned by the Indian women's movement and public debates around sexuality, *Goynar Baksho* subverts the repressive structures of patriarchal Bengali family life by exploring non-normative female sexuality. For another, we see a recurrence of the border consciousness found in such English-language films directed by Aparna Sen as *Mr. and Mrs. Iyer* (2002) and *15 Park Avenue* (2005). The latter dramatize unconsummated romance and irrational yearnings as ways to bear witness to the exclusion of the Muslim other and the victimization of the vulnerable, both in Hindu-dominant India and across the post-9/11 world (De 2016, 152–155). In a similar vein, *Goynar Baksho* engenders female spectrality as a subversive way into territorial tensions in the Bengal region. Like other transnational feminist counternarratives of divided South Asia, it depicts how personhoods fall out of place as families and communities are torn from their roots and unevenly urbanized. This fiction film inhabits West Bengali partition and ghost genres to retell the Hindu Bengali experience from the margins of linguistic and sexual territories. To this end, partition ghost stories by the Bengali male writer Sirshendu Mukherjee are mixed in with cinematic traditions. Where *Goynar Baksho* differs from Aparna's feminist repertoire of the 1980s and '90s is that the regionalism is updated for a globalized infrastructure, that of multiplex Indian cinema.

Made in a trendy format of ghost comedy, *Goynar Baksho* is dense with sensational appeals such as animation, digital morphing, and Dolby-enhanced Bangla rap. The format participates in a transformation under way in both Kolkata and other regional Indian film economies that strive to keep pace with the global Bollywood model. The goal of the regional cinemas is to reach diasporic Indian markets through producing ethnic identities replete with the erotic exuberance of neoliberal consumerism (Gopal 2012). Since the liberalization of national economic policies in 1991, Indian media spaces have been overrun with erotic commodities. Reaching across unevenly developed spaces, the erotic images evoke desires not only to acquire objects but also to "gaze upon" lives and worlds removed from consumer subjects "in terms of class, region, and nation" (Mankekar 2004, 408). In this media field, images of peoples and ghosts from Bengal's fractured past seemed to supply just the right erotic mix of pleasures for audiences with means. Metropolitan consumers were in the position not only to access the visual window to a regional exuberance removed from the urban present (in expensive theaters or on streaming platforms) but also to acquire the objects and services in reinvented authentic forms (i.e., to buy classical-style jewelry or consume pricey traditional cuisine). Thus, *Goynar Baksho* was particularly timely in its entry into the commodity field of a new Bengali cinema wanting to "realign the past to cleave more closely to [West] Bengal's recent insertion into a global present" (Gopal 2012, 164). Moreover, horror comedy being in the air of the Kolkata cinema may well have expedited Aparna Sen's access to the cutting-edge production house Shree Venkatesh Films. Another blockbuster horror comedy titled *Bhooter Bhabisyat* (The Future of the Past; 2012; dir. Anik Dutta), released the previous year, had already branded the genre with ethnocentric Bengali nostalgia by pitting the violent neocolonial identity of a *non-Bengali* urban developer against heritage Kolkata architecture and the ghosts of regional inequities. Aparna Sen's ghost comedy inserted into the brand a female ghost and women's concerns. Even though brand signifiers are flexibly instantiated across a range of products, however, they coalesce into a "normative expression . . . of emotional and cultural identity" (Banet-Weiser 2016, 25).

Goynar Baksho followed two Aparna Sen–directed fiction films with limited niche market appeal, the English-language production *The Japanese Wife* (2010) and the Bangla work *Iti Mrinalini* (Yours Mrinalini; 2011). Both were evaluated as showing issues in their execution. The latter, considered to have some weaknesses in the cowritten script, was slated by a reviewer as being appropriate only for Aparna's "diehard fans" of the art-house dispensation (Bhaskaran 2010). The former's reception was mixed because it followed a Bengali style of parallel cinema that was going out of mode. By depicting complex interiorities through "slow-paced editing, realistic mise-en-scène, deliberative camerawork, and the foregrounding of dialogue," *The Japanese Wife* fell out of pace with the "frenetic and highly technologized film apparatus" of the new Bengali cinema being sought for by metropolitan audiences (Gopal 2012, 158). By contrast, *Goynar Baksho*, hailed precisely for keeping up with the trend, went on to become a box-office success that ran, as remarked by a reviewer, to "packed" auditoriums (Dutta 2013). Reviewers celebrated the work as "one of the funniest, smartest movies of the year, and a viewer's delight" ("Goynar

Baksho Movie Review" 2013), with cinematographer Soumik Halder receiving a special congratulatory word for "bringing a superior edge to Bengali cinema with his artistry" (Bhaumik 2013).

On a more ambivalent note, reviews also sought a parallel/art-house touch. Some applauded the fact that the "crazy fantasy . . . [,] one of the sexiest structures in recent times," had been infused with a truly Bengali historical narrative about the "trauma of Partition, of lands and inheritances lost, of unfamiliar adjustments after years of *zamindari* [feudal landowner] grandeur" ("Goynar Baksho Movie Review" 2013). Other reviewers seemed comforted to see the erotic glamour of heritage—ornate zamindari jewelry, made by brand partner Anjali Jewelers, and traditional handwoven saris—being tempered by Aparna Sen's "signature touch . . . [of] social commentary" (Bhaumik 2013). Yet, what appeared to be catching many eyes was a *trendy gendering* of the woman filmmaker's "signature." As expressed in another wry comment, while the narrative centers on three women, "mind you, the feminism is not heavy-handed, but dovetails smoothly with the comic elements" ("Goynar Baksho Movie Review" 2013). The caveat evokes a particular trend. As serious cinema became outmoded in India, the comedic rendition of social issues grew to be an attractive value for the middle-class intelligentsia who were consuming multi-plex cinema (Dwyer 2011, 199). In this vein, *Goynar Baksho* was in stride with the new wave of multiplex cinema that took off in India from the mid-2000s through successfully marrying the "commercial aspect" with "non-mainstream" serious content. This wave diverged from earlier multiplex productions such as Aparna Sen's *Mr. and Mrs. Iyer*, in which the commercial attraction had been inadequate for success, despite critical acclaim (T. Amin 2007, 70). Far more complex were Aparna Sen's own promotional commentaries. While her voice undoubtedly aggregated with the temporality of heritage brand production, at the same time, it diverged. Her performances of authorship were explicitly haunted by the difference of the regional other her work sought to conjure.

In this light, I maintain that the production politics of *Goynar Baksho* must be situated at the crossroads of infrastructures. On the one hand, it accrues erotic brand value in production and circulation routes as a woman-empowering ethnic heritage film. On the other, the work mobilizes the inter-active commodity value of Aparna Sen herself—a famous female persona, a celebrity director, and on extratextual platforms, a longtime author of public contestations about gender. This famous female star qua author of dissident conversations on sexual justice actively stimulates an infrastructure of urban Bengali fandom through both film work and popular magazine editorial work (discussed in chapter 1). Seen another way, Aparna's star-author persona is intimately and continually known by mediatized Bengali publics. In this instance, it came to be the "locus" of small-scale star-body labor through which "cross-scalar relations" with large-scale brand criteria were managed, at least to an extent (McDowell 2001, 233). As suggested by one commentary quoted above, her "signature" touch was comfortably familiar and welcomed. Traces of tension bred at these crossroads—tensions between aggregate and dissident choice—are found in the filmic text, to be discussed in the next section. To get there, I follow the making of a brand identity for *Goynar Baksho* in relation to the complexities in the star-author's voice.

To approach filmic authorship in India's transforming media fields, we must be attentive to the overlap of filmic text with extra-cinematic mediatization. Drawing on scholarship by Jonathan Gray and John Caldwell, Aswin Punathambekar argues for "broadening our understanding of authorship" in this context (2013, 466). He calls our attention to a form of organized creative process that is best described as "authoring hype" (466). Quoting Tarun Tripathi, marketing manager at the leading Bollywood company, Yash Raj Films, Punathambekar identifies hype creation as an authorship of "branding" that positions "key attributes of the film" in relation to target audiences (467–468). It must be added that the selection of attributes worthy of hype and useful for strengthening brand value in a specific context are manufactured collaboratively by "partner" economies such as film production and television. One such preproduction hype event for *Goynar Baksho*—held at the five-star Taj Bengal hotel in Kolkata and televised by the "brand partner" cable channel ABP Ananda—is noteworthy as a selective showcase of filmic attributes ("Director Aparna Sen"). A primary attribute picked out, and evoked with a touch of comedic sexiness by the female stars present at the event, comprised the language and uncouth ways of the Hindu *bāngāl* villager from East Bengal (now Bangladesh).

Figurations of the village bāngāl, while familiar to West Bengali literature and cinema, take a circuitous route. Dipesh Chakrabarty explains that the ways and tongues of East Bengali village bāngāl men as "objects of amused contempt" and mimicry surfaced in mid-nineteenth-century urban Bangla literature and theater, coming hand in hand with the expansion of the city of Calcutta (located in the western region of Bengal) under British rule and the influx of migrants from the eastern part of the Bengal delta (1996, 2147). The comic figure of the Hindu bāngāl migrant turns in post-partition Bengali cinema into the Hindu refugee man displaced from his eastern village hearth and made into an object of "ambiguous sentiments" among West Bengali city folk. Bhaskar Sarkar delineates phases of the "good-natured" comedy around bāngāl refugees in the middle-class *bhadralok* Bangla cinema of the 1950s, replete as that is with a "discourse of respectability and refinement" (2009, 158–159). Tracking the transitions in the career of the foremost male comedian of dialect, Bhanu Bandyopadhyay, Sarkar points out that whereas Bhanu's roles soon after partition were marked by a "poignant excess," obliging spectators "to bear witness to the material and psychic tribulations of the displaced," later portrayals "became hackneyed" in a way that could be suggestive of "the cultural assimilation" of East Bengali refugees in urban Hindu Bengal (160). In an era of globalizing regionalism that realigns the rural past with gendered Bengali progress, the bāngāl *woman* was being updated into a multiplex brand: an agent desiring the linguistic heritage as a choice of lifestyle and consumption.

At the promotion of *Goynar Baksho*, young heroine Srabonti Chatterjee, herself an erotic symbol on contemporary Kolkata media platforms, declared with excitement that not only do her roots lie in Barisal (a district in Bangladesh) but also that she has been motivated by her role in the movie to authenticate her cultural ties by speaking to her father in Barisal dialect. The older heroine, Moushumi Chatterjee—in her day, a romantic glamour queen who appeared at the Taj Bengal event with Westernized hairdo and makeup—asserted in irreverent, uncouth bāngāl, "*ā maran, āmi to bāngāl-e* [literally: death to you, I am truly bāngāl]." While the women were performing their respective generational identities, and setting the stage for a multigenerational filmic narrative, they both responded to the same question posed by the reporter from ABP Ananda Television: "Are you a bāngāl?" Together, they were coauthoring hype for a female-centered brand of linguistic heritage comedy. To star-director Aparna Sen, who predictably claimed considerable camera time on the ABP Ananda coverage, the reporter's question was different. As "a film by Aparna Sen"—the typical auteurist descriptor of the motion pictures by this art-house director—brand formation had to include discussion of her signature touch.

While Aparna readily complied by hyping up the general promise of a carnivalesque village-woman comedy, she emphasized that her screenplay had altered the original novel "a bit" (*ektu badlechi*). She went on to explain that her screenplay had enlarged and sustained the spectral presence of the aged village widow till the end. By contrast, Sirshendu Mukherjee's novel had eliminated the aged ghost upon the birth of a new-generation urban heroine, whose narrative was put front and center throughout the work. Moreover, Aparna Sen expanded on the role of village-style comedy in a way that differed from the heritage approach to village dialect taken by the star-actresses, quoted above. She harped on the ghostly drama of female mischief by a *dushtu buri pishima* (naughty old aunt), and on the fact that she had deployed linguistic difference (village dialect and demeanor) to shine light on ghostly female mischief. Notwithstanding her statement of authorial intervention, Aparna Sen had begun the promotional event by reading from the original novel, hyping up the popular value of the motion picture to come. The novelist himself, a commercially successful writer of Bangla ghost stories and thrillers, was present to endorse and brand the literary film, implicitly attributing it to the marketability of the form of Bengali literature his work represented.

Both the novel *Goynar Baksho* and the sequel *Rashmonir Sonadana* (Rashmoni's Gold and Jewels), written by Sirshendu Mukherjee, depict generational change among East Bengali women. They gesture at how partition and displacement helped to unsettle patriarchy through expanding middle-class women's "domesticity to include public duties in the political, social, and economic spheres" (Basu Guha-Chaudhury 2009, 67). Yet, as partition novels born of the self-assured identity politics of neoliberal India, the Mukherjee narratives remain unilaterally developmental in aligning the Bengali rural past with the global present. The narrative teleology disappears the oppressed bāngāl village widow in favor of the Bengali New Woman. The new heroine—a self-propelled, consuming woman who rises above religious and class prejudices—lies at the temporal core of both the original novel and the sequel (even though the centrality is less obvious in the sequel). All in all, Sirshendu Mukherjee's works give a neoliberal lease on life to a male reformist stereotype. It pits the gendered backwardness of East Bengali village life, found in early twentieth-century Bengali nationalist literature, in contrast to a New Woman savior figure. A not dissimilar narrative of neoliberal progress surfacing in Aparna Sen's descriptions can certainly be traced to the filmic fiction of *Goynar Baksho*. Precisely the linear timeline of story and image was also picked out and celebrated by the reviews quoted earlier.

Yet, Aparna Sen's performance of signature, her insistence on the enlarged ghostliness of the naughty old aunt from the East Bengal village is suggestive of another temporal trace. It calls forth a slim but provocative legacy of the uncanny Bengali female in which Aparna's own star text is included. Best described in Priya Jaikumar's words as an "anti-heritage" form of spectrality that recalls with guilt an inassimilable past (2017, 237), ghost fictions appeared in Bangla films directed by such eminent parallel and mainstream directors as Satyajit Ray, Tapan Sinha, and Ajoy Kar, among others, in the post-partition decades of social turmoil in West Bengal (1950s–1970s). Female hauntings became a way to stage frictions between rural and urban habitation and crises in bourgeois masculinity (Dhusiya 2018, 24–27). The Aparna Sen starrer *Kayahiner Kahini* (Tale of the Bodiless; 1973), directed by Ajoy Kar, depicts female ghostliness in relation to tensile masculinity. Similar interrelations appear in the gender drama of *Goynar Baksho*, reworked into comedy. Telling in this light is a promotional column written by Aparna Sen for the "Bengali Movie News" section of *Times of India* to mark the theatrical premier of *Goynar Baksho* in 2013 (Sen 2013). While she reiterates her signatory decision by noting just how much she came to "love" the character of the aged aunt/ghost at the first reading, she goes on to describe how she has been "haunted" through the years by the filmic possibilities offered by the character of a village child widow/ghost. We go on to read that she has been in the imaginary grips of a drama of comedic "streetsmartness" combined with "angry" rebellion against the high-caste Hindu family structure.

Along these lines, Aparna Sen's column suggests an ambivalent practice of genre in *Goynar Baksho*. Her description braids an anti-heritage haunting by the specter of a bāngāl village widow, animated by an inassimilable systemic anger, with the timely progressivist storyline about "the changing position of women in society." The column promises a contradictory assemblage of ethnic attributes for the Bangla brand comedy. This feminist director's depiction of intent complicates hype authorship by stimulating desire for what Naomi Scheman conceptualizes as a particular form of feminist consciousness-raising, that which counter-tells women's indignant feelings in a "controversial" mode (1980, 186). In this context, the indignant controversy is linked to regional histories of othering: of Hindu family women, of the village, of bāngāl dialect. By staging such transnational feminist hauntings by shapes of geosocial marginalization, Aparna Sen's authorial voice at once dwells within, yet detracts from, the temporality of heritage consumption promised by the imminent theatrical release of *The Jewelry Box*. This conflict between consumerist progress and its elisions is traceable to the genre-mixed politics of the filmic text. The text encodes a self-critical feminist's interminable crossing of neoliberal urban India's regional peripheries: her imperfect striving to be "with specters [as a] politics of memory, of inheritance, and of generations" (Derrida 1994, viii–xix).

A Comedic Brand and Regional Specters:
Goynar Baksho

The ghost comedy maps a women-centered domestic drama in the vein of Bangla comedic and romantic social films onto a wide historical canvas. It depicts a chest of jewels passing through the hands of three generations of women and changing in significance. To the village widow-turned-ghost Pishima (Moushumi Chatterjee), inhabiting a neglected corner of her natal joint family, it is the *streedhan* (woman's wealth) that brings some measure of authority. To her niece-in-law Somlata (Konkona Sen Sharma), it is entrepreneurial capital to be deployed for setting up a sari shop to rehabilitate the fortunes of her marital family of feudal landowners, displaced by the India-Pakistan partition in 1947. To the liberated leftist grandniece Chaitali (Srabonti Chatterjee), it is meaningless until transformed into a means to support freedom fighters in the Bangladesh Liberation War of 1971. This tale of women's generations is entwined with another of conflict experienced by Somlata between obligatory duty toward her husband and Hindu domesticity and her illicit desire for a Muslim poet (Kaushik Sen) from then–East Pakistan. The dutiful Somlata's clandestine longings are kindled, first, by the comically rebellious Pishima (as a ghost), who had been confined in her youth to the austere isolation of a child-less Hindu widow under authoritarian patriarchy and, later, by her sexually liberated daughter Chaitali, who learns of the unfulfilled romance from letters left behind by the dead poet (driven to suicide out of despair about the failed romance). The same actress is cast in the double roles of a sexually repressed young Pishima and the liberated Chaitali. The narrative certainly seems to offer a sexy brand of love-and-liberation "saga," as put by one reviewer (Dutta 2013). Moreover, the travel of the jewelry box across generations and meanings showcases India's heritage of selective benevolence toward regional neighbors like Bangladesh. Mithuraaj Dhusiya classifies the film in an Indian spate of *film blanc* horror that features supernatural benevolence for the A-category box office (2018, 160). However, Aparna Sen's insistence on feminism and a haunting draw me to a textual trace of spectrality that jostles against the benevolent resolution.

As the opening credits roll, the screen comes alive with a black-and-white animation sequence unfolding to rock-and-roll beats. A jewelry chest looms onscreen and falls open, spilling out necklaces, bracelets, and a rolling rug that sprouts a tree. The lyric spins a tale of all that is held in the box: a carpet of dreams that touches your body and endless *bakambakam*, tittle-tattle of storytelling. Tripping down the carpet to scamper up the tree is the *galper berāl* (the cat of tales). The cat wags its tail to catch a flying hookah, only to morph into a portly female figure perched on the branch and puffing at the hookah. By elasticizing shapes with variable-speed cinematography, this theme animation disrupts the idea of a natural human process and concomitant conventions of time and space (Beckman 2014, 7–8). The witticism of the accompanying lyric mimics rhymes and tropes that are traditional to women's oral culture from the Bengal village, performing a way to be with the inheritance of an enchanted lifeworld at odds with urban anthropocentric orders. This opening animation sequence sets up shape-shifts as an aesthetic motif of spatiotemporal subversion, soon to foray into live action.

The narrative starts by implicitly raising controversy about the role taken by jewelry in reinforcing the sexual abjection of wealthy Hindu women. Quick shots of a village girl named Rashmoni being dressed as a child bride in resplendent gold jewelry are replaced by close-ups of her in the denuding process of high-caste Hindu widowhood: the ornaments are being seized from the child's body and her lustrous hair is being forcibly cropped. The montage rounds out with aged Rashmoni, now the neglected and lonely Pishima (aunt), secretly counting her gold ornaments and putting them on, although forbidden to do the latter by the sexually abject austerity enforced by Hindu widowhood. Despite these moments of pleasure and authority garnered from her refugee/landowner family through possession of her own streedhan, the widowed, elderly Pishima lives in isolation except for a nonhuman companion. A white cat that used to circle her lonesome existence sits by Pishima's corpse—lying in a forsaken top floor of the family abode—and it subsequently reappears to signal the coming of Pishima's ghost. The ghost who rises from Pishima's corpse with a horrific grin momentarily encodes a haunting by female abjection of heritage spaces—a rich mahogany four-poster, the grand family mansion. However, it soon morphs into a feminist spectrality raging against female abjection. Soon the specter forays into patriarchal orders, the most spectacular intrusion being an ensemble rap performance. The performance pits the angry female specter, an internal other refusing assimilation, against the identity of an agentive modern woman.

Two patriarchs, Somlata's father-in-law and older brother-in-law (Paran Bandopadhyay and Pijush Ganguly), are seated center-frame to interrogate daughter-in-law Somlata for starting a family business without permission. The ghost of Pishima is implicated in the transgressive act because she had supported Somlata's independent enterprise. A tracking camera reveals the decorously covered Somlata in one dark corner, quaking with submissive anxiety. Yet this seemingly demure woman has contravened patriarchal authority to start a clothing (sari) business intended to save the displaced family from penury. The interrogation intensifies as the feudal patriarchs press on with righteous indignation for a confession. A Dolby-enhanced rap of bāngāl verbiage spewed by the men to the accompaniment of gesticulating hands and hookahs animates the interrogation. Somlata must admit that she defiled the *bangśa maryādā* (family honor) by using inherited jewelry as capital, thus demonstrating her lowly commercial mentality. Jane Marcus notes that European literary traditions assuming bourgeois patriarchal domesticity and concomitant female humility have seen "righteous indignation . . . as the rightful emotion . . . of patriarchs in the state and the family" (1988, 122). In a similar systemic vein, women's rightful anger has been marginal to Bangla reformist social films favoring pleasant womanhood, entangled as these are with a Victorian morality deriving from British colonialism. (I discussed this generic propensity in chapter 1.) Precisely the genre of respectable pleasance is being subversively upstaged here by Somlata's decorum. While the latter appears to be respectably capitulating to patriarchal authority, she makes the backward bāngāl patriarchs into objects of ridicule removed from West Bengali urban domesticity. At the same time, Somlata is agentive in replacing feudal patriarchy with the modern heteronormative couple form. Off and on, the camera cuts to the supportive demeanor of Somlata's husband and business partner, Chandan (Saswata Chatterjee), who has joined hands with his proactive West Bengali wife to pull his idle refugee family out of poverty. The crescendo grows unpleasantly righteous, however, as Pishima's ghost enters the rapping contest.

Materializing androgynously next to Somlata's docile figure, the desexual-ized apparition (in widow's white weeds and close-cropped hair) abusively feminizes Somlata for being a hypocritical *dhangī*—in other words, a postur-ing sissy. As explained below, this abusive resistance to the posture of female humility is intertextual with the mode-retro interactions with the classic Bangla social film through which Aparna Sen, at the moment, was reworking and updating her own star persona on parallel media platforms. In the scene at hand, a steady camera at medium range shows Pishima's ghost taking charge by planting herself behind the men's chairs and beginning to rap against the righteous voices. The soundtrack blasts out a crossfire of *jiga, jiga, jiga* (ask, ask, ask) with the ghost swaying in impatient ire against Somlata's silence and the patriarchs rapping on their abusive questions. Suddenly the sonic battle gives way to ghostly whispers in the men's ears, reminding them of their vices. Male tones deflate and the faces crumble in emasculated embarrassment. As the ghost turns and elastically dissolves into the background, she dances in triumphant mischief. Although she stays within a cramped domestic space oppressed by patriarchs, this queerly unassimilated specter of the "dushtu buri pishima" from East Bengal can also expand antagonistically against the heteropatriarchal spaces and times encompassing urban Bengali womanhood.

Yet the politics of domesticity in and around the rap scene is complexly layered as the scene divides the entrepreneurial New Woman from spectral Bengali difference; at the same time, it depicts an unlikely family tie between the two. The relationship has been metaphoric of a working through of border conflict, encoded in antagonistic haunting by the regional other. Earlier in the narrative, the rowdy village apparition is seen swooping into Somlata's kitchen to shatter pots and pans while asserting unacceptable regional preferences (for smelly anchovies typical to some rural Bengali cuisines, for example). The animosity transmutes, however, into scenes of the ghost materializing to take over Somlata's account-keeping with village-style mathematical alac-rity, or actively participating in plans to expand the business by offering her jewels for liquidation as capital. These episodes have resulted from Somlata's decision to name the sari shop after Pishima and enshrine the memory of the neglected widow. They animate the urban West Bengali filmmaker's ways of being with gendered specters of inheritance: the village bāngāl, East Bengal, a little-educated woman and her desires. We also find a female-focused rework-ing of Bangla partition comedies like the classic *Ora Thake Odhare* (They Live on the Other Side; 1954; dir. Sukumar Dasgupta), which pivoted on the growth of solidarity between refugee and host-country men.

This transnational feminist drama of cross-border female friendship is further inflected by heterogeneous desires that unsettle Somlata's Hindu domestic identity. Scenes of the childless aged widow's sexy tittle-tattle with

Somlata—evoking a villager's carnivalesque "frankness . . . about the chamber intimacies of [heterosexual] private life" (Bakhtin 1984, 105)—has oriented desire away from heteronormative Hindu domesticity. In this vein, carnivalesque protest against the sexual compromises Somlata makes rages at the tragicomic moment of the ghost's final and failed performance of inassimilable systemic anger. We see Pishima's ghost peering from outside the bedroom window at Somlata making love to her husband, Chandan. Somlata has escaped back to the sanctuary of Hindu monogamy from her own illicit desire for the man from the other side of national and religious borders, the Bengali Muslim poet from East Pakistan. She has returned to the conjugal bed from her momentary deviant act of pursuing the lovelorn poet, to which she had been prompted by the ghost. Pishima's ghost had coaxed Somlata to follow her illicit desire for the Muslim *parpurush* (other man)—effectively, to disengage from heteronormative Hindu nationalism. But Somlata reverts back to bourgeois Hindu domestic relations, depicted in the scene at hand through close-ups of coital intimacy. The camera cuts to a deftly digitized spectacle of dwindling subversion as the form of Pishima's ghost shrinks and dissolves away. The ethnically tensile drama of both conflict and growing solidarity—between the ghostly bāngāl refugee and a West Bengali woman—gives way to an ethnic heritage narrative. The specter of the female other is soon to be aligned with the urban West Bengali feminist.

Thereafter, Pishima returns as a benign apparition who possesses Somlata's sexually liberated daughter Chaitali only. Chaitali has recognized the widowed Pishima's thwarted sexual energies. In the portrayal of Chaitali, we find a self-assured Indian identity politics that is noticeable as well in Sirshendu Mukherjee's neoliberal partition novels (discussed earlier). This new brand of ethnic womanhood—Chaitali speaking polished urban Indian Bengali and wearing authentic handwoven saris—is shown to reject heteronormative Hindu nationalism. As a participant in Indian leftist student movements and cross-border activism, Chaitali forges a romantic relationship across caste and class barriers. Moreover, she implicitly influences her spectral grandaunt into the benevolent mission of donating the jewelry chest to young freedom fighters battling for the liberation of Bangladesh in the war raging across India's border. The aesthetic of ghostliness has altered as well. Mischievous shape-shifts and disorderly hauntings once encoded another lifeworld in conflict with the languages and mores of Indian urban development. Now they give way to a stable alignment. In a metaphorically telling scene, we see Pishima's ghost perched on the backseat of New Woman Chaitali's motorbike to share a moment of consumerist freedom. The female specters of the nation's regional and village peripheries seem to have been assimilated into a "tutelary present" (Derrida 1994, xix) led by the New Woman savior. Note that tutelary episodes like the motorbike ride were noted by reviewers as some of the most "memorable"

(M. Bhaumik 2013). What this reception discourse ignored is the remainder of sensations, longings for different and inassimilable specters. My attempt to follow the plot of Aparna Sen's conviction about the "feminism" in this work makes me linger on the inassimilable trace.

The final shots show Somlata on the same remote terrace reading the undelivered letters written to her by the Bengali Muslim poet for whom she once had longed. The overpowering sentimentality of the dead poet's voice (a duet of recitation and song performed by actor Kaushik Sen and vocalist Rupankar Bagchi) haunts the soundtrack. The intense auditory appeal of the cresting to song evokes a Bangla tradition of literary romanticism that, according to Dipesh Chakrabarty, tends to recreate the past as a "way of vigilant waiting . . . [for] a political yield" (2004, 682). Written and translated (for English subtitles) by Aparna Sen, the lyric joins with visual technique to animate political vigilance at the vanishing point. An urban Indian feminist wants to be with regional others as she also loses touch. While the lyric sings of a "woman of mist," we see Pishima's ghost claim the screen. The camera has begun to track her departure from the mansion she possessed. A momentary close-up depicts Pishima glancing up at Somlata on the terrace and, with a wistful smile, turning away in response to a poetic cue. The soundtrack has picked up a duet of voices intoning these words: "Between us the flowing river creates a *byabadhān* [rift] / Between you and me / Between the two Bengals." It goes on to ask, "Woman from the other side / Is that why you came / To build a bridge of mist?" We are seeing a final, irreversible shapeshift: Pishima's ghost walks through the yawning doors of a gate, dwindles, and dissolves into a mist-shrouded river (fig. 22). Shots of swirling fog cut to a fleeting flashback of Somlata's momentary meeting with the Muslim poet from East Pakistan. The soundtrack is belting out an emotional ditty of how "time began a frenzied dance" because he (the poet) had fallen in love with the woman from the other side, the *kafer* (one of another faith; an infidel).

All in all, the political yield of the vigilance staged by *Goynar Baksho* is a haunting by byabadhān that exceeds benevolent bridgework. The byabadhān is a counter-telling of spatio-cultural rifts: between the two Bengals and the isomorphic geographies of religion assumed by partition (Hindu India versus Muslim East Pakistan or Bangladesh); between the villager and urbanized women; and between different linguistic lifeworlds. The latter include rifts not only between village and urban West Bengali but also between Sanskritized Hindu Bangla and Muslim or Musalmani Bangla, merely tokenized in the words *kāfer* and *pāni*. It is noteworthy that within the infrastructural and social divisions historical to West Bengali modernity, some such rifts are more easily codifiable as an aesthetic choice than others. The ethnic exclusions impacting language and cinema in the Bengal region fall into the latter category. Whereas the ethnic specter of the Hindu village-style bāngāl in this case is partially

Fig. 22: Pishima's ghost dissolves in the river of rifts (Source: *Goynar Baksho*)

embraced by this work, the specter of the Muslim Bengali turns out to be a fast-disappearing trace. Although Aparna Sen went on to combine linguistic with religious difference in her very next production, *Arshinagar* (2015), yet another prescient drama of Hindu-Muslim conflict within India, the representation of Muslim speech, incorporated urban Bengali into North Indian Urdu/Hindustani. The mixed-mode language used in *Arshinagar* converges more with the North Indian linguistic brand of Hindi/Urdu dominating Bollywood than with the language spoken across the border in Bangladesh. As historicized by Firdous Azim and Perween Hasan, the latter is a variable "mixture of Arabic and Persian words . . . with the local, spoken Bengali" (2014, 31).[4] The Hindification of Bengali is a trending brand in metropolitan West Bengali media.

Nonetheless, the above account demonstrates how a star-author persona like Aparna Sen inhabiting trends of femaleness and kin relations could partially disaggregate conceptual appeal (for example, make rift a concept to be hauntingly reckoned with among women and families of the divided region). Recognized as one star who keeps up with the times (Bakshi and Dasgupta 2017), she continuously works across parallel media platforms to engender fandom for timely tastes and controversies. The above history of partially re-authoring Bangla brand heritage remains incomplete unless we briefly follow another expressive detail of her transmedial labor. We see her star-author persona being worked through in "mode retro and pastiche" (Biswas 2000, 127). A small-scale infrastructure for sexual-political commentary is being generated in between large-scale structures of global Bengali media.

Take, for example, a head pose that appeared on billboards to advertise her editorship of the woman's magazine *Prothoma Ekhon* (First Woman Now), roughly around the time *Goynar Baksho* was released. The pose works as pastiche by showing an older Aparna Sen reproduce an irreverent head tilt not unlike her irreverent posture in the superhit working-women melodrama from 1973, *Basanta Bilap* (Lament of Spring; dir. Dinen Gupta) (fig. 23). In the same vein, in recent television interviews Aparna has been asserting that she loved playing only comic roles because they precluded *nyākāmi*, a style of coyness requiring heroines to "flirt" with the audience, eyes downcast (as helpfully explained by the star-author herself; Sen 2017). The assertion about loving comic roles, typically accompanied on the television platform by "mode-retro" clips from her comic roles, such as in *Basanta Bilap*, certainly updates Aparna Sen's star persona for a multiplex platform on which comedy is a brand value. When used as pastiche to advertise the women's magazine, however, the comic pose is being reclaimed from the prefabricated persona of transgressive coyness. It is being invested afresh with an attitude of change. Like her earlier magazine enterprises, *First Woman Now* staged the contradictions of globalizing Indian culture. It combined images and advice on women's self-help and bodily confidence with editorials by Sen about the sexualized *bhedābhed* (divisiveness) immanent to the heteropatriarchal Indian nation-state. To restate her words, the bhedābhed is leveled against the aged and childless, religious minorities, the physically and the mentally challenged, and LGBTQ communities (Sen 2014). Thus, the contradictions of geosocial awareness and heritage erotica in and around the text of *Goynar Baksho* must be situated in a thick web of mediatization. This web of appeals suggests that the large-scale media spaces of the 2000s could be unsettled from within by small-scale practitioners of dissident transnationalism but only partially and temporarily so.

Fig. 23: Aparna Sen's irreverent pose (Source: *Basanta Bilap*)

Dissident transnationalism takes a bolder generic form in Rubaiyat Hossain's *Meherjaan*. The mode of production differs as well from the corporate model of *Goynar Baksho*. The fiction film directed by Rubaiyat was independently produced and family-financed. Nonetheless, the latter intersects with the mainstream women's productions studied in this book insofar as it was made as a social genre film for theatrical release and exhibited with "brand-partner" support in metropolitan film halls of Bangladesh. The family-mode production history of *Meherjaan* helps to further explore a key question of this chapter—how women's gendered customs of infrastructure building, historic to South Asia, might enable small-scale interventions in globalizing formations and brand criteria. Rubaiyat is one among a new non-star generation of South Asian women filmmakers moving along familial, national, and global Northern transnational circuits. The cohort includes such directors of New Pakistani Cinema as Sabiha Sumar, Mehreen Jabbar, and Meenu Gaur, among others. For this generation of non-star filmmakers, the opportunities and the limits for dissident decisions arise from multiple locations and infrastructural interests. The complexity of the transnational traversal lies in the fact that both national and northern "world cinema" infrastructures can bring along conceptual borders. While these borders could grow flagrantly exclusive under postcolonial statist tensions, they could also work more flexibly to include and occlude difference. The flexibility is conditioned by transnationally trending concepts about regions of the global South, such as development or terror.

Crossing the Trans/National: Border Cinema and Rubaiyat Hossain in Bangladesh

Over the past few years, Rubaiyat Hossain has gained increasing visibility in international circuits and film festivals through the release of two critically acclaimed fiction films, *Under Construction* (2015) and *Made in Bangladesh* (2019). The latter is being distributed by the Paris-based independent distributor, Pyramide Films. Moreover, Rubaiyat Hossain's academic background places her among a privileged cohort of transnational young women from South Asia. Both her background and her pathway through filmmaking set her apart from the Bangladeshi female stars and filmmakers Kohinoor Akhter Shuchanda, Babita, and Nargis Akhter. As discussed in previous chapters, the latter work through local infrastructures or small-scale and contingent transnational infrastructures. Rubaiyat is internationally educated in women's and gender studies, South Asian studies, religious studies, and film (respectively at Smith College, the University of Pennsylvania, School of Oriental and African Studies, University of London, and New York University's Tisch School of the Arts) (rubaiyat-hossain.com/about/). However, in her own impassioned testimony to me (personal interview, 2014), Rubaiyat Hossain said she has always been a "nationalist" invested in the debates on community, identity, and difference ongoing in the public sphere of Bangladesh. I learned from her that since 2003 she had been writing commentaries on nationalism for the *Daily Star*, the leading English-language newspaper of Bangladesh. In being active for national and regional concerns, Rubaiyat Hossain's practice overlaps with Aparna Sen's. Her working of the familial mode of production intersects as well with that of Aparna Sen and others across South Asia. Unlike her recent made-for-festival films, her debut feature, *Meherjaan*, as a counternarrative spoke straight to ongoing border debates on nation and otherness in Bangladesh through a family-centric social fiction made in the Muktijuddho film genre.

Elora Halim Chowdhury (2016; 2020; 2022) notes that "Bangladeshi films about the Muktijuddho (Bangladesh Liberation War of 1971) occupy critical significance within the genre of national cinema . . . [because both war cinema and literature] have been the mediums through which a collective memory and national solidarity have been shaped" (2020, 283). If Rubaiyat Hossain's resolve to make a film in this culturally significant genre meant that she sought to participate in the collective debates about the past, her stated inclination (to me) to make a fiction film with the right conventional ingredients for theatrical release also meant she was reaching out to local urban audiences (as well as to the diasporic Bangladeshi and other transnational viewers). Along these lines, the narrative takes up familiar conventions of Muktijuddho cinema. Primary among these is the trope of the female rape victim as the *birāngona*, or war heroine. Nayanika Mookherjee explains that the birāngona as an ideal produced by state discourse in the wake of the Liberation War has been circulating and being reinvented through decades of visual arts and literature (2015, 129–135, 186–227). Idealistic constructions of the birāngona have oscillated between abjection and eroticization: on the one hand, the despondent, bleak, and mutely fearful woman and, on the other, the shockingly pleasurable "sexually transgressed, unstable raped woman" (188, 193). Other key tropes are those of Bangladeshi "male valor" (E. Chowdhury 2020, 283), hinging on the trauma of the raped Bengali woman and craving to "'flush' out the enemy," as against the monstrous enmity of the Pakistani soldier who can only and naturally be bad (E. Chowdhury 2016, 35).

Such war film conventions were particularly timely for the context in which *Meherjaan* was released. The release of the film coincided with the war crimes tribunal set up by the Bangladesh government to investigate collaborators in the genocide and crimes against humanity perpetrated during the 1971 war (E. Chowdhury 2016, 27). These trials were further monumentalizing in national memory the "negative sublime" value of existing tropes of wartime trauma and triumph. Dominick La Capra theorizes the negative sublime in relation to the Holocaust and Hiroshima. In his words, "Extremely destructive events

. . . may become occasions of negative sublimity or displaced sacralization . . . [by producing] founding traumas . . . that paradoxically become the valorized or intensely cathected basis of identity . . . rather than events that pose the problem of identity" (2001, 23). Conventions of Muktijuddho cinema tended to refer to a few sacralized concepts of national trauma and heroic identity even as they adapted to new trends of Bangla social film. The conceptual framework of *Meherjaan* stakes a radical departure from the sacralized referents. Created forty years after the Bangladesh Liberation War, this fiction film constitutes a feminist way of "working through" (22) problems of identity and difference in neocolonial South Asia and mourning the sexualized trauma of the Bengali Muslim experience in the subcontinent. The lens on trauma and healing is the story of a family torn apart by inherited and newfound familial feelings. The backdrop is the war-ravaged landscape of the Liberation War.

Rubaiyat Hossain's authorial perspective, being deeply inspired by her international academic training in feminism and critical South Asian history, infuses the sacralized conventions of national identity animating Muktijuddho cinema with what are best described in Kathleen McHugh's words as "perverse" aesthetic choices (2009a, 143). We see a cross-border romance grow between the Bangladeshi village girl Meher (Shaina Amin) and an ethical, wounded Pakistani soldier, Wasim Khan (Omar Rahim). A conscientious defector from the brutal Pakistani army, Wasim saves Meher from impending rape by other Pakistani soldiers. We also find the character of a war-rape survivor named Neela (Reetu Sattar) explicitly revolting against the stereotype of the birāngona as a mentally and morally unstable transgressor. The figuration of Neela forays into the erotic consumption of the female rape victim generic to Muktijuddho visuality by wresting the sexy look away from its clandestine appeal as well as speaking openly against the shaming of the raped female body. She appears onscreen in sleeveless blouses and trendy synthetic saris and, at the same time, characterizes wartime rape as falling in a continuum of sexual violence on women. In this vein, Neela is shown to work through the problem of identity of the traumatized rape survivor by also moving forward to become a female Muktijoddha (freedom fighter) for the liberation of Bangladesh. We find yet another complex female character working through gendered war identities in the form of the whimsical Salma Khala, played by the filmmaker Rubaiyat Hossain. Salma chooses to enter into a pleasurable *mutā* (temporary) marriage with a male Muktijoddha, a marriage that turns the fighter away from belliger-ent enmity. We also see queer male figurations in the characters of two Baul singers (hereditary mystical poets of the Bengal region) who give shelter to the wounded Wasim and join Meher in familial care work. The bulk of the story, staged as a flashback narrated by the older Meher (Jaya Bachchan), unfolds in the home of Meher's grandfather (Victor Banerjee) or on surrounding lush landscapes of the village, where the family has taken refuge from the violent

Pakistani aggression raging in the city (the pristine village, too, is soon raided by Pakistani soldiers). Elora Halim Chowdhury analyzes in persuasive detail the ethics of trauma and healing woven into this complex romantic narrative (2015; 2016; 2020). For the purposes of this book, I will stay with the production side of *Meherjaan* and related negotiations of authorial control by Rubaiyat Hossain.

In the words of the *Meherjaan* press kit, the aim of the work was to create "women's feminine re-visiting of the Bangladesh national liberation . . . as a [story about] loving the Other that advocates an aesthetic solution to violence" (qtd. in E. Chowdhury 2016, 29). The production sought to metaphorically embody an "aesthetic solution" to regional conflict through bringing together a cross-border infrastructure of personnel and aesthetic legacies. The Bangladeshi team was joined from India by actors Jaya Bachchan and Victor Banerjee and music director Neil Mukherjee, and from Pakistan by actor-dancer Omar Rahim and singer Nayyara Noor. The soundtrack combined the mystical lyrics of Bangladeshi Baul poet Lalon Shah with a song of longing and separation in the typical Urdu *ghazal* form written by Pakistan's national poet, Faiz Ahmed Faiz. This pairing of aesthetic politics with the production process is not uncommon to regionally grounded transnational cinema. It sheds light on how small-scale networking across borders could come to be integral to the practice of critical transnationalism in the once-indivisible region of northern South Asia. We see the same critical-aesthetic approach to infrastructure in the making of the border fiction *Ramchand Pakistani* (2008) by woman director Mehreen Jabbar in Pakistan. As put in a retrospective by the producer and co-scriptwriter Javed Jabbar, father of director Mehreen, the family-produced film shows how "two politically-estranged states, and professionals from different countries and fields can work constructively together to help create a shared narrative" (2018). Not only was the Pakistani team of performers and crew enhanced by the invited participation of Indians, including the alternative female star and filmmaker Nandita Das and the Kolkata-based music director Debajyoti Mishra, but *Ramchand Pakistani* was also theatrically released at a number of venues in both Pakistan and India. The shared counternarrative born of the collaboration depicts border violence through the plight of a Hindu Dalit (untouchable caste) family living in a village in Pakistan.

In the case of *Meherjaan*, we often hear that the release provoked tremendous controversy in print and social media and finally led to a ban. The story told less often is that the ban happened only *after* it had passed censorship and was successfully exhibited in several urban theaters across Bangladesh. What remains understated, in other words, is the story of Rubaiyat Hossain's successes as a woman filmmaker in Bangladesh with making a potentially controversial work in the hallowed Muktijuddho genre, with having it legitimized by the censor board, and with accessing corporate "brand-partner" conglomerates to promote and release *Meherjaan*. These successes demonstrate a key argument of this book. They illustrate how in South Asia, women, as filmic authors, work at small scale and through familial networks to claim control over large-scale structures of film production and cultural politics. If female star-authors like Aparna Sen reuse their own familial personas to negotiate fandom for social contestation and feminist cinema, non-star filmmakers like Rubaiyat Hossain operate at familial and social levels to accrue resources for cultural change. Thus, it is worth reiterating the politicized history of film business in South Asia. As discussed at length in the introduction, family-based film business stems from a cultural politics of the domestic that is resistive to colonial and neocolonial statist regimes. Bangla filmmaking in Bangladesh, in particular, was spawned by an anti-Pakistan-state language movement that brought women from elite backgrounds into familial businesses of cinema and theater. My larger point is that female authorship both in Bangladesh and across the region could well involve molding structures of resource and affect in culturally specific modes. In this respect, my archival findings complicate the center-margin approach found in some transnational studies of South Asian women's cinema.

One recent scholarly position is that women making counter-cinema in South Asia have to rely on established familial/dynastic structures because there is a lack of independent structures of funding and distribution. As such, they should be seen as "perform[ing] creative autonomy in terms of espousing alternative *content* whilst operating within corporate and mainstream structures" (Devasundaram 2020, 32; italics in original). In this view, the domains deemed most conducive to South Asian women's creative content are transnational networks spawned mostly from the global North, such as online streaming systems and women-targeted film festivals (Devasundaram 2020). My regional emphasis on women's cinema interrogates the north-south dichotomy implied by this scholarly perspective through filling in the archival gaps. The cases studied in this chapter and throughout the book demonstrate that in South Asia, women interact with and partially control gendered structures of familial and corporate opportunity, including brand formation, to author differences. Beyond this, I argue that global Northern structures of opportunity could impose their own borderly limits of timeliness and relevance. Let me elaborate.

Rubaiyat Hossain's initial failure to gather funds for *Meherjaan* turned around when Ashique Mostafa, the Bengali man she was to marry, stepped forward as a business partner for their small film company. He became the producer and forged contacts with a prospective cinematographer and a screenwriter. The more compelling story of *authoring a production mode*, told to me in impassioned bits and pieces by the filmmaker, was of how she molded the couple-mode business and a male-dominant infrastructure of skills her way. As she poured out her stories of making, Rubaiyat was effectively plotting and positioning for me her feminist vision of aesthetic independence. I heard not only that her producer husband had stayed away from the set at her insistence, tacitly conceding control, but also that she had disagreed with the script written by Ebadur Rahman (from the hundred-scene concept she had provided). I also heard that while Rahman went on to publish the screenplay he had composed as a novel under his own name, Rubaiyat Hossain forged ahead with both re-scripting and directing *Meherjaan* stage by stage. She told me repeatedly that she had put a "whole lot of herself" into the work, in terms not only of her academic training but also of her own family life and domestic surroundings. The stories of struggles and triumphs I heard are well encapsulated in Lingzhen Wang's terms as a female author's performative interactions with a male-familial structure of opportunity (2011, 25). Rubaiyat's compelling tale of a filmmaker's piecemeal claims of creative control drew me to the filmic text, to possible mimetic traces of an evolving authorial scene. What came close to me was the figuration of the whimsical story maker Salma Khala. The materiality of practice seemed to have been transformed into the allegory of a female author who orients the generic image another way. The role is played by Rubaiyat Hossain herself, albeit by her testimony, because another actress could not be found for the part.

Salma Khala, born under the historical trauma of 1947, is the romantic protagonist Meher's childlike and unstable aunt. Not only is she unmatured but also given to momentary mad bouts of weeping. She is best seen as another aesthetic trace of the psychic wounds left by partitions and warfare, a configuration paralleling the rape survivor in the Muktijuddho genre. As the aesthetic link between the two partitions of the Bengal region, Salma Khala's character revivifies the collective geopolitical memory of the Bengal region in the vein of the generational narrative in *Goynar Baksho*. A comparative consideration of the two works, *Meherjaan* and *Goynar Baksho*, reveals the different historical vantage points of cultural production in South Asia. The India-Pakistan partition and its consequences remain foremost for the West Bengali perspective depicted in *Goynar Baksho* and, in fact, for other Indian filmic narratives in this genre. By contrast, we see in *Meherjaan* an exploration of how Muktijuddho "displaced and reconstituted older meanings of Partition" by brutally reinforcing the "irresolution" of the Bengali Muslim question in South Asian and Pakistani history (Siddiqi 2017). This counter-telling is primary from the vantage point of Bangladesh.

Salma Khala drives the narrative and provokes tropic perversions of existing generic conventions. It is she who whimsically grants Meher "permission" to care for the other, the wounded Pakistani soldier Wasim, and later states with veiled approval that Meher has fallen in love. For her, Meher's story is one among many about unfulfilled romantic yearnings to cross borders and heal conflict. She tells another such story to Meher, not only providing a pretext for the outcome of Meher's relationship but also implying a metatext for the filmic narrative. This metatext of impossible heteronormative resolutions is intensified through imagery of color and space. Salma Khala hides out from the bustle of humdrum rationality to tell her love stories in a closet. There, she bonds with her niece Meher, clothed in matching pink and bold colors. At other times, Salma sits with Meher amid lush village greenery, playing with similarly colorful objects (see fig. 24). The pointedly pretty mise-en-scènes gesture at a non-normative sexual "solution" to hetero-aggressive border conflict (to restate the words of the press kit, quoted above). They attach queer meanings to excessive and form-spilling colors, as against austere straightness, in a way familiar to film theory and European art cinema (Galt 2013, 92–98). Whereas in her interactions with Meher, the female author-figure Salma Khala evokes sapphic desire, in other scenic constructions she configures onscreen the director's declared haptic choice of "feminizing the patriarchs" (Hossain, personal interview, 2014). The point, in other words, is to dismantle the phallic violence at the core of dominant masculinity and, by extension, of war. In this vein, Salma Khala touches a freedom fighter's manhood with sexual longing by waylaying him with a colorfully amorous posture. We see Salma at medium close-up seated (unaccountably) in a palanquin surrounded by a burst of bright lights and hues as she beckons the young man; soon thereafter she kindles within him the desire for a temporary mutā marriage.[5] The larger implication of the temporariness is that no heterosexual romance comes to be fulfilled and stabilized in this sexually critical narrative. As Salma's partner, the softened freedom fighter extends familial care to the wounded Pakistani soldier. He helps Wasim to escape, once the latter's refuge with the Baul singers and relationship with Meher are discovered, and he is both hounded by local fighters and chastised by Meher's joint family. Overall, Salma Khala is something of an author of feminist utopia in the vein of Monique Wittig's Les Guerilleres: the creator of a "mythic space" centering on women and bodies that lend a "female imprint" to nature and the outside world (Komar 1994, 97). Rubaiyat Hossain was clear in noting to me Wittig's influence on her aesthetic choices in Meherjaan.

Noteworthy are how tropes of village landscapes and riverine plains become key to the feminist utopia of queer longings that breach borders. In its landscape imagery, Meherjaan both intersects with yet diverges from The Jewelry Box (which came two years later), revealing how imaginative and geopolitical perspectives overlap and differ between the Bengals. Whereas in The Jewelry Box, the riverine village in Bengal constitutes a specter of lost lands and inheritances, in Meherjaan, the verdant village landscape makes up a possible site of utopian plenitude and cross-border community. Perhaps we see in the metaphoric spatiality of the latter a revivification of critical nationalism like that found in Zahir Raihan's Behula. As a mythological allegory spawned by

Fig. 24: Rubaiyat Hossain as Salma Khala with Meher amid lush greenery (Source: *Meherjaan*)

the Bangla Language Movement, *Behula* evokes the riverine plenitude of a Bengal village as a politicized trigger against destructive forces standing in for the repressive Pakistani state (discussed in chapter 2). The final shots of the Meher-Wasim romance are also set on the bank of the river down which Wasim must leave. His path of escape—having been drawn by the authorial hand of Salma Khala (in a sketch)—is strewn with signs of twigs and flowers breaking through arid landscape. Metaphoric of life, the uneven landscape stages community across division and difference. We see the transformed Muktijoddha (Salma's mutā husband) helping Wasim's departure, a boatman ferrying Wasim to safety, and Meher herself, bidding Wasim farewell with a gift of *tasbih* prayer beads. The beads not only signify protective solidarity but also a blending of her Bengaliness with Muslimness. The issue of whether a Bengali can be a Muslim is politically fraught in this context.

All in all, *Meherjaan* navigates sacralized concepts of the Bangla war film genre such that it can retell stories of historical trauma and national memory through a border-crossing utopian feminist aesthetic, which leaves female imprints on masculinized spaces and bodies. Strewn with touches of her signatory decisions, marked by the figuration of Salma Khala, Rubaiyat Hossain's debut production suggests how the filmmaker may have managed male-dominant opportunities at a small-scale, familial level. Similar successes both with the censor board and with the brand-partner economy of publicity and promotion enabled her participation in the space of mainstream theatrical cinema in Bangladesh—at least for a while.

Deliberations by the Bangladesh Cholochitra (Film) Censor Board had been opened up in a way suggestive of how critical thinkers were debating the legitimacy discourse and seeking inclusion of women's voices in the contestations around national memory at this historic moment of the war crimes tribunal. The decision to grant censorship certification to the film, despite controversial content, indicates that collective identity and difference constituted sites of hot debate both in the public and the legal spheres in Bangladesh at the moment. Another important, if more ambivalent, role was played by media infrastructures in the short but prominent life in Bangladesh of Rubaiyat Hossain's *Meherjaan*. Kaberi Gayen notes that such leading media outlets as the Bangla newspaper *Prothom Alo* and the television conglomerate Channel 1 "brand partnered" with the production and regularly ran promotions. By the time the motion picture was released, it was already recognized as an attraction by potential urban audiences (Gayen 2012, 69).

While it might well be, as implied by Kaberi Gayen, that the inclusion of the known Indian stars Jaya Bachchan and Victor Banerjee constituted the attraction of *Meherjaan*, brand partnership by the media conglomerate Channel I says something more. We see how industrially branded genres, and an underlying criterion of value, could shift to make space for difference and that small-scale social networking might also help to shift the gears. Through the previous decade, the Channel I conglomerate under the imprint of Impress Telefilms had been active in producing a brand of the Muktijuddho genre that mixed sacralized trauma imagery with the urban family values prevalent to bourgeois social films of the era. These valued attractions included couple romance, agential women, and sentimental family dynamics. The bourgeois branding of the trauma film had been spearheaded in 1998 by Humayun Ahmed's national-award-winning film *Aguner Poroshmoni*. As noted by Kaberi Gayen, Humayun Ahmed's production had succeeded in drawing the *modhyo-bitto nāgarik* (middle-class citizen) to film theaters (2012, 55). The voluminous catalog of Impress Telefilm covering productions from the late 1990s to 2010 not only showcases *Aguner Poroshmoni*; it also flexibly accumulates under the brand of a middle-class Muktijuddho genre a range of new war films made by male directors including Chasi Nazrul Islam, Taukik Ahmed, and Morshedul Islam (*Impress Telefilm* 2011, 19, 31, 73, 109). Some directors identify with mainstream Bangla cinema and others with the alternative stream of filmmaking born of the 1980s film club initiatives in Bangladesh (Raju 2015; see my discussion of the alternative stream in chapter 2). To a limited extent, *Meherjaan* participates in making war cinema into a brand of Bangla social melodrama. It depicts an upper-middle-class family, couple romance, and a number of agential women. Moreover, it participates in addressing diasporic Bangladeshi audiences, typical of the new Bangla genres, by including an expatriate character. Neela's war child, who had been given up for adoption, returns from Germany to reconnect with her past. Yet, the aesthetic complexity of *Meherjaan* lies in the way it inhabits the social war film tropes and reorients the referents. No doubt, the tropic orientation was enabled by the fact that it was produced not by Impress Telefilm but by the independent production company Khona Talkies, headed by Rubaiyat Hossain and her spouse, Ashique Mostafa (https://www.khonatalkies.com). Nonetheless, the brand-partner hype for *Meherjaan* mounted by Channel I and other big players of the Bangladesh media economy suggests a degree of liberal flexibility. The brand criteria for Muktijuddho cinema were indeed inflecting to include a different voice.

The fact that difference could be expelled as easily from a neoliberal media economy is well illustrated by the ban that followed. What the ban also reveals is how a large-scale media environment comprising visual and digital networks could be conditioned by state maneuvers. The role of the viral is especially noteworthy in a shifting media field like this. Digital networks circulate affect "with such speed and intensity as to become simultaneously viral and visceral." The speed of digital affect is felt so deeply in the body that it easily contributes to hypernationalist "moral panics" (Mankekar and Carlan 2019, 204–206, 210). Precisely a moral panic around the putative sexual transgressions constituting *Meherjaan* led to the ban. This history shows that the affective momentum of viral consumption can alter brand markets and control new trends.

The ban imposed on *Meherjaan*, after a twelve-day run "to packed audiences in six theatres all over the country" (Mookherjee 2011, 25), was motivated by public outcry. However, I have learned from sources that must remain anonymous that the precise act of the ban resulted from a collusion between the state and big businesses. Through subsequent years, distributors have persisted in refusing exhibition for fear of losing sponsors. Thus, the ban must be situated in relation to a longer history in Bangladesh of a partisan "state-sponsored thrust of capitalist development" (Raju 2015, 149) that has sought to shape and to legitimize territorial genres of national identity through the institution of mainstream cinema. However, in the *Meherjaan* case, the state-capital position on legitimate national identity was substantially shaped by the volatile affect already coursing around the war crimes tribunal. As noted by Nayanika Mookherjee, the contentions over *Meherjaan* were being fueled especially by the "nationalist politicisation of the younger *projonmo* [generation]," and underlying sexual anxieties (2011, 27). Blogospheres controlled by youth were ablaze with "gendered debate . . . directed primarily at a young film director, who also happen[ed] to be a woman" (27). Panic-stricken and virulently abusive "debate" embroiled depictions of female sexuality within the filmic text—in Meher's romance with a Pakistani soldier and in the rebellious eroticism of rape survivor Neela—with the sexuality of the young female director. These intense contestations over the cultural legitimacy of the female maker and her aesthetic choices well illustrate a central argument of this chapter—that both film genres and authorial identities are born into historical rifts and that they are contradictorily sexualized under statist and neocolonial conditions.

Yet, what of Rubaiyat Hossain's experience with filmmaking since *Meherjaan*, both in Bangladesh and in transnational circuits? An in-depth exploration of this question would take me beyond the regional historical scope of this book to film festival circuits and international funding structures. I finish the discussion with a few comparative observations only.

Rubaiyat Hossain, Bangladeshi Filmmakers, and Northern Transnationalism

If we look beyond Rubaiyat Hossain's experience with *Meherjaan*, we find that the stigma from allegedly violating community norms could also recede from the embodied identity of a woman filmmaker—as long as she makes the appropriate decisions. The exclusionary stigma, in other words, attaches to—in a sense is embodied by—the chosen forms of cultural expression. Helpful here is Birgit Meyer's insight that in the mediated lifeworlds of our times, the formation of community is a primarily aesthetic experience (2009, 6–7). The experience of community comes from sharing cultural forms that materialize as reality effects to *tangibly* mold bodies and tune the senses to a common sociopolitical environment (7). It follows that the choice of cultural forms that are effective for any given shared reality is what enables the subject's inclusion and legitimization. In the case of filmmakers like Rubaiyat Hossain, who are active across globalizing film cultures in Bangladesh and elsewhere, the criteria of effective choice arise from multiple reception communities. In one memorable conversation I had in 2014 with Rubaiyat Hossain, I heard her recount with some intensity her own deliberations on choice—that is, on which of the several themes and scripts she had prepared she finally had chosen to settle.

By then, her next fiction film, *Under Construction*, was already in post-production. Made as an art-house film for international film festivals, *Under Construction* was completed and released in 2015 not only at international film festivals but also in metropolitan theaters of Bangladesh. In all national and transnational venues, the motion picture was favorably received. A cover story on Rubaiyat Hossain published in 2016 by the Dhaka newspaper *Daily Star* embraced her assertion that she wants to establish her "identity as a Bangladeshi filmmaker" making films in Bangla. The cover story applauded her resolve in going on to make a second film—one that had "bagged prestigious awards" (Hossain 2016)—notwithstanding the controversies sparked by her debut work, *Meherjaan*. Effective for her tangible recognition as a

Bangladeshi filmmaker at this venue was the choice of a cultural form material to elite Bangladeshi sensibilities, that of a play by the iconic Bengali writer Rabindranath Tagore for adaptation to modern-day conditions. The impact of Tagore's literature—central to the 1950s Bangla Language Movement against the Pakistan state's imposition of Urdu—has been enshrined in the national anthem of Bangladesh. In her interview for the cover story of *Daily Star* in 2016, Hossain spoke at length about her authorial decision to adapt Tagore's political play *Red Oleanders* for depicting the present times in Bangladesh.

Since *Meherjaan*, Rubaiyat Hossain has made two fiction films for international festival circuits that have themes in common. They depict women's battles against private and public patriarchies in relation to the hazardous and exploitative labor conditions and class difference in Bangladesh. *Under Construction* was promoted as depicting "the struggles of a modern middle-class woman . . . to reclaim her identity, her freedom and her sexuality . . . in the urban sprawl of Bangladesh" (khonatalkies.com/underconstruction.php). It is set against the backdrop of the devastating fires that engulfed the Rana Plaza garment factory in 2013. The subsequent fiction film *Made in Bangladesh* was, by Hossain's own account, inspired by an interest she encountered while exhibiting her earlier film at international film festivals. In her own words, "In my previous 2015 film 'Under Construction' there was a character who was a female factory worker. When I was screening that film in different festivals, many people asked what would happen to her. I felt that this could be my next film" (Hurtes 2018). The narrative of *Made in Bangladesh* depicts the agency of a young female union organizer leading change at another hazardous and oppressive garment factory in Bangladesh. Taken up for distribution by the Paris-based company Pyramide Films, the production has already reached important international film festivals and elicited reviews from such prominent Western news media as the *New York Times* and the *Hollywood Reporter*. The feminist nuances of artistic choice in Rubaiyat Hossain's productions continue to escape neat categories. Nonetheless, these works being viable in northern transnational circuits have been read from Orientalist perspectives. They materialize as tangible evidence of underdevelopment and patriarchal exploitation in the global South. In the words of a reviewer for the *Hollywood Reporter*, *Made in Bangladesh* depicts not only the "human labor, sweat, and suffering" undergirding the global fashion industry but also "a sexist culture where women are expected to be passive servants" (Mintzer 2019).

Zakir Hossain Raju has noted that a complexity of the globalizing culture of independent cinema in Bangladesh is that productions today have a propensity to become realigned with dominant world cinema interests. They could be taken as contributing to the "ethnography" of a backward nation that is replete with underdevelopment and that perpetuates the "subjugation of women in a pro-Islam society" (2015, 197–198). I must add that in a global environment that propagates Islamophobia at a very large scale, the decision to depict Muslim-majority societies as security threats could offer particularly tangible ethnography for imperialist brands and policies.[6] This concern is raised by a recent docudrama titled *Shonibarer Bikel* (Saturday Afternoon, 2019), a Bangladesh-German coproduction about the terrorist attack in Dhaka (2016) directed by the prolific Bangladeshi male author Mostafa Sarwar Farooki.

Bringing together two elite feminist directors from different generations and locations of cinema, this concluding chapter has attempted to illuminate two points that are key to this book. I have sought to show that culturally established modes of film production such as star economies or familial/social networking—being habitual to women's small-scalar participation in the filmic spaces of South Asia—could be used by women to reorient dominant expectations. I have also noted that women's innovative counternarratives could have easily become realigned with choices branded apt for the times. Moreover, brand markets are shaped at the intersection of media geographies with workings of states and global politics. For feminist filmmakers situated in large-scale South Asian infrastructures, then, depictions of difference could run into neocolonial and imperial assumptions—assumptions that limit ways of seeing the regional and relating to the other.

Coda

The previous chapters assemble a wide spectrum of female filmic authors from across the northern region of South Asia. These authors are found in different industrial spaces and historical times. I began the book with one end of the spectrum of female creative labor, that of the star-author who works on both sides of the camera and uses persona in material ways to build infrastructure. Let me begin these final observations with the other end of the female creative spectrum, that of authors known as "directors."

A fair number of non-star author-directors have been discussed in the previous pages, including Nargis Akhter and Rubaiyat Hossain in Bangladesh as well as Gauri Shinde and Sai Paranjpye in India. As I have noted, new cinema in Pakistan also has a growing number of female author-directors. Beyond this, at least three among the star-author cohort this book studies, coming from educated elite backgrounds, share with non-stars the author-director's identity both in public and in scholarly discourse. They are Samina Peerzada in Pakistan, Aparna Sen in India, and Kohinoor Akhter Shuchanda in Bangladesh. Both Aparna and Shuchanda, although they came with star capital, found the opportunity to step into the director's role through support from the state or from state-led production structures lying outside their own initiative. These cases demonstrate that we find in the director-as-author identity a discursive paradigm that accrues resources and visibility for women's creative agency. As an exploratory category, then, the "woman director" is indispensable to building an archive of female filmic authorship across South Asia. In my attempt to do the brief work of gender research on forms of female authorship in this postcolonial region, however, I have come to the position that even though it is useful, the paradigm of the director-as-author is too narrow. The limitation has to do with the historical and conceptual legacies the paradigm carries.

Two interrelated conceptual histories inform the opportunity structures available to the women director-as-authors studied in this book. One is specific to postcolonial nation-states, and the other is shared with Euro-American contexts. The first concept is that women bring the authentic female voice and often, though not invariably, women's stories into the "biographies" (Gyanendra Pandey, qtd. in Rajadhyaksha 2000) of modernizing and liberalizing nation-states. Infrastructures premised on this concept typically rise from state-initiated projects of developing or reforming film industries to produce socially meaningful cinema in the local languages. They evolve into industrial production practices that intermingle social meaning and realistic imagery with high-end entertainment value. The inclusion of women is key to the modernist agendas of representation and liberalization at all stages. Previous chapters have contextualized these processes in Bangladesh (Dhaka) and India (Kolkata and Mumbai), discussing in what ways opportunities for women director-authors evolve alongside. The role taken by national infrastructures (and their global networks) in enabling women directors in South Asia, far from being unusual, is specific to the history of anti-imperial mobilization. As Lingzhen Wang notes, in "third world countries women first articulated their critical voices through anticolonialism and nationalism," rather than solely through "women's rights-oriented movements" as in the West (Wang 2011, 16). Along similar lines, this book has argued that female director-authors across South Asian societies make sexually nuanced claims on the modes by which femaleness is being fictionalized and embodied (on- and offscreen). In other words, they work from ambivalent positions within patriarchal frameworks of nation and state rather than from margins that are radically oppositional. The serious critiques of sexuality in relation to patriarchal nationalisms we find in fictions directed by Aparna Sen and Rubaiyat Hossain, or the tongue-in-cheek subversion of gender strata and consumerism offered by the Sai Paranjpye–directed social comedy are cases in point.

What has proved to be the limitation of the woman director identity for my research is the concept of creative work it brings along. The concept is that of what counts as authorial work and which type of creative voice lays claim to it within the nation or in front of the world. This limitation has to do with the second conceptual legacy shaping infrastructural support for director-authors in South Asia. This is the legacy of "auteurism" shared with Euro-American film cultures. The legacy is best described in the words of James Naremore as that in which "directorial names . . . have been fundamental to the establishment of movies as 'respectable' art" distinguishable from mass entertainment (2004, 9–16). Even though auteurism is debated on a theoretical level and practiced in ambiguous forms, it brings along the conceptual heft of an international formation of modern cinema culture. Canonizing the director, the cultural formation comes with the assumption that the directorial author thoughtfully controls the meaning and style of fiction film production. The legacy devalues entertainment cinema as tasteless and thoughtless (escapist), unless and until the entertainment medium itself is uplifted from mass-oriented conditions through added production and exhibition value. Moreover, it suppresses the fact that film is a collaborative medium in favor of conceiving it as the author-director's unifying medium.

By generating the concept of the woman author qua director as the only respectable authorial identity, auteurism comes to be especially constraining to the excavation of historically different forms of female authorship and fictional modes in a postcolonial terrain like South Asia, for here, mass entertainment cinema carries the stigma of moral contagion and regional barbarism. The stigma stems, as argued by William Mazzarella, from colonial film censorship of the unpredictable "sensory erotics" in the social fiction films being produced in early twentieth-century British India (2013, 10). As far as my own research went, the paradigm of the woman author-director as the only lens for building an archive of female authorship from across historical spaces and times was soon impossible to cling to. As previous chapters have elaborated, too many details of creative entrepreneurship simply spilled out. I came to note the many female voices and bodies speaking in different fictional modes into the biographies of filmic spaces, nations and states, regional places, and familial communities. Thus, this book has argued for a number of transborder modes through which the horizon of female authorial study should be expanded in relation to postcolonial/neocolonial terrains like South Asia—including the author-director mode but not limited by it.

The first mode is found in the substantial histories of female stars growing to be filmic authors of femaleness and gendered genres, thereby blurring the sexual border between respectable creativity and mass entertainment. This book has explored a wide range of female star-authors who come at once from historically respectable backgrounds—and not. They include Sangeeta, Shamim Ara, Kanan Devi, Babita, Shuchanda, Samina Peerzada, and Aparna Sen. These case studies maintain that we must eschew the common tendency to see star labor and female authorial labor as separate categories of film work, or for that matter, to settle for the stereotype that female stars past their prime step into production work and management labor (a patriarchal stereotype I came across in the course of my research and found *not* to be true, as illustrated by a number of star-author case studies in this book).

This means, second, that we approach women's cinema as a modality of collaborative authorship in which the borders between creative labor and entrepreneurial labor cross-permeate, entwining the specializations of female filmmakers and collaborative crew with the desires of target audiences. An approach like this to female authorship as process leads, on one side, to the issue of women's authority over decisions in relation to scales of the film business. Throughout the three parts of this book, I have demonstrated that production arrangements in which material and immaterial resources (i.e., social values and aspirations) are managed by women at the smaller spatial levels of familial labor and star-body labor sustain more heterogeneous sexual meanings and contestations than do large-scale frameworks of discourse and resource. On another side, it leads us to reading as archives of transborder practice fiction films with which women's names are connected in some production capacity—whether as director, producer, scriptwriter, costume designer, or shot and set designer. Sometimes these authorial connections surface only if we do the gender work of researching around the text for orbital visual and print material.

Third, my endeavor to expand the lens of women's authorial practices through female-focused attention to historical difference has taught me to be attentive to the different disruptive modalities of female-focused aesthetics found in women's cinemas across South Asia. Therefore, I have looked not only for the recognizably subversive but also for conservative fiction films concerned with women and gender issues. As the case studies in this book illustrate, I have sought for ways into these archives of female creative labor by animating the contradictions rather than settling for the narrative closures. This way of reading has been partly inspired by Christine Gledhill's thoughtful feminist approach to mainstream Hollywood cinema (1994, 118–121).

In a nutshell, this book argues for understanding female authorial labor as an archive comprising different ways in which women interact with and unsettle specific gendered hierarchies in the interrelated fields of production and of filmic aesthetics. To open the archive with an eye to difference, we must be alert to the historical fact that aesthetic politics emerge not only in the form of socially subversive analytical reasoning but also in the form of dissident bodily cognition. In doing this research, I have also learned to fail in finalizing the concept of female filmic authorship and wrapping my archive with hermeneutic neatness. Instead, I have come to acknowledge that research for archival difference in women's cinema has to be a "question of the future . . . of a promise and of a responsibility" (Derrida and Prenowitz 1995, 27).

Notes

Introduction

1. Zebunnisa Hamid argues that the New Pakistani Cinema burgeoning since 2001 constitutively differs from the "old" popular film traditions of the Lahore studios (2020a).

2. For representative works in this field, see Sangeeta Datta (2000); Geetha Ramanathan (2006); Priya Jaikumar (2007); Rashmi Sawhney (2015); Elora Halim Chowdhury (2022); the special issue of *Bioscope* on contemporary women filmmakers in South Asia, edited by Valentina Vitali (2020); and the recent volumes on the Hindi film director Zoya Akhtar edited by Aakshi Magazine and Amber Shields (2022), and on contemporary Hindi women filmmakers edited by Aysha Iqbal Viswamohan (2023).

3. For a succinct history of the auteur paradigm and author theory, see James Naremore ([1999] 2004). I discuss the auteur paradigm at greater length in the coda to this book.

4. This book uses "Bangla" to refer to the language as well as to motion pictures and texts produced in the language. "Bengali" is used to refer to the people of Bangladesh and West Bengal, India, as well as to the geographic locations. In the star and producer biographies compiled by Md. Fokrul Alam in *Amader Chalachittra* (Our Cinema), published by the Bangladesh Film Archive, we find many accounts of women from respectable family backgrounds working alongside husbands, fathers, and avuncular figures. In the oral history given to me, Md. Fokrul Alam, whom I met at the Bangladesh Film Archive in Dhaka, added to the list of women film workers named in the book. However, some incoherent and provocative details complicate his oral history.

5. Most of the West Bengali print materials discussed in this book were obtained from the Jadavpur University Film Archive, Kolkata, India, to which I was introduced by Moinak Biswas. I thank Professor Biswas and the film studies faculty at Jadavpur University for their generous support of my research.

6. In developing my intersubjective method, I am indebted to Ortner's observation that as we try to push lifeworlds and people into the "molds of our texts," they push back: "The final [analytical] text is a production of our pushing and their pushing back" (1995, 189).

7. Samina Peerzada argues for this conviction on public platforms as well. See, for example, her comments on the panel discussion on "Portrayal of Women in TV and Film" at the Faiz International Festival in 2016. Samina asserts that she has performed stock roles in commercial cinema because she felt that to make a public impact she had to "be someone" (*kuchh honā hai*).

8. See Michael Feingold, "Nora Gets Her Gun," *Village Voice*, Tuesday, November 9, 2004; and "Southasian Children's Cinema Forum: Promoting Quality Indigenous Cinema for Children and Young People," *The Second Round Table on Southasian Children's Films*, 2013 (Kerala: Eighteenth International Kerala Film Festival): 3, 10. 25.

9. See also Christine Gledhill (1991, xiv–xvi) who elaborates on the production of star fame in more recent multimedia contexts by drawing on Richard Dyer's notion of the film star as an "intertextual construct." According to Gledhill, star texts, industries, and target audiences are linked intertextually in a continuous process of social meaning production.

10. Richard deCordova notes that with the inception of a discourse on the pose struck by individual actors/stars in early Hollywood, the role of human labor behind the cinematic apparatus came to be foregrounded (1991, 19). See also Roland Barthes, who implicitly points to labor by saying that the pose constitutes one's active physical transformation, a making of "another body for myself" (1981, 10).

11. See, for example, "Morning with Farah," https://www.youtube.com/watch?v=pDjCjr8a5D8&t=498s.

12. Walter Benjamin (1968, 255). Drawing on Susan Buck-Morss, Laura Marks expounds on Benjamin's thoughts on the multiple lives of commodities. Marks points to how "fetish" and "fossil" are used in their tactile anthropological senses to describe how cultural commodities "condense cryptic histories" of bygone wish images (2000, 88–89). They offer the material to which new historical significance could be invested by situated bricoleurs.

13. For example, see Brinda Bose (1997), Sangeeta Datta (2000), Mantra Roy and Aparajita Sengupta (2014), and Rashmi Sawhney (2015). My own earlier work on Aparna Sen also fails to factor in her historical status as a star (De 2011; 2012; 2016). A noteworthy departure from this scholarly legacy is Kaustav Bakshi and Rohit Dasgupta (2017).

14. For new work in Indian female star studies, see Monika Mehta and Madhuja Mukherjee, *Industrial Networks* (2020).

15. For this idea, I am partially indebted to Debashree Mukherjee's approach to historical analysis as a "libidinal coupling of texts, images, data, and memories" (2020a), and to Monica Dall'Asta and Jane Gaines's notion of constellating pasts and presents (2015). See also Christine Gledhill and Julia Knight's introduction to the volume *Doing Women's Film History*, 1–12.

16. See Debashree Mukherjee (2020a, 13–14) for a succinct overview of these fields and how they develop in Indian studies. See also Iftikhar Dadi (2022) and

Zakir Hossain Raju (2015) for historiographies of Pakistani and Bangladeshi cinema, respectively, and Lotte Hoek (2014) for an extended anthropological analysis of film production in Bangladesh.

17. Ravi Vasudevan makes this point succinctly in his discussion of a "family form encompassing public universe" that began evolving in popular Hindi cinema from the 1930s onward (2010, 48, 45). Drawing on Christine Gledhill's theorization of Hollywood melodrama as the protean narrative genre of post-sacred, modernizing societies, Vasudevan argues that in colonial/postcolonial South Asia, the melodramatic mode adapts to difference. It takes on "disaggregated, heterogeneous dimensions" (2010, 39) in various genres of family form cinema engaged in interrogating "social transformation in a colonial and postcolonial world" (2000, 131). See also Vasudevan (1989) and Christine Gledhill, "The Melodramatic Field: An Investigation," in *Home Is Where the Heart Is* (1987, 5–39).

18. Christine Gledhill (2000, 220–243) argues that the modality of melodrama having a wide "socio-cultural embrace generates a wide diversity of genres . . . drawing social, popular, and high-art cultures into its orbit" through the momentum of social movements and expanding forms of mass media (229, 234–236). I make the same argument about the family form of social melodrama in South Asia. See also Ravi Vasudevan's discussion of the India avant-garde director Ritwik Ghatak's use of the "Manichean, melodramatic method" in realist family drama (2010, 30).

19. Sinha refers to late nineteenth-/early twentieth-century politics. For analyses of the woman-and-family question in different historical contexts of anticolonial nationalism in South Asia, see Partha Chatterjee, *The Nation and Its Fragments* (1993); Tanika Sarkar, *Hindu Wife, Hindu Nation: Community, Religion, and Cultural Nationalism* (2002); Deniz Kandiyoti, ed., *Women, Islam, and the State* (1991); Ayesha Jalal, *Self and Sovereignty: Individual and Community in South Asian Islam since 1850* (2000); Shahnaz Rouse, *Shifting Body Politics: Gender, Nation, State in Pakistan* (2004); Sonia Nishat Amin, *The World of Muslim Women in Colonial Bengal, 1876–1939* (1996); and Mahua Sarkar, *Visible Histories, Disappearing Women: Producing Muslim Womanhood in Late Colonial Bengal* (2008).

20. In taking this approach, I am inspired by Derrida's observation that histories of concepts must inflect "archive desire" to the possibilities and futures of concepts, to "all that ties knowledge . . . to the promise" (Derrida and Prenowitz 1995, 24).

21. See Erik Barnouw and S. Krishnaswamy ([1963] 1980) for an overview of the early family mode of the film business and the joint family studios of pre-partition India; Madhuja Mukherjee (2009) for an in-depth study of the "New Theatres" joint family–style studio in Calcutta; Md. Fokrul Alam (Feb. 2014) for similar familial arrangements in Dhaka; and the new-generation, young filmmaker Iram Parveen Bilal for the respect she currently garners as something of a "female and maternal figure" among her crew and cast in Lahore (2014, 251).

22. I am greatly indebted to the anonymous reviewer who called on me to engage more deeply in scalar analysis, and to Danny Nasset, who encouraged me at an earlier stage of this book project to take up the question of scales.

23. I thank the anonymous reviewer who asked me to account for difference in the "nature of capital" enabling women to become filmmakers in South Asia. My

effort to think about capital and women's film work comparatively is indebted to that question.

24. For an extended discussion of "affective economies," seen in relation to commodity circulation in post-liberalization India/diaspora, see Purnima Mankekar (2015, 12–18, 114–116); (2004, 405–415).

25. For scholarly debates on women's cinema and historically specific counternarratives, see also Teresa de Lauretis, 1987; Anneke Smelik, 1998; Catherine Grant, 2001; Kathleen McHugh, 2009; Lingzhen Wang, 2011; and Elora Halim Chowdhury, 2022.

26. For these key characteristics of transnational cinema, I am indebted to Katarzyna Marciniak, Anikó Imre, and Áine O'Healy, "Introduction: Mapping Transnational Feminist Media Studies" (2007, 4–9).

27. Elora Halim Chowdhury and Niyogi De, "Introduction: Transregional Archives, Cinematic Encounters: Filmscapes across South Asia," 2020. In *South Asian Filmscapes: Transregional Encounters*, edited by Elora Halim Chowdhury and Esha Niyogi De, 3–21. Seattle: University of Washington Press. See Harry Harootunian for a compelling critique of the "spatial containers" constraining area studies (2012, 7).

Chapter 1. Decoupled Maternities

1. In his conversation with me in 2014, the octogenarian actor Nirmal Kumar, a salaried employee at the New Theatres Studio in Kolkata in the late 1940s, told a nostalgic story about an actress who frequently brought along for her male coworkers delectable dishes such as goat meat curry prepared with her own hands. He also noted that, coming from the red-light quarters of the Bowbazaar neighborhood, the actress had to travel a distance to get to the studio on time. Nonetheless, she seems to have felt obliged to put in the extra effort to prepare the food, perhaps as a way of belonging and being accepted by her elite male peers.

2. Reading the cinematic image as archeology, Laura Marks argues that just as a "fossil is the indexical trace of an object that once existed," the photographic image becomes a "witness" to the life of an object. Thus, "fossil" is an apt metaphor for "certain inexplicable but powerful images" that, being incommensurable with the "present" the imagery explicates, bear witness to "unresolved pasts" (2000, 84). I argue that, in this case, the career narrative of Kanan's teleological rise to patriarchal respectability is ruptured by the unresolved traces of her struggle to author a cinema that decenters patriarchal control. These traces are fossilized in the life anecdotes that illuminate certain cine-objects that are at odds with generic norms.

3. As noted by Tarun Majumdar in a phone conversation with me in 2014.

4. For a more detailed discussion of this fiction film, see my 2016 essay "Kinship Drives, Friendly Affect: Difference and Dissidence in the New Indian Border Cinema."

5. See Anugyan Nag and Spandan Bhattacharya's recent extensive study of the changing media landscape of Bangla "Tollywood" cinema in Kolkata, *Tollygunge to Tollywood* (2021).

Chapter 2. Public Maternities

1. For historiographies of the Bangla Language Movement and political and economic conflicts that led to the formation of Bangladesh, see Willem Van Schendel, *A History of Bangladesh* (2009); Rounaq Jahan, ed. *Bangladesh: Promise and Performance* (2000); Afsan Chowdhury, *Bangladesh 1971* (2007).

2. Elora Shehabuddin argues that educated women like Rokeya Sakhawat Hossain, by choosing to express themselves in Bangla rather than in Arabic or Persian—considered by many male Muslim elite to be closer to Islamic culture than to Hinduism (as Bangla was perceived to be)—helped the "Bengalicisation of the Muslim middle class" at the turn of the twentieth century. She suggests that women's expressions in Bangla may well have been an "act of resistance against the class and religious strictures" that governed elite women's lives (2014, 54). Firdous Azim and Perween Hasan add that Bengali Muslim women's writings at the turn of the twentieth century refrained from promoting the "image of the genteel woman who was a companion for the educated men" as did the nationalist writings of elite Hindu women from the same period (2014, 38–39).

3. A production titled *Rupban* (1965; dir. Salahuddin)—the filmic version of a *jatra* depicting the travails of a self-sacrificial twelve-year-old girl married to a newborn prince—is seen as the savior of a waning Bangla film market in the 1960s. It created new markets by drawing villagers to urban cinema halls (Kabir, qtd. in Raju 2015, 87).

4. Sohela Nazneen notes the rise of several different women's activist groups and "ideological positions" in response to Islamicist developmentalism between the 1970s and the 1990s. These include the Marxist or left-leaning groups Bangladesh Mohila Parishad and Karmojibi Nari (Working Women), liberal feminist organizations like Women for Women, and the critical feminist group Naripokkho, concerned with issues of female sexuality and bodily integrity (2017, 8). A female-focused urban action text such as *Tin Konna* was intertextual with these overlapping yet contradictory positions. Note that across US and Chinese contexts, transgressive heroine action has staged responses to feminist movements as well as women's increased workforce participation (Tasker 1993; Hunt 2007).

5. Cinema work, argues Debashree Mukherjee, comprises "a set of practices through which media and subjects are mutually constituted in an ongoing process of individuation"; in this vein, the film actress as a "cine-worker" practices her bodily craft at the intersection of her institutional location and related objects (technical and structural) in what is a perpetual bodily process of becoming while "struggling to stay relevant" (2020a, 12). The actresses Shuchanda and Babita (as well as newcomer Champa) become cinema workers claiming infrastructural support by the way they stay relevant at once to familial propriety and to gendered change. Yet, star personas are a distinct case of the cine-worker. Since they engage in layered performances appealing to diverse fans, they are in a position to partially inflect the institutions of cinema and society they inhabit, and even raise implicit questions of what is relevant and for whom.

6. Declaring *Jibon Theke Neya* to be "a turning point in Pakistani cinema," film critic Alamgir Kabir explains, "Through the metaphor of a family viciously

dominated by a dictatorial woman [who controls the keys to the home], Zahir has tried to symbolise the decade-long dictatorship of Ayub Khan," the then-president of Pakistan (qtd. in Hayat 2013a, 122). In her testimonies about dialogues with Zahir Raihan about his scripts, Shuchanda notes that he would regularly work with her or ask her for feedback, on whose basis he edited the drafts (qtd. in Hayat 2013a, 111).

Chapter 3. Performing Bodies

1. According to Brian Larkin (2013, 329, 333), "Infrastructures are matter that enable the movement of other matter . . . [in other words] they are objects that create the grounds on which other objects operate." Since infrastructures form the grounds of mobility, they also "operate on the level of fantasy and desire . . . [constructing] subjects not just on a technopolitical level but also through this mobilization of affect." In the case of cinema, the physical infrastructure of studios and exhibition halls is inextricable from the human infrastructure of personnel and audiences in enabling commodity movement. The latter's fantasies and distastes condition the former's survival or change.

2. In the *Platinum Jubilee Directory* of Pakistani cinema, published in 1987, censor board chairman Abdur Rashid distinguishes Urdu films from productions in other languages by saying that in them "the story does seem to figure," suggesting that these were being submitted to the "Script Scrutiny Committee whose task it is to pass a story for picturisation" (Rashid 1987, 68). An interview given by Shamim Ara to the Urdu periodical *Film Asia* states that not only had she submitted *Lady Smuggler* to the censor board, but she was also preparing to take the production to the Moscow Film Festival on behalf of her nation (Shamim Ara 1987). See chapter 5 for a discussion.

3. According to Kamran Asdar Ali, Urdu magazines and women's "digests" expanded in number from the late 1960s, hand in hand with heterogeneous urbanization (2004, 127–130). Urdu medium education for women and a lower-middle-class female workforce (bank clerks and schoolteachers) burgeoned in the cities and small towns, producing consumers of female-oriented "pulp fiction." See also Ayesha Jalal (1991).

4. Helpful here is Richard Dyer's argument that leisure-time entertainment is an enabling rather than a wasteful process. It is process wherein socially meaningful emotions could be co-created by consumers not only outside the "daily round . . . characterized by . . . insistence" (2002, 7) but also in protest against everyday experience. Considering Hollywood, Dyer emphasizes the prominent role taken by professional entertainers from such "structurally subordinate groups [as] women, blacks, or gays" in shaping socially meaningful entertainment (20). The latter point resonates with the role taken by hereditary entertainers in the Lahore studios.

5. Noorjehan's creative authority in turning the film song into a cinematographic art form has also been vindicated by veteran PTV (Pakistan Television Corporation) producer Khwaja Najam-ul-Hasan. Both in a personal interview given to me in 2013 and on television talk shows, he has recounted in detail his firsthand experience of

her command of the tools and techniques of lighting and camera work in relation to sound.

6. Debashree Mukherjee's recent analysis of the *abhinetri* films produced in Bombay from the 1920s through the 1940s complicates the symbolic politics surrounding public female performers (2020a, 163–178). However, these politics of representation did not, in the long run, stem the marginalization of female entertainer classes in Bombay.

7. Classic *baithakī mahfil* performances in Hindi films include Meena Kumari's performance in *Pakeezah* (1972; dir. Kamal Arohi); and Rekha's performance in *Umrao Jaan* (1981; dir. Muzzaffar Ali). See the detailed discussion in Bhaskar and Allen, *Islamicate Cultures*, 44–64.

8. Translated by Malik Hussain Bakshi.

9. The Hindi version is titled *Ek Chadar Maili Si* (1986; dir. Sukhwant Dhadda), starring Hema Malini and Rishi Kapoor.

10. Translated by Gwendolyn Sarah Kirk.

11. See "Fariha Jabeen, Sangeeta & Hina Rizvi" in BOL Nights with Ahsan Khan, February 3, 2020. https://www.youtube.com/watch?v=xyvFuT1hQJ0/.

12. According to Lauren Berlant, "juxtapolitical" entertainment is proximal to the political sphere of social movements but not obviously critical of dominant paradigms. This form of entertainment generates "fantasies of . . . refunctioning [oppressive] historical conditions" (2008, 2–10). See also Lalitha Gopalan's analysis of the Indian Rape Revenge heroine as a genre that "throw[s] up the aggressive strands of feminism" at a time of women's movement in India (2002, 51).

Chapter 4. Timing Bodies

1. I am indebted to the anonymous reviewer who encouraged me to think more closely on a regional level about historical times in relation to women's film work and capital.

2. Coonoor Kripalani 2014, 212–213. Salima Hashmi of Lahore, daughter of the National Poet of Pakistan Faiz Ahmed Faiz, told me about a letter in her possession written by Jaddanbai to her father. Jaddanbai writes to thank Faiz for penning a song lyric for her and sends along a gold watch as a token of her gratitude. In Bombay, Jaddanbai as a singing star and entrepreneur-author set up the Sangeet Movietone Company. In 1935, through the production of *Talash-e-Haq*, she launched her daughter Baby Ranee (to become the famous star Nargis). The matrilineal launch was received by the public with much fanfare. As reported by *Times of India*, the "fame . . . in every mouth" of the star-mother precedes the child star's "melodious voice and very capable acting" ("Read What the Three Great Papers Say," *Filmindia* 2).

3. See Dadi 2022, 2–4. See also Gazdar 1997, 22–59; and A. Said 1962, 785–797.

4. The three previous chapters demonstrate that there was press coverage of the work being done and voiced by female star-entrepreneurs in Calcutta, Lahore, and Dhaka. My case studies show that in some cases more than others, "fugitive" gender research is doubtless needed to dig out the accounts of women's production work

from available print media and plot their paths to aesthetic practice. Nonetheless, the accounts do exist in the print and visual archives.

5. *Report of the Working Group on National Film Policy* 1980, 16. Madhava Prasad notes that by the late 1970s, a parallel production logic had emerged in which "commercial viability" and the "ability to command private finance" were increasingly important because state sponsorship was proving inadequate while also being debated (1998b, 135–136).

6. Arjun Appadurai contends that locality is "primarily relational and contextual . . . a complex phenomenological quality, constituted by a series of links between the sense of social immediacy, the technologies of interactivity, and the relativity of contexts." Thus, in a mediatized world, the "flow of images, news, and opinion now provides part of the engaged cultural and political literacy" people bring to places and neighborhoods (1996, 178).

7. Tejaswini Ganti has persuasively demonstrated that the Bollywood industry has undergone a major gentrification since the turn of the millennium (from around the time cinema was recognized by the Indian state as a valued national industry). In her words, "Hindi cinema, along with the film industry more broadly, has acquired greater cultural legitimacy from the perspective of the state, the English-language media, and English-educated/speaking elite" (2012, 3).

8. Pillaai 2007, 57–64. Reported by Jitesh Pillaai, this cover story, titled "The Director's Cut: Seven of India's Most Influential Filmmakers Get Together to Talk Shop and Lots More," hails this "momentous occasion" as the first one on which the leading Bollywood trade periodical *Filmfare* "embarked on assembling the country's seven most influential directors under one roof" (57). The coverage is significant for my argument for two reasons. First, it shows the emergence of a high-end author-director cinema in Bollywood with the expansion of the multiplex infrastructure, reported on in other issues published the same year, 2007. Second, it shows that Bollywood Hindi directors are being taken to represent the most influential directors of the country as a whole, in other words, Hindi cinema is standing in for national Indian cinema.

9. Gopal notes that under the repressive "emergency" rule declared by the Indian state to "deal with escalating social tensions . . . [s]tudying women was regarded" by the state "at least temporarily as an *alibi* for political activity" (Gopal 2019, 43).

10. A recent stride is a collection of essays on Zoya Akhtar as a filmmaker in Bollywood, edited by Magazine and Shields (2022). It includes some discussion on production and an interview with Akhtar.

11. Writing in 1981 for the Directorate of Film Festivals publication titled *Film India: The New Generation*, Gopal Dutt notes that "state finance is provided for films made by newcomers or films that may not sell," and that national and international award-winning films funded by the National Film Development Corporation do not reach audiences because "established distributors will not buy them" (Dutt 18–21).

12. Gopal 2019; S. Sen 2000; Sawhney 2007. The male buddy movie recurs in both mainstream middle cinema, such as *Anand*, directed by Hrishikesh Mukherjee (1971), and blockbusters such as *Sholay* (1975; dir. Ramesh Sippy) and *Amar Akbar Anthony* (1977; dir. Manmohan Desai).

13. See Urvashi Butalia, "Let's Ask How We Contribute to Rape," December 2012, updated December 4, 2021. The Nirbhaya case refers to a fatal gang rape perpetrated on December 2012 upon a young woman in New Delhi. "Nirbhaya," meaning "fearless," was the pseudonym used in press reportage because revealing the name of a rape victim is against Indian law. Later she was identified as twenty-three-year-old Jyoti Singh ("What Is Nirbhaya Case?" 2019).

14. Kuhu Tanvir (2014) notes that Amitabh Bachchan, building on his working-class "angry young man" image of the 1970s, was the most popular male star until the 1990s. With the liberalization of the Indian economy in the early 1990s, his hero persona began to be overtaken by the (more gentrified) softer male body of the Muslim star Shah Rukh Khan, who rose to visibility, however, by playing largely upper-class Hindu men. Since then, Shah Rukh and the other two Muslim male icons of Bollywood, Salman Khan and Aamir Khan, have faced stiff competition from Hindu stars with the toned muscularity of modern men glamorizing right-wing Hindu iconography. Foremost is Hrithik Roshan, also Amitabh's son Abhishek Bachchan. Meanwhile, Amitabh Bachchan has made a comeback both on the big screen and, notably, as the anchor of the widely consumed television game show *Kaun Banega Crorepati* (Who Will Become a Millionaire?). Today, his iconicity is hailed by the Indian press as embodying "new India": "not brute force but the subtle power of information . . . the mentor [who] has power but does not need to reveal it" ("Living Myth" 2022). In *English Vinglish*, Amitabh Bachchan appears precisely as this iconic soft-power male mentor embodying new India but with costuming that incorporates a classic Hindu nationalist palette. See Dwyer 2021.

15. According to Walter Benjamin, "By focusing on hidden details of familiar objects . . . the ingenuous guidance of the camera . . . extends our comprehension of the necessities that rule our lives" in the form of an "immense and unexpected field of action." The capacity of the camera to *exhibit* objects and details makes it a transformative "instrument of magic" (1968, 236, 225).

Chapter 5. Families Out of Bounds

1. Exchanges between the film cultures of East and West Pakistan during the 1960s are well documented in the pages of the periodical *Eastern Film* published in Karachi, West Pakistan. They regularly carried columns describing new theatrical releases of Bangla fiction films in Dhaka as well Bengali star activity. See, for example, the columns titled "Dacca Spotlight" and "Dacca Doings" by Shahab and Said Haroon, respectively, in the December 1966 issue of *Eastern Film*.

2. The *kirpan*, or ritual dagger, is an essential article of faith worn on the body by practicing Sikhs. See http://www.sikhiwiki.org/index.php/Kirpan/.

3. For a detailed discussion on the difference of this action-heroine aesthetic from the American and Hollywood aesthetic, see my "Women's Action Cinema in Pakistan: Fighting Bodies and Arts of Difference," *Third Text* (2021).

4. The Pakistani practice of coproduced action cinema dates back to the 1970s, suggesting the widespread release in Pakistan of Hollywood and Hong Kong motion pictures even before the video age. An Iranian-Pakistani coproduction bearing the colorful title *Jane Bond 008 Operation Karachi*, directed by Reza Fazeli, was released

as early as 1971. A genre of action heroine popularly called "Jane Bond" arose in Hong Kong in the 1960s. See Paul Fonoroff, "Film Studies: Jane Bond," *South China Morning Post*, January 31, 2008. https://www.scmp.com/article/624985/film -studies-jane-bond/. Moreover, a rush of coproduced action-heroine films directed by men followed Shamim Ara's *Miss Hong Kong*; for example, *Miss Bangkok* (1986), directed by Iqbal Akhter and Noor Uddin Jehangir.

5. Buck-Morss explains that *aisthitokos* is the ancient Greek word for that which is "perceptive by feeling"; thus, the "original field of aesthetics is not art but real-ity—corporeal, material nature" (1992, 5–6). She draws on this earlier meaning to understand Walter Benjamin's perspective on the aesthetic potential of the new technologies, that of restoring the "instinctual power of the human bodily senses," as against organizing the real and instinctual in an alienating way in terms of political or cultural assumptions.

Chapter 6. Families Torn and Found

1. Priya Jaikumar, "Translating Silences: A Cinematic Encounter with Incom-mensurable Difference," in *Transnational Feminism in Film and Media* (2007, 217). Jaikumar discusses the critically acclaimed feminist fiction film *Khamosh Pani* (Silent Waters), directed in 2002 by the Pakistani woman filmmaker Sabiha Sumar and produced by her couple-mode film company, Vidhi Films, with funding from Switzerland, France, Germany, and Sweden. This drama of a mother-son relation-ship fraught by the intensely divisive politics of Islamizing Pakistan is situated by Jaikumar at the "thresholds of shared spaces in feminism, social theory, and film text where gender relations are imagined and unmade nationally and globally" (210).

2. Humaira Saeed, "*Ramchand Pakistani, Khamosh Pani*, and the Traumatic Evocation of Partition," *Social Semiotics* (2009, 490). Saeed argues that these films demonstrate how cultural production contributes to the "memory and history work" of excavating partition trauma (484). Treatments of such themes in the Bollywood mode are found in big-budget productions such as the multiplex-oriented romantic spy-thriller *Raazi* (2018) by woman director Meghna Gulzar. For a discussion, see Saradindu Bhattacharya, "Gender, Genre, and the Idea of the Nation: 'Reading' Popular Cinema in an Indian Classroom," *Pedagogy* 1, no. 3 (2021): 549–558.

3. See Elizabeth Ezra and Terry Rowden "Introduction: What Is Transnational Cinema?" *Transnational Cinema: The Film Reader*, 2006; White, *Women's Cinema, World Cinema*, 2015; and Rosanna Maule, "Her Blog: Women's Cinema in the Digital Age," in *Contemporary Women's Cinema, Global Scenarios and Transnational Contexts*, ed. Veronica Pravadelli, 2018.

4. We find in this filmic history the rift within a shared linguistic register that began, according to Azim and Hasan, in the colonial period. Even though the majority of Bengali-language speakers in the region were Muslim, Bengali language development came to be collaboratively controlled and Sanskritized by British colonial educators and the Hindu gentry in a way such that the Muslim Bengali "remained unrecognized and outside the field of modernization" (2014, 30–31). Bangladeshi cinema historians Zakir Hossain Raju (2015, 104–110) and Alamgir

Kabir (1979, 16–18) show that these linguistic-religious fissures came to intersect with infrastructures of resource and opportunity in studio-era Kolkata cinema. Bengali Muslim elite were virtually excluded from participation in the Calcutta film publics in the 1930s and 1940s, the one exception being Obaidul Haq, who had to disguise his name in the attempt to make a film.

5. *Mutā* marriage is a tradition of "temporary marriage" that has been variously constituted in Islamic jurisprudence and in different Shiite and Sunni social practices. For a detailed historiography of the tradition, see Khalid Sindawi, *Temporary Marriage in Sunni and Shiite Islam: A Comparative Study* (2013).

6. Responding to Michael Hardt and Antonio Negri's formulation of the US projects of imperialism and democracy in the era of late globalization, Partha Chatterjee argues that the "liberal evangelical creed of taking democracy and human rights to the backward cultures is still a potent ideological drive, and that even the instrumental use of ideological rhetoric for realist imperialist ends remains entirely available" (2004, 4155). Nivedita Menon points to the emergence of a "transnational public sphere whose moral values proceed from the assumption of the existence of a unified civil society" whose organizations are implicitly engaged in "assessing the incomplete modernities of particular nation formations" (2004, 225). Scholars Sheema Kermani, Asif Farrukhi, and Kamran Asdar Ali, and Nayanika Mookherjee, among others, note that in the transnational sphere today Pakistani society tends to be placed in a "security . . . Islamic threat paradigm" (Kermani, Farrukhi, and Asdar Ali 2015), and Bangladeshi society as a "central laboratory for the developmentalist genre . . . [classified under] notions of disaster and impoverishment" (Mookherjee 2006, 77).

Bibliography

"Abosheshe *Lady Smuggler* Udhdhār/Finally *Lady Smuggler* Rescued." 1990. *Saptahik Purnima*. January 10: 46–47.

Ahmad, Ali Nobil. 2016a. "Introduction: Pakistani Cinema Dossier." *Screen* 57, no. 4 (Winter): 459–479.

Ahmad, Ali Nobil. 2016b. Introduction to *Cinema and Society: Film and Social Change in Pakistan*, edited by Ali Khan and Ali Nobil Ahmad, 3–24. Karachi: Oxford University Press.

Ahmad, Sadaf. 2009. *Transforming Faith: The Story of Al-Huda and Islamic Revivalism among Urban Pakistani Women*. Karachi: Oxford University Press.

Alam, Md. Fokrul. 2011. *Amader Chalachittra* [Our cinema]. Dhaka: Bangladesh Film Archive Publications.

Alam, Md. Fokrul. 2023. WhatsApp Message. July 15.

Ali, Kamran Asdar. 2004. "Pulp Fictions: Reading Pakistani Domesticity." *Social Text 78*, vol. 22, no. 1 (Spring): 123–145.

Ali, Kamran Asdar. 2020. "Female Friendship and Forbidden Desire: Two Films from 1960s Pakistan." In *South Asian Filmscapes: Transregional Encounters*, edited by Elora Halim Chowdhury and Esha Niyogi De, 43–59. Seattle: University of Washington Press.

Amin, Sonia Nishat. 1996. *The World of Muslim Women in Colonial Bengal, 1876–1939*. The Hague: Brill.

Amin, Tushar A. 2007. "Different Beat: Multiplex Films Get the Mainstream Edge." *Filmfare*. November 1: 68–70.

Anderson, Aaron. 2009. "Asian Martial-Arts Cinema, Dance, and the Cultural Languages of Gender." In *Chinese Connections: Critical Perspectives on Film, Identity, and Diaspora*, edited by Tan See-Kam, Peter X Feng, Gina Marchetti, 190–202. Philadelphia: Temple University Press.

Anwer, Megha, and Anupama Arora. 2021. Introduction to *Bollywood's New Woman: Liberalization, Liberation, and Contested Bodies*, edited by Megha Anwer and Anupama Arora, 1–26. New Brunswick: Rutgers University Press.

Appadurai, Arjun. 1996. *Modernity at Large: Cultural Dimensions of Globalization.* Minneapolis: University of Minnesota Press.

Armaan, Robi. 1990. "Apriyo Satyoti Janye Gyalo Fazle Rabbi Robi/The Unhappy Truth Is Told by Fazle Rabbi Robi." *Saptahik Punima.* January 18, 44–45.

Asif. 1964. "Shamim Ara: A Versatile Artiste." *Eastern Film* 5, no. 8 (March): 9–13.

Athique, Adrian Mabbott, and Douglas Hill. 2007. "Multiplex Cinemas and Urban Redevelopment in India." *Media International Australia* 124: 108–118.

Awaal, Arpana. 2018. "From Villain to Hero: Masculinity and Political Aesthetics in the Films of Bangladeshi Action Star Joshim." *Bioscope* 9, no. 1: 24–45.

Azim, Firdous, and Perween Hasan. 2014. "Construction of Gender in the Late Nineteenth Century and Early Twentieth Century in Muslim Bengal: The Writings of Nawab Faizunnessa Chaudhurani and Rokeya Sakhawat Hossain." In *Routledge Handbook of Gender in South Asia*, edited by Leela Fernandes, 28–40. London: Routledge.

"*Babitār Ekānto Shākhātkār* [Babita's Exclusive Interview]." 1989. By Robi Armaan. *Saptahik Purnima.* October: 41.

Bagchi, Jasodhara. 1990. "Women in Calcutta: After Independence." In *Calcutta the Living City.* Vol. 2: *Present and Future.* 42–49.

Bakhtin, Mikhail. 1984. *Rabelais and His World.* Translated by Hélène Iswolsky. Bloomington: Indiana University Press. Reprint from MIT Press, 1968.

Bakshi, Kaustav, and Rohit K. Dasgupta. 2017. "From Teen Kanya to Arshinagar: Feminist Politics, Bengali High Culture and the Stardom of Aparna Sen." *South Asian History and Culture* 8, no. 2, 186–204.

Balki, R. 2018. "Gauri Shinde and R. Balki@Algebra Bangalore." https://www.youtube.com/watch?v=4_5lRKH4Jkg/.

Bandopadhyay, Parthopratim. 1985. "*Parama Prasange* [On the topic of *Parama*]." *Chitravas*, 27–30. Kolkata: North Calcutta Film Society/Mudrakar Press.

Bandopadhyay, Sanat. 1985. "Parama." *Chitravas*, 30–32. Kolkata: North Calcutta Film Society/Mudrakar Press.

Banerjee, Koel, and Jigna Desai. 2021. "Mompreneur in the Multiplex: Entrepreneurial Technologies of the 'New Woman' Subject in the Age of Neoliberal Globalization." In *Bollywood's New Woman: Liberation, Liberalization, and Contested Bodies*, edited by Megha Anwer and Anupama Arora, 27–39. New Brunswick: Rutgers University Press.

Banet-Weiser, Sarah. 2016. "Brand." In *Keywords for Media Studies*, edited by Laurie Ouelette and Jonathan Gray, 24–27. New York: New York University Press.

Banet-Weiser, Sarah. 2018. *Empowered: Popular Feminism and Popular Misogyny.* Durham: Duke University Press.

Barnouw, Erik, and S. Krishnaswamy. [1963] 1980. *Indian Film.* 2nd ed. New York: Oxford University Press.

Barthes, Roland. 1981. *Camera Lucida: Reflections on Photography.* Translated by Richard Howard. New York: Hill and Wang.

Barthes, Roland. 1982. "The Photographic Message." *A Barthes Reader*, edited by Susan Sontag, 194–210. New York: Hill and Wang.

Basu Guha-Choudhury, Archit. 2009. "Engendered Freedom: Partition and East Bengali Migrant Women." *Economic and Political Weekly* 44, no. 49: 66–69.

Batool, Farida. 2004. *Figure: The Popular and the Political in Pakistan*. Lahore: ASR Publications.

Bean, Jennifer M. 2002. "Technologies of Early Stardom and the Extraordinary Body." In *A Feminist Reader in Early Cinema*, edited by Jennifer Bean and Diana Negra, 404–443. Durham: Duke University Press.

Beckman, Karen. 2014. "Animating Film Theory: An Introduction." In *Animating Film Theory*, edited by Karen Beckman, 1–24. Durham: Duke University Press.

Bedi, Rajinder Singh. 1967. *I Take This Woman* [Ek Chadar Maili Si]. Translated from Urdu by Khushwant Singh. New Delhi: Orient Paperbacks.

Benjamin, Walter. 1968. *Illuminations: Essays and Reflections*. Edited by Hannah Arendt. New York: Schocken Books.

Berlant, Lauren. 2008. *The Female Complaint: The Unfinished Business of Sentimentality in American Culture*. Durham: Duke University Press.

Bhaskar, Ira, and Richard J. Allen. 2009. *Islamicate Cultures of Bombay Cinema*. New Delhi: Tulika Books.

Bhaskaran, Gautaman. 2010. "Review: Iti Mrinalini." *Hindustan Times: Entertainment*. November 6.

Bhattacharya, Saradindu. 2021. "Gender, Genre, and the Idea of the Nation: 'Reading' Popular Cinema in an Indian Classroom." *Pedagogy* 1, no. 3: 549–558.

Bhattacharya, Sutapa. 1985. "*Narider Drishtite Parama* [*Parama* in Women's Eyes]." *Chitravas*, 38–39. Kolkata: North Calcutta Film Society/Mudrakar Press.

Bhaumik, Kaushik. 2001. "The Emergence of the Bombay Film Industry, 1913–1936." Unpublished diss. D. Phil Thesis. St. Anthony's College, Oxford University, UK.

Bhaumik, Moinak. 2013. "Goynar Baksho Decoded." *The Telegraph: Entertainment*. https://www.telegraphindia.com/entertainment/goynar-baksho-decoded/.

Bhowmick, Bikash Chandra. 2009. *Women on Screen: Representing Women by Women in Bangladesh Cinema*. Dhaka: Bangladesh Film Archive.

Bhuiyan, Naresh. 1981. "*Hit-Floper Pare* [After hits and flops]." *Chitrali* (August): 27–28.

Bilal, Iram Parveen. 2014. "To Direct Patriarchy." In *Celluloid Ceiling: Women Directors Breaking Through*, edited by Gabrielle Kelly and Cheryl Robson, 243–253. Twickenham, UK: Supernova Books.

Birla, Ritu. 2009. *Stages of Capital: Law, Culture, and Market Governance in Late Colonial India*. Durham: Duke University Press.

Biswas, Moinak. 1990. "Modern Calcutta Cinema." In *Calcutta the Living City*. Vol. 2: *The Present and Future*, edited by Sukanta Chaudhuri, 302–315. New Delhi: Oxford University Press.

Biswas, Moinak. 2000. "The Couple and Their Spaces: *Harano Sur* as Melodrama Now." In *Making Meaning in Indian Cinema*, edited by Ravi S. Vasudevan, 122–142. New Delhi: Oxford University Press.

Biswas, Moinak. 2003. "Historical Realism: Modes of Modernity in Indian Cinema 1940–1960." Unpublished diss. Monash University, Melbourne, Australia.

Bose, Brinda. 1997. "Sex, Lies, and the Genderscape: The Cinema of Aparna Sen." *Women: A Cultural Review* 8, no. 3: 319–326.

Bruno, Giuliana. 2011. "Surface, Fabric, Weave: The Fashioned World of Wong Kar-wai." In *Fashion in Film*, edited by Adrienne Munich, 83–105. Bloomington: Indiana University Press.

Buck-Morss, Susan. 1992. "Aesthetics and Anaesthetics: Walter Benjamin's Artwork Essay Reconsidered." *October* 62 (Autumn): 3–41.

Burton, Antoinette. 2010. "Foreword: 'Small Stories' and the Promise of New Narratives." In *Contesting Archives: Finding Women in the Sources*, edited by Nupur Chaudhuri, Sherry J. Katz, and Mary Elizabeth Perry, vii–x. Urbana: University of Illinois Press.

Butalia, Urvashi. 2012. "Let Us Ask How We Contribute to Rape." *The Hindu*. December 25. Updated December 4, 2021. https://www.thehindu.com/opinion/op-ed/lets-ask-how-we-contribute-to-rape/article4235902.ece/.

Butler, Alison. 2002. *Women's Cinema: The Contested Screen*. London: Wallflower.

Caron, David. 1998. "Intrusions: Families in AIDS Films." *L'Esprit Créateur* 38, no. 3: 62–72.

Chakrabarti, Baidurya. 2021. "Beyond the Couple Form: The Space of the New Woman in Yash Raj Films." In *Bollywood's New Woman: Liberalization, Liberation, and Contested Bodies*, edited by Megha Anwer and Anupama Arora, 54–65. New Brunswick: Rutgers University Press.

Chakrabarty, Dipesh. 1996. "Remembered Villages: Bengali Memories in the Aftermath of the Partition." *Economic and Political Weekly* 31, no. 32: 2143–2145, 2147–2151.

Chakrabarty, Dipesh. 2004. "Romantic Archives: Literature and the Politics of Identity in Bengal." *Critical Inquiry* 30, no. 3: 654–682.

Chakrabarty, Dipendu. 1985. "*Parama*: Je Chabi Gelāo Jayna Phyalāo Jayna [*Parama:* The movie that can neither be swallowed nor discarded]." *Chitravas*, 33–37. Kolkata: North Calcutta Film Society/Mudrakar Press.

Chakravarty, Sumita S. 1993. *National Identity in Indian Popular Cinema, 1947–1987*. Austin: University of Texas Press.

"*Champa: Bhetare O Bāire* [Champa: inside and outside]." 1988. *Saptahik Purnima* (April): 35–36.

Chatterjee, Partha. 1993. *The Nation and Its Fragments: Colonial and Postcolonial Histories*. Princeton: Princeton University Press.

Chatterjee, Partha. 2004. "Empire after Globalisation." *Economic and Political Weekly* 39, no. 37 (September 11–17, 2004): 4155–4164.

Chatterjee, Sushmita. 2016. "'English Vinglish' and Bollywood: What Is 'New' about the 'New Woman'?" *Gender, Place, and Culture: A Journal of Feminist Geography* 23, no. 8: 1179–1192.

"Chinese Premier Chou En Lai Thrilled." 1964. *Eastern Film*. April: 6.

Chitrali. 1985. "Dui Bon Shuchanda O Babita." *Chitrali* Report. November 29:4.

Choudhury, Juton. 2013. "Nargis Akhter *Sakhatkar* [Interview]. *Anandadhara: A Mediaworld Publication*. Year 16. Issue 358: 68–69.

Chowdhury, Afsan. 2007. *Bangladesh 1971.* Dhaka: Maola Bradarsa.

Chowdhury, Elora Halim. 2010. "Feminism and Its 'Other': Representing the 'New Woman' of Bangladesh." *Gender, Place, and Culture* 17, no. 3: 301–318.

Chowdhury, Elora Halim. 2015. "When Love and Violence Meet: Women's Agency and Transformative Politics in Rubaiyat Hossain's *Meherjaan.*" *Hypatia* 30, no. 4: 760–777.

Chowdhury, Elora Halim. 2016. "War, Healing, and Trauma: Reading the Feminine Aesthetics in Rubaiyat Hossain's *Meherjaan.*" *Feminist Formations* 28, no. 3: 27–45.

Chowdhury, Elora Halim. 2020. "Ethical Encounters: Friendship and Healing in Contemporary Films about the Bangladesh Liberation War." In *South Asian Filmscapes: Transregional Encounters*, edited by Elora Halim Chowdhury and Esha Niyogi De, 283–300. Seattle: University of Washington Press.

Chowdhury, Elora Halim. 2022. *Ethical Encounters: Transnational Feminism, Human Rights, and War Cinema in Bangladesh.* Philadelphia: Temple University Press.

Chowdhury, Elora Halim, and Esha Niyogi De. 2020. "Introduction: Transregional Archives, Cinematic Encounters: Filmscapes across South Asia." In *South Asian Filmscapes: Transregional Encounters*, edited by Elora Halim Chowdhury and Esha Niyogi De, 3–21. Seattle: University of Washington Press.

Clifford, James. 1986. "Introduction: Partial Truths." In *Writing Culture: The Poetics and Politics of Ethnography*, edited by James Clifford and George E. Marcus, 1–26. Berkeley: University of California Press.

Clover, Carol J. 1987. "Her Body, Himself: Gender in the Slasher Film." *Representations* 20 (Autumn): 187–228.

Cook, Pam. 1991. "Melodrama and the Woman's Picture." In *Imitation of Life: A Reader in Film and Television Melodrama*, edited by Marcia Landy, 248–262. Detroit: Wayne State University Press.

Cook, Pam. 1998. "No Fixed Address: The Women's Picture from Outrage to Blue Steel." In *Contemporary Hollywood Cinema*, edited by Steve Neale and Murray Smith, 229–246. London: Routledge.

Cooper, Timothy. 2015. "The Black Market Archive: The Velocity, Intensity, and Spread of Pakistani Film Piracy." In *Dissonant Archives: Contemporary Visual Culture and Contested Narratives in the Middle East*, edited by Anthony Downey. 401–418. London: I. B. Tauris.

"Cover Story: Gorgeous *Amar Kache Nandanikata* [Gorgeous is aesthetic to me]. 2009. *Apsara.* March 13: 1.

Dadi, Iftikhar. 2016a. "Lineages of Pakistani Cinema: Mode, Mood, and Genre in *Zehr-e-Ishq*/Poison of Love 1958." *Screen* 57, no. 4: 480–487.

Dadi, Iftikhar. 2016b. "Modernity and Its Vernacular Remainders in Pakistani Cinema." In *Cinema and Society: Film and Social Change in Pakistan*, 77–100. Karachi: Oxford University Press.

Dadi, Iftikhar. 2022. *Lahore Cinema: Between Realism and Fable.* Seattle: University of Washington Press.

Dall'Asta, Monica, and Jane M. Gaines. 2015. Prologue. "Constellations: Past Meets Present in Feminist Film History." In *Doing Women's Film History: Reframing Cinemas, Past and Future,* edited by Christine Gledhill and Julia Knight, 13–28. Urbana: University of Illinois Press.

Datta, Sangeeta. 2000. "Globalisation and Representation of Women in Indian Cinema." *Social Scientist* 28, nos. 3–4: 71–82.

Dayan, Daniel. 1976. "The Tutor-Code of Classical Cinema." In *Movies and Methods: An Anthology,* Vol. 1, edited by Bill Nichols, 438–450. Berkeley: University of California Press.

De, Esha Niyogi. 2011. *Empire, Media, and the Autonomous Woman: A Feminist Critique of Postcolonial Thought.* Delhi: Oxford University Press.

De, Esha Niyogi. 2012. "'Choice' and Feminist Praxis in Neoliberal Times: Autonomous Women in a Postcolonial Visual Culture." *Feminist Media Studies* 12, no. 1 (2012): 17–34.

De, Esha Niyogi. 2016. "Kinship Drives, Friendly Affect: Difference and Dissidence in the New Indian Border Cinema." In *Dissident Friendships: Feminism, Imperialism, Transnational Solidarity,* edited by Elora Halim Chowdhury and Liz Philipose, 143–159. Urbana: University of Illinois Press.

De, Esha Niyogi. 2020. "Female-Star-Authorship across South Asia: Genres and Controversy on Pakistani and Indian Screens." *Feminist Media Studies.* 1–18. DOI: 10.1080/14680777.2020.1815231/.

De, Esha Niyogi. 2021. "Women's Action Cinema in Pakistan: Fighting Bodies and Arts of Difference." *Third Text* 35, no. 3: 373–388.

De, Hiren. 1982. "*Chabir Byabsha*/Film Business." *Chitrali* (September): 53–57.

deCordova, Richard. 1991. "The Emergence of the Star System in America." In *Stardom: Industry of Desire,* edited by Christine Gledhill, 17–29. London: Routledge.

deCordova, Richard. 2001. *Picture Personalities: The Emergence of the Star System in America.* (rprt ed.) Urbana: University of Illinois Press.

de Lauretis, Teresa. 1987. *Technologies of Gender: Essays on Theory, Film, and Fiction.* Bloomington: Indiana University Press.

Derrida, Jacques. 1993. *Aporias: Crossing Aesthetics.* Translated by Thomas Dutoit. Stanford: Stanford University Press.

Derrida, Jacques. 1994. *Specters of Marx: The State of Debt, the Work of Mourning, and the New International.* Translated by Peggy Kamuf. New York: Routledge.

Derrida, Jacques, and Eric Prenowitz. 1995. "Archive Fever: A Freudian Impression." *Diacritics* 25, no. 2: 9–63.

Devasundaram, Ashwin Immanuel. 2020. "Interrogating Patriarchy: Transgressive Discourses of 'F-Rated' Independent Hindi Films." *Bioscope* 11, no. 1: 27–43.

Devi, Kanan. 1956. "Rise of Star System: Eclipse of the Bengal Industry." *Indian Talkie 1931-'56: Silver Jubilee Souvenir.* Bombay: Film Federation of India.

Devi, Kanan. 1973. *Sabāre āmi Nomi* [My obeisance to all]. Transcription by Sandhya Sen. Kolkata: M. C. Sarkar and Sons.

Dhusiya, Mithuraaj. 2018. *Indian Horror Cinema: (En)gendering the Monstrous.* London: Routledge.

Dinnie, Keith. 2008. *Nation Branding: Concepts, Issues, Practice*. Amsterdam: Butterworth-Heinemann.

"Director Aparna Sen about Her New Bengali Film 'Gainer Baksha." 2012. ABP Ananda Promotion. https://www.youtube.com/watch?v=Y3QpC2boFH8&t=9s/.

Dutt, Gopal. 1981. "The Film Framework: Government Support." In *Film India: The New Generation 1960–1980*. 18–33. New Delhi: Directorate of Film Festivals.

Dutta, Anjan. 2013. "Goynar Baksho Decoded 1." *The Telegraph: Entertainment.* https://www.telegraphindia.com/entertainment/goynar-baksho-decoded-1/cid/1555754/.

Dwyer, Rachel. 2011. "*Zara hatke* ("somewhat different"): The New Middle Classes and the Changing Forms of Hindi Cinema." *Being Middle-Class in India: A Way of Life*, edited by Henrike Donner, 184–206. London: Routledge.

Dwyer, Rachel. 2021. "New Myths for an Old Nation: Bollywood, Soft Power, and Hindu Nationalism." In *Cinema and Soft Power: Configuring the National and Transnational in Geo-Politics*, edited by Stephanie Dennison and Rachel Dwyer, 184–208. Edinburgh: University of Edinburgh Press.

Dyer, Richard. 2002. *Only Entertainment*. 2nd ed. 1992; London: Routledge.

"Eid Mubarak." 1987. *Film Asia*. August 2, no. 8: 25. Translated from Urdu by Lubna Saira.

"Ekhan Babita Anyarakam Ekjan/Now Babita Is Another One." 1990. *Saptahik Purnima*. January 28: 45–46.

Elsaesser, Thomas. 1985. "Tales of Sound and Fury: Observations on the Family Melodrama." In *Movies and Methods*. Vol. 2, edited by Bill Nichols, 165–189. Berkeley: University of California Press.

Ezra, Elizabeth, and Terry Rowden. 2006. "Introduction: What Is Transnational Cinema?" *Transnational Cinema, The Film Reader*. 1–12. New York: Routledge.

Farzeen, Sana. 2019. "Zoya Akhtar: No One in the Industry Cares about Gender." *Indian Express*. March 11. https://indianexpress.com/article/entertainment/bollywood/zoya-akhtar-gender-women-in-industry-feminists-family-5617474/.

Feingold, Michael. 2004. "Nora Gets Her Gun." *Village Voice*. November 9. https://www.villagevoice.com/2004/11/09/nora-gets-her-gun/.

Feldman, Shelley. 2001. "Exploring Theories of Patriarchy: A Perspective from Bangladesh." *Signs* 26, no. 4: 1097–1127.

Film India: The New Generation 1960–1980. 1981. New Delhi: Directorate of Film Festivals.

Filmotsav '86 Brochure: A Third World Women's Film Programme. 1986. January 13–20. Hyderabad.

Fonoroff, Paul. 2008. "Film Studies: Jane Bond." *South China Morning Post*. January 31. https://www.scmp.com/article/624985/film-studies-jane-bond/.

From Colourless to Colourful: Platinum Jubilee Film Directory 1913–1987. 1987. Edited by A. R. Slote. Karachi: Falak Printing Press.

Gaines, Jane. 1990. "Introduction: Fabricating the Female Body." In *Fabrications: Costumes and the Female Body*, edited by Jane Gaines and Charlotte Herzog, 1–27. London: Routledge.

Gaines, Jane. 2012. "The Genius of Genre and the Ingenuity of Women." In *Gender Meets Genre in Postwar Cinemas*, edited by Christine Gledhill, 15–28. Urbana: University of Illinois Press.

Gaines, Jane. 2018. *Pink-Slipped: What Happened to Women in the Silent Film Industries?* Urbana: University of Illinois Press.

Gaines, Jane, and Radha Vatsal. 2011. "How Women Worked in the US Silent Film Industry." *Women's Film Pioneers Project*. https://wfpp.cdrs.columbia.edu/essay/how-women-worked-in-the-us-silent-film-industry/.

Galt, Rosalind. 2013. "'brash . . . indecent . . . libertine': Derek Jarman's Queer Colors." In *Color and the Moving Image: History, Theory, Aesthetics, Archive*, edited by Simon Brown, Sarah Street, and Liz Watkins, 93–103. New York: Routledge.

Ganti, Tejaswini. 2012. *Producing Bollywood: Inside the Contemporary Hindi Film Industry.* Durham: Duke University Press.

Gargi, Charu. 2013. "*A Room of One's Own* Revisited: Women Professionals in Mainstream Hindi Cinema: Aruna Raje." *Deep Focus Cinema* 1, no. 3: 46–52.

Gayen, Kaberi. 2012. *Muktijuddher Chalachitre Nari Nirman* [The construction of women in muktijuddho film]. Dhaka: Bangladesh Film Archive.

Gazdar, Mushtaq. 1997. *Pakistani Cinema 1947–1997.* Karachi: Oxford University Press.

Ghosh, Rituparno. 2008. "Ghosh and Company: Aparna Sen and Kalyan Roy." *Star Jalsha Television Chat Show*. November 9.

Gledhill, Christine. 1987. "The Melodramatic Field: An Investigation." In *Home Is Where the Heart Is: Studies in Melodrama and the Woman's Film*. 5–39. London: British Film Institute.

Gledhill, Christine. 1991. Introduction to *Stardom: Industry of Desire*, xiii–xx. London: Routledge.

Gledhill. Christine. 1994. "Image and Voice: Approaches to Marxist-Feminist Film Criticism." In *Multiple Voices in Feminist Film Criticism*, edited by Diana Carson, Linda Dittimar, and Janice R. Welsch, 109–124. London: University of Minnesota Press.

Gledhill, Christine. 2000. "Rethinking Genre." In *Reinventing Film Studies*, edited by Christine Gledhill and Linda Williams, 221–243. London: Arnold.

Gledhill, Christine, and Julia Knight. 2015. Introduction to *Doing Women's Film History: Reframing Past and Future*, edited by Christine Gledhill and Julia Knight, 1–12. Urbana: University of Illinois Press.

Gokulsing, K. Moti, and Wimal Dissanayake. 2004. *Indian Popular Cinema: A Narrative of Cultural Change.* Stoke on Trent: Trentham Books.

Gooptu, Sharmistha. 2010. *Bengali Cinema: An Other Nation.* London: Routledge.

Gooptu, Sharmistha. 2017. "Kanan Devi: A Bengali Star." *South Asian History and Culture* 8, no. 2: 143–154.

Gopal, Sangita. 2012. *Conjugations: Marriage and Form in New Bollywood Cinema.* Chicago: University of Chicago Press.

Gopal, Sangita. 2019. "Media Meddlers: Feminism, Television, and Gendered Media Work in India." *Feminist Media Histories* 5, no. 1: 39–62.

Gopalan, Lalitha. 2002. *Cinema of Interruptions: Action Genres in Contemporary Indian Cinema*. London: British Film Institute.

"*Goynar Baksho* Movie Review." 2013. *Times of India*. April 12. Updated May 17, 2017. https://timesofindia.indiatimes.com/goynar-baksho/movie-review/19594636.cms/.

Grant, Catherine. 2001. "Secret Agents: Feminist Theories of Women's Film Authorship." *Feminist Theory* 2, no. 1: 113–130.

Gul, Aijaz. 2008. *Malika-e-Tarannum Noorjehan: The Melody Queen*. Delhi: Vitasta Publishing.

Gul, Aijaz. 2016. "Mandwa to Screen 'Muthi Bhar Chawal' on 26th." November 24. https://www.thenews.com.pk/print/167204-Mandwa-to-screen-Muthi-Bhar-Chawal-on-26th/.

Hallet, Hilary A. 2013. *Go West, Young Women! The Rise of Early Hollywood*. Berkeley: University of California Press.

Hameed, Yaseen. 2021. "Classic Film Review: Mutthi Bhar Chawal." *Desimovies.biz*. https://www.youtube.com/watch?v=0c4EK77Va7U/.

Hamid, Zebunnisa. 2020a. "Behind the Scenes: Women Filmmakers of New Pakistani Cinema." *Bioscope* 11, no. 1: 15–26.

Hamid, Zebunnisa. 2020b. "The Birth of a Cinema in Post-9/11 Pakistan." In *South Asian Filmscapes: Transregional Encounters*, edited by Elora Halim Chowdhury and Esha Niyogi De, 216–230. Seattle: University of Washington Press.

Hardt, Michael. 1999. "Affective Labor." *Boundary 2*, vol. 26, no. 2: 89–100.

Haroon, Said. 1966. "Dacca Doings." *Eastern Film*. December: 34–35.

Harootunian, Harry. 2012. "'Memories of Underdevelopment' after Area Studies." *Positions: East Asia Cultures Critique* 20, no. 1 (Winter):7–35.

Hasan, Sheikh Mehdi et al. 2020. "*Dukkho: Sadheen Deshe Raihanke Haralam* [Grief: we lost Raihan in the independent nation]" (Shuchanda interview). *Bangladesh Pratidin*. October 8: 79–80.

Hawkes, Sarah, and Tasnim Azim. 2000. "Health Care Systems in Transition III. Bangladesh Part II. Bangladesh's Response to HIV-AIDS." *Journal of Public Health Medicine* 22, no. 1: 10–13.

Hayat, Anupam. 2013a. "*Ganaandolan Bhittik Chalachitra* [Social movement–based cinema]." In *Bangladesher Anyo Cinema* [The alternative cinema of Bangladesh]. 95–128. Vol. 1, edited by Sushil Saha. Dhaka: Abhijan Publishers.

Hayat, Anupam. 2013b. *Ganamadhyam O Nari: Sangbadpatro, Betar, Television, Chalochitro, O Bigyapon* [Mass media and women: newspapers, radio, television, film, and advertising]. Dhaka: Samachar.

Hirschkind, Charles. 2006. "Cassette Ethics: Public Piety and Popular Media in Egypt." In *Religion, Media, and the Public Sphere*, edited by Birgit Meyer and Annelies Moors, 29–51. Bloomington: Indiana University Press.

Hoek, Lotte. 2009. "'More Sexpression Please!' Screening the Female Voice and Body in the Bangladesh Film Industry." In *Aesthetic Formations: Media, Religion, and the Senses*, edited by Birgit Meyer, 71–90. New York: Palgrave.

Hoek, Lotte. 2014. *Cut Pieces: Celluloid Obscenity and Popular Cinema in Bangladesh*. New York: Columbia University Press.

Hoek, Lotte. 2015. "Cross-Wing Filmmaking and Their Traces in the Bangladesh Film Archive." *Bioscope: South Asian Screen Studies* 5, no. 2: 99–118.

Hoek, Lotte. 2016. "*Aina*, Afzal Chowdhury's Cinematography, and the Interlinked Histories of Cinema in Pakistan and Bangladesh. "*Screen* 57, no. 4: 488–491.

Hossain, Rafi. 2016. "Rubaiyat Hossain–*Under Construction*." *Daily Star: Cover Story*. February 20. https://www.thedailystar.net/showbiz/cover-story/rubaiyat -hossain-under-construction-574879/.

Hossain, Rubaiyat. Blog. https://rubiyat-hossain.com/about/.

Hunt, Leon. 2007. "Zhang Ziyi, 'Martial Arthouse,' and the Transnational *Nuxia*." In *Women Willing to Fight: The Fighting Woman in Film*, edited by Silke Andris and Ursula Fredrick, 144–160. Newcastle: Cambridge Scholars Publishing.

Hurtes, Sarah. 2018. "Interview with Rubaiyat Hossain: 'I Believe in a Feminist Intervention in Cinema.'" https://rm.coe.int/interview-rubaiyat-hossain/16808ae844/.

IANS (Indo-Asian News Service). 2012. "After a Slow Start, *English Vinglish* Gains Momentum." *Firstpost*. October 17. https://www.firstpost.com/entertainment/ after-a-slow-start-english-vinglish-gains-momentum-493550.html/.

Impress Chalachitra Album/Impress Telefilm's Movie Album 2000–2010. 2011. Edited by Luftor Rahman Riton. Dhaka: Impress Telefilm Ltd.

Inam, Sabeen. 2009. "De-Certification of Samina Peerzada's *Inteha* . . . Legal Analysis." March 2. http://sabeeninam.blogspot.com/2009/03/de-certification-of -samina-peerzadas.html/.

Jabbar, Javed. 2018. "Ramchand Pakistani—10 Years On." *Instep*. September 9. https://www.thenews.com.pk/tns/detail/566275-%C2%ADramchand-pakistani -10-years/.

Jackman, David. 2017. "Living in the Shade of Others: Intermediation, Politics and Violence in Dhaka City." PhD Diss. University of Bath.

Jaffery. 1965. "Shamim Ara: Past, Present . . . and Future." *Eastern Film* 6, no. 11: 8–11.

Jaffery. 1966. "Shamim Ara: Seen from a Different Angle." *Eastern Film* 7, no. 12: 16–19.

Jahan, Rounaq. 2000. *Bangladesh: Promise and Performance*. London: Zed Books.

Jaikumar, Priya. 2007. "Translating Silences: A Cinematic Encounter with Incommensurable Difference." In *Transnational Feminism in Film and Media*, edited Katarzyna Marciniak, Anikó Imre, and Áine O'Healy, 207–226. Houndmills, Basingstoke, UK: Palgrave Macmillan.

Jaikumar, Priya. 2017. "*Haveli*: A Cinematic Topos." *Positions* 25, no. 1: 223–248.

Jalal, Ayesha. 1991. "The Convenience of Subservience: Women and the State of Pakistan." In *Women, Islam, and the State*, edited by Deniz Kandiyoti, 72–114. London: Macmillan.

Jalal, Ayesha. 2000. *Self and Sovereignty: Individual and Community in South Asian Islam since 1850*. London: Routledge.

Jalal, Ayesha. 2017. "In Conversation with Ayesha Jalal: Separating a Once Historically Indivisible People." *Daily Star: Star Weekend*. August 25. https://www.the dailystar.net/star-weekend/separating-once-historically-indivisible-people-1453531/.

Jameson, Fredric. 1991. *Postmodernism, or, the Cultural Logic of Late Capitalism*. Durham: Duke University Press.

Jamil, Khaula, and Aaliyah Tayyebi. 2015. "On This Day Today: Karachi's Iconic Cinema Was Set Ablaze." *Images*. September 21. https://images.dawn.com/news/1173889/.

Jayamanne, Laleen. 2001. *Towards Cinema and Its Double: Cross-Cultural Mimesis*. Bloomington: Indiana University Press.

John, Mary E. 1998. "Globalisation, Sexuality, and the Visual Field: Issues and Non-Issues for Cultural Critique." In *A Question of Silence: The Sexual Economies of Modern India*, edited by Mary E. John and Janaki Nair, 368–396. New Delhi: Kali for Women.

Johnston, Claire. [1973] 2021. "Women's Cinema as Counter-Cinema." In *Film Manifestos and Global Cinema Cultures*, edited by Scott MacKenzie, 347–355. Berkeley: University of California Press.

Kabeer, Naila. 1991. "The Quest for National Identity: Women, Islam, and the State in Bangladesh." In *Women, Islam, and the State*, edited by Deniz Kandiyoti, 115–143. Philadelphia: Temple University Press.

Kabir, Alamgir. 1979. *Film in Bangladesh*. Dhaka: Bangla Academy.

Kanpuri, Zakhmi [Jameel Ahmed]. 2012. *Yaadgar Filmen*. Karachi: City Book Point. Translated from Urdu by Malik Hussain Bakshi.

"*Katha*: A Tale Well Told." 1984. *The Telegraph*. August 31: 10.

Kazi, Durriya. 2006. "Portrayal of Women in Pakistani Cinema." http://durriyakazi.blogspot.com/2012/03/portrayal-of-women-in-pakistani-cinema.html/.

Kermani, Sheema. 2015. "Tehrik-e-Niswan's *Tilismati Tees Aur Aik Saal* (Magical Thirty and One Years)." In *Gender, Politics, and Performance in South Asia*, edited by Sheema Kermani, Asif Farrukhi, and Kamran Asdar Ali, 3–34. Karachi: Oxford University Press.

Kermani, Sheema, Asif Farrukhi, and Kamran Asdar Ali, eds. *Gender, Politics and Performance in South Asia*. Karachi: Oxford University Press

Khalid-Bin-Habib. 2006. "Nargis Akhter: Empathy with Women." *Daily Star*. March 8.

Khan, Ali. 2016. "Film Posters: Reflections of Change in the Pakistani Film Industry." In *Cinema and Society: Film and Social Change in Pakistan*, edited by Ali Khan and Ali Nobil Ahmad, 209–262. Karachi: Oxford University Press.

Khan, Ali, and Ali Nobil Ahmad. 2016. "Violence and Horror in Pakistani Cinema." In *Cinema and Society: Film and Social Change in Pakistan*, edited by Ali Khan and Ali Nobil Ahmad, 115–136. Karachi: Oxford University Press.

Khan, Nighat Said. 1992. *Voices Within: Dialogues with Women on Islam*. Lahore: ASR Publications.

Khan, Omar Ali. 2020. Movie Review: *Society Girl* (1976). Desimovies.biz. https://www.desimovies.biz/blogs/desimovies-biz/society-girl-1976./

Khan, Sher. 2014. "Wishing for Shamim Ara's Speedy Recovery." *Express Tribune Epaper*. June 12. https://tribune.com.pk/story/720362/wishing-for-shamim-aras-speedy-recovery/.

Khan, Tamanna. 2010. "Making Movies for a Cause." [Interview with Nargis Akhter.] *Star Weekend Magazine* 9, no. 27: 24–25.

Khandakar, Mahmudul Hassan. 2011. *Cinema Theke Chitrali* [From *Cinema* to *Chitrali*]. Dhaka: Oitijjhya.

Khona Talkies Website. https://www.khonatalkies.com/.

Kirk, Gwendolyn Sarah. 2016. "Uncivilized Language and Aesthetic Exclusion: Language, Power, and Film Production in Pakistan." PhD diss. University of Texas at Austin.

Komar, Kathleen. 1994. "Feminist Curves in Contemporary Literary Space." In *Reconfigured Spheres: Feminist Explorations of Literary Space*, edited by Margaret R. Higonnet and Joan Templeton, 89–107. Amherst: University of Massachusetts Press.

Kripalani, Coonoor. 2014. "Why Are You Making Such a Big Deal Just Because I'm a Woman? Women Directors of Popular Indian Cinema." In *Celluloid Ceiling: Women Directors Breaking Through*, edited by Gabrielle Kelly and Cheryl Robson, 210–221. Twickenham: Supernova Books.

Kuhn, Annette. 1988. *Cinema, Censorship, and Sexuality 1909–1925*. New York: Routledge.

Kuhn, Annette. 2007. "Photography and Cultural Memory: A Methodological Exploration." *Visual Studies* 22, no. 3: 283–292.

Kulkarni, Onkar. 2012. "*English Vinglish* Gets a Slow Start." *Indian Express*. October 12. http://archive.indianexpress.com/news/english-vinglish-gets-a-slow-start/1015887/.

La Capra, Dominick. 2001. *Writing History, Writing Trauma*. Baltimore: Johns Hopkins University Press.

Larkin, Brian. 2008. *Signal and Noise: Media, Infrastructure, and Urban Culture in Nigeria*. Durham: Duke University Press.

Larkin, Brian. 2013. "The Politics and Poetics of Infrastructure." *Annual Review of Anthropology* 43: 327–343.

Lash, Scott, and Celia Lury. 2007. Introduction: Theory: Some Signposts. *The Global Culture Industry: The Mediation of Things*. Cambridge: Polity Press.

"The Living Myth of Amitabh Bachchan." 2022. *The Indian Express*. https://www.newindianexpress.com/opinions/2022/oct/27/the-living-myth-of-amitabh-bachchan-2512073.html/.

Lugones, Maria, in collaboration with Pat Alake Rosezelle. 1995. "Sisterhood and Friendship as Feminist Models." In *Feminism and Community*, edited by Penny A. Weiss and Marilyn Friedman, 135–145. Philadelphia: Temple University Press.

Magazine, Aakshi, and Amber Shields. 2022. *Refocus: The Films of Zoya Akhtar*. Edinburgh: University of Edinburgh Press.

Mahar, Karen Ward. 2006. *Women Filmmakers in Early Hollywood*. Baltimore: Johns Hopkins University Press.

Mahmood, Saba. 2005. *Politics of Piety: Islamic Revival and the Feminist Subject*. Princeton: Princeton University Press.

Majeed, Alauddin. 2013. "Chalacitre Narinirmatader Shaphalya" [Women filmmakers' success]. *Bangladesh Pratidin*. August 29: 10.

Majumdar, Neepa. 2009. *Wanted Cultured Ladies Only! Female Stardom and Cinema in India, 1930s–1950s*. Urbana: University of Illinois Press.

Majumdar, Neepa. 2017. "Gendered Borderlands: Screens as Contact Zones in Contemporary Women's Cinema in India." In *Contemporary Women's Cinema:*

Global Scenarios and Transnational Contexts, edited by Veronica Pravadelli, 45–58. Milan-Udine: Mimesis International.

"Malika- e-Tarrannum: A Heart Set Aflame." 1985. *SHE*. January–February 1985: 70–73, 182–183.

Mankekar, Purnima. 2004. "Dangerous Desires: Television and Erotics in Late Twentieth-Century India." *Journal of Asian Studies* 63, no. 2: 403–431.

Mankekar, Purnima. 2015. *Unsettling India: Affect, Temporality, Transnationality*. Durham: Duke University Press.

Mankekar, Purnima, and Hannah Carlan. 2019. "The Remediation of Nationalism: Viscerality, Virality, and Digital Affect." In *Global Digital Cultures: Perspectives from South Asia, edited by* Aswin Punathambekar and Sriram Mohan, 203–222. Ann Arbor: University of Michigan Press.

Marciniak, Katarzyna, Anikó Imre, and Áine O'Healy. 2007. "Introduction: Mapping Transnational Feminist Media Studies." In *Transnational Feminism in Film and Media*, edited by Katarzyna Marciniak, Anikó Imre, and Áine O'Healy, 1–20. Houndmills, Basingstoke, UK: Palgrave Macmillan.

Marcus, Jane. 1988. *Art and Anger: Reading like a Woman*. Columbus: Ohio State University Press.

Marks, Laura. 2000. *The Skin of the Film: Intercultural Cinema, Embodiment, and the Senses*. Durham: Duke University Press.

"Marriot Road Whole-Sale Market." 1983. *SHE*. November 1983: 57.

Maule, Rosanna. 2018. "Her Blog: Women's Cinema in the Digital Age." In *Contemporary Women's Cinema: Global Scenarios and Transnational Contexts*, edited by Veronica Pravadelli, 231–250. Milan-Udine: Mimesis International.

Mazumdar, Ranjani. 2007. *Bombay Cinema: An Archive of the City*. Minneapolis: University of Minnesota Press.

Mazzarella, William. 2013. *Censorium: Cinema and the Open Edge of Mass Publicity*. Durham: Duke University Press.

McDowell, Linda. 2001. "Linking Scales: or How Research about Gender and Organizations Raises New Issues for Economic Geography." *Journal of Economic Geography* 1, no. 2 (April): 227–250.

McHugh, Kathleen. 2009a. "Jane Campion: Adaptation, Signature, Autobiography." In *Jane Campion: Cinema, Nation, Identity*, edited by Hilary Radner, Alistair Fox, and Irène Bessière, 139–156. Detroit: Wayne State University Press.

McHugh, Kathleen. 2009b. "The World and the Soup: Historicizing Media Feminisms in Transnational Contexts." *Camera Obscura* 72, vol. 24, no. 3: 111–150.

Mehta, Monika, and Madhuja Mukherjee. 2020. *Industrial Networks and Cinemas of India: Shooting Stars, Shifting Geographies and Multiplying Media*. New York: Routledge India.

Menon, Nivedita. 2004. *Recovering Subversion: Feminist Politics Beyond the Law*. Urbana: University of Illinois Press.

Meyer, Birgit. 2009. "Introduction: From Imagined Communities to Aesthetic Formations: Religious Formations, Sensational Forms, and Styles of Binding." In *Aesthetic Formations: Media, Religion, and the Senses*, edited by Birgit Meyer, 1–30. New York: Palgrave.

Mintzer, Jordan. 2019. "'Made in Bangladesh' Film Review: TIFF 2019." *Hollywood Reporter*. https://www.hollywoodreporter.com/review/made-bangladesh-review-1236014/.

Mookherjee, Nayanika. 2006. "Muktir Gaan: The Raped Woman and Migrant Identities of the Bangladesh War." In *Gender, Conflict, and Migration*, edited by Navnita Chadha Behara, 72–96. New Delhi: Sage Publications.

Mookherjee, Nayanika. 2011. "'Love in the Time of 1971: The Furore over 'Meherjaan.'" *Economic and Political Weekly* 41, no. 12: 25–27.

Mookherjee, Nayanika. 2015. *The Spectral Wound: Sexual Violence, Public Memories, and the Bangladesh War of 1971*. Durham: Duke University Press.

Moors, Annelies. 2006. "Representing Family Law Debates in Palestine: Gender and the Politics of Presence." In *Religion, Media, and the Public Sphere*, edited by Birgit Meyer and Annelies Moors, 115–131. Bloomington: Indiana University Press.

Morcom, Anna. 2009. "Indian Popular Culture and Its 'Others': Bollywood Dance and Anti-*Nautch* in Twenty-First-Century Global India." In *Popular Culture in a Globalized India*, edited by Moti K. Gokulsingh and Wimal Dissanayake, 125–138. London: Routledge.

Morcom, Anna. 2013. *Illicit Worlds of Indian Dance: Cultures of Exclusion*. London: Hurst Publishing/Oxford University Press.

Mottahedeh, Negar. 2008. *Displaced Allegories: Post-Revolutionary Iranian Cinema*. Durham: Duke University Press.

Mukherjee, Debashree. 2015. "Scandalous Evidence: Looking for the Bombay Film Actress in an Absent Archive (1930s–1940s)." In *Doing Women's Film History: Reframing Cinemas, Past and Future*, edited by Christine Gledhill and Julia Knight, 29–41. Urbana: University of Illinois Press.

Mukherjee, Debashree. 2020a. *Bombay Hustle: Making Movies in a Colonial City*. New York: Columbia University Press.

Mukherjee, Debashree. 2020b. "Somewhere between Human, Nonhuman, and Woman: Shanta Apte's Theory of Exhaustion." *Feminist Media Histories* 6, no. 3: 21–51.

Mukherjee, Madhuja. 2007. "Early Indian Talkies: Voice, Performance, and Aura." *Journal of the Moving Image*: 1–18. http://jmionline.org/articles/2007/early-indian-talkies-voice-performance.

Mukherjee, Madhuja. 2009. *New Theatres Ltd.: The Emblem of Art, the Picture of Success*. Pune: National Film Archive of India.

Mukherjee, Sabyasachi. 2012. "Sabya and *English Vinglish*." *Telegraph Online*. March 10. https://www.telegraphindia.com/entertainment/sabya-english-vinglish/cid/388846/.

"*Mukhomukhi* [Face-to-Face]." (Shuchanda Interview). 1988. *Saptahik Purnima* (August): 41–42.

Munich, Adrienne. 2011. "The Stars and Stripes in Fashion Films." In *Fashion in Film*, edited by Adrienne Munich, 260–280. Bloomington: Indiana University Press.

Nabi, Hira. 2017. "Transient Spaces and Places: Inside an 80s Cinema Hall in Lahore." *Bioscope* 8, no. 2: 268–279.

Naficy, Hamid. 2012. *A Social History of Iranian Cinema*. Vol. 4: *The Globalizing Era, 1984–2010*. Durham: Duke University Press.

Nag, Anugyan, and Spandan Bhattacharya. 2021. *From Tollygunge to Tollywood: The Bengali Film Industry Reimagined*. Hyderabad: Orient Blackswan.

Nandy, Ashis. 2001. "The City as the Invitation to an Antique Death: Pramathesh Chandra Barua and the Origins of the Terribly Effeminate, Maudlin, Self-Destructive Heroes of Indian Cinema." In *An Ambiguous Journey to the City: The Village and Other Odd Ruins of the Self in Indian Imagination*. New Delhi: Oxford University Press. 42–71.

Naremore, James. [1999] 2004. "Authorship." In *A Companion to Film Theory*, edited by Toby Miller and Robert Stam, 9–24. London: Blackwell Publishing.

"Nari Diboshe Protyasha [The Hope of International Women's Day]." 2007. *Manab-jibon*. Year 10, no. 22. March 8: 16.

Nasreen, Gitiara, and Fahmidul Haq. 2008. *Bangladesher Cholochitro Shilpo: Sankate Janosangskriti* [The film industry of Bangladesh: popular culture in crisis]. Dhaka: Srabon Prokashoni.

National Film Development Corporation Limited Pakistan. 1981. *Cinema of Pakistan 1970–1980*. Islamabad: NAFDEC.

Nazneen, Sohela. 2017. *The Women's Movement in Bangladesh: A Short History and Current Debates*. https://library.fes.de/pdf-files/bueros/bangladesch/13671.pdf/.

"On Flogging . . . A Life-Long Punishment." 1984. Newsmonth: Issues. *SHE*. March: 11.

Orsini, Francesca. 2002. *The Hindi Public Sphere 1920–1940: Language and Literature in the Age of Nationalism*. New Delhi: Oxford University Press.

Ortner, Sherry B. 1995. "Resistance and the Problem of Ethnographic Refusal." *Comparative Studies in Society and History* 37 (1): 173–193.

Pamment, Claire. 2015. "A Split Discourse: Body Politics in Pakistan's Popular Punjabi Theatre." In *Gender, Politics, and Performance in South Asia*, edited by Sheema Kermani, Asif Ali Farrukhi, and Kamran Asdar Ali, 203–234. Karachi: Oxford University Press.

Pamment, Claire. 2017. *Comic Performance in Pakistan: The Bhānd*. London: Palgrave Macmillan.

Paranjpye, Sai. 2021. "A Patchwork Quilt by Sai Paranjpye." May 16. *Undecided in Dubai*. Blog. https://undecidedindubai.wordpress.com/2021/05/16/a-patchwork-quilt-sai-paranjpye/July 6.

Patwari, Shahnewaj, and Abu N.M.A. Ali. 2020. "Muslim Women's Right to Divorce and Gender Equality Issues in Bangladesh: A Proposal for Review of Current Laws." *Journal of International Women's Studies* 21, no. 6: 50–79.

Peerzada, Samina. 1986. "Two's Company." [Interview with Moneeza Hashmi.] *SHE*. February 1986: 50–53.

Peerzada, Samina. 2016. "Portrayal of Women in TV and Film." Panel Presentation. Faiz International Festival. Lahore, Pakistan. https://www.youtube.com/watch?v=EYVWpo0Y4Jo&t=9s/.

Pillaai, Jitesh. 2007. "The Director's Cut: Seven of India's Most Influential Filmmakers Get Together to Talk Shop and Lots More." *Filmfare*. October 2007: 57–74.

Portelli, Alessandro. 2006. "What Makes Oral History Different." *The Oral History Reader*, 2nd ed., edited by Robert Perks and Alistair Thomson, 32–42. London: Routledge.

Prasad, Madhava. 1998a. *Ideology of the Hindi Film: A Historical Construction*. New Delhi: Oxford University Press.

Prasad, Madhava. 1998b. "The State in/of Cinema." In *Wages of Freedom: Fifty Years of the Indian Nation-State*, edited by Partha Chatterjee, 123–146. New York: Oxford University Press.

Prasad, Madhava. 2011. "Genre Mixing as Creative Fabrication." *Bioscope* 2, no. 1: 69–81.

Prasanga: Tin Konna [Topic: Tin Konna]. 1986. *Purbani*. Magh [January] 16. p. 15.

Punathambekar, Aswin. 2013. "Authoring Hype in Bollywood." In *A Companion to Media Authorship*, edited by Jonathan Gray and Derek Johnson, 465–484. Hoboken: Wiley Blackwell.

Rajadhyaksha, Ashish. 2000. "Realism, Modernism, and Post-Colonial Theory." In *World Cinema: Critical Approaches*, edited by John Hill and Pamela Church Gibson, 29–39. Oxford: Oxford University Press.

Rajadhyaksha, Ashish. 2003. "The 'Bollywoodization' of the Indian Cinema: Cultural Nationalism in a Global Arena." *Inter-Asia Cultural Studies* 4, no. 1: 25–39.

Rajadhyaksha, Ashish, and Paul Willemen. 1999. *The Encyclopedia of Indian Cinema*. Rev. ed. London: Fitzroy Dearborn Publishers.

Raju, Saraswati, and Tanusree Paul. 2016–2017. "Public Spaces and Places: Gendered Intersectionalities in Indian Cities." *India International Centre Quarterly* (Winter 2016-Spring 2017): 128–138.

Raju, Zakir Hossain. 2013. "*Chalachitre Sramajibi Manush: Prekshapat Bangladesh* [Laborers in Cinema: Context Bangladesh]." In *Bangladesher Anyo Cinema* [The alternative cinema of Bangladesh]. Vol. 1, edited by Sushil Saha, 129. Dhaka: Abhijan Publishers.

Raju, Zakir Hossain. 2015. *Bangladesh Cinema and National Identity: In Search of the Modern?* London: Routledge.

Ram, Anjali. 2021. "Out of India: Educating the New Women in *Queen, English Vinglish*, and *Badrinath ki Dulhania*." In *Bollywood's New Woman: Liberation, Liberalization, and Contested Bodies*, edited by Megha Anwer and Anupama Arora, 133–145. New Brunswick: Rutgers University Press.

Ramanathan, Geetha. 2006. *Feminist Auteurs: Reading Women's Films*. London: Wallflower Press.

Rangayan, Sridhar, and Saagar Gupta. 2013. "Queen of Humour: A Candid Interview with Award-Winning Writer and Filmmaker Sai Paranjpye." *The South Asianist* 2, no. 3: 153–171.

Rashid, Abdur. 1987. "Censor Bureau Chief's Report on Film." In *From Colourless to Colourful: Platinum Jubilee Film Directory 1913–1987*, edited by A. R. Slote, 61–70. Karachi: Falak Printing Press.

Ray, Satyajit. 1976. "An Indian New Wave?" In *Our Films, Their Films*. Calcutta: Orient Longman. 90–92.

"Read What the Three Great Papers Say." 1935. *Filmindia* 1, no. 4 (July 31): 2.

Rehman, Nasreen. 2020. "Pakistan, History, and Sleep: Hasan Tariq, a Progressive Patriarch, and *Neend.*" In *South Asian Filmscapes: Transregional Encounters*, edited by Elora Halim Chowdhury and Esha Niyogi De, 97–118. Seattle: University of Washington Press.

Report of the Film Enquiry Committee. 1951. New Delhi: Govt. of India Press.

Report of the Working Group on National Film Policy. 1980. New Delhi: Govt. of India, Ministry of Information and Broadcasting. May 1980.

"Revival of the 'Society Girl': A Tribute Offered to Sangeeta, the Determined, Resolute Face of Pakistani Cinema." 2014. *Express Tribune.* May 1. https://tribune.com.pk/story/702827/revival-of-the-society-girl/.

Rizvi, Wajiha Raza. 2014. "Visual Pleasure in Pakistani Cinema (1947–2014)." *IJAPS* 10, no. 2: 73–105.

Rouse, Shahnaz. 2004. *Shifting Body Politics: Gender, Nation, State in Pakistan.* New Delhi: Women Unlimited.

Roy, Abhijit. 2000. "The New Popular and the *Bhadralok.*" Unpublished paper. Inaugural Conference of the Sarai Programme. New Delhi: Center for the Study of Developing Societies.

Roy, Mantra, and Aparajita Sengupta. 2014. "Women and Emergent Agency in the Cinema of Aparna Sen." *South Asian Popular Culture* 12, no. 2: 53–71.

Roy, Sudeshna. 2017. "Sudeshna Roy's *Mayer Biye* Inspired from Aparna Sen's Life." *TOI* January 12. https://timesofindia.indiatimes.com/entertainment/bengali/movies/news/sudeshna-roys-mayer-biye-inspired-from-aparna-sens-life/articleshow/48985332.cms/.

"Sabita." 1987. *Weekly Akhbar-e-Jehan, Karachi.* March 20–27: 56.

Sadana, Rashmi. 2012. *English Heart, Hindi Heartland: The Political Life of Literature in India.* Berkeley: University of California Press.

Saeed, Fouzia. 2002. *Taboo! The Hidden Culture of a Red Light Area.* Karachi: Oxford University Press.

Saeed, Humaira. 2009. "*Ramchand Pakistani, Khamosh Pani,* and the Traumatic Evocation of Partition." *Social Semiotics* 19, no. 4: 483–498.

Sagar, Faridur Reza. 2011. Preface to *Impress Telefilm's Movie Album 2000–2010.* Dhaka: Impress Printing Limited. 3.

Said, Ahmad. 1962. "Film." *Nuqūsh* 92: 785–797. Translated from Urdu by Gwendolyn Sarah Kirk.

Said, Edward. 1979. *Orientalism.* New York: Vintage Books.

"Sakhatkar Nargis Akhter." 2003. *Binodon Bichitra* 3 (April 2003): 30–31.

Sangeeta. 2016. Interview by Hina Altaf Khan. July 25. https://www.youtube.com/watch?v=Ft1VF_eP92syt+92s/. Accessed on April 15, 2017, but no longer available.

Sanyal, Sunanda. 1985. "*Narider Drishite Parama* [*Parama* in Women's Eyes]." *Chitravas,* 40. Kolkata: North Calcutta Film Society/Mudrakar Press.

Sarkar, Bhaskar. 2009. *Mourning the Nation: Indian Cinema in the Wake of Partition.* Durham: Duke University Press.

Sarkar, Mahua. 2008. *Visible Histories, Disappearing Women: Producing Muslim Womanhood in Late Colonial Bengal.* Durham: Duke University Press.

Sarkar, Tanika. 1995. "Hindu Conjugality and Nationalism in Late Nineteenth-Century Bengal." In *Indian Women: Myth and Reality*, edited by Jasodhara Bagchi, 98–116. Hyderabad: Sangam Books.

Sarkar, Tanika. 2002. *Hindu Wife, Hindu Nation: Community, Religion, and Cultural Nationalism*. Bloomington: Indiana University Press.

Sawhney, Rashmi. 2007. "Apotheosis or Apparition? Bombay and the Village in 1990s Women's Cinema." *Film Studies* 11 (Winter): 1–11.

Sawhney, Rashmi. 2015. "Revising the Colonial Past, Undoing 'National' Histories: Women Filmmakers in Kannada, Marathi, and Bengali Cinema." In *Doing Women's Film History: Reframing Cinemas, Past and Future*, edited by Christine Gledhill, 151–165. Urbana: University of Illinois Press.

Scheman, Naomi. 1980. "Anger and the Politics of Naming." In *Women and Language in Literature and Society*, edited by Sally McConnell-Ginet, Ruth Borker, and Nelly Furman, 22–35. New York: Praeger.

Schleier, Merrill. 2008. *Skyscraper Cinema: Architecture and Gender in the American Film*. Minneapolis: University of Minnesota Press.

Schubart, Rikke. 2007. *Super Bitches and Action Babes: The Female Hero in Popular Cinema, 1970–2006*. Jefferson, NC: McFarland.

Sedgwick, Eve Kosofsky. 2003. *Touching Feeling: Affect, Pedagogy, Performativity*. Durham: Duke University Press.

Sen, Aparna. 1984. "Interview." *Filmfare* 33, no. 18: 78–85.

Sen, Aparna. 1993. "*Sampadakyo* [Editorial]." *Sananda*. Kolkata: Anandabazar Patrika. January 22: 4.

Sen, Aparna. 1999. "Friendships Survive." *The Indian Panorama 1999*. New Delhi: Directorate of Film Festivals.

Sen, Aparna. 2004. "Aparna Sen." *Screen Weekly*. November 19. http://www.screen india.com/fullstory.php?content_id=9446/.

Sen, Aparna. 2013. "Goynar Baksho Almost Never Got Made: Aparna Sen." *Times of India: News: Entertainment: Bengali Movies*. Updated: January 11, 2017. https://timesofindia.indiatimes.com/entertainment/bengali/movies/news/goynar -baksho-almost-never-got-made-aparna-sen/articleshow/19509886.cms/.

Sen, Aparna. 2014. "Editorial: Rituparno ke khola chitti [An open letter to Rituparno]." *Prothoma Ekhon*. January 1.

Sen, Aparna. 2017. "Uncut Aparna." Television Interview. ETV Bangla. https://www.youtube.com/watch?v=nQCwslKNMBU/.

Sen, Samita. 2000. "Toward a Feminist Politics? The Indian Women's Movement in Historical Perspective." *Policy Research Report on Gender and Development. Working Paper Series No. 9*. Washington, D.C.: World Bank Development Research Group/Poverty Reduction and Economic Management Network.

Sengupta, Mekhala. 2015. *Kanan Devi: The First Superstar of Indian Cinema*. Noida, India: Harper Collins.

Sevea, Iqbal. 2014. "'*Kharaak Kita Oi!*': Masculinity, Caste, and Gender in Punjabi Films." *Bioscope* 5, no. 2: 129–140. https://doi.org/10.1177/0974927614548645/.

Shamim Ara. 1964. "Shamim Ara: Pages from My Diary." *Eastern Film* 6, no. 1 (August): 37–40.

Shamim Ara. c. 1993. Exclusive Interview. BBC Urdu. https://www.youtube.com/watch?v=yfiUUbPBvzI&t=243s/.

Shamim Ara. 1987. Interview. *Film Asia.* June 6, no. 5: 27. Translated from Urdu by Lubna Saira.

"Shamim Ara: Scanning New Horizons." 1963. *Eastern Film* 8, no. 4 (March): 8–10.

Shahab. 1966. "Dacca Spotlight." *Eastern Film.* December: 26–29.

Shehabuddin, Elora. 2008. *Reshaping the Holy: Democracy, Development, and Muslim Women in Bangladesh.* New York: Columbia University Press.

Shehabuddin, Elora. 2014. "Feminism and Nationalism in Cold War East Pakistan." *South Asia Chronicle* 4: 49–68.

"*Shilper Sathe Mitali* [Bond with the Arts]." (Nargis Akhter Interview). 2010. *Binodon* 8, no. 3: 32–33.

Shohat, Ella. 1997. "Post-Third-Worldist Culture: Gender, Nation, and the Cinema." In *Feminist Genealogies, Colonial Legacies, Democratic Futures*, edited by M. Jacqui Alexander and Chandra Talpade Mohanty, 183–209. New York: Routledge.

Shohat, Ella. 2006. "Post-Third-Worldist Culture: Gender, Nation, and the Cinema." In *Transnational Cinema: The Film Reader*, edited by Elizabeth Ezra and Terry Rowden, 39–56. New York: Routledge.

Siddiqi, Dina. 2017. "Ghosts of 1947." *Daily Star.* August 26.

Siddique, Salma. 2019. "Archive Filmaria: Cinema, Curation, and Contagion." *Comparative Studies of South Asia, Africa and the Middle East* 39, no. 1: 196–211. DOI: 10.1215/1089201X-7493898.

Sindawi, Khalid. 2013. *Temporary Marriage in Sunni and Shiite Islam: A Comparative Study.* Weisbaden, Germany: Harrassowitz Verlag.

Singer, Ben. 2001. *Melodrama and Modernity: Early Sensational Cinema and Its Contexts.* New York: Columbia University Press.

Singh, Kuldip. 1992. "Obituary: Kanan Devi." *Independent.* July 21. https://www.independent.co.uk/news/people/obituary-kanan-devi-1534655.html/.

Sinha, Meenakshi. 1985. "*Narider Drishtite Parama* [*Parama* in Women's Eyes]." *Chitravas*, 41. Kolkata: North Calcutta Film Society/Mudrakar Press.

Sinha, Mrinalini. 2014. "Gendered Nationalism." *Routledge Handbook of Gender in South Asia*, edited by Leela Fernandes, 13–27. London: Routledge.

Smelik, Anneke. 1998. *And the Mirror Cracked: Feminist Cinema and Film Theory.* New York: St. Martin's Press.

"Southasian Children's Cinema: Promoting Quality Indigenous Cinema for Children and Young People." 2013. *The Second Round Table on Southasian Children's Films.* Kerala: Eighteenth International Kerala Film Festival. 3, 10, 25.

Speaking Chic. 2012. "Bollywood Fashion: Sabyasachi Dresses Sridevi as Typical Shypical Housewife in *English Vinglish.*" *Speaking Chic: Food, Travel, Fashion.* October 8. https://speakingchic.com/2012/10/bollywood-fashion-sabyasachi-dresses-sridevi-as-typical-shypical-housewife-in-english-vinglish/.

Spivak, Gayatri Chakravorty. 1999. *A Critique of Postcolonial Reason: Toward a History of the Vanishing Present.* Cambridge: Harvard University Press.

Spivak, Gayatri Chakravorty. 2008. *Other Asias.* Malden: Blackwell Publishing.

Stoler, Ann Laura, with Karen Strassler. 2006. "Memory-Work in Java: A Cautionary Tale." In *The Oral History Reader*. 2nd ed, edited by Robert Perks and Alistair Thomson, 283–309. London: Routledge.

Sundaram, Ravi. 2009. *Pirate Modernity: Delhi's Media Urbanism*. New York: Routledge.

Tanvir, Kuhu. 2013. "Pirate Histories: Rethinking the Indian Film Archive." *Bioscope: South Asian Screen Studies* 4, no. 2: 115–136.

Tanvir, Kuhu. 2014. "Snapshots of Bollywood Masculinity in the Age of Hindutva." *Special Effects*. https://www.fsgo.pitt.edu/.

Tasker, Yvonne. 1993. *Spectacular Bodies: Gender, Genre, and the Action Cinema*. Reprint ed. London: Routledge, 2000.

Tasker, Yvonne. 2004. "Introduction: Action and Adventure Cinema." In *Action and Adventure Cinema*, edited by Yvonne Tasker, 1–14. London: Routledge.

Taussig, Michael. 1992. *Mimesis and Alterity: A Particular History of the Senses*. Reprint ed. New York: Routledge, 2018.

Toor, Saadia. 2011. *The State of Islam: Culture and Cold War Politics in Pakistan*. London: Pluto Press.

"Top Fifteen Films Driven by Film Leads." 2018. *Box Office India Trade Network*. May 23. https://boxofficeindia.com/report-details.php?articleid=3954/.

"Uro Katha." 1982. *Chitrali*. September 1982: 47–48.

Van Schendel, Willem. 2009. *A History of Bangladesh*. Cambridge: Cambridge University Press.

Vasudevan, Ravi. 1989. "The Melodramatic Mode and the Commercial Hindi Cinema: Notes on Film History, Narrative, and Performance in the 1950s." *Screen* 30, no. 3 (Summer): 29–50.

Vasudevan, Ravi. 2000. "The Politics of Cultural Address in a 'Transitional' Cinema: A Case Study of Indian Popular Cinema." In *Reinventing Film Studies*, edited by Christine Gledhill and Linda Williams, 130–164. London: Arnold.

Vasudevan, Ravi. 2010. *The Melodramatic Public: Film Form and Spectatorship in Indian Cinema*. Ranikhet: Permanent Black.

"Video: *Shamajik Chhobir Chahida Beshi*/More Demand for Social Films." 1990. *Saptahik Purnima*. January. 10: 43.

Viswamohan, Aysha Iqbal, ed. 2023. *Women Filmmakers in Contemporary Hindi Cinema: Looking through Their Gaze*. Cham, Switzerland: Palgrave MacMillan.

Vitali, Valentina. 2008. *Hindi Action Cinema: Industries, Narratives, Bodies*. Delhi: Oxford University Press (rprt. Indiana University Press).

Vitali, Valentina. 2020. "Why a Special Issue on Women's Cinema?" *Bioscope* 11, no. 1: 7–14.

Wang, Lingzhen. 2011. "Introduction: Transnational Feminist Reconfiguration of Film Discourse and Women's Cinema." In *Chinese Women's Cinema: Transnational Contexts*, edited by Lingzhen Wang, 1–43. New York: Columbia University Press.

Weiss, Anita M. 2012. "Islamic Influences on Social-Legal Conditions of Pakistani Women." In *Islam and Society in Pakistan: Anthropological Perspectives*, edited by Magnus Marsden, 52–75. Karachi: Oxford University Press.

"What College Students Want." 2007. *Filmfare*. January 2007: 94–96.

"What Is Nirbhaya Case?" 2019. *TOI-Online.* December 19, 2019. https://timesof india.indiatimes.com/india/what-is-nirbhaya-case/articleshow/72868430.cms/.

White, Patricia. 2015. *Women's Cinema, World Cinema: Projecting Contemporary Feminisms.* Durham: Duke University Press.

"Why Don't Our Film Heroes Have a Goal?" 1989. *Film Asia* 4, no. 11 (November); 1–4. Translated by Lubna Saira.

Williams, Linda. 1994. "Introduction." In *Viewing Positions: Ways of Seeing Film.* Rutgers University Press. 1–20.

Zia, Afiya Shehrbano. 2009. "The Reinvention of Feminism in Pakistan." *Feminist Review* 91: South Asian Feminisms: Negotiating New Terrains. 29–46.

Ziad, Abdullah. 2010. *Bangladesher Challochitra: Panch Doshoker Etihash.* Dhaka: Mostafa Jehangir Alam, Jyotiprokash.

Personal Interviews and Conversations

Ahmed, Syed Hafeez. 2015. Skype Interview. Washington, DC. April 10.

Ahmed, Syed Hafeez. 2018. Phone Interview. September 23.

Ahmed, Syed Hafeez. 2019. Phone Interview. November 8.

Akhter, Nargis. 2014. Personal Interview with Esha Niyogi De. Dhaka, Bangladesh. February 18.

Akhtar, Shameem. 2014. Personal Interview with Esha Niyogi De. Dhaka, Bangladesh. February 10.

Alam, Md. Fokrul. 2014. Personal Interview. Dhaka: Bangladesh Film Archive. February 12.

Alam, Md. Fokrul. 2014. Personal Interview. Dhaka: Bangladesh Film Archive. March 29.

Ali, Sarwat. 2013. Personal Interview by Esha Niyogi De. Islamabad, Pakistan. November 16.

Haq, Mofidul. 2014. Personal Interview with Esha Niyogi De. Dhaka, Bangladesh. April 8.

Hashmi, Mira. 2013. Personal Interview with Esha Niyogi De. Islamabad, Pakistan. December 10.

Hashmi, Salima. 2013. Personal Interview with Esha Niyogi De. Islamabad, Pakistan. December 18.

Hossain, Rubaiyat. 2014. Personal Interviews with Esha Niyogi De. Dhaka, Bangladesh. Feb. 14 and 19.

Jevanjee, Kamila. 2019. Personal Interview. Los Angeles. June 7.

Khan, Irshad Ahmed. 2014. Personal Interview. London. November 10.

Khan, Raja Riaz, 2016. Personal Interview. Lahore, Pakistan. September 7.

Kirk, Gwendolyn Sarah. 2021. Personal Interview with Esha Niyogi De. April 10.

Kumar, Nirmal. 2014. Personal Interview with Esha Niyogi De. Kolkata, India. March 25.

Majumdar, Tarun. 2014. Phone Conversation with Esha Niyogi De. May 10, 2014.

Mokammel, Tanvir. 2014. Personal Interview with Esha Niyogi De. Dhaka, Bangladesh. February 6.

Najam-ul-Hasan, Khwaja. 2013. Personal Interview by Esha Niyogi De. Islamabad, Pakistan, November 14.

Peerzada, Samina. 2013. Personal Interviews. Islamabad, Pakistan. December 10, 18.

Roy, Sudeshna. 2014. Personal Interview with Esha Niyogi De. Kolkata, India. April 24.

Sagar, Faridur Reza, and Gita Hasan. 2014. Personal Interview with Esha Niyogi De. Dhaka, Bangladesh. January 30.

Sen, Aparna. 2009. Personal Interview with Esha Niyogi De. Kolkata, India. March 22, 2009.

Sen, Aparna. 2012. Personal Interview with Esha Niyogi De. Kolkata, India. August 10, 2012.

Sen, Aparna. 2013. Phone Interview with Esha Niyogi De. Kolkata, India. September 25, 2013.

Sen, Aparna. 2014. Personal Interview with Esha Niyogi De. Kolkata, India. April 25. 2014.

Shinde, Gauri. 2013. Personal Conversation with Esha Niyogi De. Mumbai, India. October 30.

Select Filmography

Chanway [O, Moon]. 1951. Directed by Noorjehan. Lahore: Shah Noor Films. 2 hrs. 19 mins.

Chashme Buddoor [Far Be the Evil Eye]. 1981. Directed by Sai Paranjpye. Mumbai: P.L.A. Productions. Motion Picture. 2 hrs. 13 min. https://www.youtube.com/watch?v=beHF6uxhzZA&t=126s/

English Vinglish. 2012. Directed by Gauri Shinde. Mumbai: Hope Productions. Motion Picture. 2 hrs. 14 mins. DVD.

Goynar Baksho [The Jewelry Box]. 2013. Directed by Aparna Sen. Kolkata: Shree Venkatesh Films. Motion Picture. 2 hrs. 21 mins. DVD.

Hajaar Bachhar Dhorey [Symphony of Agony]. 2005. Directed by Kohinoor Akhter Shuchanda. Dhaka: Shuchanda Cholochitra. 2 hrs. 16 mins. https://www.youtube.com/watch?v=xVzOSYWf6Nk&t=449s/

Inteha [The Limit]. 1999. Directed by Samina Peerzada. Lahore: Samina Peerzada Productions. 2 hrs. 12 mins. https://www.dailymotion.com/video/x1zvz4e/

Lady Smuggler. 1987. Directed by Shamim Ara. Lahore: Shamim Ara Productions. 2 hrs. 42 mins. https://www.youtube.com/watch?v=XIao8ZxYwl0&t=8706s/

Mayer Biye [Mother's Marriage]. 2015. Directed by Sudeshna Roy and Abhijit Guha. Kolkata: Eskay Movies and Sony 8. DVD. 1 hr. 35 mins. https://www.youtuber.com/watch?v=OR01nRCguZA&t=139s/

Megher Koley Rod [Sunshine in the Clouds]. 2008. Directed by Nargis Akhter. Dhaka: FemCom Productions. 2 hrs. 31 mins. https://www.youtube.com/watch?v=DU7mTQN9Fps/

Meghla Akash [The Cloudy Sky]. 2001. Directed by Nargis Akhter. Dhaka: FemCom Productions. 2 hrs. 17 mins. DVD.

Meherjaan. 2011. Directed by Rubaiyat Hossain. Dhaka: Khona Talkies. 1 hr. 59 mins. https://alexanderstreet.com/page/streaming-video/

Mej Didi. [Middle Sister]. 1950. Directed by Sabyasachi Collective. Kolkata: Sreemati Pictures. 1 hr. 58 mins. https://www.youtube.com/watch?v=1pRn4R7dzlw&t=5887s/

Miss Colombo. 1984. Directed by Shamim Ara. Lahore: Shamim Ara Productions. 2 hrs. 40 mins. https://www.youtube.com/watch?v=YBCQNId6zJk/

Miss Hong Kong. 1979. Directed by Shamim Ara. Lahore: Shamim Ara Productions. 2 hrs. 28 mins. https://www.youtube.com/watch?v=yijmqki03iQ/

Mutthi Bhar Chawal [A Handful of Rice]. 1978. Directed by Sangeeta. Lahore: P.N.R. Productions, Mehtab Bano. https://www.youtube.com/watch?v=kGotUaod VQw&t=379s/

Parama. 1985. Directed by Aparna Sen. Kolkata: Usha Enterprises. 2 hrs. 19 mins. DVD.

Paromitar Ek Din [House of Memories]. 2000. Directed by Aparna Sen. Kolkata: Suravi Production. 2 hrs. 13 mins. DVD.

Society Girl. 1976. Directed by Sangeeta. Lahore: P.N.R. Productions, Mehtab Bano. 2 hrs. 17 mins. https://www.youtube.com/watch?v=fGBwahISNC0&t=11s/

Tin Konna [Three Sisters]. 1985. Directed by Shibli Sadique. Dhaka: Shuchanda Cholochitra. 2 hrs. 35 mins. https://www.youtube.com/watch?v=ttgOOpon Mfs&t=4905s/

Index

207, 210; ghost fictions, 209, 210; trauma films, 201; urban auteur cinema, 53. *See also* Bangladeshi cinema; Kanan Devi; Kolkata cinema; Sen, Aparna

Bengali language, 244–245n4. *See also* Bangla Language Movement

Bengali Muslims, 14, 223, 225, 245n4. See also *Meherjaan*

Benjamin, Walter, 186, 236n12, 243n15, 244n5

Berlant, Lauren, 241n12

bhānd comedy, 113, 124, 126, 129, 176, 187, 188

Bhattacharya, Haridas, 47–48; *Asha*, 48, 49

Bhooter Bhabisyat (The Future of the Past; dir. Anik Dutta, 2012), 205

Bhutto, Benazir, 6

Bhutto, Zulfikar Ali, 116

bikalpa dhārā (alternative film stream), 70–71

Bilal, Iram Parveen, 138, 237n21

Binodon (periodical), 89

birāngona (war heroine), 219, 220

Biswas, Moinak, 14, 37, 81

Bollywood: Bollywoodization of Hindi cinema, 140, 144, 165; branding and scale, 25, 138, 158; female-authored fiction films, 145–47; female-confidence fiction, 157–58; gentrification of, 145, 242n7; *hatke* niche films, 135, 146; infrastructure, 145, 162, 242n8; male dominance, 142, 162; male stars, 142, 162, 243n14; in Pakistan, 138; and partition trauma films, 203; youth-oriented films, 154–55. *See also* Mumbai film industry; Shinde, Gauri

border-crossing, 5, 22–23, 28, 118–19. *See also* transnational cinema

Box Office India Trade Network, top fifteen female-lead films, 153–54

brand culture, 20–22, 27, 29; in Bangla cinema, 64, 90, 216; in Bollywood cinema, 26, 103, 140, 147; and globalization, 160, 230; heritage brand, 206, 208, 210, 216; hype creation, 207, 208, 210, 227; male branding, 65;

nation as brand, 140, 145, 152, 158. *See also* brand partners

brand partners, 147, 155, 160, 163, 206, 207, 218, 221, 225–27

bricolage (genre mixing), 9, 16, 19, 68, 191, 202, 236n12

British colonialism, 14, 16, 212, 244n4

Buck-Morss, Susan, 194, 236n12, 244n5

buddy genre, 148–50, 183, 242n12

caiti (song style), 45

Calcutta Film Society, 53, 54. *See also* Kolkata cinema

Chakrabarty, Dipesh, 75, 207, 215

Chakraborty, Sabyasachi, 65

Champa, Gulshan Ara Akhter, 14, 25, 69, 85; in *Tin Konna*, 73, 74, 76, 85

Channel 1 (Bangladesh), 226, 227

Chanway (O, Moon; dir. Noorhehan, 1951), 108–9

Chaowa Pawa (dir. Tarun Majumdar, 1959), 51

Chaplin, Charlie, 187

Charlie's Angels (TV series), 183

Chasme Buddoor (Far Be the Evil Eye; dir. Sai Paranjpye, 1981): aesthetic, 148–49; conventions of middle cinema, 146, 149–52; Dadi Amma and Neha, *151*; female personifications, 150–51; funding, 144; Gul Anand as producer, 148–49, 152; positive press, 148; as social comedy, 26, 140, 146

Chatterjee, Moushumi, 208, 210

Chatterjee, Partha, 245n6

Chatterjee, Saswata, 212

Chatterjee, Soumitra, 39

Chatterjee, Srabonti, 208, 210

Chatterji, Basu, 148, 149

Chitrabani (periodical), 50, 143

Chitrali (periodical), 72, 74, 173; "Two Sisters" report, 83, 84

Chitravas (periodical), 59–60

Choti Si Baat (dir. Basu Chatterji, 1976), 149

Chowdhury, Elora Halim, 70–71, 91, 219, 221

Christians, 45, 115, 117, 180–81, 182

narrative, 155–57, 159–60; production company, 163; script, 163; shot compositions, 159, 160; Sridevi in, 154, 155, 158, 160, 162, 163, 164; success of, 153, 154–55

entertainment professionals, 110–11, 113, 137, 141–42, 241n6

eroticism, 130, 155, 227, 205

Ershad, Hussain Muhammad, 177

Eskay Movies, 64

ethnographic perspective, 4, 10–11, 105, 107, 131, 144, 147, 229–30

Evernew Studios (Lahore), 119

Faiz, Faiz Ahmed, 107, 221, 241n2

fame, 4, 7–8, 13, 34. *See also* stardom

family subject films, 33, 124, 237n18. *See also* motherliness genre

family system of production, 16–20, 141, 222, 237n21; brand identities, 21; couple and partner mode, 18, 19, 22, 24, 48, 132, 141, 162, 163, 222, 244n1; early-twentieth-century United States, 18–19; female-led, 114; joint family studio era, 16, 24, 36, 37, 237n21; Lahore studios, 17, 189; as male-dominant, 83–84; sororal, 69, 74–75, 84; and transnational cinema, 189, 218. *See also* Lahore studio culture

fandom, 3, 72, 108, 122, 206

Farooki, Mostafa Sarwar, 230

female authorship, 10–11, 88, 231, 231–34; archive of, 160, 200, 233, 234; Bangladesh, 66, 69, 88–89, 93, 222; cross-generational and cross-border, 22–23, 29; Hindi film, 26–27, 139–41, 144, 147, 165, 202; Pakistan, 137; and publicity, 194–97; and scale of capital supporting production, 19, 21–22, 33, 103, 169, 178; social films, 13–14; transnational, 183. *See also* female-star-authorship; women film directors; *and names of individual film authors*

female body, 25–26, 78, 105, 120, 146, 149, 179; in *Chasme Buddoor*, 150, 151; in *English Vinglish*, 155, 157, 158; in *Meherjaan*, 220; in *Miss Colombo*, 182; in *Miss Hong Kong*, 126, 127, 128–29, 130; politics of, 103

female-confidence fiction, 157–58

female friendship, 187, 189, 213

female-lead productions, 26, 117, 153–54, 161–62. *See also* *English Vinglish*; *Inteha*

female mobility, 104, 132, 151

female-star-authorship, 4, 8–10, 11, 12–13, 21, 35–36, 141, 231, 233. *See also* Babita, Farida Akhtar; Kanan Devi; Peerzada, Samina; Sangeeta; Sen, Aparna; Shamim Ara; Shuchanda

female star persona, 78, 80, 99, 137, 239n5; Aparna Sen, 9, 24, 52, 54, 55, 59, 60–61, 65, 206, 216–17; Kanan Devi, 46; Samina Peerzada, 7–8, 9, 131–32; Sangeeta, 120–21; Shamim Ara, 122, 124, 200

FemCom, 69, 91, 93

feminist cinema, 5, 160, 222; Indian women's wave of 1980s, 34–35; melodramas, 39, 55, 114, 131; women's counternarratives, 23, 202, 203, 204, 230

feminist theater movement, 5, 6

15 Park Avenue (dir. Aparna Sen, 2005), 204

film archives, 2–3, 92, 173, 192, 235nn4–5

Film Asia (periodical), 174, 190, 194–95, 240n2

film capital, 19, 22, 25, 33, 89–90, 99, 103, 176, 189

film censorship: Bangladesh, 91, 93, 95, 96, 99, 124, 226; colonial, 233; depiction of marital rape, 133; of *Inteha*, 5, 6–7, 8, 133; Pakistan, 106, 107, 112, 124, 127, 129, 130, 174, 175, 240n2

Film Development Corporation (Dhaka), 173, 198

Film Directory (Pakistan), 107, 174, 175, 240n2

film entrepreneurship: directors' mode, 52, 53, 99, 144, 201; entrepreneurial authorship, 71, 72, 241nn2,4; maternal politics, 66, 69; Noorjehan compared with Kanan Devi and Shuchanda, 109; portrayed in *Tin Konna*, 82–83. *See also* family system of production; female authorship; female-star-authorship; women's film companies

Kakhano Megh Kakhano Brishti (Sometimes Clouds, Sometimes Rains; dir. Moushumi, 2003), 91

Kamran, Murtaza, 132–33

Kanan Devi, 15, 109–10; in *Asha*, 48, 49; on Bengali cinema in Calcutta, 143; comparison with Aparna Sen, 35, 40–41; costume and set designs, 37; entertainer background, 111; film company, 24, 36, 42, 50; fossilized traces of, 42, 238n2; husband of, 47–48, 48; Life Story, 41–42, 45, 47–48, 48–51; maternal dramas, 41, 48; obituary by Kuldip Singh, 45; projects with Barua, 45, 50–51; as singing star, 41, 45–47. See also *Mej Didi*; Sreemati Pictures

Kanpuri, Zakhmi (Jameel Ahmed), *Yaadgar Filmen*, 115

Kapoor, Sashi, 54

Kar, Ajoy, 38, 49, 51, 209

Karanth, Prema, 34

Katha (dir. Sai Paranjpye, 1982), 152

Kaun Banega Crorepati (Who Will Become a Millionaire? TV game show), 243n14

Kaveeta (Nasreen Rizvi), 114, 115

Kayahiner Kahini (Tale of the Bodiless; dir. Ajoy Kar, 1973), 209

Kermani, Sheema, 5, 245n6

Khamosh Pani (Silent Waters; dir. Sabiha Sumar, 2002), 244n1

Khan, Aamir, 162, 243n14

Khan, Ayub, 95, 105

Khan, Irshad Ahmed, 124

Khan, Nighat Said, 107

Khan, Omar Ali, 115, 116, 117

Khan, Raja Riaz, 190, 191, *192*

Khatta Meetha (dir. Basu Chatterji, 1978), 148, 149

Khona Talkies, 227

Kirk, Gwendolyn Sarah, 17

Kolkata (Calcutta) cinema, 24, 35, 66, 143, 205, 245n4. See also Bengali cinema; Kanan Devi

Kuhn, Annette, 127, 191

Kumar, Nirmal, 40, 47, 238n1

Kumar, Uttam, 39

Kunwari Bewa (dir. Najam Naqvi, 1956), 195

labor, filmic, 16–18, 22, 29, 50, 68, 139, 141–42, 231; authorial, 2, 10, 140, 145, 233, 234; Bollywood, 160, 162, 165; creative, 1, 9, 11–12, 17, 23, 52, 59, 104, 132; production, 19, 37, 109–10, 160, 199–200. *See also* female authorship; female-star-authorship

La Capra, Dominick, 219–20

Lady Commando (dir. Shamim Ara), 192

Lady Smuggler (dir. Shamim Ara, 1987): as action-heroine film, 179, 183–86; Bangla dubbed version, 170, 172, 173, 176,186, 197, 199; Bangla film poster, 197, *198*; cast and crew, *192*; censor board submission, 240n2; closing shots, 189; comedy sequences, 187, 188; as coproduction, 170, 172–73, 183, 185, 192–93, 197–200; dance numbers, 185–86; directors and coproducers, 175, 183, 186–87, 197–99; and pirate mode creativity, 176, 183, 193; poster-booklet, 183, *184*, 192, 193, 197; prison scenes, 186–88, 200; production archive, 190–91; publicity, 186, 194–200; and *Sholay*, 183, 185; theft of film reel, 198–99; video copies, 175–76. See also *Miss Colombo*

Lahore studio culture, 103, 106, 119; female star-authors in, 10, 104, 131; kin relations in, 17, 189; and new cinema, 137; partition and, 143; poster and billboard painters, 114; talkies and female stars, 110, 111. See also *Mutthi Bhar Chawal*; Pakistani cinema; Urdu cinema

Lajmi, Kalpana, 34, 146

Lakhon mein ek (One among a Million; dir. Raza Mir; 1967), 193

Larkin, Brian, 170, 240n1

Lash, Scott, 21, 90

linguistic nationalism, 2, 67, 144. See also Bangla Language Movement

literary film, 88–89, 91, 118, 208; children's, 39. See also *Mej Didi*; *Mutthi Bhar Chawal*

lovemaking scenes, 59, 93, 95–96

Lury, Celia, 21, 90

Made in Bangladesh (dir. Rubaiyat Hossain, 2019), 218, 229

Mahar, Karen, 16–17

mahi munda (tomboy theater and dance), 126

mainstream cinema, 1, 12, 29; Bangladesh, 66, 69–70, 71, 90, 92, 226–27. *See also* middle cinema; social comedy

Majumdar, Neepa, 13, 39, 110, 141, 142

Majumdar, Tarun, 47, 49, 51

male stars, 38, 44, 74, 141, 142, 162, 243n14. *See also* Bachchan, Amitabh

Manju Dey Productions, 39

Manmoyee Girls School (dir. Jyotish Bannerjee, 1935), 45

Margarita with a Straw (dir. Shonali Bose, 2014), 157

Marks, Laura, 236n12, 238n2

Mary (Filipina tour operator/coproducer), 185, 190, *191*

masala films, 183

masculinity, 38, 43, 156, 158, 180, 209, 224. *See also* emasculation

mass entertainment cinema, 53, 232–33. *See also* director's cinema

Mayer Biye (Mother's Marriage; dir. Sudeshna Roy, 2015), 24, 64–65

McDowell, Linda, 18

McHugh, Kathleen, 5, 220

Meera (Pakistani actress), 133

Megher Koley Rod (Sunshine in the Clouds; dir. Nargis Akhter, 2008), 25, 69, 92, 96–98; DVD, 96; maternal savior figure, 97, 98; partnership with Malaysia, 96–97; Rodela hands divorce papers to Nijhum, *98*

Meghla Akash (The Cloudy Sky; dir. Nargis Akhter, 2001), 25, 69; aesthetics, 94, 95–96; as AIDS-awareness cinema, 94–95; censorship, 93; funding, 96; maternal savior figure, 94–95; song and dance, 96

Meherjaan (dir. Rubaiyat Hossain, 2011): aesthetic choices, 220, 221, 224; brand partners and promotions, 221–22, 226, 227; censor board approval and ban, 29, 221, 226–27; characters and narrative, 220–21, 223, 223–25; compared with *Goynar Baksho*, 28–29, 223, 224; as counternarrative, 219; and

female sexuality, 227–28; funding, 222; as independent family production, 218, 222–23, 227; as Muktijuddho film, 28, 219–20, 225; as regional transnational cinema, 29, 201; Rubaiyat Hossain as Salma, 220, 223; script, 223; as social melodrama, 226–27; sound track, 221; use of color, 224

Mehta, Depa, *Fire* (1996), 61

Mehta, Vijaya, 34

Mej Didi (Middle Sister; 1951), 42–47; camerawork, 51; couple scenes, 51; direction and production credits, 47; mother figuration, 43–45, 46, 48; role of Kanan Devi, 24, 47, 48, 50, 51; script, 48; song interludes, 44, 45, 46

Meyer, Birgit, 228

middle cinema, 26, 148–52, 226, 242n12. *See also* mainstream cinema

Ministry of Information and Broadcasting (India), 53

Mishra, Leela (Indian actress), 150

Miss Bangkok (dir. Iqbal Akhter and Noor Uddin Jehangir, 1986), 244n4

Miss Colombo (dir. Shamim Ara, 1984), 28, 169–70, 184; as action-heroine film, 178–80; cast, 178; and Islamization, 182; location shots, 178; narrative, 178, 180; Nayyar Sultana as Mother Superior, *181*; and pirate mode creativity, 176, 182, 193; script, 178; transnational spectacles, 176, 178; video copies, 175–76

Miss Hong Kong (dir. Shamim Ara, 1979/1980), 26, 104, 107, 125–26, 171; comedy in, 126; dance-fight edits, 129–30; fight scenes, 127–29; narrative, 126; New Woman in, 127, 135; poster for, 126, 127, *128*; transborder aesthetic, 131

missionaries, 180–81

Modern Girl, 133, 135. *See also* New Woman

Mohiuddin, Ghulam, 116

Mookherjee, Nayanika, 219, 227, 245n6

Morcom, Anna, 111, 130

Mostafa, Ashique, 222, 227

state-supported film industry, 25, 52, 53, 61, 89, 144, 165
Street Singer (dir. Phani Majumdar, 1938), 45
Shuchanda Cholochitra, 71–72, 74, 85–86, 89, 199; inaugural event, 83, 84. *See also* Shuchanda
Sultana, Nayyar, 131, 180, *181*
Sumar, Sabiha, 20, 138, 218, 244n1
Sumita Devi, 84
Supriya Devi, 39
Suvidha (magazine), 64

Tagore, Rabindranath: *Red Oleanders*, 229; song repertoire, 45–46
Taka Ana Pai (1970), 71
Talash-e-Haq (1935), 241n2
talkies, 110
tapori (vagabond), 79
Tasker, Yvonne, 78, 179
Teen Yaari Katha (Three Male Friends' Tale; 2012), 65
Telegraph (Kolkata), 148
television, 64, 93, 243n14; serials, 15, 106, 147; telefilm source of *Chasme Buddoor*, 149–50, 152; Urdu, 105–6, 131
36 Chowringhee Lane (dir. Aparna Sen, 1981), 54–55, 59
Times of India, "Bengali Movie News," 209–10
Tin Konna (Three Sisters; 1985); and action-heroine genre, 25, 69, 73, 77–78, 80; audiovisual spectacle, 80–81; "family feud" episode, 87–88; female personifications, 78–80, 78–82, 85; motherliness in, 81–82; narrative, 76–77, 84; posters announcing, 72–74, *73*, 78, 82, 90; Shuchanda as script writer and producer, 71, 76, 83; as sororal mode production, 69, 74–75, 84; and women's activist groups, 239n4. *See also* Shuchanda
Toor, Saadia, 135
transnational cinema, 19–23, 169–70; Bollywood, 22; coproductions, 171–72, 173, 175, 180, 192–93, 197, 200, 243–44n4; defined, 201; and

feminist critiques, 5, 203, 204, 217–18; and fictive kinship ties, 189–90; influence of pirate video, 28, 170, 178, 188; location scenes, 178; *Meherjaan* and *Ramchand Pakistani*, 221; *Mutthi Bhar Chawal*, 118–19; and pirate mode creativity, 3, 28, 170, 175–76, 189, 202; regional, 27, 29, 201, 210, 222
trauma films, 202, 203, 226. *See also* *Goynar Baksho*; *Meherjaan*; Muktijuddho film genre

Udayan (periodical), 67
Umrao Jaan (1981; dir. Muzzaffar Ali), 241n7
Under Construction (dir. Rubaiyat Hossain, 2015), 218, 228–29
Urdu cinema, 106–7, 139; action-heroine films, 169; in Calcutta, 143; censorship, 240n2; critiqued, 174; cross-lingual collaboration, 173, 243n1; Hindi film tropes in, 177; 1960s social films, 25, 26, 104, 105, 131, 135; star-heroines, 105; and Urdu television, 131; women's, 103, 114, 124. *See also* Lahore studio culture; Pakistani cinema

Vasudevan, Ravi, 13, 44
video format, 72, 74, 77, 96, 125, 132. *See also* video piracy
video piracy, 3, 89, 106, 107, 172, 174–75; and transnational cinema, 27–28, 170–71, 178, 198–99, 200; and video circulation, 177, 181–82. *See also* pirate-mode cinema
Vidhi Films, 244n1
violence against women, 4–5, 94, 133, 135; Nirbhaya gang rape, 153, 243n13; sexual harassment, 94, 151; wartime, 201, 219
viral media and the nation, 11, 29, 227

Wang, Lingzhen, 10, 223, 232
War on Terror, 29, 138
wartime genocide and rape, 201; Liberation War genre, 201, 219
Weber, Lois, 19

Weekly Akhbar-e-Jehan (Pakistan), 196
West Bengal, 66, 67, 204; Bangla
films, 209; theme of Hindification of
Bengali, 216. *See also* Bengali cinema;
Kolkata cinema
widowhood, 211; remarriage, 147. See
also *Goynar Baksho*
Wittig, Monique, *Les Guerilleres*, 224
women film directors, 1, 91, 99, 231–33.
See also Akhter, Nargis; female authorship; female-star-authorship; Hossain,
Rubaiyat; Kanan Devi; Noorjehan,
Madam; Paranjpye, Sai; Peerzada,
Samina; Roy, Sudeshna; Sangeeta;
Sen, Aparna; Shamim Ara; Shinde,
Gauri; Shuchanda
women's cinema, 24, 29, 36–39, 64; as
"counter-cinema," 5; as feminist, 34,
204; meaning of term, 1; in Pakistan,
1; as subversive, 2; as transborder, 9,
22. *See also* feminist cinema
women's film companies, 51–52, 114,
241n2. *See also* Babita Movies;
FemCom; Shamim Ara Productions; Sreemati Pictures; Shuchanda
Cholochitra

women's film history, 23, 27. 67, 104,
109
women's magazines, 196, 216, 217,
240n3
women's movement: Bangladesh, 70, 85;
India, 52, 53, 103, 140, 144, 146, 152,
241n12; Pakistan, 5–6, 125
women's wave, 34–35
working girl melodrama, 26, 104,
115–17, 121, 217. See also *Society Girl*
Working Group on National Film Policy
(India), 53
world cinema, 90, 92, 218, 229; Bangladeshi, 25, 89, 90, 92

Yash Raj Films, 207
Yatrik Collective, 49, 51

Zaman, Samia (Bangladeshi director), 91
Ziad, Abdullah, 90, 171–72, 173
Zia-ul-Haq: anti-obscenity measures,
187; regime, 6, 106, 124–25, 127,
135, 177, 182. *See also* Islamization:
Pakistan
zina (illicit intercourse), 112, 125, 188

ESHA NIYOGI DE is a senior lecturer in the Writings Programs division at the University of California, Los Angeles. She is the author of *Empire, Media, and the Autonomous Woman: A Feminist Critique of Postcolonial Thought.*

The University of Illinois Press
is a founding member of the
Association of University Presses.

_____

Composed in 11.5/13 Adobe Garamond Pro
with Gotham display
by Lisa Connery
at the University of Illinois Press

University of Illinois Press
1325 South Oak Street
Champaign, IL 61820–6903
www.press.uillinois.edu